W9-AVF-303

Transatlantic Rebels

Transatlantic Rebels

Agrarian Radicalism in Comparitive Context

Edited by THOMAS SUMMERHILL
and JAMES C. SCOTT

Michigan State University Press
East Lansing

Copyright © 2004 by Thomas Summerhill and James C. Scott

 Michigan State University Press is a member of the Green Press Initiative and is committed to developing and encouraging ecologically responsible publishing practices. For more information about the Green Press Initiative and the use of recycled paper in book publishing, please visit www.greenpressinitiative.org.

∞ The paper used in this publication meets the minimum requirements of ANSI/NISO Z39.48–1992 (R 1997) (Permanence of Paper).

Michigan State University Press
East Lansing, Michigan 48823-5245

Printed and bound in the United States of America.

10 09 08 07 06 05 04   1 2 3 4 5 6 7 8 9 10

Library of Congress Cataloging-in-Publication Data

Transatlantic rebels : agrarian radicalism in comparative context / edited by Thomas Summerhill and James C. Scott.
    p. cm
Includes bibliographical references.
  ISBN 0-87013-727-1 (pbk : alk. paper)
  1. Agriculture—Economic aspects—America—History—Congresses.
2. Agriculture—Economic aspects—Europe—History—Congresses.
3. Agriculture—Social aspects—America—History—Congresses.
4. Agriculture—Social aspects—Europe—History—Congresses.
  HD1748.J33 2000
  338.1/097 22

                                            2004012346

Cover and book design by Sans Serif, Inc.

Visit Michigan State University Press on the World Wide Web at:
www.msupress.msu.edu

Contents

Acknowledgments

The essays contained herein were first presented at the Jack and Margaret Sweet Symposium at Michigan State University in 2000, and examine in detail an often unexplored phenomenon: the transfer of agrarian ideas across the Atlantic Ocean since the first European contact with the native peoples of the Americas. I would like to thank a number of people for making the volume possible. Above all, Jack and Margaret Sweet provided a generous gift to the Department of History that underwrote the "Transatlantic Rebels" symposium and the publication of this anthology. In an era in which the humanities are dreadfully underfunded, their appreciation for the significance of history as a discipline is truly inspiring.

I would also like to thank my friend and coeditor, Professor James C. Scott of Yale University, for accepting the department's invitation to serve as visiting Sweet Lecturer. He and I developed the concept for the symposium during my tenure as a fellow at the Yale Program in Agrarian Studies, of which he is director. During the planning and execution of the conference and, later, the putting together of this anthology, his insight and support have been—as usual—exceptional. Both Jim and I relied heavily on the organizational and scholarly talents of Daniel J. Lerner, our assistant, to make the symposium come off successfully. I cannot credit him enough for his energy, aplomb, and professionalism.

Within the MSU community, several individuals deserved special thanks. I cannot thank enough the chair of the Department of History, Lewis Siegelbaum, for acting as senior faculty advisor for the Sweet program—and as the gracious host to our visiting scholars. His help in all phases of the project has been invaluable. The associate dean of the College of Arts and Letters, Patrick McConeghy, likewise took time out of his busy schedule to help make the symposium a success. And, of course, Margaret Jeffrey navigated the administrative shoals with her renowned expertise.

I would also like to thank the contributors to this volume—Rusty Bittermann, David A. Y. O. Chang, Gregory Crider, Louis Ferleger, Reeve Huston, Marixa Lasso, James McCann, Sarah T. Phillips, Daniel Samson, and Susan Sleeper-Smith—for the work they did to revise their essays for publication. Each addresses particularly well the comparative themes of the symposium. Because of limited space, we had to choose those essays that spoke most directly to each other; however, the other presenters—Shelby

Balik, Terry Bouton, Yeong-Shyang Chen, Laurent Dubois, Thomas Humphrey, Marilda Aparecida de Menezes, Marcy Norton, and the late David Walker—each produced sterling papers which either will or ought to be published in the near future. And commentators Peter Beattie, Leslie Butler, Deborah Fitzgerald, Steven Hahn, Jonathan Prude, and Robert C. Ritchie generously offered stimulating, constructive criticism to panelists. My personal thanks also go to several other friends and colleagues—Harold Forsythe, Maureen Flanagan, Paul S. Landau, Leslie Moch, Charles Radding, Harry Reed, David Robinson, and Terry Shaffer.

Finally, I would like to thank Martha Bates and Julie Loehr of Michigan State University Press for their enthusiastic support of this collection.

Thomas Summerhill
East Lansing, Michigan

Foreword

The fascinating and mind-opening collection of work you have just opened represents a particularly fine example of what the best of comparative history has to offer. Its cumulative effect on me, and I suspect on most readers, was to make it henceforth virtually impossible to understand much of eighteenth- or nineteenth-century history on either side of the Atlantic as "national" history. The borders were so porous, the material and human traffic across them so brisk, the ideas such increasingly common property, and the connections so continuous and robust that transatlantic history is the only plausible point of departure. It took a very discerning eye to see the powerful connection between such otherwise disparate work—not to mention a broad knowledge of current work in the field and no little organizational talent to bring all this together. For the idea and the execution, we have Thomas Summerhill to thank.

Transactions across the Atlantic are not exactly news! They are the staple of the colonial and much of the immediate postcolonial history of the New World from the Arctic Circle to Tierra del Fuego. But notice the sorts of transactions that have typically come under this rubric. To oversimplify greatly, the things in motion were usually ideas (e.g., the "Rights of Man" and John Locke's "Two Treatises of Government"); they were typically moving from Europe to the New World (e.g., and especially, Britain to North America); and they generally moved between elites (e.g., Montesquieu to Jefferson).

What is remarkable about the studies in *Transatlantic Rebels* is the novelty of what is moving and the direction of the movement, as well as what we might call the "parties" to transatlantic transactions. I want briefly to highlight each.

First, ideas. We are familiar enough with the intercontinental movement of ideas: liberalism, socialism, emancipation, democracy, etc. Such ideas move most swiftly and effectively when carried by powerful actors: the French ideas of rights and citizens carried by Napoleon's armies across Europe; Leninist Socialism backed by Soviet power; and today, capitalism and liberal economic policies backed by the United States through the International Monetary Fund and the World Bank. But in this volume, it is crops and techniques of cultivation, rumors, radical plebian ideas, workers, sailors, and prisoners which are moving. Suddenly, the traffic across the water becomes vastly more . . . well, democratic and comprehensive. Suddenly, it becomes difficult to understand how slaves, farmers, rioters, rebels, revolutionaries, or reformers thought, acted, or even scratched the earth without this traffic.

Second, direction. Here the traffic is decidedly two-way, and the impact occasionally more decisive in Europe and Africa from "New World" imports than the other way around. Maize and potatoes arguably changed Europe as much, initially, as Old World agricultural practices and crops transformed the New World. In the case of maize, for example, the effect of maize was swiftly felt in Southeast Asia where, because it thrived at higher altitudes, it allowed groups fleeing the state to run further up the watershed. It was, in other words, a new and valuable "escape crop" adopted with alacrity. Radical agrarian ideas and revolutionary sentiment, as this volume amply demonstrates, moved as often from the New World to the Old (e.g., the Haitian Revolution, the Creole revolutions of Latin America, as well as 1776 in the United States) as the other way around.

Absorbing the aggregate effect of these papers suggests a continuous circulation of material, intellectual, technical, and social patterns that makes neither world comprehensible without seeing its history as the vector sum of such flows.

Well, not quite . . . for another great advantage of this work is its appreciation of how everything that moves is transformed in the process. Objects as palpable as maize are adapted to new cultivation techniques, different social uses, and a new habitat. The same, of course, goes for agrarian socialism, revolution, democracy, emancipation from slavery, and new social forms. Virtually every study here casts a subtle eye on the process by which goods, ideas, and people in circulation can be understood only in their new setting and the novel uses to which they are put.

Similar efforts are under way to dissolve untenable national "containers" in understanding Pacific, Southeast Asian, and Indian Ocean history. Increasingly, it is understood that water frequently "joins" rather than dividing—even when the expanse is substantial—and this volume seems a model worthy of emulation elsewhere.

James C. Scott
Agrarian Studies, Yale University

Agricultural Dynamics of the Columbian Exchange

Susan Sleeper-Smith

The arrival of Christopher Columbus triggered bio-social changes that would prove as consequential as those created by the migration of people across the Bering land bridge. In 1492 two dramatically different worlds were reunited. In *The Columbian Exchange,* Alfred Crosby concludes that this reunion triggered the death of thousands of indigenous people who possessed no immunity to the deadly diseases that traveled silently west with the explorers.[1] Coastal Indian villages were left vacant by epidemic outbreaks of smallpox, whooping cough, chicken pox, and measles. Virulent pathogens became the real conquistadors.[2]

Environmental historians, like Crosby, have drawn attention to the often unintended consequences of contact, and they have established a new perspective on European conquest that emphasizes the importance of biological factors and refutes stereotypical reasoning about European superiority. But this environmental perspective also presents disadvantages. This is history that positions Europe's human beings, domesticated animals, pathogens, and weeds as victors and reinforces notions of indigenous decline and demise. Biological findings, devoid of cultural context, create a context of demographic takeover and fail to describe a viable process of mutual exchange.

1

They crossed oceans and Europeanized vast territories, often in informal cooperation with each other—the farmer and his animals destroying native plant cover, making way for imported grasses and forbs, many of which proved more nourishing to domesticated animals than the native equivalents; Old World pathogens, sometimes carried by Old World varmints, wiping out vast numbers of aborigines, opening the way for the advance of the European frontier, exposing more and more native people to more and more pathogens . . . Europe has exported something in excess of sixty million people in the past few hundred years. The great mass of these white emigrants went to the United States, Argentina, Canada, Uruguay, and New Zealand. . . . In contrast, very few aborigines of the Americas, Australia, or New Zealand ever went to Europe. Those who did often died not long after arrival. . . . The vast expanses of forests, savannahs, and steppes in the Lands of the Demographic Takeover were inundated by animals from the Old World, chiefly from Europe . . . [h]orses, cattle, sheep, goats, and pigs . . . which were completely lacking in these species at the time of first contact with the Europeans.[3]

The Columbian Exchange has been too narrowly remembered. Human and animal populations changed dramatically in the Americas, but it was indigenous people that often encouraged and promulgated these changes. Historians rarely focus on how crops from the Americas not only transformed European agriculture, but created new global markets for products like tobacco and furs. As we shall see, this occurred despite the frequent and determined opposition of European farmers and even Europe's rulers.

This article establishes a broader, more dynamic Columbian Exchange, in which the agricultural knowledge of indigenous people and their skill in extracting natural resources shaped the exchange process. First, this research explores how crops of the Americas transformed Europe's agricultural landscape. Second, it examines the role that Native people played in helping Europeans adapt to the Americas. Third, it demonstrates that the exploitation of natural resources was contingent upon indigenous knowledge of the natural landscape. It was the resources of the Americas—trapping, timbering, and naval stores—that fueled the development of modern Europe.[4]

I. Transforming Europe's Agricultural Landscape

By 1970, Christopher Columbus was mugged on the road to discovery, accosted by social historians who looked at the past from the bottom up and robbed "great" men, like Columbus, of their historical importance. But attempting to understand how "everyday" people affected the course of events has proven a more challenging and often elusive task for social historians.[5] The difficulty of uncovering and then evaluating the lives of people who left few written records has been partially overcome by learning to deconstruct established texts, or by turning to new types of evidence, such as material culture. Attempting to understand the influence of Indians is further complicated by their oral culture; they left few written documents for historians to examine.

In the 1960s, at the dawn of the "New Indian history," when social historians evaluated the agricultural expertise of Native people, they were shocked by the variety and abundance of Indian crops. After all, Indians were presumed to be nomadic. When environmental historians addressed agriculture as part of the Columbian Exchange, the contributions of America's indigenous people to the world's food supply became apparent. Clearly, it was the Americas that held the agricultural advantage, and the crops that traveled across the Atlantic to Europe were far greater in number and nutritional advantage than those that came from Europe.

Unfortunately, even this more "optimistic" scenario about the exchange process reinforced the notion that Europeans secured the agricultural

Table 1. Transatlantic Agricultural Exchange

Americas to Europe	*Europe to the Americas*
American persimmon	apple
beans	beet
bell and hot pepper	cabbage
blueberry	celery
cranberry	cucumber
maize (corn)	eggplant
manioc	grapefruit
papaya	lemon
pineapple	peach
pumpkin	plum
squash	olive
sweet potato	sugarcane
tobacco	
tomato	
white potato	
wild rice	

advantage. Crops that were nutritionally advantageous went from the Americas to Europe, rather than from Europe to the Americas. Indians gave Europeans maize and, in exchange, received lemons. Potatoes went east while oranges went west. Even the ways in which Europeans then re-exported Indian crops to other colonies on other continents suggests that Europe controlled external redistribution patterns.

While historians lauded the agricultural contributions of indigenous cultures, these contributions often remain contextualized within a framework of winners and losers. Agricultural exchange lists made Indians look good, and there was limited interest in tampering with such "good news." Few social historians possessed either the desire, agricultural expertise, or cultural knowledge to refute this ascendant star of Indian agriculture. Historians focused on the transatlantic exchange of maize, and it became the most lauded of indigenous crops. It was praised for producing the greatest bulk of seed per acre of all cereals on earth, and there was irrefutable evidence for its genesis in the Americas. Maize was initially cultivated in Mexico and then exported to South America. Some 5,500 years ago, Peruvian farmers produced the greatest varieties—including those with the largest seeds and the largest cobs. Following European arrival, the Spanish took maize to Europe. It quickly became an important southern European staple, especially in Italy. The Portuguese then reexported maize to Africa.[6]

Crops from the Americas were often cultivated first in southern Europe: in Italy, Spain, and Portugal. It appears that Spanish and Portuguese sailors carried the seeds and provided the agricultural expertise required to plant these crops. Their knowledge was probably acquired directly from the Indians. It was the Spanish and Portuguese and Italians who were cultural innovators, rather than their northern counterparts. It is, therefore, not surprising that a vegetable such as the tomato became a staple of Italian cuisine so early in the exchange process that it is rarely associated with its origin in the Americas.

Maize was quickly adopted by southern European farmers, but that willingness to experiment, to adopt new crops should not be generalized to Europe's northern farmers. Northern communities resisted agricultural innovation because their fields were far less productive than those of their southern counterparts. Southern European farmers produced an agricultural surplus which, coupled with high levels of agricultural productivity, facilitated experimental behavior. Farmers who opposed agricultural innovation often had very practical reasons. Their lands fed their families, and they lived in a fifteenth-century world where crop failures resulted in starvation. Farming rested on traditional knowledge.

> Farmers [must] know how to treat the soil before planting, when to plant, how deep to plant, when to weed, when to fertilize, how to protect the crop from predators and disease, when to harvest, what to harvest, and how to store the crop. Since each crop has its own needs, knowledge of how to cultivate one crop cannot be applied to the cultivation of another. Clearly, it would take many generations of experimentation before humans learned how to grow plants reliably.[7]

Most crops from the Americas were initially cultivated in southern Europe, and their diffusion northward often occurred generations later. Even crops that became the staple of entire communities, regions, and nations followed a circuitous path, and in the course of their progress a great deal of confusion, including fiction, evolved about their cultivation. The potato, for example, followed a far more complicated process of acceptance. The potato is native to the highlands of Bolivia and Peru and, like maize, was a staple of the Incas. But, unlike maize, there was no ready European reception for the potato. European farmers had to be supplied with more than just seeds or tubers; the potato required specialized planting knowledge and had to be changed to produce a shorter period of maturation before it could be planted in northern Europe. Adaptation of the potato was also hindered by conservative eating habits.[8] Maize was also a cereal crop, and people found its preparation and taste similar to other foods in their diets; but potatoes were entirely different.

Knowledge about the potato was disseminated by botanists who first cultivated and then wrote about the plant. But they also created fictions about the potato. The first written description in 1596, by the London botanist John Gerard, reported the potato's origin as Virginia. This error was furthered complicated by the belief that Sir Walter Raleigh had transported the potato to England or Ireland. In 1601, a Leyden professor reported on the potatoes being grown in southern Italy, where they were raised as pig feed. It was not until another century later, in 1700, that potatoes were first grown in Ireland, and even then, potatoes were not cultivated in the rest of Europe until the middle of the eighteenth or beginning of the nineteenth century.[9]

Europeans were not enthusiastic sponsors of agricultural innovation; they did not eagerly adopt the crops of the Americas, and in many instances new crops were actively opposed. For instance, tobacco was vigorously and vociferously opposed by both the king of England and the Roman Catholic Church. However, tobacco received a warm reception among Europe's lower classes, especially among sailors who became addicted to its use. Smoking was widespread among the Spanish and Portuguese, who learned how to smoke from the people of the West Indies and South America. But when Pochontas's husband, John Rolfe, exported the first crop of tobacco to England, it so displeased King James I that the king published a pamphlet in which he described smoking as a "base hurtful corruption" and condemned it as "A custome lothsome to the eye, hatefull to the nose, harmefull to the braine, dangerous to the Lungs, and in the black stinking fume thereof, neerest resembling the horrible Stigian smoke of that pit that is bottomlesse." Despite the king's warnings, smoking prevailed, and consumption expanded when European physicians described tobacco's curative powers against a wide variety of disease. A well-respected physician at the University of Seville reported that "tobacco cured coughs, asthma, headaches, stomach cramps, gout, and women's diseases." Tobacco's curative powers were exaggerated, and medicinal use gained some adherents, but that audience was limited. Instead, tobacco use initially spread through the practice of taking snuff, and became popular among the upper classes in the seventeenth century. During the nineteenth century, when first cigars and then cigarettes were introduced, smoking become fashionable with large segments of the European population.[10]

Most crops from the Americas found initial acceptance in the gardens and laboratories of botanists, and most of these crops underwent adaptation and change before they were extensively cultivated throughout Europe. Only when we are able to fully assess the transfer of agricultural knowledge from the horticulturalist to the farmer will the exchange process be fully understood.

II. The Indian as Agricultural Mentor

Northern European farmers resisted agricultural innovation, and it is not surprising that the agricultural baggage of the Pilgrims, Puritans, and Virginians included their most prized crops: barley and wheat. These crops failed to produce a harvest, and ironically it was maize that allowed English immigrants and their families to survive. Despite the popularity of maize in southern Europe, English farmers lacked experience growing maize, and these immigrant farmers acquired that knowledge directly from

Native people. Unfortunately, Indians have been denied any agricultural role because we stereotypically depict Englishmen as skilled and innovative agriculturalists, while Indians are viewed as nomadic hunters. The "Ecological Indian" is depicted as uninterested in economic gain—people who were quickly displaced from the land and then disappeared. These stereotypes deserve reexamination if we are to understand how and why the Columbian Exchange was mutually constitutive.[11]

The level of interaction between the English and Indians was both immediate and prolonged. Immigrants whose food supply depended on growing wheat in coastal Massachusetts were destined for starvation. Therefore, English needs were immediate, and the transfer of knowledge required to teach Europeans to grow and successfully harvest unfamiliar crops took place on an ongoing and daily basis. It is this level of agrarian interaction that requires further study. We ought to revisit familiar sites, reexamine traditional documents, and listen carefully so we can hear the long-silenced voice of the Indian as agricultural mentor. In doing so, we must simultaneously examine the degree to which Indians were voluntary and often eager participants in agricultural as well as other economic ventures with their newly arrived European neighbors.

No interaction is more famous than that of Squanto and the Pilgrims of Plymouth Plantation. Squanto's role as a colonial Indian helpmate is well known, but his stereotypically flawed depiction as the friendly Native masks the extent to which his actions were indicative of deliberate Indian strategies.[12] A close examination of William Bradford's diary reveals that the Indians chose Squanto to live among the Pilgrims, and Bradford himself describes how Squanto then provided the detailed type of practical information that ensured that English colonists would learn how to grow Indian crops.[13]

Plymouth, like other communities, was founded along the coastline, and incorporated Indian fields that were abandoned when epidemic diseases decimated village populations, with death tolls soaring to over 90 percent of the inhabitants. The Puritan's late fall arrival meant that they could neither plant nor harvest crops, nor build the shelters necessary to escape New England's harsh winter weather. English death tolls were also horrendous, and within two to three months of their arrival, over half of the Plymouth community died. During January and February, two to three people died each day. In March, when the survival of the colony appeared dim, several area Indians visited the Pilgrims. An Abenaki from Maine, Samoset, brought with him the Patuxet Indian named Squanto. The visitors negotiated an alliance between the Pilgrims and the neighboring Wampanoag Indians. If Samoset had intended for the English settlement to fail, there was little that Plymouth could have done to successfully ward off an attack. Also, the English were unable to hide the dismal prospect for their future. Fewer than half the people had survived the winter, most were sickly, they had no tools (they had been stolen by the Indians), and the seeds they brought to plant would not germinate in the harsh New England soils. In fact, Bradford's diary clearly describes what happened when they tried to plant their English seeds. "Some English seed they sew, as wheat & peas, but it came not to good, either by the badness of the seed, or lateness of the season, or both, or some other defect."[14]

The key to Plymouth's survival was Squanto. He facilitated the transfer of agricultural knowledge between the immigrants and the Indians because he spoke English. Along the northern Atlantic coastline, English-speaking Indians were not unusual. Hobamack was a Squanto contemporary who also lived among the English and served as a guide and interpreter for Plymouth Colony.[15] Linguistic familiarity with European languages developed among Indians early in the sixteenth century, and was facilitated by the annual visit of European fishermen who worked the Grand Banks. Many of the fishermen who ventured as far south as Cape Cod lived on shore for part of the spring and most of the summer. These men, estimated to be as many as 20,000 fishermen each summer, built dories in which to fish, as well as temporary shelters and drying racks. Men were often left through the winter to secure the site for the return of fishing crews the next spring. Indians not only fished side-by-side with these foreigners, but also traded with them, and Europeans visited with Indians during the winter months.[16]

Bradford describes Squanto as directing both the agricultural and fishing efforts at Plymouth, and from the advice that Squanto offered, we can assume that he had long fished the coastal waters. Plymouth was a less-than-desirable agricultural site, and if the settlement was to survive, the Pilgrims would have to learn how to fish as well as plant. "He directed them how to set their corn, where to take their fish, and to procure other commodities, was also their pilot to bring them to unknown places for their profit. . . ."[17]

Squanto was the community's lifeline, and the advice he offered was garnered in a world distant from New England's Atlantic coastline. The Plymouth Separatists had selected a problematic agricultural site—an area that lacked naturally fertile soils. Squanto showed the Pilgrims how to fertilize the soil with fish to ensure the successful harvesting of their crops. In April 1621, Bradford recorded,

Afterwards they (as many as were able) began to plant their corne, in which servise Squanto stood them in great stead, showing them both ye manner how to set it, and after how to dress & tend it. Also he tould them excepte they gott fish & set with it (in these old grounds) it would come to nothing, and he showed them yet in ye midle of Aprill they should have store enough come up ye brooke, by which they began to build, and taught them how to take it, and wher to get other provisions necessary for them; all which they found true by triall & experience.[18]

It is unlikely that North American Indians used fertilizer; rather, they moved their fields when they failed to produce adequately. Fertilization was a technique Squanto may have learned while living in England. As a young man, he had been captured by an English captain named Hunt, who intended to sell him along with other Indians as slaves in Spain. Squanto escaped capture in England and lived for a while in London. He was later hired as part of an expeditionary force sent on a private voyage of exploration by Sr. Ferdinando Gorges. In the end, Squanto served as both a skilled interpreter and agricultural instructor.[19] As a negotiator of agricultural exchange, Squanto made it possible for the English to survive in a land where the seeds they brought failed to germinate, and where new agricultural techniques would have to be patiently acquired from the Indians. It is not surprising that Bradford described Squanto as "a special instrument sent of God for their good beyond their expectation."[20]

Plymouth Plantation represents one of the best-known but least-understood instances of agricultural exchange. Thanksgiving has transformed Squanto into a familiar figure, but traditional narratives fictionalize that event; they praise Indian-settler cooperation and minimize Pilgrim dependency on the Indians. Even my brief but more nuanced interpretation of Bradford's diary reveals the extent to which settlers depended on Squanto to learn how to plant; how and where to catch the unusual fish indigenous to this section of the North Atlantic, particularly lobster, cod, clams, and mussels; how to harvest wild foods that were safe to eat, especially berries and mushrooms; and how to hunt and trap.

Indian expertise made it possible for English coastal settlements to prosper. Social histories have not fully examined the face-to-face exchange necessary to transfer agricultural and environmental knowledge from one culture to another. A fuller exploration of the interactions and associations that began at the moment of encounter will show how agricultural exchange was paramount to the survival of these colonial communities.[21] Europe's crops were rarely amenable to initial American cultivation, and

Indians showed the English how to successfully grow crops indigenous to the American landscape. There were other Indians, like Squanto, who helped broker this exchange of agricultural information, but many of these were probably women, since agriculture was a female responsibility.[22]

A more accurate history of the Columbian Exchange deserves to be written. The records of colonial America are replete with references to Indians: as interpreters, neighbors, and farmers. Rarely do historians explore those casual references. For instance, economic development was hampered by monetary dependency, but these limitations were lessened by the colonists' use of Indian wampum as a form of payment. Closer examination of New England's probated wills and inventories reveals numerous attempts to expand the currency by relying on wampum, obtained through trade with the Indians. The colonists also relied on Indian corn as a form of currency. In the 1630s, the Massachusetts Bay General Court countered a serious shortage of coinage by decreeing that Indian corn should "pass in payment of new debts" at a rate of four shillings to the bushel.[23]

This reference to Indian corn and the use of wampum represents some of the many anecdotal niches in larger narratives about American history. But the processes of how maize came to be cultivated or how wampum was held as accumulated wealth were indicative of a series of face-to-face interactions that requires further analysis. Indian crops ensured the survival of the colonies, and it was these crops that eventually enabled colonial farmers to successfully compete in an emerging transatlantic economy.

III. The Demise of the Ecological Indian and the Agricultural Origins of American Capitalism

Together, Europeans and Indians transformed North America's natural landscape and allowed market forces to determine how the land would be used to procure material goods. Indians were not only skilled agricultural instructors, but they were highly proficient in harvesting natural resources, such as furs. Indians were eager, rather than reluctant, trading partners, and although their motivation usually differed from that of their European neighbors, the results were not dissimilar. During the first decades of settlement, North America's natural landscape was rapidly transformed into commodifiable products.

The colonial period contains numerous literary tracts describing the lushness of New England's landscape. These writers described a densely forested environment with "goodly groves of trees . . . delicate faire large plaines, sweete cristall fountaines, and cleare running streames. . . ."[24] Thomas Morton depicted the land as " . . . Natures Master-peece: Her chiefist Magazine of all where lives her store: if this Land be not rich, then is the whole world poore."[25] Ministers preached weekly sermons that provided God's blessing for exploiting the land. They quoted from the Bible and expressed sentiments similar to those of Massachusetts Bay founder John Winthrop, who told his listeners:

> The whole earth is the lords Garden, and he hath given it to the sons of man with a generall Condition, Gen: 1:28 Increase and multiply, replenish the earth and subdue it . . . The lord revealeth his Secretts to . . . his prophets among us, whom her hath stirred up to encourage his servants to this plantation . . . We shall come in with the good leave of the Natives, who finde benefitt already by our neighborhood and learne of us to improve but to more use . . . which will yeild them more benefitt . . . all the land.[26]

Poets and writers created sexual images that encouraged the physical conquest of the land. Thomas Morton transformed nature into a female presence to be fully enjoyed by Puritan men once their labor had transformed virgin forests into tillable lands. For Morton, New England became New Canaan, a reference that described a wedding feast at which Christ transformed the water into wine. Morton invited his readers to possess a land that longed for conquest, comparing the land to a virgin bride that longed to greet her lover in their nuptial bed.

New English Canaan

or

New Canaan

The Authors Prologue

> If art & industry should doe as much
> As Nature hath for Canaan, not such
> Another place, for benefit and rest,
> In all the universe can be possest,
> The more we proove it by discovery,
> The more delight each object to the eye
> Procures, as if the elements had been
> Bin reconcil'd, and pleas'd it should appeare,
> Like a faire virgin, longing to be sped,
> And meete her lover in a Nuptiall bed. . . . [27]

These several examples were part of a growing chorus of New England voices, and each encouraged and urged people to rejoice in commodification of the natural landscape. They were joined by an indigenous response, more sublime but equally enthusiastic, about extracting resources from the land to secure highly desired manufactured goods: particularly cloth and such iron tools as awls and hoes, knives and hatchets.[28] That voice has been silenced by the powerful image of the environmentally conscious Indian, but it is a voice that can be easily detected in the stories that Indians shared with Europeans.

Convinced of the superiority of their world, the Indians believed that the Europeans had been pushed west by the innate inferiority of Europe's lands. This Indian exchange with a Jesuit missionary reveals both the sense of indigenous superiority and the extent to which the natural landscape became the common ground of encounter.

> They believe that Lake Superior is a Pond made by the Beavers . . . this God (the great Hare) they add, while chasing a Beaver in Lake Superior, crossed with a single stride a bay of eight leagues in width. In view of so mighty an enemy, the Beavers withdrew to another Lake . . . when they afterward, by means of the Rivers flowing from it, arrived at the North Sea with the intention of crossing over to France; but finding the water bitter, they lost heart, and spread throughout the Rivers and Lakes of this entire Country. And this is the reason why there are not Beavers in France, and the French came here to get them.[29]

Numerous tales about the beaver were recorded by European missionaries, particularly the Jesuits. These are amusing tales; but sadly, they also describe a world in which many fur-bearing animals became marketable commodities. The beaver was enthusiastically exchanged by Indians for more highly valued trade goods. Indians often proclaimed that trade goods "cost them almost nothing." Indians were delighted to find themselves confronting Europeans who "have such a fondness for the skin of this animal [they] fight to see who will give the most . . . to get it." From an Indian perspective it was a seller's market, where "The Beaver does everything perfectly well, it makes kettles, hatchets, swords, knives, bread, in short it makes everything."[30]

The most unexplored implications of the Columbian Exchange are environmental, and deal with how Indians exploited natural resources to secure manufactured goods. That exchange occurred on a daily, face-to-face basis and was monetarily lucrative to both sides. In New England, that exchange process proved so profitable that Plymouth colony paid off its

English creditors within five years by securing furs from the Abenaki, on the Kennebec River in Maine. In this five-year period, from 1631 to 1636, the Plymouth settlers shipped 8,000 beavers and 1,156 otters to England. Even then, they exported only a small share of the annual Abenaki harvest; most Abenaki peltry was traded to the French.[31]

Beaver and small luxurious furs like otter, black fox, and marten found a ready market in Europe. As early as 1826, the Iroquois shipped 8,000 skins to Fort Orange (Albany, New York) and New Amsterdam, and by the 1650s they took approximately 46,000 pelts a year to Fort Orange. The French were even better supplied by their Native partners, and within six years of Quebec's founding almost 25,000 beaver skins were annually shipped to French hatters. At trading villages maintained by the Indians, the annual harvest of peltry was equally impressive. At Tadoussac, on the north shore of the St. Lawrence River, Indian traders annually brought as many as 12,000 to 15,000 pelts to exchange in one of the continent's largest open-air summer markets.[32]

Although this article focuses primarily on New England, similar symbiotic relationships also developed between the Indians of the Southeast and the English.[33] Between 1700 and 1715, the deerskin trade annually netted Charleston 54,000 skins, and by 1740 the trade was up to 152,000 skins per year. In the twenty years between 1739 and 1759, Cherokee hunters alone reduced the southeastern deer population by 1.25 million.[34]

During the seventeenth century, Indians and colonists created an ecological revolution that transformed not only the landscape but also human consciousness. The southern New England Indians had long cleared fields in the lowland forests, where they had planted corn, beans, and squash, while they relied on the upland forests to hunt the animals they needed for clothing and food. Once the European immigrants learned how to successfully grow Indian crops, frequently on abandoned Indian lands, they further transformed the land by applying more intensive methods of cultivation. The broadcasting of seeds on plowed cultivated fields made the land prone to erosion by wind and water, exhausted the soil more quickly, and forced farmers to either abandon fields or fertilize to attain the desired yields. Simultaneously, the English introduced livestock, as well as weeds and vermin. By the end of the seventeenth century, these changes had dramatically transformed New England ecology, undercutting resources and transforming the natural landscape.[35] Through depletion of the beaver population, the Indians transformed the land. Beaver created complex pond ecosystems in the forests that left tree stumps and brush for grouse, rabbits, and birds; watering spots for deer and moose; and foraging sites for foxes, raccoons, and bears. The Indians simplified these ecosystems by trapping beaver and breaking down their dams. As old beaver sites became the pasture sites of New England farms, it became easier to extract pines for masts and oak for barrel staves.

What was radical about the Columbian Exchange was that Indians and Englishmen jointly created this resource-extractive economy. Colonial participation in an emerging North Atlantic economy resulted from the extraction of resources from the land. In New England, the attainment of wealth resulted from the appropriation and exploitation of natural resources, rather than from agricultural success. From the day that the English arrived along the Atlantic coast, Indians taught them what to grow in New England's rocky soil, but more importantly, taught them how to exploit the land to accumulate wealth. However much we may mythologize New England farmers as small independent producers who owned their land and equipment and worked their farms with family labor, they were simultaneously a crucial part of the transatlantic economy. Without Indians, there would have been a prolonged period of subsistence farming.

The English persisted because of what Indians taught them about farming, but the profits they made and the surplus capital (or credit) they accumulated resulted from what they extracted from the land. They succeeded because they had access to resources that Europe had long ago depleted—particularly timber and furs. With Indian assistance, natural resources became cash crops.

The role that Indians played in the extraction of natural resources should also begin to revise the ongoing debate about agrarian transformation. Rather than argue about whether these seventeenth-century New Englanders were nascent capitalists, we might rather consider how the extraction of natural resources by Indians encouraged capitalist development. Capitalism depends on the accumulation of wealth or capital through the appropriation of the surplus value of free wage laborers.[36] But for Americans, the most efficient way to accrue resources resulted from the appropriation and exploitation of natural resources. The capitalist transformation that took place in the rural American North during the century after the 1750s occurred following a thorough commodification and transformation of the land, a process in which Indians remained active participants. Indians and Europeans had so thoroughly and effectively commodified the land that Americans developed few prohibitions about exploiting the land. To continue to promote the image of the Ecological Indian to change

American behavior, or to foster badly needed environmental legislation further, has not only obscured the ability of the Indian to adapt to a continually changing world, but has masked the central role that Indians played in the Columbian Exchange.

Notes

1. Alfred W. Crosby, *The Columbian Exchange: Biological and Cultural Consequences of 1492* (Westport, Conn.: Greenwood Press, 1972), 219.
2. The impact of virgin soil epidemics has generated a contest between ethnologists from the American Historical School, who do not see disease playing a major role in the early precontact period (Kroeber to Helm), and more recent ethnohistorians and demographers who do (Henry Dobyns, S. F. Cook, and William Borah). Ann Ramenofsky in *Vectors of Death* offers a compromise between the two schools of thought, and although she supports catastrophic population losses prior to the onset of large-scale European migration, she contends that not all population declines were permanent, and that they differed on a village-by-village basis. Russell Thornton in *American Indian Survival* supports population decline as preceding American settlement, but suggests that initial population losses, although dramatic, did not decimate American Indians as a distinct population. Ann R. Ramenofsky, *Vectors of Death: The Archaeology of European Contact* (Albuquerque: University of New Mexico Press, 1987). Russell Thornton, *American Indian Survival: A Population History Since 1492* (Norman: University of Oklahoma Press, 1987).
3. Alfred W. Crosby, "Ecological Imperialism," in *Major Problems in American Environmental History,* ed. Carolyn Merchant (Lexington, Mass.: D. C. Heath and Co., 1993), 15.
4. To more fully explore the agricultural dynamics of a broad-based Columbian Exchange requires that we divest ourselves of the image of the Ecological Indian. *The Ecological Indian,* the title of Shepard Krech's recent book, disputes the depiction that Indians, particularly prior to contact, lived harmoniously with nature. Shepard Krech III, *The Ecological Indian: Myth and History* (New York: W. W. Norton and Co., 1999). His perspective reflects the recent literature that contends that Indians did not passively adapt to their regional environments, and that while they had a vast and impressive store of knowledge about the natural landscape, they could not always foresee the consequences of their acts. For a discussion of this emerging perspective,

see Richard White and William Cronon, "Ecological Change and Indian-White Relations," in *Handbook of North American Indians,* vol. 4 of *History of Indian-White Relations,* ed. Wilcomb Washburn (Washington, D.C.: Smithsonian Institution, 1988), 417–29; Sam D. Gill, *Mother Earth: An American Story* (Chicago: University of Chicago Press, 1987); Lynn Hirschkind, "The Native American as Noble Savage," *Humanist* 43, no. 1 (April 1983): 16–18, 38; William Cronon and Richard White, "Indians in the Land," *American Heritage* 37 (August 1986): 18–25; William M. Devevan, "The Pristine Myth: The Landscape of the Americas in 1492," *Annals of the Association of American Geographers* 82, no. 3 (1992): 369–85; Karl W. Butzer, "No Eden in the New World," *Nature* 362 (4 March 1993): 15–17; Jared Diamond, "The Golden Age That Never Was," *Discover* 9 (December 1988): 71–79.

5. An extensive literature has emerged that examines the origins and ramifications of social history; those that help illuminate the points made in this essay include James Henretta, "Social History as Lived and Written," *American Historical Review* 84 (December 1979): 1293–1322; Eric Hobsbawn, "From Social History to the History of Society," *Daedalus* 100 (fall 1971): 20–45; Peter Stearns, "Coming of Age," *Journal of Social History* 10 (winter 1976): 246–55.

6. Otto T. Solbrig and Dorothy J. Solbrig, *So Shall You Reap: Farming and Crops in Human Affairs* (Washington, D.C.: Island Press, 1994), 54–56.

7. Ibid., 64.

8. Ibid., 165–66.

9. Ibid., 168–69.

10. Ibid., 172–74.

11. The textbooks used for college-level American history surveys have begun to present a more nuanced interaction, but even the most highly respected texts suggest that Indian cooperation quickly moved toward coercion. In one recent and respected textbook, Indians are depicted as initially cooperative, but ultimately forced to meet European demands through coercion. The 1998 edition of *The Enduring Vision* states that "the Indians taught the newcomers to grow corn . . . the Pilgrims traded their surplus corn with nonagricultural Indians for furs . . . they foreshadowed the coercive methods that later generations of Americans used to gain mastery over the Indians." Paul S. Boyer, Clifford E. Clark Jr., Sandra McNair Hawley, Joseph F. Kett, Neal Salisbury, Harvard Sitkoff, Nancy Woloch, *The Enduring Visions: A History of the American People,* 3d ed. (Boston: Houghton Mifflin, 1998), 36.

12. There is an extensive Native American literature that demonstrates how the stereotyping of Indians as helpmates is common to "notions of the good Indian." Rayna Greene has written extensively about this phenomenon, and shows how "The only good Indian—male or female, Squanto, Pocahontas, Sacagawea, Cochise, the Little Mohee or the Indian Doctor—rescues and helps white men." Rayna Green, "The Pocahontas Perplex: The Image of Indian Women in American Culture," *Massachusetts Review* 16 (autumn 1975): 703.

13. Bradford's History "Of Plimoth Plantation" from the original manuscript, with *A Report of the Proceedings Incident to the Return of the Manuscript to Massachusetts* (Boston: Wright and Potter Printing Co., 1899).

14. Ibid., 121.

15. Ibid., 124.

16. There were two types of fishing, green and dry, and both involved interaction with Native people. Green fishing took place almost completely at sea. Dry fishing was a land-based operation, and was a more profitable economic enterprise. Lodges were constructed along the shoreline in which the fishermen lived during the spring and summer months, rather than aboard ship. Nearby staging areas were built where cod was processed and dried. These men fished in small boats or dories, launched from the shoreline, which were built by the carpenters who were part of these transatlantic fishing expeditions. When the ships returned to France, these extensive land-based operations were often guarded by resident fishermen, for whom these temporary arrangements became a permanent residence. One of the earliest descriptions of fishing along the Atlantic coast was completed by Nicolas Denys, *The Description and Natural History of the Coasts of North America* (1672; reprint, Toronto: Champlain Society, 1908), esp. 273–74. For a description of the bartering process between Natives and Europeans, see H. P. Bigger, *The Early Trading Companies of New France* (Clifton, N.J.: Augustus M. Kelley Publishers, 1972). A brief but accurate discussion of sixteenth-century North American fishing is contained in W. J. Eccles, *France in America* (East Lansing: Michigan State University Press, 1990), 10–13.

17. Bradford, "Plimoth Plantation," 121.

18. Ibid.

19. According to Bradford, Samoset told him that Squanto had been in England and "could speake better English then him selfe." Bradford, "Plimoth Plantation," 114–15.

20. Ibid., 116.

21. Thomas R. Wessel, "Agriculture, Indians, and American History," *Agricultural History* 50 (January 1976): 10; Percy W. Bidwell and John I. Falconer, *History of Agriculture in the Northern United States, 1620–1860* (1941; reprint, Washington, D.C.: Carnegie Institution of Washington, 1925), 41.

22. Most Indian societies followed the same fundamental divisions of labor, with women as the primary agriculturalists. However, kinship systems were substantially different, and there were both patrilineal and matrilineal systems. The most prominent indigenous example of a society that was both matrilineal and matrilocal was the Cherokee. Theda Perdue describes produce as the property of Cherokee women because they were the principal farmers. Theda Perdue, "Cherokee Women and the Trail of Tears," *Journal of Women's History* 1 (spring 1989): 14–30. For a review of the current scholarship on Indian women, see the introduction to *Negotiators of Change* by Nancy Shoemaker (New York: Routledge Press, 1995), and Laura F. Klein and Lillian A. Ackerman, eds., *Women and Power in Native North America* (Norman: University of Oklahoma Press, 1995).

23. J. K. Hosmer, ed., *Winthrop's Journal: History of New England, 1630–1649* (New York: Barnes and Noble, 1953), 2:6; Jack Weatherford, *Native Roots: How The Indians Enriched America* (New York: Fawcett Columbine, 1991), 114.

24. Thomas Morton, *New English Canaan or New Canaan* in *Tracts and Other Papers Relating Principally to the Origin, Settlement, and Progress of the Colonies in North America from the Discovery of the Country to the Year 1776*, vol. 2, ed. Peter Force (Gloucester, Mass.: Peter Smith, 1963), 41–42.

25. Morton, *New English Canaan*, 42.

26. John Winthrop, "Winthrop's Conclusions for the Plantation in New England [January 15, 1648–9]," in *Old South Leaflets*, ed. Burt Franklin (New York: Burt Franklin, n.d.).

27. Morton, *New English Canaan*, 10.

28. Guns are not included in this list because it is clear from trade-good inventories that guns constituted a small portion of the goods acquired. In the Great Lakes, for instance, guns constituted less than 5 percent of the goods traded at posts like Detroit and Michilimackinac. Dean L. Anderson, "The Flow of European Trade Goods into the Western Great Lakes Region, 1715–1760," in *The Fur Trade Revisited: Selected Papers of the Sixth North American Fur Trade Conference, Michilimackinac Island, Michigan, 1991*, ed. Jennifer S. H. Brown, W. J. Eccles,

and Donald P. Heldman (East Lansing: Michigan State University Press, 1994), 93–116.

29. *Jesuit Relations and Allied Documents, 1896–1901,* 54:201–3. There are numerous beaver tales among the Native American people of the Great Lakes region. The oldest and best known of these tales originated with the giant beaver tales of the Northeastern Algonquin. This huge animal also transformed the topographical landscape through the creation of large lakes, rivers, and ponds. Jane C. Beck, "The Giant Beaver: A Prehistoric Memory," *Ethnohistory* 19 (spring 1972): 109–22.

30. James Axtell, *Natives and Newcomers: The Cultural Origins of North America* (New York: Oxford University Press, 2001), 107.

31. Ruth A. McIntyre, *Debts Hopeful and Desperate: Financing the Plymouth Colony* (Plymouth, Mass.: Plimoth Plantation, 1963).

32. Axtell, *Natives and Newcomers,* 106.

33. Timothy Silver, *New Faces on the Countryside: Indians, Colonists, and Slaves in South Atlantic Forests, 1500–1800* (New York: Cambridge University Press, 1990).

34. Axtell, *Natives and Newcomers,* 107.

35. For a discussion of the ecological transformation of New England, see William Cronon, *Changes in the Land: Indians, Colonists, and the Ecology of New England* (New York: Hill and Wang, 1983).

36. The idea that exchange was central to the emergence of capitalism and that commodification of everything, even labor, rather than class struggle, led to increased commerce is advanced by Wallerstein in *Historical Capitalism.* Both Holton's *Transition from Feudalism to Capitalism* and Fox-Genovese's *The Fruits of Merchant Capitalism* offer critiques of this perspective. Immanuel Maurice Wallerstein, *Historical Capitalism* (with *Capitalist Civilization*) (London: Verso, 1995); Elizabeth Fox-Genovese and Eugene D. Genovese, *The Fruits of Merchant Capitalism: Slavery and Bourgeois Property in The Rise and Expansion of Capitalism* (New York: Oxford University Press, 1983), 15, 190–93; R. J. Holton, *The Transition from Feudalism to Capitalism* (Basingstoke, England: Macmillan, 1985).

Rural Protest on Prince Edward Island in Transatlantic Context: From the Aftermath of the Seven Years' War to the 1840s

Rusty Bittermann

In the summer of 1832, rural inhabitants of Rustico, on the north coast of Prince Edward Island, met to consider a collective problem. Most were tenants, most were in arrears with their rents, and, like tenants elsewhere on the Island, most feared that their landlords might seize their farms and possessions for nonpayment of rent. They questioned the validity of the title deeds on which landlords claimed the right to grant leases and demand rents, and doubted the wisdom of imperial policies that had created a colony where most of the population were tenants, clearing and improving the properties of proprietors who, from a tenant perspective, had done nothing to earn their entitlement to the land. Those assembled at the Rustico meeting drew up a list of resolutions to address the land question on the Island, and to indicate their position regarding a widespread anti-proprietorial movement that was gaining momentum in the colony. Their ten resolutions, which were subsequently published in a local paper, addressed specific grievances concerning the nature of land tenure on the Island and its consequences for settlers. The preamble to these resolutions, however, contextualized them in broader terms, and linked their actions with developments that spanned the Atlantic. It noted, among other things, that reform appeared "to be the order of the day in almost all parts of the civilized world," and it cast their demands for an end to landlordism as part of these progressive changes.[1]

The history of rural protest on Prince Edward Island in the late eighteenth and early nineteenth centuries provides many examples of activists connecting their struggles on the Island with events occurring elsewhere in the Atlantic world. At times, external developments played an important role in justifying demands for reform, and in providing hope. As well, agrarian leaders in the colony made use of tactics and organizational strategies that had been developed in other struggles. The history of rural protest in this period also reveals connections between the language and rationale of rural protest on Prince Edward Island and broader transatlantic discussions of social justice, though there are many silences in this zone and others. The dangers and difficulties of challenging the status quo do not tend to encourage full disclosure of influences.

While agrarian activists on Prince Edward Island gained strength and inspiration from progressive political developments in other parts of the Atlantic world in the late eighteenth and early nineteenth centuries, they also drew opposition because of them. Radical challenges elsewhere buttressed resistance to demands for land reform on Prince Edward Island, as those standing to lose from popular mobilization often perceived Island developments in terms of revolutionary challenges in other areas of the Atlantic world. Events in France, Ireland, and elsewhere in the late eighteenth and early nineteenth centuries helped to make conservatives involved with Island affairs ever vigilant to nip popular stirrings in the bud. As well, revolutionary precedents provided the material with which to label and damn those threatening the status quo on the Island, regardless of whether or not the parallel was apt.

Compared to Britain's other North American colonies, Prince Edward Island, on the inner reaches of the Gulf of St. Lawrence, was a small, relatively insignificant place. Unlike the adjacent, comparably sized island of Cape Breton, Prince Edward Island lacked the year-round ice-free ports that in times of war made Cape Breton strategically important. Although most of the Island was suitable for agriculture, with some of the best agricultural soils in the region, the growth of a European settler population was slow, both during its years as a French colony and in its early years as a British possession following the Seven Years' War. Given Prince Edward Island's position within Britain's Atlantic empire, the external events that most directly shaped agrarian protest in the colony tended to be those occurring in the imperial center. Certainly this was the case with the most substantial rural protest movement in Island history, the Escheat Movement of the 1830s and early 1840s—the inspiration for the anti-landlord protest meeting at Rustico.[2] The Escheat Movement, which was grounded in half a century of resistance to landlordism in Prince Edward Island, took form and prospered in an imperial context shaped by the successful mass struggles for Catholic emancipation in the 1820s and passage of legislation providing for parliamentary reform and slave emancipation in 1832 and 1833. Indeed, at times, leaders of the Escheat Movement explicitly cast the struggle for agrarian reform on the Island in terms of an extension of the logic and promise of these developments. In the early 1840s, though, when Robert Peel's Conservatives ended a decade of Whig rule, formal politics in Britain swung to the right. These changes in the imperial center dimmed the prospects for agrarian reform on the Island, and the Escheat Movement lost its momentum.

It is difficult to assess the effect that varying currents of change elsewhere in the Atlantic world had on the complex history of rural protest in Prince Edward Island in the eighteenth and nineteenth centuries. In part, this is because it is hard to weigh the impact of developments that were interpreted and used quite differently by different sectors of Island society. In addition, linkages to external developments that provided strength at one moment sometimes became a source of weakness at another. As well, of course, external influences unfolded within the context of the ever-changing specifics of Island society, with its own locally grounded dynamics of change. What is clear, however, is that the actions of those who challenged landlordism on Prince Edward Island—and the responses of those who opposed them—were intimately connected, in many ways, to a broader transatlantic politics that transcended the boundaries of locality, colony, nation-state, and empire that commonly shape and confine contemporary historical analysis.

The roots of the discontent articulated at the Rustico meeting lay with policies the British government established for Prince Edward Island after acquiring sovereignty over the territory in the victory over the French in the Seven Years' War.[3] In the imperial reorganization that followed the war, Ile St Jean—or the Island of St John, as the British called it at that time—became part of a new British imperial frontier, stretching from the Floridas north to the Great Lakes, across the lands to the west of the Appalachians, and east to the Gulf of St. Lawrence.[4] Imperial planners charged with managing these acquisitions had to secure parts of the frontier with British settlement and, where possible, do so in ways that would not add to British debts, and indeed, preferably, reduce them. The policy eventually adopted for Prince Edward Island sought to privatize the costs of establishing British settlers in the new colony, and as well to provide rewards to prominent Britons who had played significant roles in the successful military struggle against the French, giving private individuals the possibility of reaping profits from many of the potential gains of settlement.[5] The result was the land system that residents of the Rustico region met to protest in the summer of 1832.

In the British colonization plan implemented in 1767, the Island's 1.4 million acres were divided into 67 lots (townships) of roughly 20,000 acres each, and distributed to grantees—usually as a whole or half township.[6] This approach to organizing colonization was consistent with policies adopted by the French in their possessions prior to the war, and with policies the British had previously employed—and continued to employ—both for the northeast coast of North America and more generally, as well as with some of the colonial policies of other European powers.[7] It was not a novel way of proceeding, nor should the problems and tensions that followed have been a surprise. The grantees acquired their lots, or partial lots, subject to conditions: they were required to bring in foreign Protestants— people drawn from Europe or other parts of North America—at a rate of 100 settlers per township. One-third of the grantees' holdings were to be settled in the proper proportions within four years, and all within ten. Grantees were also required to pay annual quit rents to the Crown at a rate of from two to six shillings per acre.[8] At the time that this policy was initiated, Prince Edward Island was part of the colony of Nova Scotia, which had been enlarged by the addition of territory conquered from the French in the Seven Years' War. In 1769 the Island became a separate colony, and the quit rents stipulated in the grants were then earmarked to help sustain the costs of the new colony's government, which came to include a governor, crown officials, appointed executive and legislative councils, and an elected House of Assembly.[9]

As had often been the case with other imperial initiatives of this sort, few grantees attempted to meet the obligations in their conditional grants, and fewer yet succeeded. Although quit rents trickled in from some grantees, most did not pay.[10] Perhaps half a dozen of the hundred or so proprietors who received grants of full or partial lots made attempts in the decade after 1767 to develop their properties as required by their deeds.

Some spent considerable sums and undertook initiatives that brought settlers to the Island, but these efforts focused on advancing commercial and religious projects, rather than fulfilling the conditions of the grants.[11] No proprietors fully complied with the conditions, and few came even remotely close to doing so. In consequence, the property claims of the Island's landlords had a questionable legal basis. Rural protest repeatedly raised this issue in the years of struggle against the proprietorial system. Indeed, the legality of landlords' claims remained a fundamental matter of dispute until 1875, when compulsory land-purchase legislation provided the means to eliminate the last of the large estates.[12]

The first formal land protest within the colony emerged in the years after the American Revolution. The population of the Island at the time was probably around 3,000 and growing.[13] Included were some Micmac aboriginal inhabitants and some Acadians, who had escaped deportation during the Seven Years' War or had returned to the Island after the war.[14] Others were settlers drawn from Ireland and Scotland and England, from adjacent parts of British North America, and from among the Loyalist refugees who moved north in the aftermath of the warfare to the south.[15]

When British officials divided and distributed Island property, they did so as if the Island were uninhabited, ignoring the Micmac and the pre-Conquest Acadian settlers, even though official surveys made note of the improvements left by previous settlement.[16] As a result, Acadian and aboriginal inhabitants of the Island found themselves living in violation of the new imperial property regime from the time it was proclaimed. In theory, these residents might have sought out their new landlord or landlords, if they could have identified them, and arranged mutually acceptable terms for the sale or lease of land that they already occupied. In practice, such a procedure was highly unlikely.

Many of the new settlers arriving in the wake of the Conquest also occupied land outside the property regime established by imperial planners, as they tended to respond to the opportunities of the landscape—taking up good lands where they could, even if there were no landlord or agent with whom to formalize their legal position, or sometimes *particularly* if there were no signs of landlord activity.[17] Settlers who were able to acquire lands by entering into agreements with landlords often assumed burdens more onerous than they had anticipated, as the costs of establishing their farms left them without the means to meet rents or payments for the purchase of land.

The protest movement that emerged in the late eighteenth century was thus grounded in Island problems and articulated preexisting tensions between the needs of Island inhabitants and the property relations favored by imperial planners and landlords; it sought to change the colony's land regime to conform with the needs and wishes of much of the Island's population. In this sense, it was a northern version of a common North American frontier experience of settler resistance to metropolitan organization and domination.[18] It emerged in the aftermath of the American Revolution, in part because with the arrival of new settlers, landlords and government officials paid more attention to the colony.[19] The imperial plan, which formerly many settlers had ignored safely, began to become more than a plan on paper. As landlords moved to manage their Island holdings more actively, there were fewer spaces within the colony where settlers might squat and make a livelihood without troubling with formal property claims. Increasingly, settlers had to choose between acknowledging landlord claims or resisting them in a more or less direct fashion.

Protest against the colonial land regime was also fueled by contemporary developments in adjacent colonies. In Nova Scotia and in the new colony of New Brunswick (carved out of Nova Scotia after the American Revolution), government authorities acted to enforce the terms of conditional deeds similar to those granted on Prince Edward Island. When proprietors of large estates failed to meet the terms of their grants, escheat courts examined the evidence and, where appropriate, reasserted Crown ownership of the lands. In these colonies, escheat actions brought hundreds of thousands of acres back into the public domain, making them available for settlers who received freehold grants directly from the Crown. Nova Scotia's escheat courts were particularly active in the wake of the American Revolution, as the government sought to prepare the colony for the arrival of Loyalist settlers.[20]

The ideas and activism of the new immigrants coming to the Island from elsewhere in the Atlantic world in the years after the war were central to the emergence of a formal protest movement. Of particular importance was the arrival of Joseph Robinson, a Loyalist from South Carolina who had served with distinction as a lieutenant colonel in the Revolutionary War. Robinson was a well-educated man who had once possessed a backcountry plantation. On Prince Edward Island, he became a tenant, holding his lands by lease from Sir James Montgomery, Lord Advocate for Scotland in the years prior to the American Revolution and one of the few proprietors actively involved in managing their Island properties.[21] Robinson became involved in the struggle against landlordism on the Island when he successfully ran for a seat in the colony's House of Assembly in 1790 as part of a slate of candidates advocating the escheat of proprietorial holdings, such as those belonging to Montgomery.[22] Six years later, he assumed a leading role in challenging landlordism on the Island. Using a tactic fully in keeping with Anglo-American traditions of protest prior to the Revolution, Robinson issued a manifesto in 1796 that described the incompatibility between the views and needs of settlers and those of landlords, and called for an end to the existing land system.[23]

Robinson argued that farm making in a northern wilderness context was too difficult and costly to permit settlers to pay rents. As a consequence, settlers would inevitably fall into arrears and lose their lands and improvements. As well, he challenged the validity of landlords' property claims, arguing that their titles had been forfeited when they failed to comply with the conditions of their grants. Placing Island circumstances in the broader context that he was familiar with, Robinson noted that a similar proprietorial system in the Carolinas had been swept away in the early eighteenth century, and that comparable measures had recently been effected in the adjacent colonies of Nova Scotia and New Brunswick. The legitimate claims of ownership, he maintained, using an argument that echoed throughout the Atlantic frontier in the late eighteenth and early nineteenth centuries, were the claims of those who were investing their labor in the land.[24] Robinson advocated petitioning the House of Assembly for the establishment of a court of escheat that would investigate the status of landlords' grants and set the stage for a redistribution of their lands to those who farmed them, after the Crown had resumed title.

Robinson's closest ally in the land-reform campaign was yet another of the new immigrants who had arrived in the closing years of the eighteenth century. Robert Hodgson, who was an Englishman and a carpenter by trade, organized a campaign to press the House of Assembly to establish a court of escheat. Hodgson worked with other assemblymen and local magistrates to organize meetings about the Island to discuss Robinson's manifesto and draw up petitions. These, ultimately, were sent to the House of Assembly, which in turn prepared a report on the Island land situation. The House sent this to the imperial government, along with a petition for the establishment of a court of escheat. Settlers also initiated plans, never realized, to send Robinson to London to present their case.[25]

The tactics of the escheat movement engendered by Robinson and Hodgson, combining initiatives of the Assembly with public meetings and petitions, were consistent with British traditions of constitutional protest. Indeed, the role of magistrates in calling public meetings suggests that Robinson and Hodgson, and their allies, acted carefully to ensure that the protest stayed within these limits. Not all of the tactics of protest that emerged in conjunction with Robinson and Hodgson's initiatives, though, were so prudent. Widespread rent resistance developed in the wake of the petition campaign, and so too did resistance to militia service.[26] In the late summer of 1797, militiamen in the east of the colony linked military service with land grievances. After obeying a call to assemble for a militia muster, they refused to form ranks or follow orders. Instead, rank-and-file militiamen held a meeting separate from their officers and then sent delegates to relay their thinking: they would only obey militia laws if they were granted freehold titles to their lands. Similar militia protests followed in other locales, including Rustico.[27]

While those with an interest in challenging landlordism on the Island gained strength from the circulation of peoples and ideas in a broader Atlantic world, their adversaries grounded crucial aspects of their response in a critical reading of unfolding events in the same sphere. The conjunction of direct action with political initiatives calling for an escheat of landlords' lands soon had some of the Island's proprietors, and their allies, linking Island events to a more general pattern of revolution that was unfolding on both sides of the Atlantic. People such as Robinson, one local landlord asserted, were disseminating principles "which may vie with the like which have laid France to ruins."[28] They were, another landlord complained, "coniving [*sic*] in the peasantry being invited to discuss so delicate a subject" as property rights and "a division of lands," and in consequence, their tenants were developing "wild ideas about natural rights."[29] The author in the first case was John MacDonald, chief of the cadet branch of Clan Ranald. An Island landlord, MacDonald, like many Highland tacksmen, had been educated in mainland Europe and had firsthand knowledge of contemporary developments there.[30] Even the Island's governor, Edmund Fanning, who had reason to downplay the disturbances in his reports to his superiors in London as they did not reflect well on his administration, suggested that agitators on the Island, as "in many other parts of the world," were "exciting a contempt of constituted authorities."[31] He himself had had direct experience of the consequences of this in North Carolina, where he had been a victim of Regulator attacks.[32]

The most overt manifestations of this post-Revolution rural protest soon died down. Once the House of Assembly's report and petition calling for the establishment of a court of escheat had been sent to London, the next step was to wait for the imperial authorities' decision. Although few Islanders likely realized it, the report had been drafted in ways that undercut the possibility of sweeping land reform. It did this, in part, by focusing in great detail on the issue of landlord quit-rent arrears and how they might be recovered.[33] Four years later, the colony was still waiting for the imperial response.[34] Meanwhile, the militia revolts had been immediately suppressed both by a show of force and by gentler persuasion. The rural units were confronted with an armed force drawn from among the "principal gentlemen" of the colony's capital, Charlottetown, aided by a detachment of light horse belonging to Charlottetown's militia; but the authorities negotiated a face-saving compromise that allowed the men of the rebellious units to back down and avoid punishment.[35] Landlords quickly moved to dampen rent resistance by initiating legal proceedings against tenants who were in arrears.

In addition to the demoralizing effects of the government's and landlords' displays of power, organized protest may have diminished because of a crisis in leadership after the Assembly took up the land question. In part, the movement seems to have lost momentum because some of those supporting calls for an escheat did so in aid of more limited personal goals. Some achieved their ends by gaining elective office. Others hoped to buy out landlords' grants once the threat of an escheat scared them into disposing of their lands cheaply. And some government officials gained what they wished when imperial attention to recovering quit-rent arrears produced monies that were applied to back salaries owed to them. Given the role played in the late-eighteenth-century escheat movement by members of the elite guided by such commercial and pecuniary motives, recent historical interpretations have suggested that there was never really a popular protest movement at all, just "contending factions of elites" vying "for their own political, economic, and social advantage."[36] There is some truth in this contention, but it misses more than it captures. The tactics of the leaders of the land agitation of the 1790s were predicated on harnessing a preexisting popular dissatisfaction with landlordism which was *not* their creation.[37] And in the event, these popular forces proved hard to control.[38] Joseph Robinson experienced this directly, as he was the commanding officer of the first militia unit to refuse to follow its officers' orders in the summer of 1797. Although he agreed with the concerns of his men, it seems unlikely that he would have approved of their means for agitating them, given the consequences they held for him and the resonance it must have had with his own bitter experiences of civil war in the American South during the Revolution. Surely, too, as rural protest moved beyond constitutional tactics, Robinson, and other prominent Islanders who had helped to launch the formal challenge to landlordism, must have been troubled by the strident claims of other educated, worldly members of the elite who claimed that they had put themselves at the head of forces similar to those which had brought revolution to other settings. Whether the claim was true or not, it was a warning and an accusation that could not be lightly dismissed, given the transatlantic context in which it was made.

For a variety of reasons, then, formal land protests lost their momentum in the closing years of the eighteenth century. The land question, though, persisted as an issue in electoral politics, and those hoping for land reform remained a latent political force. It was not long before others chose to fill the vacuum left by the escheat leadership of the 1790s. One of the men who came to be most closely associated with the new challenge of the early nineteenth century was yet another recent immigrant, James Bardin Palmer, who attempted to link organizational tactics drawn from elsewhere in the Atlantic world with the challenges he encountered in Prince Edward Island. Palmer was a Dublin attorney who had lived and worked in London before accepting a job as a land agent and emigrating to the Island in 1802. An ambitious man with grand ideas about developing Island resources, he took his ideas to the electorate the year he arrived on the Island. Although he failed to win a seat in the Assembly, he gained insight into the political significance of the land question.[39]

On the eve of the next general election, held in 1806, Palmer helped to found an organization called the Society of Loyal Electors, which in time revived formal consideration of the land question. In this election, Palmer won a seat in the House of Assembly. According to Palmer, the inspiration for the Loyal Electors was the Dublin Society, founded in that city in 1731 to provide a forum for middle-class improvers interested in the new intellectual developments and dissatisfied with the status quo.[40] The Dublin Society served as a model for similar organizations in the British Isles and Europe, as well as for the Society of Loyal Electors on Prince Edward Island.[41] In keeping with the social basis of the Dublin Society, the early membership of the Society of Loyal Electors was drawn primarily from merchants, professionals, and artisans living in the capital, Charlottetown, where it met on a monthly basis. Its urban nature was reflected not just in its membership, but as well in the language of its organization. Its officers included a "Lord Mayor," "aldermen," and other titles associated with city government.[42]

Although begun as an improvement-oriented urban society that reflected its Old World origins, the Society of Loyal Electors changed its character over time. The shift was propelled, it seems, by a search for issues that would help elect more of its members to the House of Assembly and, correspondingly, by the inclusion of more people from the countryside among its membership. Early in the second decade of the nineteenth century, the society began to establish branches in rural communities, and to translate the writings of some of its members into Gaelic and French to make them more widely accessible.[43] With these changes, the society increasingly became a vehicle for the demands that had been articulated by the escheat movement of the 1790s, although these were never its only concerns. The society's electoral appeal grew as it changed its membership and orientation, and although it failed to gain dominance in the House of Assembly elections of 1812, it doubled its representation.

The election of 1812 was bitterly fought, and in a number of cases, members of the Island's elite who opposed the society's candidates were driven from the hustings by angry mobs.[44] The social and political tensions the election highlighted, coupled with the coming of war between Britain and her colonies and the republic to the south, set the stage for conservative efforts to suppress the Society of Loyal Electors before its challenge could develop further.

From the point of view of the Island's power holders, the activities of the Society of Loyal Electors, like those of the escheat advocates of the 1790s, fit within a broader pattern of revolutionary challenge. The society's activities, though, were even more disturbing than the challenges of the 1790s, as the society was a permanent, formal organization that appeared to be orchestrating a broad challenge to the status quo. According to Island cleric Abbé LeSeuer, the situation in Prince Edward Island in the spring of 1812 was similar to "the state of France in the years 1789 and 1790," when the populace was being inflamed by rhetoric concerning the rights of the poor. When LeSeuer argued that the organization fanning the flames needed to be suppressed, or things would "soon turn out here as they did in my unfortunate country," he spoke with authority, as he and his brother had fled France after witnessing the outbreak of revolution.[45] Chief Justice Caesar Colclough spoke from experience, too, when he suggested that the subversive model for what was happening on the Island lay not with the activities of French Jacobins, but with the United Irish. Reports that the Society of

Loyal Electors were "attempting to gain over the soldiery" who were stationed on the Island resonated with his memories of insurrection at home, when he had assisted in the repression that followed.[46] Others among the Island's elite focused on how the Charlottetown Society of Loyal Electors had organized the establishment of affiliated societies in the countryside, and drew parallels with the activities of British Corresponding Clubs.[47]

No doubt, the Society of Loyal Electors drew from many models. Its repertoire of oppositional tactics included effective use of the Island's new newspaper, the *Weekly Recorder*, monthly meetings at a Charlottetown tavern, the establishment of corresponding branch societies, the circulation of papers and manifestos, celebratory dinners, and election campaigns—all in keeping with broader transatlantic developments.[48] Islanders who were well informed concerning these developments imagined Island possibilities in terms of what they suggested, for better or for worse.

Over time, the Society of Loyal Electors had increasingly become a political organization agitating for a change in the status quo. Even some of those seeking to cast its activities in the most favorable light were willing to acknowledge this. One of these was William Roubel, a British attorney who, like Palmer, had come to the Island as a land agent and became a leading light in the society after joining in 1809.[49] Roubel suggested that the society was an island parallel to the political club which had supported John Archer Houblon's successful election to the House of Commons in 1810.[50] In a time when "party" and "faction" were still negative labels, Roubel's defensive claims conceded a great deal; they also reveal, yet again, the significance of the political traditions new immigrants brought with them.

As with the escheat agitation of the 1790s, conservative forces effectively used negative associations grounded elsewhere in the Atlantic world to assist in suppressing formal protest related to the land question. Letters of alarm from prominent Islanders played a role in inducing the British Colonial Office to remove the governor who had permitted the establishment of the Society of Loyal Electors, and to replace him with a new man who would look closely at its activities. Governor Charles Douglas Smith, who arrived in the colony in 1813, soon decided that the society was a "club" of "very dangerous principles" that must be extirpated. It was, he argued, formed "upon the plan and *principles* of the United Irish and connected I am strongly persuaded with the Irish in the United States of America."[51] In a subsequent dispatch, he emphasized the need to support landed proprietors "against the attempts of democratic levellers" who kept "stirring up sedition" by agitating the "question of an Agrarian Law."[52]

In the context of the War of 1812 and its aftermath, Smith moved to destroy the society's influence and suppress agrarian protest. This included curtailing the role of the House of Assembly in Island politics. After trying to control the behavior of the House and failing, Smith chose to govern without it for most of his twelve-year regime. The paranoid tone of his administration was in keeping with that prevailing in Britain at the time, and in other British North American colonies as well.[53] In his pursuit of sources of revenue that did not require convening the House of Assembly, Smith promoted rigorous collection of quit rents. As well, he took the radical step of escheating two lots, and would have proceeded against other proprietors had he not been stopped by London. Although Smith intended that his escheat actions would thwart democratic power by enhancing the resources available to the governor, he inadvertently renewed popular faith in the possibility of a general escheat.

By the mid-1820s, the call for land reform through an escheat was beginning to reemerge in the political arena. In part, this was because Smith was removed from office in 1824, and his replacement, John Ready, helped to provide a context that seemed favorable to reform. Ready had served as a government official in Lower Canada in the years after the war, and had developed a sympathy with the positions of politicians such as John Neilson and Louis-Joseph Papineau, who were pressing for democratic reform there.[54] Ready's positions reflected broader changes in imperial policy as well. As governor of Prince Edward Island, he helped to renew reform possibilities by reactivating the House of Assembly and giving it a place of importance in Island politics. Although escheat was an issue in the 1824 election, and there were calls to form a party around the issue,[55] the election victories went primarily to men who had helped to get rid of the previous governor, even though many had little or no sympathy for land reform. It was clear, however, that the land question was not going to fade away. Following the election of 1824, Angus Macaulay, once a prominent member of the Society of Loyal Electors, presented a petition to the House calling for a general escheat.[56] Macaulay was an important rural leader and had been Speaker of the Assembly. The petition he presented carried the signatures of 800 residents, demanding that the Assembly act to eliminate landlords' titles and regrant proprietorial holdings in small tracts to those who worked them.[57]

The 1830s saw these early popular rumblings develop into a powerful Island-wide protest movement that moved well beyond the scope of previous rural protests. Local Island matters were some of what shaped this development. Significant shifts in property distribution occurred in the early nineteenth century as a number of big holdings changed hands, in part because of the threat of escheat. Many of the original grantees sold out altogether, and their lots were acquired by newcomers in the Island property market, as well as by landlords interested in enlarging their existing holdings. One result was an increasing concentration of property ownership. By 1830, the six biggest landlords owned four or more 20,000-acre townships each, and collectively held roughly half of the colony's 1.4 million acres.[58] Although these property transfers did not eliminate landlords with little concern for actively managing their holdings, they helped to generate a greater level of landlord interest in making profits from their Island properties. There were significant changes in settlement patterns as well, as thousands of emigrants from the British Isles made their way to the British North American colonies in the aftermath of the Napoleonic Wars. This, coupled with natural growth, pushed the Island's population to around 30,000 by 1830.[59] These local-level changes in the ownership and demand for land, which reflected broader imperial shifts in the allocation of capital and labor, heightened land tensions on the Island.

Political developments in the empire and in the Atlantic world more generally helped to set the context for the development of a vibrant rural protest movement on the Island in the 1830s. Daniel O'Connell's successful mass campaigns for Catholic emancipation made it possible for Island Catholics, who represented roughly half of the colony's population, to vote for the first time when new members of the House of Assembly were selected in 1830. O'Connell's successes served as well to demonstrate the efficacy of collective action. So too did the struggle for parliamentary reform in Britain, a cause which Island papers tracked while also paying close attention to revolutionary challenges on the European mainland, beginning with the July Revolution in France.[60] Following passage of the Reform Act of 1832, it became a reference point for judging the pace of political changes on the Island.[61] The momentous 1833 legislation abolishing slavery within the British Empire further broadened the grounds for hope, as it represented an abridgement of the property rights of British citizens, and politically powerful ones at that. If Parliament was willing to infringe on planters' property claims in order to right wrongs elsewhere in the empire, it suggested a new context in which those struggling against proprietors on Prince Edward Island might also finally succeed in ending landlordism.

The rural protest movement that emerged in the 1830s and came to be known as the Escheat Movement began to take form in the period between passage of the Catholic Emancipation Bill in 1829 and passage of the parliamentary reform and slave emancipation acts in 1832 and 1833. The Island's House of Assembly played an important role in its genesis, and the man who was most central to this was William Cooper, an Englishman elected to the House in 1832. Cooper had immigrated to the colony in 1819, after twenty years at sea with the British navy and as a sea captain in the international trades. He moved to the Island to serve as a land agent on the estate of Lord Townshend, one of the Island's many absentee proprietors.[62] Townshend's previous agent had been killed by an angry tenant, seeking to resist the agent's seizure of his horse for back rents, and Cooper's task was to pick up where he left off.[63] Cooper proved remarkably successful in what must have been a difficult task, and ultimately gained the support of Lord Townshend's tenantry, who in time would be central to his electoral success.

Cooper's popularity probably reflected both his personal skills and the appeal of the policies he adopted. His vision of landlord-tenant relations was paternal and grounded in the notion of reciprocity; tenants owed landlords rents, but landlords were responsible for providing services in exchange. As Townshend's agent, Cooper arranged for the construction of a grist mill, found markets for rural products, and accepted rent payments in timber, agricultural goods, or labor. As well, Cooper lived among the tenantry and acted as a local peacemaker, doctor, and sustainer of those in need. Cooper's initiatives involved Townshend in the economic risks of rural industry in ways that simple rent collection did not. When these affected Townshend's rental income in the economically troubled years of the late 1820s, Townshend chose to dismiss him.[64] Subsequently, Cooper ran for a seat in the House of Assembly and used it as a forum to articulate proposals for radical land reform.

Not surprisingly, Cooper's first speeches in the House of Assembly on the land question framed the subject in terms of a failed paternal order. Landlords, he argued, had turned their backs on the "people they ought to support and cherish," and refused to use their property to provide "employment and bread to the industrious."[65] In subsequent declarations, he expanded on these ideas: "In the old fashioned times the lands were considered to be for the use of the people, to give them employment and subsistence, to raise and maintain a hardy race for the support and defense of the country." This, though, had become a thing of the past in the Old World, as "according to the improved system, the land is not for use of the people, but for the proprietor—and as the lands will yield more if cultivated by a few useful hands, without women or children, the supernumeraries are turned off to the manufacturing towns and the colonies, and villages are turned into sheep pastures and pleasure grounds." The same thinking, he argued, would soon be applied to Prince Edward Island; once its lands were cleared and improved, "the present inhabitants will be turned off to make room for large farms, which will either sell or let at a great advantage."[66] Cooper's arguments were grounded in a transatlantic vision of the erosion of an organic social order, and were a call for Islanders to resist the spread of the logic of clearances from the Old World to the New World. Given that many of the settlers on the Island had been compelled to leave the British Isles because of the agrarian transformation Cooper described, his warnings must have had a powerful resonance.

Cooper argued that the appropriate response to the threats posed by the decline of a paternalistic order was to turn to the state for protection. In Prince Edward Island, this included making use of the possibilities afforded by popular representation in the House of Assembly. One of Cooper's many strengths as a leader was his recognition of the usefulness of his Assembly seat in mobilizing support for radical land reform and maintaining a focused campaign. During the first escheat movement of the 1790s, rural calls for radical land reform were muted, to a large extent, when they were translated into legislative action. A similar dynamic was at work in the House of Assembly in the 1830s, as rural demand for a general escheat that would end landlordism altogether was transformed into a call for the escheat of grants where there had been little settlement.[67] Such a policy, which fit well with the agenda of those interested in promoting economic development or in gaining access to wilderness lands, offered little to redress the grievances of the existing settler population, as escheats would only occur on properties where they did not live. In the early 1830s, the disjuncture between rural demands for sweeping land reform and what in fact the Assembly was doing became a public issue, as Cooper denounced the land policies the House was considering, and published his position in the leading Island paper at the close of the 1832 session. This set the stage for organizing an out-of-House movement to sustain radical land reform.[68]

The rural protest movement that began to take shape at this juncture combined local-level organizing with very effective use of Island newspapers. Cooper's home community of Bay Fortune, in the east of the Island, provided a model for how other rural communities might use the Island's newspapers to help them agitate for land reform. At the end of the 1832 session, a committee of Bay Fortune residents called a local public meeting—not the first such—to consider the land question. It then sent the resolutions they passed, calling for a general escheat of proprietorial grants, to an Island paper.[69] Its initiatives helped to inspire other communities to do the same. When the residents of Rustico gathered in the summer of 1832, they were following the example established by Bay Fortune and, by this time, half a dozen other communities. These simple tactics of holding community-level public meetings, developing resolutions, and arranging for their publication built on the possibilities afforded by the growth of newspaper publishing in the 1830s and proved very effective in mobilizing the rural population and coordinating the rural activism.

As the conversation on land reform developed in meetings, petitions, re-ports to the newspapers, and debate in the House of Assembly, so too did the ideological foundation of protest. Joseph Robinson's escheat manifesto of 1796 had challenged the legitimacy of the original township grants, as the landlords had not fulfilled the terms of their deeds, and had suggested that only those who invested their labor in the land were entitled to the rights of ownership. The idea that property rights should be grounded in labor emerges in his manifesto, but Robinson did not push the point, and modified it somewhat with his other observations.[70] Cooper and other leaders of the Escheat Movement that began in the 1830s spoke much more explicitly about the relationship between property and labor, and about the fit between this and a properly organized civic order. Cooper's first major speech on the land issue in the House of Assembly focused on the need for a general escheat in order to protect "the liberties of the peo-ple." As well, he argued, an escheat was necessary to secure the property of those who had "planted their labour where the forest grew . . . and made a garden in the wilderness."[71] Citing classical precedents, Cooper extolled the thinking of the Gracchan Law that limited the amount of land a Roman family could hold; similar restrictions were needed on Prince Ed-ward Island.[72] "[T]here cannot," he argued, "be a greater monopoly of the labour of man, than by holding the possession of large tracts of land," and if "the people" were to provide "the bulwark and support of Government," the state needed to intervene to restrict the "injustice" that would emerge from such a monopoly. As he phrased it in a subsequent speech, the "majority of mankind must have an interest in the soil" if they were to "support and defend" the state.[73]

The language and arguments that Cooper and others employed to sustain the Escheat Movement belonged to a broader transatlantic conversation concerning a just social order.

Like producers elsewhere, Escheat activists argued that the security and independence of the populace, and ultimately the health of the polity, lay in ensuring broad access to the land.[74] The republicanism of their vision of an appropriate ordering of society was often framed, as it was by radicals in the imperial center, in terms of a correct interpretation of British constitutional principles.[75] Like many working people elsewhere around the Atlantic, Escheaters drew strength from the notion that producers had a right to the product of their labor, and that a just order would ensure this.[76] And, in keeping with the positions adopted by settlers in other North American locales, they used a labor theory of value to cast their efforts in the land struggle as a defense of property.[77] He who "cultivates a farm by the sweat of his brow," they argued, "is fairly and honestly entitled to it."[78] The Island's tenants had "made all the property out of a wilderness, where there was none before; and all the claim the landlords set up [is] to the property which we have made by our hard labour."[79] It followed that the objectives of the Escheat Movement were consistent with upholding property rights within a just social order, as Escheaters sought "to secure to every man the possession of the property made by his labour."[80] Like those elsewhere who viewed the world in similar ways, Escheaters expressed these sentiments in an inclusive vocabulary of class. The struggle for land reform pitted, in their words, "the people" against their oppressors, "the many" against "the few," the "labouring class" against "land jobbers," the "productive classes" against parasites, and/or the "working bees" against the "drones."[81]

Escheat leaders drew as well from the language and logic of the struggle to abolish slavery. In their view, Island tenants deserved to participate in the developments that had at last liberated slaves within the British Empire. It was time, they argued, for the state to turn its attention to assisting them to "shake off proprietary fetters."[82] William Rankin, who immigrated to the Island from Demerara in the 1830s, sustained this message in his short-lived pro-Escheat paper, the *Prince Edward Island Times*. The "progress of improvement," he noted, was transforming the lives of slaves in the West Indies while "chains and manacles of oppression" that rivaled slavery continued to persist on Prince Edward Island.[83] The precedent of British emancipation legislation proved particularly useful for countering the claim that the Escheat Movement's challenge to the property rights of landlords put it outside the realm of legitimate political discussion. After 1833, Escheators could note that, although the antislavery crusaders, such as William Wilberforce and Thomas Buxton, had been vilified for their attack on property rights, their initiatives had ultimately become law, and that they would be remembered as progressive leaders who had contributed to "freeing millions of the human race from bondage."[84] Those who opposed the emancipation of Island tenants, like those who had opposed the emancipation of slaves in the West Indies, were, they argued, "a race of arrogant, upstart gentry" who wished to be supported forever "by the hard labour of the oppressed and degraded Agriculturalists."[85]

The tactics of rural protest on Prince Edward Island in the 1830s and early 1840s focused on formal politics and court challenges, as well as on local resistance. In this they had more in common with the actions which tenants in the Hudson Valley would deploy than with contemporaneous rural protests in the regions of the British Isles where most of the population had originated, and where redress of grievances was most commonly sought through direct action.[86] Prince Edward Island had had its own House of Assembly since 1773, and this, coupled with a relatively broad franchise, created a forum for rural grievances. Electoral changes introduced in 1833, which set the term of the House of Assembly at four years, gave Escheators the opportunity to bring voter pressure to bear on legislative proceedings. This they ultimately did quite successfully by establishing their own political party. The bill which created quadrennial elections was passed in the wake of the British parliamentary Reform Bill, and the member of the Assembly who introduced the bill pressed his case, arguing that it was fully consistent with the political philosophy of "friends and supporters of freedom in Great Britain," as well as with the aspirations of liberals shedding blood for political freedom in Italy, Poland, and Russia.[87]

Direct action in the form of a rent strike was also part of the Escheat Movement's repertoire of resistance from the beginning. When, following the close of the spring session of the legislature in 1832, the citizens of Bay Fortune met to consider the land question, they included a call to stop paying rents in their published resolutions. This was true of other meetings held elsewhere as well in the wake of publication of the Bay Fortune proceedings. In some communities, "bonds" or "agreements" were established at this time to bind tenants to the strategy of rent resistance.[88] Refusal to pay rents soon led to confrontations with land agents and the forces of the law as tenants moved from resisting payment to blocking attempts to seize property or serve eviction notices.[89] The historical record is, understandably, relatively silent concerning the organization of this resistance and the exact role of Escheat leaders in it, but the scale of the resistance (which at times saw large armed crowds turn back sheriffs and their deputies), as well as its extent and locales point to the intimate connections between the well-documented political initiatives and the direct actions. At various times, direct action effectively halted the collection of rents on much of the Island, and made some areas unsafe for those seeking to collect rents or enforce legal actions relating to the land question.

The formal political challenge, too, came to hold the possibility of a direct confrontation with the forces of constituted authority, as there was no precise demarcation between mobilizing a population to protest an injustice by petition, assembly, and electoral action, and mobilizing a population to gain its ends by force, if necessary.[90] The Escheat Movement, like the movements associated with Mackenzie and Papineau in Upper and Lower Canada that were demonstrating their power in the 1830s—the Reform Bill agitation in Britain, the mass movements orchestrated by Daniel O'Connell, and the Chartist protests—brought large crowds together in mass rallies to, among other things, demonstrate physical power. The rally that would prove to be the largest of the Escheat rallies was held the same week that the first edition of the Chartist newspaper appeared on British streets, and days before reform challenges in the Canadas slipped into insurrection.[91] This mass rally of November 1837, with marching contingents from various parts of the Island and the pageantry of flags and banners and rounds of musket fire, was the expression of a substantial challenge to the authority of the state.

Although the escheat agitation of the 1830s began with the hope that the Island's House of Assembly could be electorally reconstructed to reflect the demands of land reformers, the task proved more difficult than its leaders had first imagined. Frustrated over Assembly policies that seemed to fly in the face of the wishes of the rural populace, Escheat activists in communities around the Island took steps in the winter of 1836 that led to the establishment of what became, in essence, an alternative assembly. Communities selected "delegates" to represent their interests at Escheat "conventions," which in turn assumed leadership in a number of areas concerning the land question. These included raising monies for a legal defense fund and to send delegates to represent their cause with government officials in London and Quebec City, orchestrating electoral campaigns, hammering out collective policy on the land question, printing pamphlets to send to the British Parliament, exploring the possibility of founding their own newspaper, establishing lists of their foes, and orchestrating what would later be known as "boycotts." Some of these initiatives were handled by community-level Escheat organizations, but a central "Managing Committee" coordinated local efforts and dealt with broader issues.[92]

These initiatives might have provided the organizational basis for armed challenges such as those which developed in Upper and Lower Canada in the winter of 1837. Indeed, one of the main reform leaders in Lower Canada publicly drew the parallels with Prince Edward Island just before the outbreak of violence, and suggested that rural protestors in Lower Canada would do well to emulate the militancy of the activists on Prince Edward Island.[93] The strength of agrarian organization on Prince Edward Island, though, had much to do with why protest there stopped short of armed rebellion. Escheat leaders recognized the futility of insurrection in such a small colony, and they had the authority to persuade their followers not to engage in actions that would, in their words, "expose their dwellings to desolation and themselves to all the horrors of military execution."[94] As well, the Escheat Movement had sufficient strength to deter others from acts of provocation, for, as the Island's governor noted in the winter of 1837, authorities in Prince Edward Island lacked sufficient troops to deal with any "serious tumult," and reinforcements could only be sent at the times of year when the ice was out and shipping possible.[95]

In the aftermath of the bloody suppression of the rebellions in Upper and Lower Canada, conservative forces on the Island sought, as they often had in the past, to damn rural protesters in the colony by association. This time, the tactic proved remarkably unsuccessful, and when elections for the House of Assembly were held in the fall of 1838, the men who had been the leaders of Escheat's alternative assembly shifted over to assume control of the official House of Assembly. Although the Escheat Movement employed a wide variety of tactics in its assault on landlordism, much of its energy had been directed toward formal political mobilization, and a guiding assumption of the movement had been that it was possible to achieve land reform by constitutional means. During the four years following the election of 1838, advocates of a radical land reform had the representation and the leadership to push relentlessly for real reform. The experience revealed the limitations of the political system, which they had believed would respond to strong expressions of the public will. Time and again, the House of Assembly's legislative initiatives were blocked by the appointed upper house, or by the Colonial Office in London, which ultimately had the final say on all legislation concerning property.

Direct appeals to the imperial government also proved fruitless. Just prior to the 1838 election, the Escheat "convention" had dispatched Cooper to London to present the case for land reform to the Colonial Secretary, Lord Glenelg. Although Cooper met with Daniel O'Connell and Joseph Hume and began to forge relationships with them, he made little headway with the Colonial Secretary, who had been informed by letter from the colony's governor that any claims Cooper might make that he represented the majority of the Island's rural population were "entirely without foundation."[96] With election results that proved the contrary, Cooper returned to London in his capacity as Speaker of the new House of Assembly, but again was rebuffed at the Colonial Office. His fallback plan, which was to bring the grievances of the Island's rural population to the attention of the British Parliament, proved difficult, as by the time Cooper was in a position to do so, Parliament had been dissolved and an election called. Its results brought a decade of Whig rule to an end. The Escheat Movement's main ally, Joseph Hume, lost his seat, and although another vigorous advocate of reform, Dr. Bowring, agreed to act in his stead, the chances of success in the first years of Robert Peel's ministry were not good, to say the least.[97]

Within the year, the Escheat Party too lost its majority, and with it its momentum. The movement that Cooper led had developed energy in the early years of the 1830s, as the struggle for reform seemed to be moving from success to success in the imperial center and elsewhere. It survived the crisis of the winter of 1837–38 in British North America by opting not to challenge the status quo by force of arms. Thus, as the followers of Mackenzie and Papineau went into voluntary and involuntary exile, to prison, and to the gallows,[98] Escheators more clearly defined a constitutional strategy, which permitted them to assume power in the colony's House of Assembly. Ultimately, however, power did not lie there, or with the appointed upper house, or with government officers on the Island, but with the British Parliament. Escheat's strategy had come to entail using political mobilization on the Island, and their position as the elected representatives of the Island's population, to make a moral claim. The changing political context in Britain, though, closed down whatever opportunities there might have been for success by such means.

With the loss of hope, the Escheat Movement began to come undone. "Prince Edward Island's Chartists," as one of their conservative opponents labeled them, had grappled with the problems of choosing between physical force and moral force, and having opted for the latter, ran out of options when the imperial state said "no" to their demands and showed itself willing to sustain that position by force. In the early years of the Escheat Movement, Cooper had drawn a parallel between the circumstances on Prince Edward Island and those in Ireland, suggesting that the rural residents of both were the victims of insidious land monopolies. He suggested as well that while "bullets and bayonets" might momentarily silence rural protest, force was not a viable long-term state policy.[99] He was right—in the long term. In the short term, however, the imperial government was willing to adopt such policies, both at home and in British North America. "The order of the day," as the Rustico activists had phrased it, was definitely not "reform," and as a result, the possibilities for effective formal rural protest on Prince Edward Island were sharply reduced. As with its rise, the Escheat Movement's demise, like the ebb and flow of rural protest in earlier periods of Island history, was intimately connected with broader patterns of change in the Atlantic world.

Notes

1. John Crisp to the Editor, *Royal Gazette* (Charlottetown), 21 August 1832, p. 2. The *Royal Gazette* functioned as a commercial paper, as well as the record of official news.
2. I use capitals to distinguish the rural protest movement that began in the 1830s—the Escheat Movement—from other calls for an escheat (a process whereby land title is resumed by the state) of some or all of the proprietorial holdings in the colony.
3. To avoid confusion, I refer to the colony as Prince Edward Island throughout this paper. See D. C. Harvey, *The French Regime in Prince Edward Island* (New Haven: Yale University Press, 1926), 141–60.
4. D. W. Meinig, *The Shaping of America: A Geographical Perspective on 500 Years of History*, vol. 1, *Atlantic America, 1492–1800* (New Haven: Yale University Press, 1986), 267–307; Bernard Bailyn, *Voyagers to the West: A Passage in the Peopling of America on the Eve of the Revolution* (New York: Alfred A. Knopf, 1986), 7–24.
5. J. M. Bumsted, *Land, Settlement, and Politics on Eighteenth-Century Prince Edward Island* (Kingston and Montreal: McGill-Queen's University Press, 1987), 12–26. For land policies and the activities of land speculators elsewhere on this new frontier, see Charlton W. Tebeau, *A*

History of Florida (Coral Gables, Fla.: University of Miami Press, 1971), 80; Thomas Perkins Abernethy, *Western Lands and the American Revolution* (New York: Russell and Russell, 1959), 1–58; Matt Bushnell Jones, *Vermont in the Making, 1750–1777* (1939; reprint, Hamden, Conn.: Archon Books, 1968), 40–66.

6. Andrew Hill Clark, *Three Centuries and the Island: A Historical Geography of Settlement and Agriculture in Prince Edward Island, Canada* (Toronto: University of Toronto Press, 1959), append. B.

7. Harvey, *The French Regime in Prince Edward Island*; Andrew Hill Clark, *Acadia: The Geography of Early Nova Scotia to 1760* (Madison: University of Wisconsin Press, 1968); Richard Colebrook Harris, *The Seigneurial System in Early Canada: A Geographical Study* (1966; reprint, Kingston and Montreal: McGill-Queen's University Press, 1984); Alan Taylor, *Liberty Men and Great Proprietors: The Revolutionary Settlement on the Maine Frontier, 1760–1820* (Chapel Hill: University of North Carolina Press, 1990); Oliver A. Rink, *Holland on the Hudson: An Economic and Social History of Dutch New York* (Cooperstown, N.Y.: New York State Historical Association, 1986); Michael Kammen, *Colonial New York: A History* (New York: Charles Scribner's Sons, 1975); Sung Bok Kim, *Landlord and Tenant in Colonial New York: Manorial Society, 1664–1775* (Chapel Hill: University of North Carolina Press, 1978); Reeve Huston, *Land and Freedom: Rural Society, Popular Protest, and Party Politics in Antebellum New York* (New York: Oxford University Press, 2000); Aron M. Sakolski, *Land Tenure and Land Taxation in America* (New York: Robert Schalkenbach Foundation, 1957), 18–58.

8. Clark, *Three Centuries and the Island*, 42–50.

9. Bumsted, *Land, Settlement, and Politics*, 27–44.

10. Ibid., 30, 40.

11. Ada MacLeod, "The Glenaladale Pioneers," *Dalhousie Review* 11 (1931–32): 311–24; J. M. Bumsted, "Highland Emigration to the Island of St. John and the Scottish Catholic Church," *Dalhousie Review* 54 (1978): 511–27; J. M. Bumsted, "Sir James Montgomery and Prince Edward Island, 1767–1803," *Acadiensis* 7, no. 2 (1978): 76–102; F. L. Pigot, "Thomas Desbrisay," *Dictionary of Canadian Biography* (Toronto: University of Toronto Press, 1983), 5:249–50; H. T. Holman, "Robert Clark," *Dictionary of Canadian Biography* (Toronto: University of Toronto Press, 1979), 6:152–53; Bumsted, *Land, Settlement and Politics*, 45–64; Bailyn, *Voyagers to the West*, 59–61.

12. Margaret E. McCallum, "'The Sacred Rights of Property': Title, Entitlement, and the Land Question in Nineteenth-Century Prince Edward

Island," in *Essays in the History of Canadian Law*, vol. 8, *In Honour of R. C. B. Risk*, ed. G. Blaine Baker and Jim Phillips (Toronto: University of Toronto Press, 1999), 365. For the importance that similar questions about the legitimacy of landlord titles held to contemporaneous land struggles in New York, see Huston, *Land and Freedom*, 19–20, 33–35, 83, 97–98, 101, 121, 165, 180, 193; Charles W. McCurdy, *The Anti-Rent Era in New York Law and Politics, 1839–1865* (Chapel Hill: University of North Carolina Press, 2001), 4, 97–100, 275, 282–84.

13. Clark, *Three Centuries and the Island*, 56–60.

14. Earle Lockerby, "The Deportation of the Acadians from Ile-St. Jean, 1758," *Acadiensis* 27, no. 2 (1998): 45–94.

15. Orlo Jones and Doris Haslam, eds., *An Island Refuge: Loyalists and Disbanded Troops on the Island of Saint John* (Charlottetown: Abegweit Branch of the United Empire Loyalist Association of Canada, 1983); Bumsted, *Land, Settlement and Politics*, 98–120.

16. Lockerby, "The Deportation of the Acadians from Ile-St. Jean, 1758," 86–88.

17. These shifts, to find the best land and/or avoid landlords, included moves to adjacent colonies. John MacDonald to Nelly, 6 March 1784, ms. 2664/8/3–4, Public Archives of Prince Edward Island [hereafter PAPEI]; Hill Memorial, [n.d.] Colonial Office Papers (CO) 226/17/143–4; MacLeod, "The Glenaladale Pioneers," 319.

18. Richard Maxwell Brown, "Back Country Rebellions and the Homestead Ethic," in *Tradition, Conflict, and Modernization: Perspectives on the American Revolution*, ed. Richard Maxwell Brown and Don E. Fehrenbacher (New York: Academic Press, 1977), 73–98; Edward Countryman, "Out of the Bounds of the Law: Northern Land Rioters in the Eighteenth Century," in *The American Revolution: Explorations in the History of American Radicalism*, ed. Alfred F. Young (DeKalb: Northern Illinois University Press, 1976), 39–61; Gregory H. Nobles, "Breaking into the Backcountry: New Approaches to the Early American Frontier, 1750–1800," *William and Mary Quarterly* 46, no. 4 (October 1989): 641–70.

19. A series of questionable land-policy initiatives, beginning in the early 1780s and orchestrated by the Island's first governor, Walter Patterson, left the issue of land titles and ownership even more muddied than they previously had been, and contributed to settlers' land grievances as well. For a discussion of the details of Patterson's initiatives, see Bumsted, *Land, Settlement and Politics*, 83–138.

20. Margaret Ells, "Clearing the Decks for the Loyalists," Canadian Historical Association, *Annual Reports* (1933): 43–58.

21. For Robinson's biography, see J. M. Bumsted, "Joseph Robinson," *Dictionary of Canadian Biography* (Toronto: University of Toronto Press, 1983), 5:720–21; Edward J. Cashin, *The King's Ranger: Thomas Brown and the American Revolution on the Southern Frontier* (Athens: University of Georgia Press, 1989); [John Hill's biographical sketch of Robinson], CO 226/18/215. For Montgomery, see Bumsted, "Sir James Montgomery and Prince Edward Island."

22. John Hill memorandum, [n.d.], CO 226/17/110.

23. "To the Farmers in the Island of St. John, in the Gulf of St. Lawrence," ms. 2702/684. PAPEI.

24. Brown, "Back Country Rebellions and the Homestead Ethic"; Alan Taylor, "Agrarian Independence: Northern Land Rioters After the Revolution," in *Beyond the American Revolution: Explorations in the History of American Radicalism*, ed. Alfred F. Young (DeKalb: University of Northern Illinois Press, 1993), 221–45.

25. [John Hill's biographical sketch of Robinson], CO 226/18/215–6; J. M. Bumsted, "Robert Hodgson," *Dictionary of Canadian Biography* (Toronto: University of Toronto Press, 1983), 5:424–25.

26. Enclosure, John MacDonald to Portland, 24 November 1798, CO 226/16/142–3; [John Hill's biographical sketch of Robinson], CO 226/18/215; John Hill memorandum, [n.d.], CO 226/17/138.

27. Fanning to Portland, 30 September 1797, CO 226/15/264–7; Joseph Robinson's Report, 25 August 1797, CO 226/15/268–9.

28. MacDonald to Fanning, 15 April 1797, CO 226/15/211.

29. Hill memorandum, [n.d.], CO 226/17/126–7.

30. F. L. Pigot, "John MacDonald of Glenaladale," *Dictionary of Canadian Biography* (Toronto: University of Toronto Press, 1983), 5:514.

31. Fanning to Portland, 30 September 1797, CO 226/15/267.

32. J. M. Bumsted, "Edmund Fanning," *Dictionary of Canadian Biography* (Toronto: University of Toronto Press, 1983), 5:308.

33. Contextualization of this report is provided by J. M. Bumsted, "The Land Question on Prince Edward Island and the Quit Rent Controversy of 1802–1806," *Acadiensis* 29, no. 2 (2000): 3–16.

34. Prince Edward Island, *Journals of the House of Assembly* (*JHA*), 16 July 1801.

35. Fanning to Portland, 30 September 1797, CO 226/15/215.

36. J. M. Bumsted, "The Origins of the Land Question on Prince Edward Island, 1767–1805," *Acadiensis* 11, no. 1 (1981): 45.

37. Arturo Warman has aptly compared the situation confronting the historian in these circumstances to the problems of following a play in which the most important actor says nothing. The persistent influences of a silent peasantry have provided, Warman has suggested in the case of Mexico's development, the essential continuities and determinants of national history. Landlords and the bourgeoisie may have had all the lines, but their behavior reflected the position of the rural masses who physically dominated the stage. Arturo Warman, *"We Come to Object": The Peasants of Morelos and the National State*, trans. Stephen K. Ault (Baltimore: Johns Hopkins University Press, 1980), 4. James C. Scott has suggested a coral metaphor to make the same point. Like the millions of polyps whose actions go into the construction of reefs, peasant actions in aggregate create a political presence which makes some routes possible and leads to the wreck of those attempting others. James C. Scott, *Weapons of the Weak: Everyday Forms of Peasant Resistance* (New Haven: Yale University Press, 1985), xvii.

38. Loyalist elites in Saint John encountered similar problems in controlling their followers during the turbulent 1780s. D. G. Bell, *Early Loyalist Saint John: The Origin of New Brunswick Politics, 1783–1786* (Fredericton: New Ireland Press, 1983), 129–33.

39. H. T. Holman, "James Bardin Palmer," *Dictionary of Canadian Biography* (Toronto: University of Toronto Press, 1987), 6:565–59; "Report by Major J. B. Palmer on Conditions in Prince Edward Island," 20 August 1805, DesBarres Papers, MG 23/F1–5/14/2708–17, National Archives of Canada.

40. Palmer Deposition, 16 May 1811, CO 226/28/66; James Meeman and Desmond Clarke, eds., *The Royal Dublin Society, 1731–1981* (Dublin: Gill and Macmillan, 1981); J. C. Beckett, *The Making of Modern Ireland, 1603–1923* (London: Faber and Faber, 1981), 175–76.

41. Ulrich Im Hof, "German Associations and Politics in the Second Half of the Eighteenth Century," in *The Transformation of Political Culture: England and Germany in the Late Eighteenth Century,* ed. Eckhart Hellmuth (London: Oxford University Press, 1990), 211.

42. Charles Wright deposition, 23 April 1812, CO 226/26/195–6.

43. Holland to Smith, 21 December 1814, CO 226/31/15.

44. Charles Stewart to Montgomery, 20 April 1812, CO 226/26/28; Colclough to Hill, 28 April 1812, CO 226/26/225–6.

45. LeSeuer to Attorney General Charles Stewart, 24 April 1812, CO 226/30/83–5.

46. Colclough to Robert Montgomery, 26 March 1812, CO 226/26/235.

47. Hill and Montgomery, "Statement Relative to Prince Edward Island," [n.d.], CO 226/26/165; Cambridge to Richardson, 9 March 1818, CO 226/34/391. There were parallels here as well with Jacobin modes of organization, as Abbé LeSeuer may have noted. See Michael L. Kennedy, *The Jacobin Clubs in the French Revolution: The First Years* (Princeton, N.J.: Princeton University Press, 1982), 3–30.

48. Charles Tilly, "Britain Creates the Social Movement," in *Social Conflict and the Political Order in Modern Britain*, ed. James E. Cronin and Jonathan Schneer (London: Croom Helm, 1982), 21–51.

49. J. M. Bumsted, "William Roubel," *Dictionary of Canadian Biography* (Toronto: University of Toronto Press, 1987), 6:662–63.

50. Roubel deposition, 30 July 1813, CO 226/28/63; Gerrit P. Judd, *Members of Parliament, 1734–1832* (Hamden, Conn.: Shoe String Press, 1972), 106.

51. Emphasis in the original. Smith to Bathurst, 29 July 1813, CO 226/29/67–70.

52. Smith to Bathurst, 13 September 1814, CO 226/29/82.

53. Eric Hobsbawm aptly characterizes the second decade of the nineteenth century in Britain as the "hysterical 1810s." E. J. Hobsbawm, *The Age of Revolution, 1789–1848* (New York: New American Library, 1962), 251.

54. Elinor Vass, "John Ready," *Dictionary of Canadian Biography* (Toronto: University of Toronto Press, 1988), 7:740–42.

55. *Prince Edward Island Register* (Charlottetown), 4 December 1824.

56. Prince Edward Island, *JHA*, 1825, 1st session, pp. 44, 59; CO 226/43/5–6.

57. Prince Edward Island, *JHA*, 1825, 1st session, p. 44; CO 226/43/5–6.

58. CO 226/47/166–8.

59. Clark, *Three Centuries and the Island*, 66.

60. *Royal Gazette*, 21 September, 19 October, 26 October, 9 November 1830; 15 February, 19 April, 7 June, 14 June 1831; 1 May, 14 August 1832.

61. See, for instance, Dalrymple and Cooper's remarks in *Royal Gazette*, 15 January, 2 April 1833.

62. Harry Baglole, "William Cooper," *Dictionary of Canadian Biography* (Toronto: University of Toronto Press, 1976), 9:155–58; Harry Baglole, "William Cooper of Sailor's Hope," *The Island Magazine* (fall–winter 1979): 3–11.

63. D. A. Sutherland, "1810–1820: War and Peace," in *The Atlantic Region to Confederation*, ed. Phillip A. Buckner and John G. Reid (Toronto and

Fredericton: University of Toronto Press and Acadiensis Press, 1994), 234–35.

64. My description of Cooper's behavior as a land agent draws primarily from "Report of a Select Committee of the Inhabitants of Lot or Township number 56 in Prince Edward Island. Submitted to the Inhabitants at a Public Meeting the 16th of January 1838," CO 226/56/177–88; statement of Archibald Steele et al., from the September 1837 *Colonial Herald* (Charlottetown), CO 226/55/316.

65. *British American* (Charlottetown), 13 April 1833.

66. *Legislative and Other Proceedings on the Expediency of Appointing a Court of Escheats in Prince Edward Island* (1836).

67. Similar shifts emerged in the translation of tenant demands into legislative and gubernatorial initiatives in New York in the 1840s. Huston, *Land and Freedom*, 99, 154–56, 180; McCurdy, *The Anti-Rent Era*, 33.

68. Mr. Cooper's Speech on the Escheat Question, *Royal Gazette*, 3 April 1832.

69. *Royal Gazette*, 24 April 1832. Rural people who were literate in English assumed the task of reading and translating these newspaper reports to others in their communities. See, for instance, John Arbuckle to T. H. Haviland, 25 January 1838, CO 226/55/297.

70. The printed text that historians now have to work with was not the version that circulated in the countryside, and some members of the Island elite claimed that the printed version was altered before publication—perhaps toned down. Hill's biographical sketch of Joseph Robinson, CO 226/18/215.

71. Mr. Cooper's Speech on the Escheat Question, *Royal Gazette*, 3 April 1832.

72. *Colonial Herald*, 10 February 1838. For French and American parallels regarding use of classical agrarian law as a precedent, see R. B. Rose, "The 'Red Scare' of the 1790s: The French Revolution and the 'Agrarian Law,'" *Past and Present* 103 (May 1984): 113–30; Paul Conkin, *Prophets of Prosperity: America's First Political Economists* (Bloomington: Indiana University Press, 1980), 224–25. Apparently conflating the Roman land unit, the *iugera*, with acres, Cooper incorrectly claimed that the limit was 500 acres, rather than approximately 330 acres. The 500-acre figure subsequently became the ceiling that the Escheat Movement used as an appropriate limit for land accumulation. Yet later, it was embodied in the compulsory land purchase legislation of 1875.

73. *British American*, 13 April 1833.

74. Malcolm Chase, *"The People's Farm": English Radical Agrarianism, 1775–1840* (Oxford: Clarendon Press, 1988); Jamie L. Bronstein, *Land Reform and Working-Class Experience in Britain and the United States, 1800–1862* (Stanford, Calif.: Stanford University Press, 1999); Thomas R. Knox, "Thomas Spence: The Trumpet of Jubilee," *Past and Present* 76 (1977): 75–98; Dorothy Thompson, *The Chartists: Popular Politics in the Industrial Revolution* (New York: Pantheon, 1984), 299–306; Conkin, *Prophets of Prosperity*, 222–58; Sean Wilentz, *Chants Democratic: New York City and the Rise of the American Working Class, 1788–1850* (New York: Oxford University Press, 1984), 335–43; Huston, *Land and Freedom*, 8, 112–13.

75. John Belchem, "Republicanism, Popular Constitutionalism and the Radical Platform in Early Nineteenth-Century England," *Social History* 6 (1981): 1–32. See, for instance, John LeLecheur's demand for "pure and unadulterated British laws" in the *Colonial Herald*, 3 October 1838.

76. Edward Pessen describes these ideas as the "solid rock" underlying radical labor's "idea of the good society" in Jacksonian America. Edward Pessen, *Most Uncommon Jacksonians: The Radical Leaders of the Early Labour Movement* (Albany: State University of New York Press, 1967), 174. Thomas Summerhill notes the parallels between the producer ideology of tenants and small farmers in upstate New York and that espoused by labor radicals, and notes Thomas Devyr's role in trying to build a link between urban and rural laborers. Thomas Summerhill, "The Farmers' Republic: Agrarian Protest and the Capitalist Transformation of Upstate New York, 1840–1900" (Ph.D. diss., University of California, San Diego, 1993), 55, 127. See also Huston, *Land and Freedom*, 111–12; Taylor, "Agrarian Independence"; Wilentz, *Chants Democratic*, 157–58, 178; Alan Dawley, *Class and Community: The Industrial Revolution in Lynn* (Cambridge, Mass.: Harvard University Press, 1976), 63–65; Paul G. Faler, *Mechanics and Manufacturers in the Early Industrial Revolution: Lynn, Massachusetts, 1780–1860* (Albany: State University of New York Press, 1981), 175–88; Bruce Laurie, *Working People of Philadelphia, 1800–1850* (Philadelphia: Temple University Press, 1980), 75–77, 108–9; Patricia Hollis, *The Pauper Press: A Study in Working Class Radicalism in the 1830s* (Oxford: Oxford University Press, 1970), 203–58; J. F. C. Harrison, *Robert Owen and the Owenites in Britain and America: The Quest for the New Moral Order* (London: Routledge and Kegan Paul, 1969), 69–72.

77. Alan Taylor, "Agrarian Independence," 224–25.
78. *Royal Gazette*, 1 May 1832.
79. *Royal Gazette*, 29 March 1836.
80. *Colonial Herald*, 31 March 1838.
81. *Royal Gazette*, 3 April 1832; *British American*, 13 April 1833; *Royal Gazette*, 25 November 1834, CO 226/55/309; "To the Reformers of Prince and Queen's County," *Prince Edward Island Times*, 16 April 1836; "A Native Elector" to "The Electors of the Second Electoral District of Prince County," *Colonial Herald*, 7 May 1842. Asa Briggs, "The Language of 'Class' in Early Nineteenth-Century England," in *Collected Essays of Asa Briggs*, vol. 1, *Words, Numbers, Places, People* (Brighton: The Harvester Press, 1985), 1:3–33; Raymond Williams, *Keywords: A Vocabulary of Culture and Society* (New York: Oxford University Press, 1976), 51–59.
82. *Colonial Herald*, 22 August 1838.
83. *Prince Edward Island Times*, 26 July 1836; J. M. Bumsted, "William Rankin," *Dictionary of Canadian Biography* (Toronto: University of Toronto Press, 1988), 7:734–35.
84. *Colonial Herald*, 5 May 1838.
85. *Colonial Herald*, 3 October 1838.
86. Huston, *Land and Freedom*; Eric Hobsbawm and George Rudé, *Captain Swing: A Social History of the Great English Agricultural Uprising of 1830* (1968; reprint, New York: W. W. Norton, 1975); Eric Richards, "How Tame were the Highlanders During the Clearances?" *Scottish Studies* 17 (spring 1973): 35–50; James Hunter, *The Making of the Crofting Community* (Edinburgh: John Donald, 1976); T. M. Devine, "Unrest and Stability in Rural Ireland and Scotland, 1760–1840," in *Economy and Society in Scotland and Ireland, 1500–1939*, ed. Rosalind Mitchison and Peter Roebuck (Edinburgh: John Donald, 1988), 126–39; Michael Beames, *Peasants and Power: The Whiteboy Movements and Their Control in Pre-Famine Ireland* (Sussex: Harvester Press, 1983); P. E. W. Roberts, "Caravats and Shanavests: Whiteboyism and Faction Fighting in East Munster, 1802–11," in *Irish Peasants: Violence and Political Unrest, 1780–1914*, ed. S. D. Clark and J. S. Donnelly Jr.(Madison: University of Wisconsin Press, 1983), 64–101; David Williams, *The Rebecca Riots: A Study in Agrarian Discontent* (Cardiff: University of Wales Press, 1955); David Jones, *Before Rebecca: Popular Protests in Wales, 1793–1835* (Bristol: Allen Lane, 1973); Pat Molloy, *And They Blessed Rebecca: An Account of the Welsh Toll-Gate Riots, 1839–1844* (Llandysul, Wales: Gomer Press, 1983).

87. *Royal Gazette,* 5 February 1833, p. 2.

88. *Abstract of the Proceedings of the Land Commissioners' Court Held During the Summer of 1860 to Inquire into the Differences Relative to the Rights of Landowners and Tenants in Prince Edward Island* (Charlottetown, 1862), 154; "Report of a Select Committee of the Inhabitants of Lot or Township number 56 in Prince Edward Island. Submitted to the Inhabitants at a Public Meeting the 16th of January 1838," CO 226/56/180–1; *British American,* 27 October 1832.

89. For the role of women in this direct action, see Rusty Bittermann, "Women and the Escheat Movement: The Politics of Everyday Life on Prince Edward Island," in *Separate Spheres: The World of Women in the Nineteenth-Century Maritimes,* ed. Suzanne Morton and Janet Guildford (Fredericton: Acadiensis Press, 1994), 23–38.

90. T. M. Parssinen, "Association, Convention and Anti-Parliament in British Radical Politics, 1771–1848," *English Historical Review* 88 (1973): 504–33; Tilly, "Britain Creates the Social Movement," 44–45; John Belchem, *Industrialization and the Working Class: The English Experience, 1750–1900* (Aldershot: Scholar Press, 1990), 73–83; J. T. Ward, *Chartism* (London: Batsford, 1973), 111–42.

91. *Colonial Herald,* 25 November 1837, in CO 226/56/141–2; Dorothy Thompson, *The Chartists,* ix; Alan Greer, *The Patriotes and the People: The Rebellion of 1837 in Rural Lower Canada* (Toronto: University of Toronto Press, 1993); Colin Read and Ronald J. Stagg, eds., *The Rebellion of 1837 in Upper Canada* (Don Mills, Ont.: The Champlain Society, 1985); Allan Greer, "1837–38: Rebellion Reconsidered," *Canadian Historical Review* 76, no. 1 (March 1995): 1–18.

92. *Prince Edward Island Times* (Charlottetown), 12 July 1836; *Royal Gazette,* 25 April 1837; *Colonial Herald,* 25 November 1837, in CO 226/56/141–2; Petition to Harvey, CO 226/54/95; *Colonial Herald,* 13 January 1838, 10 February 1838, 17 February 1838, 10 March 1838, 4 July 1838.

93. Fernand Ouellet, *Lower Canada, 1791–1840: Social Change and Nationalism,* trans. Patricia Claxton (Toronto: McClelland and Stewart, 1980), 293–97.

94. *Colonial Herald,* 14 April 1838.

95. Fitzroy to Glenelg, 29 November 1837, CO 226/54/304; Fitzroy to Glenelg, 30 January 1838, CO 226/55/76–81.

96. Fitzroy to Glenelg, 6 May 1838, CO 226/55/318–21.

97. Bowring to Macfarlane, 23 November 1841, Prince Edward Island, *JHA,* 1842, append. K; Betty Fladeland, *Abolitionists and Working-Class*

Problems in the Age of Industrialization (Baton Rouge: Louisiana State University Press, 1984), 98.

98. George Rudé, *Protest and Punishment: The Story of the Social and Political Protesters Transported to Australia, 1788–1868* (Oxford: Clarendon Press, 1978), 42–51, 82–88, 96–99.

99. *British American*, 13 April 1833, p. 290.

The United States as a Postcolonial State, 1789–1865

Thomas Summerhill

This article will reconsider the early history of the United States as a case study of postcolonial nationhood in the Americas. In particular, it attacks the notion of American exceptionalism as an ethnocentric myth with dubious empirical foundations. The foundations of my argument are the persistence of a landed elite that derived power from illiberal labor forms—slavery, tenancy, etc.—in both the North and South, the dominance of extractive agriculture and industries, the struggle for power between landed and financial capital that expressed itself in conflicts between the central government and the states over class prerogatives, the dominant role of European capital in the development of the nation, and the conquest and subjugation of native peoples. I conclude that the United States evinced sufficient similarities to Latin American nations before the Civil War to be considered a variant of the same processes. Since farming defined American culture during this period, this is a decidedly agrarian story, one that promises to offer new ways of understanding the transformation of rural into industrial societies.

I. Exceptionalism, Dependency, and Ethnocentrism

Since the United States escaped dependency in the mid-nineteenth century, it takes a deft analysis of existing literature to outflank the exceptionalists and demonstrate that the nation bore the marks of other postcolonial states in the hemisphere between 1789 and 1865. It has been far easier to point to the Protestant ethic and a liberal constitution as the source of America's success than to analyze rigorously the interplay between international political and economic changes and the struggle within the United States between creole agrarians and capitalists to direct the nation's future. Historical forces, not the innate virtues of American institutions, played the decisive role in determining the nation's course—with the climax coming, I argue, with the Panic of 1837 and its destruction of the alliance between free-soil laborers and Southern planters. With agrarians divided, the bourgeoisie of the North staged a generation-long revolution that culminated in the defeat of the slave South and the beginning of America's second industrial revolution. It was after the panic that Northern capital began to exercise sufficient national power to overcome economic dependency on Britain, which the cotton South fostered. Only then did America establish itself as an independent nation.[1]

One of the most enduring historical paradigms is that the United States stands as an "exception" in the development of world capitalism, and more particularly, that the republic's egalitarian social, economic, and political institutions enabled the nation to avoid after 1789 the dependency that ultimately plagued its sister republics in Latin America. The fact that Americans staged the first modern revolution lends rhetorical force to this position; indeed, aspects of it are essential for understanding the peculiarities of American history. Certainly, the Revolutionary generation considered themselves to be imbued with extraordinary virtue as a people—the few skeptics, mostly federalists, were dismissed as aristocrats—and subsequent authors from Alexis de Tocqueville to Frederick Jackson Turner agreed that the United States had almost mystically arisen as a nation thanks to the liberating forces of cheap land, commerce, and democracy. Turner's frontier thesis suggested that pioneer white farmers had tamed the virgin landscape and built republican institutions in the wilderness that were unsullied by unnatural restraints that tainted European monarchies. Though Turner has been assailed repeatedly, rarely have scholars discarded the mythology from which he wove his tale: that white Anglo-Americans were more prepared for freedom than the people who confronted them on the continent, in neighboring nations, or in Europe.[2]

American exceptionalism as an analytical trope is therefore intimately entwined with a nationalistic language of conquest. Scholars have attempted periodically to assail exceptionalism, and have produced a series of articles that ponder the relative merits of the concept and the utility of applying comparative methods to the study of the United States. As Raymond Grew has observed, however, when comparative history is either proposed or practiced by U.S. historians, they fail to use the comparisons to "pose new questions and suggest unexpected relationships," and undertake narrow, "topical" studies that fit within narrative frameworks, not theoretical ones. The exceptions to exceptionalism have been studies of labor and slavery. Labor historians have endeavored for two decades to free American workers from their purported "classlessness." Sean Wilentz perhaps put it best when he noted that scholars must stop seeking socialist labor movements to prove class consciousness, and instead trace the ways in which workers expressed class solidarity within the particular social and political environment of early America. Studies of North American slavery likewise have evolved toward comparative analysis in ways that allow scholars to demonstrate that slave regimes in the Americas shared certain fundamental features while allowing regional or national variations in class structure to determine the ultimate shape of each society. Still, labor organization and slavery have been considered outside of the main trajectory of American historical development because they ran counter to the liberal consensus; thus, the opening wedge of "unexceptionalism" has not taken root in the broader literature.[3]

The only way to confront exceptionalism directly is to examine the political economy of the nation from its founding to the Civil War in reference to the other young republics of the Americas. Above all, class relations (especially the agrarian-capitalist conflict among the creole elite), the continued presence of unfree labor and the exploitation of non-white peoples in extractive agriculture and industries, and the preponderance of foreign capital in the national economy and the reliance on international markets need to be carefully examined.[4] Some scholars have attempted such an analysis with mixed results. Anthony McFarlane, for example, argued that the American Revolution touched off liberal revolutions throughout the Atlantic world by providing ideological inspiration for rebels and bankrupting European regimes, which had participated in the conflict—particularly France. McFarlane conceded that from 1774 to 1826,

American colonies joined a general republican outburst led by creole elites. However, McFarlane drew a dichotomy between the United States and its sister republics, suggesting that British political traditions, a liberal constitution, and the enterprise of the largely Protestant population made the American republic peculiarly free and, therefore, dynamic. Latin American nations, he suggested, labored under the burden of Catholicism, militarism, and the assumption of power of a small coterie of creole elites. McFarlane's Weberian approach led him to assume that order was the sine qua non of American political, economic, and social life; hence, his treatment of the early republican history of the United States ignored its internal conflicts, militarism, and unfreedom.[5]

The work of such scholars as Lester Langley and Peggy Liss is more promising. They argue that the United States shared certain characteristics with its Latin American neighbors during the period, particularly the commitment of creole elites to Enlightenment principles of political economy and anticolonialism. Langley develops McFarlane's themes with greater attention to the historical context within which colonial elites operated. He suggests that attempts by Britain (1763–75) and Spain (1783–1808) to rationalize their colonial administrations had like effects in each part of the Americas: creole leaders responded with republican, free-trade rhetoric that targeted the colonial system as arbitrary and capricious. Such men represented the economic vanguard of their nations—a new class poised to prosper if the patronage of the old regime were dismantled. The North American colonists responded first and more decisively to imperial reforms. Better yet, their stress on constitutional redress fitted easily within Anglo-American protest traditions, lending a legitimacy to the Revolution. His contention that the colonies succeeded because they were racially homogenous and geographic mobility mitigated class antagonism is dubious, but he nonetheless recognizes the relative peacefulness of the transition from colony to state. The Constitution confirmed the ideals of the Revolution and brought order to North America. In Latin America, he argues, Spain moved during the American Revolution to appease creole elites, a move that did not quell republicanism or calls for free trade, but which elevated would-be revolutionaries sufficiently to curb rebellion. Only when France toppled Ferdinand VII in 1808 did the Spanish colonies revolt. Langley contended that the rebellion therefore was not ideologically grounded, but was in response to a particular event. Latin American creoles also had to rely on mestizos, Indians, and blacks to promote their cause, creating unstable alliances that led to increasing civil unrest, civil war, and militarism. By the 1820s, as Latin American republics faced economic crises, their institutions, if liberal in design, were not accepted as legitimate by the population. Hence, the governments never achieved stability, leaving the nations susceptible to economic imperialism.[6]

The comparative approach that Langley and McFarlane adopt—which treats the colonies primarily as extensions of their mother country—limits the analysis they can make in ways that Liss avoids by conceptualizing the Americas as an integrated economic and political universe. Liss contends that the economies of the British and Spanish colonies were closely linked after the mid-eighteenth century. The relative weakness of the Spanish imperial apparatus left the Latin American colonies without sufficient shipping and other resources to carry on active trade. Furthermore, Spanish administration maintained strong mercantilist policies that linked colonies to the mother country with little interregional trade. The American Revolution became an important transformative moment for creole elites in the entire hemisphere. North Americans, imbued with Enlightenment ideals and English opposition traditions, shaped a revolutionary ideology that enabled them to rally rich and poor to establish independence. Their free-trade principles became influential in Latin America; almost as soon as the Revolution began, American ships began appearing in Spanish ports, interacting with creole merchants, and establishing ideological connections that helped create a Latin American language of revolution. When Spain attempted to increase colonial efficiency, creoles countered that the restrictive trade policies of Madrid were undermining free trade. Conceiving themselves as "Americans," they sought reforms that would bring them into a wider commercial world. But the historical context had changed. The influence of American traders tended to subordinate Latin American commerce; more problematic, the beginning of the Napoleonic wars brought British merchants to the Caribbean. They dumped British manufactured goods in the region, hurting domestic industries and draining specie. As a result, Latin American republics that declared independence from 1810 to 1826 began at a disadvantage economically, which prevented the kind of stability that marked the United States' transition to freedom.[7]

These comparative studies have begun to chip away at the overemphasis on American exceptionalism in important ways. Still, scholars make several assumptions that prematurely date American independence from "dependency," or oversimplify the process. First, while they make the important point that the United States quickly became a creditor of Latin American nations, they do not note that North America remained heavily in debt to Europe. Second, they do not explore the agrarian roots of that dependency (stressing the commercial dominance of the United States over Latin America). Third, they pay too little attention to the persistence of unfree labor systems in the United States and the impact of class antagonisms on the development of the nation. Fourth, the continued split between agrarians and capitalists tends to be obscured behind discussions of the remarkable commercial revolution from which both groups benefited. Finally, they remain Eurocentric in focus, and underplay the relationship between Native Americans and whites in shaping the United States; therefore, they underestimate the impact of Indians on the creation of the North American political economy.[8]

Only by incorporating the class, race, and ethnic conflicts that shaped the nation can scholars escape the theoretical restraints that underlie exceptionalism, and liberate themselves from the teleological conclusion that since the United States developed into an industrialized imperial power, it must have had particular advantages at the beginning that its neighbors did not share. The history of the United States from 1789 to 1865 gives a different picture if one chooses to look. First, the creole elite agreed to replace the feeble Articles of Confederation with the Constitution, but soon fell into a fratricidal struggle between Hamiltonians (mostly Northern commercial men) and Jeffersonians (Southern planters and frontier farmers) over the power the federal government enjoyed under the terms of the document. Class became the defining factor in the political resolution of the conflict, as agrarian uprisings rippled along the Appalachian chain and brought the Jeffersonians to power. Second, the nation was overwhelmingly dependent on foreign capital for development, and was rocked by depressions whenever European markets fluctuated. As a result, international events determined internal development—only in response to such pressures did the United States begin to crawl out of its subordinate position in the global community. And this occurred only after the decisive defeat of the agrarian interest by the capitalist class. Third, economic and political democracy were not nearly as pervasive as most scholars would have us believe. Through slavery, tenancy, and the harnessing of Native American labor through a variety of economic devices, unfreedom—not freedom—defined the experience of a substantial number of Americans before the Civil War.

II. Early National America:
Jefferson, Hamilton, and Dependency

The celebration of the liberalism (and exceptionalism) of the American Revolution was renewed with the publication of Gordon Wood's magisterial *The Radicalism of the American Revolution*. In it, Wood countered a generation of New Left historiography that argued that the war with England unleashed democratic forces that challenged the patriot leadership and sharply divided the nation along class lines. Rather, Wood contended, the true radicalism of the American Revolution was that both elite and working-class Americans agreed that Lockean liberalism offered the surest path to independence. With all Americans committed to upward mobility, he noted, the nation entered a commercial revolution after the passage of the Constitution in 1789, and moved seamlessly, classlessly into modernity by the 1830s. America had no Terror, no Thermidor, no Napoleon, because all citizens embraced individualism and happily went about the business of making money. Even politics, he averred, became entrepreneurial: those denied economic rewards by their lowly birth could, by the Age of Jackson, count on entrée into the halls of power through machine politics. Any conflicts along the way sprang not from ideological disagreements, but from differences over means to the same end. If nothing else, this interpretation conflates commerce and capitalism. Were it made for any other nation in the Atlantic world, Wood's argument would seem smug, nationalistic, and ahistorical because it masks the political struggles that flared between classes, races, ethnic groups, men and women, and farmers and workers throughout the period. Despite his efforts, the preponderance of evidence demonstrates that power was central to the Revolution, the Constitution, and America's subsequent growth. The Revolution was about "home rule" and "who should rule at home."[9]

The Revolution drew several groups into an alliance to defeat British imperialism—a task made imperative by the fact that patriots, neutrals, and loyalists were equally balanced in the population. We know the most about the Northern merchants and Southern planters who led the Revolution— men like Washington, John Adams, Jefferson, Hancock, Franklin. They fought the war for a variety of reasons; but most important, each had specific economic or political grievances against England that stemmed directly from the French and Indian War. Washington and Franklin, for example, were investors in competing land companies that sought, right up to Lexington and Concord, to outmaneuver each other to secure claims in the Ohio country. The British Proclamation Line of 1763 prevented them and other whites from venturing across the Appalachians; after all, the Native American nations of the interior were members of the new British empire that stretched from India to the far reaches of Canada with the defeat of France. Jefferson and Washington each understood well the dim future of tobacco in the played-out soils of Virginia, and English taxes stood to drive the planter class to which they belonged out of business. Adams and Hancock represented the merchant interests of New England whose markets were threatened by the proposed British trade monopolies. They found ready allies in tobacco planters and urban artisans, who feared that the new English tax structure would undercut their ability to participate freely in markets. Artisans like Samuel Adams and Thomas Paine embraced Smithian free-trade doctrines along with their social betters to protect colonial manufacturers from British "dumping." Each of these men also spoke for "outsiders" who did not enjoy the patronage of the Crown, which blended into criticisms of monopoly and corruption.[10]

Far more uncertain were the loyalties of court favorites, farmers, unskilled workers, slaves, and Native Americans. Loyalists came from a variety of groups, but the strongest defenders of the Crown were men who enjoyed political position in the colonial administration, or who had particularly strong links to English trade. Farmers, no friends of the Crown, were not unified in support of Whigs. In South Carolina, for example, backcountry farmers did not immediately rally to the Whig cause—for good reason. Lowcountry planters and merchants who led the Revolution believed that frontiersmen attacked property rights and acted as uncivilized as Indians. Pioneers despised the unequal representation in the colonial legislature that enabled lowcountry planters and merchants to pass discriminatory legislation that left marketing, credit, and defense in the Piedmont in dreadful condition. On the great estates of New York's Hudson and Mohawk valleys, tenant and debtor farmers frequently sided against their landlords. But ethnicity was also vital to their decision. Catholic Scots, for example, remained loyal, while Presbyterian Scots took up arms against Britain (and this was only one of many such divisions in the colony). In South Carolina, New York, and other frontier areas, a vicious civil war broke out during the Revolution. In North Carolina, many Regulators who had protested the land system and political corruption before the Revolution remained neutral rather than choose between an empire that prevented westward expansion or elite patriots with no love of backcountry culture and mores. Unskilled workers found unattractive the Lockean message of the revolutionaries. Slaves, meanwhile, were offered emancipation if they joined British forces. Many did, exposing Whig hypocrisy—especially since many wavering planters in the South joined the patriot cause after Dunmore's Proclamation in order to protect rights of property in man. In the North, however, African Americans made significant gains, including (though accidentally) the right to vote in New Jersey.[11]

Scholars have devoted less energy to establishing the position that Indians took during the conflict; generally, Indians supported the Crown because of fears of colonial encroachments on their territory. Indian fundamentalism in the mid-eighteenth century had spread among the Shawnee, Cherokee, Creek, and other nations bordering the Appalachians (Pontiac's Rebellion in 1763 and a series of Cherokee wars confirmed that Indians viewed colonial settlement plans with alarm). But the territorial issue was only part of the story. While the Covenant Chain between the Iroquois and the English kept those empires aligned during the Revolution, Indian nations subordinate to the Iroquois took the opportunity to cut their own deals with the Americans. In the Southwest, Choctaws, Creeks, and Cherokees split. The British had established strong relations only with the Cherokees, and the influence of French and Spanish traders (particularly in deerskins) meant that even Cherokee loyalty to the Crown was uncertain. Native American hunting and cattle raising, furthermore, played an important role in the economy of the trans-Appalachian region, giving them considerable political leverage in addition to their ability to field warriors. The British failed to adequately support the Iroquois, allowing the Continental army to scour New York of Indians. But along the rest of the backcountry, Native Americans remained a strong political force. Indeed, the very nature of Indian society made difficult any North American attempt to either defeat or incorporate them into the new republic. Most Indian nations adopted other Indians, blacks, and whites into their clans to replace lost relatives. Indian culture therefore blurred the lines between "Indian" and "colonial" in fascinating ways that gave them remarkable protection from outright extermination. Indian law, furthermore, was not constitutional, but instead was governed by negotiated settlements between clans and families. As a result, Indian nations tended to adapt to new political circumstances with much greater flexibility than whites; while this did not ensure that Indians would be able to resist white encroachment, it did prolong that process considerably. Cherokees, Creeks, Choctaws, Shawnees, and others remained important players in cattle, deerskins, and agriculture throughout the Revolutionary period. By 1782, it could be argued, they were in a stronger position relative to the colonists than at any time in their history; with the backing of British arms, they faced an economically feeble United States that had deep internal splits and little ability to move against Native America.[12]

The subsequent transformation of the United States into a world power makes it easy to lose sight of the fact that victory in the Revolution came only with the support of the French and Spanish, particularly at the Battle of Yorktown, where the French fleet prevented the British from supporting Cornwallis. At the same time, the French and Spanish opened their Caribbean and Latin American ports to North Americans, allowing trade in flour and other supplies that helped the struggling United States survive economically. Nonetheless, the colonies faced a grave crisis at the end of the war. The Continental Congress was powerless to force states to repay war debts, could not levy taxes, did not enjoy full control of relations with the Indians, did not have the power to establish a national currency, and had no power to create a military force to defend independence. The states had reserved all of those rights to prevent the re-creation of a tyrannical central government. Furthermore, to bring artisans and farmers into the patriot camp, Revolutionary leaders had agreed to democratize state governments. Small producers were far more radical than elite leaders, and did not wish to concede power to a central government that might then become a tool for oppression. To them, defense of property meant the protection of individual households from any encroachment, and the preservation of patriarchal authority. Though not opposed to commerce (especially free trade), they nonetheless did not wish to see the imposition of economic dependency by the new republic's elite. But the end of the war brought renewed trade with England, which began dumping manufactured goods on the United States, causing an economic slump made worse by dependence on English markets for agricultural products and credit. Compounded by debts to France and Spain, the new nation plunged into depression.[13]

The Constitutional Convention in Philadelphia in 1787 marked the final transformation of the Revolution from a decentralized, chaotic independence movement that included a plethora of interests to an assertion of order by creole elites. Three circumstances prompted calls for the convention. First, the new nation found itself surrounded by three powers and hostile Indians after the war. Second, stripped of British markets, devastated by war, and crippled by war debt, the young nation fell into economic depression after 1782. Finally, the economic downturn exposed the primary weakness of the Articles of Confederation. As debts mounted, states passed individual currency laws. In Rhode Island, where voting was well distributed, debtors secured legislation that made paper money legal tender. Farmers rejoiced, while creditors went bankrupt—especially those who had debts to British or French traders. In Massachusetts, the coast was overrepresented in the legislature, and merchants secured laws that made all debts payable in specie. This brought on Shays's Rebellion in 1786, as backcountry farmers suspended the courts, mobilized a Regulator force, and made entreaties to British agents in Canada for support. To this was added vigilantism in the countryside, aimed at Tories and Indians, and anger that confiscated loyalist estates were sold to the wealthy rather than being redistributed systematically among the people. Without popular conventions, a group of men calling themselves "federalists" gathered in Philadelphia to reform the articles and to defend property. Backcountry farmers and urban artisans were decidedly underrepresented at the gathering.[14]

The Constitution reordered American government in significant ways. The constitutional convention in Philadelphia had not been called for by the people. Delegates arrived from states with no authority to rewrite the Articles of Confederation. Yet they did. Prominent merchants, planters, landholders, and Revolutionary leaders, the men constructed a new government that ignored the primary demand of the people during the Revolution: the protection of personal liberties. Rather, the document began the process of defining not only the nation as a state but also which individuals would be citizens. Propertyless men, slaves, free blacks, and women were not granted citizenship, and therefore, by default, were defined as dependents. And, importantly, Indians were defined as separate peoples (not just separate nations), a fiction that ultimately enabled North American creole elites to avoid contending with the complexities of race, class, and citizenship that bedeviled their Latin American contemporaries. Mostly, however, the Constitution dealt with foreign relations, commerce, and the relationship between the central government and the states. To keep the states of the young republic from cutting their own deals financially and diplomatically in the world, the federal government would enjoy exclusive control over those functions. The Constitution centralized control over the economy, interstate commerce, foreign debt, relations with Europe, acquisition of western lands, and relations with Native Americans. Importantly, democracy was curbed with a bicameral national legislature, an executive with veto power, and a tiered federal court system. Furthermore, senators, the president, and judges were all appointed. Scholars consider the Constitution a liberal document because it was written in response to the New England disorders and because it primarily addressed economic issues. But it might be more accurate to say that it protected commerce, and *under the right conditions* could be the foundation for a capitalist state.[15]

There is reason to view the Constitution in this way. It had to unite both North and South, and perforce had to avoid controversial issues—particularly slavery. The document did not encourage capitalist development, though planters participated in the world capitalist market. Southern representatives to the convention recognized, even before the expansion of cotton in the early nineteenth century, that the concentration of financial capital in the North (generated though shipping, trading, and manufacturing) posed a threat to the agricultural economy of the South. Southern planters feared the creation of too strong a federal government because a large military and bureaucracy would lead to high taxes, the bane of farmers. No less important, Northerners had fought the Revolution to protect manufacturing—high tariffs could trigger trade wars and undermine profits. Indeed, Virginian James Madison, who helped pen the Federalist Papers, saw in the Constitution not the framework for a capitalist state, but a government strong enough to protect the young republic while it established an agrarian economy. To him and his mentor, Thomas Jefferson, the nation needed to expand over space, offering commercial opportunities to yeoman farmers so that the nation could avoid industrial development and the impoverishment of the people—and the ultimate destruction of free government. Regularizing trade relations and the acquisition of western lands was one way they could help prevent such a fate. Jefferson wrote the Northwest Ordinances in 1787, which established the land policy for the federal government and proscribed slavery north of the Ohio River. Though these acts seemed democratic, blunting democracy worked to the advantage of the Southern elite: the three-fifths clause gave them undue representation in Congress; states elected senators and presidential electors; and federal taxes would be levied on commerce, not land. State legislatures were more likely to protect planter and (ultimately) yeoman interests. Commerce and limited government received their blessing.[16]

Unease with the document permeated both the North and the South, especially among backcountry farmers and urban working men. The Constitution met stiff resistance from anti-federalists because it curbed democracy in profound ways, shifted power away from states, and addressed commerce, not civil liberties. The fact that convention delegates had not been popularly elected added to concerns that the "few" were trying to take control of the government to subjugate the "many." A remarkable political campaign by the federalists overcame resistance on a state-by-state basis, but not before democratic elements extracted the Bill of Rights. The amendments not only secured individual liberties, but expressly stated that any rights not granted to the federal government were reserved by the states. For the moment, therefore, the interpretation of the Constitution had not been decisively won by either Northern or Southern elites, and the laboring classes shared Southern wariness of a strong government.[17]

The federalists understood power well, and elected General Washington president without resistance. The results were not surprising, given the deferential politics of the early national United States. Though more men could vote than in most European or Latin American nations, the best men in the community—in elaborate election rituals of treating, speechifying, drinking, bribery, and at times intimidation—dominated politics. Patron-client relationships mapped out networks of power, with civil and militia offices distributed out to men in accordance with their social station. At first, then, federalists enjoyed the support of the strongest political brokers in the republic. Washington's aide during the war, Alexander Hamilton, was made secretary of the treasury; General Henry Knox became secretary of war; and Thomas Jefferson, the wartime governor of Virginia and minister to France, was appointed secretary of state. They entered office with considerable unity between North and South, financial and planter interests. And all had participated in military affairs at some level during the Revolution.[18]

The creole elite that swept into power in 1789 had a great deal of revolutionary prestige, but the split between agrarian and commercial interests destroyed unity and allowed class conflicts to be renewed in the polity. Hamilton's plan for the retirement of the national debt and his proposal for a national bank made clear that Northern financial interests believed that the new government should be used in partnership with private capital to develop the nation. First, Hamilton proposed to use the taxing powers of the government to repay all Continental debts at face value. Since most bonds, land scrip (which had been given to soldiers in lieu of pay), and other government securities had been sold by the original holders at below par, the speculators who bought up the notes stood to reap a windfall. Hamilton also called for high tariffs to protect manufacturers and encourage industry. Joining the cry against the plan was Madison. As a representative of the agrarian South, he concluded that Hamilton meant to line the pockets of the Northern capitalists at the expense of the rest of the populace. He introduced legislation in Congress that would pay the original holders of securities half of their value. He failed because too many Congressmen had heard of Hamilton's plan and had bought up the discounted paper.[19]

The split in elite ranks widened over the national bank. In its simplest form, the bank would be used to sink the national debt and stabilize the currency. Hamilton, however, made two proposals that unnerved Jefferson and his allies. First, the Constitution made no provision for chartering a national bank. The enlargement of federal power in this arena, Jefferson argued, would concentrate too much power over the economy into the hands of the bank. Hamilton planned to allow private investors to purchase stock and sit on the board, which would include public appointees, as well. He also proposed to pay interest on the stock in land. A small group of investors, many of whom might be foreign, would have control over the finances of the nation and have no checks on their power. Jefferson penned an eloquent plea for a strict constructionist interpretation of the Constitution—that no power not specifically granted to the federal government was reserved by the states. Only strict adherence to the document could preserve the liberties of the people against usurpation by interest groups. The blurring of public and private interests (especially coming in the wake of the debate over the national debt, which amounted to the federal government giving capital to private investors) could only help a single group in the country at the expense of all others. Washington, however, chose to support Hamilton's plan, beginning a protracted political power struggle between the elite leaders of the United States.[20]

The Jeffersonians considered Hamilton's plan a dangerous step toward reabsorption into the British Empire, since England remained the nation's leading trading partner. In short, they believed that by concentrating wealth among a single class in a single region, Hamilton would encourage a dependent relationship between producers and capital; unless prosperity was broad-based and labor independent from capital, the Jeffersonians reasoned, the republic would become corrupt and fail. They had ample evidence in the 1790s that something was amiss in the halls of government. The French Revolution helped the United States economically by stimulating demand for food and fiber in Europe. But diplomatically and politically, it tore the nation apart. On the high seas, both Britain and France seized American ships, interrupting trade. The republic attempted to maintain neutrality, but eventually signed the humiliating Jay Treaty with England in 1798, which made the United States appear to be little more than a client state. Worse, Hamilton's plan for retiring the debt included provisions for excise taxes, particularly on whiskey. Frontier farmers in Pennsylvania, Virginia, and the Carolinas rebelled, and were put down by federal troops with Washington and Hamilton at the head. Whiskey rebels demanded other reforms: clear title to their land, the opening of the Mississippi to American trade, and the removal of Indians—only Anthony Wayne's victory at the Fallen Timbers in 1794 neutralized the threat. They were joined by land rioters in Maine, New York, and South Carolina who protested the unequal distribution of land and elite attempts to force pioneers into market production. The fact that most of the landlords were federalists added to the general feeling that federalism meant the recreation of a British-style aristocracy and a rapprochment with the mother country.[21]

Jefferson and his allies tapped agrarian and class unrest brilliantly during John Adams's administration, and created a single-party system that remained in power until 1824 with virtually no dissent. The systematic federalist suppression of artisans' Democratic-Republican clubs for supporting the Whiskey Rebellion and the French Republic, which resulted in the Alien and Sedition Acts in 1798, gave Jefferson and Madison the opportunity to write the Kentucky and Virginia Resolutions, which outlined a state's right to overturn a federal law by not enforcing it. They therefore appealed to the laboring classes while still promoting an economic agenda that benefited the planter aristocracy of the South; indeed, Jefferson's sentimental paeans to a nation of yeoman farmers included a stern reminder that the government must provide support for commerce to make sure that husbandmen produced for the market, and therefore became virtuous citizens. Men must be made to work, he reasoned, or they would live like Indians. The authority of the state would be used to make sure they did. And, the sudden boom in cotton offered hope that plantation slavery could thrive once again, adding urgency to Southern denunciations of protectionism. Jefferson proposed free trade as the surest way to keep government small and commerce active for agriculturalists. Other nations had industrialized and therefore needed American food. Necessarily, they had to defend their source of provisions—the United States—which would enable Americans to eschew a large military force to protect itself, stymie the creation of a strong central state, and prevent the development of a wage labor system. Playing on the federalist attacks on civil liberties, the heavy investment in the United States by English capital, federalist support for Britain against republican France, the building of a large navy to protect shipping, perceived Indian menaces, and social disorder aimed at federalist elites, Jefferson brought planters, labor, farmers, and middling merchants into an alliance, and swept into office in the 1800 presidential election.[22]

The agrarian republic that Jefferson envisioned was by definition dependent, and it must be underscored here that between 1800 and 1816, the United States could easily have fallen into the kind of dependency that marked Latin American countries. At any point, Great Britain could have retaken its former colonies. But the English could just as effectively control the United States with capital, diplomacy, and limited military force. Jefferson at first seemed able to outflank international developments, securing the Louisiana Purchase in 1803; the cornerstone of his agrarian nation would be the land it held. But Jefferson scuttled most of the ships built under Adams and declared neutrality. American shipping was so defenseless that Barbary pirates attacked merchantmen with impunity. England and France continued to seize ships and sailors on the high seas. In 1807, a British ship sailed into Norfolk harbor, crippled a U.S. ship, and impressed sailors within sight of land. When Jefferson, true to his free-trade doctrines, declared an embargo, both Britain and France happily found other sources for food and raw materials. Having devastated New England shippers, Jefferson rekindled sectional hostilities by precipitating an economic crisis. Then, in the spirit of patriotism, he encouraged home manufactures, which in turn sparked the industrial revolution that would destroy any hope of an agrarian republic. By the War of 1812, Northern industries were spinning Southern cotton into cloth to be sold back to planters for their slaves; the shoe industry had sprouted for similar reasons; and in the North, the proceeds of the trade began to be turned into capital investments in canals and roads. Still, only England's unwillingness to decisively defeat American troops during the War of 1812 stood between the United States and formal subordination to Britain.[23]

Internally, the administrations of Jefferson and Madison revealed the rigidity of Jeffersonian ideology on issues of citizenship and nationalism. While in Latin America creole elites had included other races in the polity, and therefore political conflict between groups was ingrained in the political system (which therefore destabilized it), the Constitution had excluded these groups, despite their presence in society. The violence of the period purposefully was externalized. However, scholars need not treat it as substantially different from the civil wars of Latin America. Jeffersonian struggles were likewise over power, were militaristic, and exposed the hierarchical nature of American republicanism (and its unfreedom). Least understood and most eventful was the beginning of the settlement of the Ohio country. When Jefferson took office in 1800, Native Americans had been quiescent since their defeat in 1794; but led by Tecumseh and the Shawnee Prophet, Indians begun to forge a pan-Indian alliance stretching from Lake Erie to the Georgia backcountry. The British supported the alliance, though they were too occupied in Europe to give effective aid. The source of resistance was the settlement plan contained in the Northwest Ordinances, a striking exercise in cartographic state making. The Midwest was to be platted into squares, with villages in each township to serve as commercial and civic centers for white pioneers.[24]

The plan was distinctly Jeffersonian, and aimed at both Indians and poor whites. Indians would have to cede their territory to the state (particularly their "unused" commons—their hunting grounds) and take up an agricultural life. In his most expansive moments, Jefferson held out hope that Indians would give up their wandering ways to assimilate into U.S. society. Poor whites, in Jefferson's mind, likewise needed the guiding hand of the state. To him, the frontier decivilized whites, creating a class of woodsmen, cattlemen, hunters, and outlaws who lived entirely too much like Indians (or with them). By mapping the countryside and fixing commerce to the land, Jefferson intended to force whites to adopt the values promoted by the state. Indians, of course, rejected the Jeffersonian landscape and resented the refusal of the federal government to honor treaties that recognized Indian sovereignty over the land, not to mention native culture, politics, and economy. As for whites, the state could not rely on them to defend the Jeffersonian world. Hence, the army became the vehicle for the repression of Indians and the ordering of white society (with race the rhetorical device used to cultivate divisions between red and white). The frontier was not democratic, for democracy might result in a multiracial, antistate alliance against the United States.[25]

Jefferson and Madison each took steps to ensure that state interests triumphed in the West. Jefferson watched with detachment the activities of Aaron Burr, James Wilkinson, and others in the Southwest, but recognized that their filibustering in Louisiana and Texas would secure that territory for the United States. Prompted by Albert Gallatin, the National Road was proposed to link the East and West across the Appalachians. By purchasing Louisiana, Jefferson also opened the Northwest to commerce. He then brought pressure on Indians to cede territory to enable road construction and settlement to begin. Indians responded by growing increasingly radical, with dissent coalescing around the Ghost Dance movement. Indians staged their uprising in 1812 in coordination with the British in Canada, only to be defeated by William H. Harrison at the Battle of Tippecanoe. In the South, divisions within nations like the Cherokee and Creeks prevented unified action; the Cherokee, in particular, believed Jefferson was interested in allowing Indians to create autonomous states within the United States, and began establishing cotton plantations using slave labor, and participating in commerce. After the War of 1812, they developed a constitutional government based on the U.S. model. Their inaction enabled Andrew Jackson to stage a rogue attack, using Tennessee militia to exterminate Creeks in Alabama, and eventually to invade Spanish Florida—again without sanction—ostensibly to defeat the Seminoles. Since the United States did not declare war in any of these cases, despite treaties that recognized Indian sovereignty, the only way to properly interpret these actions is to see them as civil wars that were not simply over land, but over the very definition of who would be included in the state, and under what terms. No case can be made for Native Americans not being part of the national economy. Their pastoral economy was thriving by the early national period; in the Midwest they were busy working as contract labor in mines, and they still acted as important traders in the Far West. But they resisted the state. By the end of his term, Jefferson no longer argued for assimilation.[26]

Other groups found themselves similarly excluded. Despite Jefferson's agrarian doctrines, small farmers discovered that their interest in equal access to productive resources would not be fulfilled. The Jeffersonian revolution in 1800 had drawn small producers into an alliance with a new class of self-made commercial men—millers, merchants, lawyers—who had benefited from the commercial expansion of the 1790s (caused by demand for agricultural products during the Napoleonic wars), but resented the continued political domination of the federalist elite. In addition to Southern planters and urban artisans, these anti-aristocratic forces made a potent electoral force. In office, however, the Jeffersonians concentrated on commerce and state building. Though debtor farmers in Maine, tenants in New York, and others across the nation continued to protest oppressive land policies, they had no political allies to help generate an insurgency. As a result, agrarian reform on anything other than the statist model embodied in the Northwest Ordinances ground to a halt. In industry, Jefferson's calls for home industries encouraged the construction of factories. In turn, skilled workers lost their jobs or faced lower wages. Unionization began in places like New York. Employers counterattacked by dragging laborers into court on charges of interfering with trade, and conspiracy. For white farmers and laborers, therefore, the Jeffersonian period proved to be a decidedly dark moment, for the class interests of the state clearly did not comport with their own. Blacks found themselves even more disenfranchised. Gabriel Prosser's rebellion in Virginia in 1800 was organized by free blacks who demanded rights of citizenship based on the labor theory of value and the principles of the American Revolution. Prosser and his followers were put down forcefully, and slave laws tightened throughout the South. Whatever gains African Americans had made during the Revolution were lost. The expansion of cotton, which exploded across the Southwest after the War of 1812, engrafted unfreedom onto the land once again.[27]

Between 1816 and 1830, the United States began its commercial expansion and industrial development that formed the foundation of its future prosperity. Historical developments, not a liberal ethos, were the cause. The Constitution stabilized economic interaction between separate states, and channeled conflict into the law. Hamilton's bold plan to retire the national debt had prevented the kind of economic chaos that bankrupted Latin American republics soon after independence. And Jefferson's inability to systematically promote an agrarian agenda because of foreign wars ironically set in motion the kinds of development Hamilton sought. But as late as 1816, the new nation still was weak enough to be militarily seized by a European power. After that date, conquest was unlikely, but social unrest at home and the continued influence of foreign capital prevented the nation from becoming economically independent. Despite the elaborate mythology about the creation of a domestic market, petty-commodity production dominated much of the nation's agricultural economy, the plantation economy was geared toward external markets, and the North did not have sufficient infrastructure to maintain internal trade. The United States was subject to the wiles of the international market.[28]

III. The Beginning of American Independence

From 1820 to 1865, the internal logic of the state order that emerged from the interaction of Hamiltonian and Jeffersonian policies both built and destroyed the Union. First, a commercial agricultural economy based on unfree labor expanded across the South, creating a separate planter class antagonistic to the emerging bourgeoisie of the industrial Northeast. In the Midwest and the Mid-Atlantic states, an agricultural economy geared toward Southern, English, and Caribbean markets developed. As a number of scholars have demonstrated, agricultural expansion in the North (with the exception of New England) was not necessarily liberating for small farmers. Land speculators engrossed large tracts of land; tenancy and debt prevailed across significant parts of the region. Agricultural production did bring wealth to the young nation—cotton alone fueled most of its growth—yet it also knit the United States and British economies virtually into one. By the mid-1830s, British policies dictated American economic fortunes, and British capital underwrote land speculation, canal and railroad construction, industrial enterprise, banking, and even state governments. American historians tend to dissect federal policies to explain the development of the nation during the antebellum years, but it is far more fruitful to think of American politics as being shaped by English economic demands: British cotton markets encouraged reliance on the crop at the same time that it fostered economic crises in the United States, exposing social cleavages that destroyed the basic Jeffersonian political economy (and the agrarian-labor alliance that supported it), which accepted dependency as a prima facie condition of nationhood.[29]

The problem of American dependency was masked by internal political conflict and westward expansion, each of which was shaped by sectional conflict. The expansion of the cotton economy had been stunning, and slavery spread rapidly into the Southwest. Lingering resentment in the North against the agrarian policies of the Virginia dynasty, however, was compounded by the Panic of 1819, a commercial crisis that struck merchants and financiers hard. (Given the structure of the early national economy, commercial interests, not producers, bore the brunt of most downturns.) In this atmosphere, Missouri petitioned to enter the Union as a slave state in 1819. Most of the territory stood north of the Ohio River, arousing fears in the North that the South was hemming in Northern expansion. The Missouri Compromise of 1820 resolved the crisis, but shook the planter-farmer-laborer alliance that held the Jeffersonians in power. In New York, for example, Martin Van Buren rallied Bucktail Republicans— laborers and farmers committed to Jeffersonian ideals, but wary of the monopolization of economic and political power by elites—around the issue of universal suffrage, which was instituted in New York in 1821 at the same time that the state began the process of emancipating its slaves. Other Northern states followed, adding to Southern fears that a Northern majority in the House of Representatives would eventually turn against slavery. The election of John Quincy Adams to the presidency signaled the rebirth of federalist policies in new form. Under Adams, the American System—a program for the construction of internal improvements with governmental support—thrived, and Northern capital appeared again on the rise. The opening of the Erie Canal in 1825 symbolized, it appeared, the triumph of a new order in the North.[30]

The rapid expansion of industry, and governmental support for internal improvements raised fears among planters, farmers, and laborers of a monopolization of wealth and power by "non-producers"—capitalists and political insiders. Andrew Jackson, working with Van Buren, John C. Calhoun of South Carolina, and Thomas H. Benton of Missouri, forged a new electoral coalition of Northern working men, Southern planters, and Western pioneers to win the presidency in 1828. Their program emulated Jeffersonian attacks on the strong central state, high tariffs, and "aristocracy." Of particular note was Jackson's success at winning over the "free-soil" workingmen of Northeastern cities. Followers of Thomas Skidmore, they called for government ownership of land, and the right of all families to occupancy. Skidmore attacked everything from inheritance to the industrialization of the crafts. To him, each signaled the destruction of a producers' republic and the beginning of wage slavery. Meanwhile, Calhoun articulated the doctrine of nullification, a refinement of the Virginia and Kentucky Resolutions, claiming that the sovereign bodies in the United States were the state conventions that approved the Constitution, and they reserved the right to nullify "unconstitutional" federal laws. His target was the tariff passed in 1828 that favored Northern industry. Nullifiers sought a constitutional corrective to the rapidly expanding Northern majority in the House; they believed that eventually the South would no longer be able to hold a veto power in the Senate and would have to succumb to capitalist legislation. Westerners, rankled by the dominance of Eastern bankers over the economy, happily joined the alliance. The Democracy became intimately associated with "producers of wealth."[31]

Opposing the Jacksonians was a collection of disparate political factions representing former federalists, supporters of the American System, and the emerging bourgeoisie in the North. Each had vested interests in the creation of a capitalist economy, and by 1832 came together in the Whig Party. The Whigs did not enjoy the support of small producers; rather, they represented "the best men" in the community: self-made entrepreneurs, professionals, and early industrialists. Their ranks were swelled after the Second Great Awakening, with its emphasis on moral free agency, gave the bourgeoisie a language through which their class consciousness could be expressed. They embraced individualism, but saw no contradiction in their belief that the powers of the central government should be used to enforce morality. Their ideology threatened the independent household (and its system of dependencies) that supported yeoman and artisan households by positing that all individuals—young or old, male or female, black or white—should be liberated to participate rationally in the marketplace. Under their influence, the Whigs became the party of reform—from temperance to abolition. As the party most linked to capital, the Whigs may well have helped the Jacksonians maintain electoral cohesion by opposing unions, plantation slavery, and the cultural habits of immigrants—especially Irish Catholics. In addition, they did not support state's rights, threatening the agrarians of the South. Their connection to antislavery made them seem too radical for Americans committed to the Union; they seemed determined to unsettle the long-standing compromise between the North and the South based on the agrarian-labor alliance.[32]

Under Jackson, a neo-Jeffersonian revival occurred, with federalism and wage slavery the targets of Democratic wrath. Jackson continued the Jeffersonian policy of expansion, now justified by the racialist ideology of Manifest Destiny. Manifest Destiny posited that the white U.S. republic was blessed by God, and charged with the Protestant duty to tame the landscape with democracy and commerce. Any "uncivilized" groups—blacks, Indians, Mexicans, Catholics—would have to give way before the surge of progress. Thus, when the Cherokees secured a favorable ruling in the Supreme Court declaring that they enjoyed sovereignty over their land, Jackson ignored it. The Indians were removed from the Southeast in 1838 and completely pushed outside of the boundaries of the nation. U.S. designs on Northern Mexico—especially Texas, which was suited to cotton production—led to Jackson's interference in the territory. In the end, white Texans won independence in 1836 and joined the Union in 1845. Blacks, led by Nat Turner, revolted in Virginia in 1832, only to be brutally suppressed. Slavery, which many Southerners still viewed as an unfortunate evil, became harsher across the South. The pro-slavery argument—which posited that slavery was a humane, republican, Christian institution—began to take shape. Combined with the Nullification crisis of 1832, itself spurred by fears of Northern aggression toward slavery, the notion of slavery as a positive good took shape. So long as Whiggery could also be identified with wage slavery, the Democrats could confidently expect to hold power.[33]

The agrarian-labor alliance appeared to be in the ascendant at the precise moment that the American economy began to boom. The source was cotton, which by the mid-1830s made up 60 percent of the nation's exports. Furthermore, 60 percent of the crop went to Britain, while other nations and the North absorbed the remaining supply. The nation's economy, therefore, was heavily dependent on foreign markets, and in particular, English trade policies. Far from establishing the independence of the United States, cotton wove the young nation more tightly into an Atlantic economy that it could not easily control. Other economic factors were at work. Because of the opium trade, China accepted increasingly less silver in trade. American specie reserves expanded, especially since Mexican coinage—legal tender in the United States—continued to flow into the country. Meanwhile, for a complex set of reasons related to balancing cotton imports, Britain exported specie to the United States at the same time. America underwent inflation, which was partly offset by public land purchases. British capital financed unprecedented investment in railroads, canals, and Western state bonds. Jackson's economic policies neither helped nor hurt the situation, but they did have important political consequences. He vetoed the charter of the Second Bank of the United States as an antimonopoly measure designed to shift economic control to the states. In 1836, fearful that the boom was draining working capital from the West, he issued the Specie Circular in an effort to restrain speculation. Finally, the federal government pledged to distribute its own specie surplus to the states.[34]

The denouement for the agrarian-labor alliance came with the Panic of 1837, which exposed the class antagonisms within the Jacksonian ranks between working men and farmers, and the planter aristocracy. The panic unemployed thousands of artisans and sparked a retooling of industry that made more workers redundant. Unions in the 1830s, backed by the Jacksonian Democrats, had made substantial strides in protecting the crafts system from further erosion. The panic, however, left unions in tatters. Working men rallied around the Democratic banner, revitalizing free soil under the leadership of George Henry Evans and the National Reformers. In 1838, free-soil Democrats, calling themselves "Locofocos," routed regular Democrats and won elections in New York and other cities. Van Buren, who had to maintain a strong constituency in New York if he wanted re-election in 1840, swung behind the agrarian program of the Locofocos. He knew the consequences. Because of abolitionist agitation, which began in 1831 with the publication of William Lloyd Garrison's *Liberator,* the subsequent effort to let the Republic of Texas join the Union, and the gag rule in Congress, Southern Democrats were in no mood to tolerate free-soil apostasy. The Democracy, and its cross-class and cross-sectional coalition, shattered. In 1838, the hardest hit of all groups, small merchants, jumped to the Whig banner. In 1840, working men and Westerners rallied behind Whig William H. Harrison. The Whigs had reaped a windfall. Long associated with neofederalism and bourgeois reform, they now presented themselves as the economic saviors of the nation. The rising tide of Irish Catholic immigration—which swelled Democratic ranks and undercut skilled trades—pushed native-born Protestant artisans toward an alliance with Whigs, especially since the antislavery forces in the party had no quarrel with free soil. Novelist James Fenimore Cooper marked the passing of the alliance between the landed gentry and the laboring classes by penning a school primer, *The American Democrat,* which decried the middle class as charlatans and called on Americans to renew the ties that bound together agrarian society. He was dismissed as a cranky aristocrat.[35]

The depression continued until the discovery of gold in California in 1848; meanwhile, Texas was admitted as a slave state in 1845, and the Southern Democrat James K. Polk led the nation to war with Mexico, conquering the entire Southwest—all of which would be slave territory under the terms of the Missouri Compromise. Van Burenites attempted to neutralize the slave power's gambit by advancing the Wilmot Proviso in 1846, which called for free soil in any territories won in the war with Mexico. The bill twice passed the House, where the North enjoyed a clear majority, only to lose in the Senate, where the South still retained a balance of seats. For Northern laborers and farmers (including Anti-Renters in New York), the issue was not the expansion of capitalism, but the protection of the artisan and yeoman household from extinction. Wage slavery seemed imminent, given the continued hard times. In 1848, Van Buren led free-soil workingmen into alliance with bourgeois reformers in the Free Soil Party. While the working class and the middle class were locked in battle in Europe, therefore, in America the revolution in 1848 pitted labor and capital against the old landed elite. America's second revolution occurred as a result of a split between working-class and elite agrarians, because of the dominant position of slave states in the national government.[36]

IV. Epilogue

The gold rush ended the depression by freeing up credit across the nation. Furthermore, it freed American businessmen from reliance on foreign capital. In conjunction with the repeal of the British Corn Laws in the 1840s, which allowed greater U.S. grain exports to England, the nation became less dependent on the policies of the British government. Cotton boomed as well, making the entire nation's economy vibrant. But California gold came at a cost. In order to prevent the territory from being seized by Britain, France, Russia, or even Mexico, Whig president Zachary Taylor asked that California be admitted as a free state, violating the Missouri Compromise. Calhoun and the Southern wing of the Democratic Party threatened secession, and the nation teetered on the brink of civil war. Only the Compromise of 1850, which replaced the Missouri Compromise with "popular sovereignty"—the right of a territory to declare itself slave or free at the time of admission to the Union—prevented secession. But by 1854, the compromise was a shambles, with civil war in Kansas between free and slave settlers sucking the nation into a deeper sectional crisis. Southern agrarians, now isolated from Northern working-class agrarians, took the radical step of proposing that all labor should be enslaved in order to protect workers from the poverty caused by a free-labor system. Though this helped cement Southern nationalism, it forfeited any chance of reconciling Northern workingmen and the planter class. As a result, the Republican party, which in its economic policies was strongly federalist and pro-capital, succeeded in its rhetorical appeal to free laborers. In the charged atmosphere of the 1850s, the planter elite appeared to be a far more dangerous opponent of laboring men; hence, by 1860, small producers went to war to defeat the agrarian South.[37]

The defeat of the South in the Civil War might seem inevitable, given the strength of Northern industry and the weaknesses an agrarian, decentralized government like the Confederate States of America labored under in prosecuting a modern war. But the South nearly won. Had Britain intervened on the side of its cotton "colony," the United States might well have been divided, or forced to negotiate reunion with slavery and dependency central tenets of the agreement to remain a nation. When Britain chose not to provide military support (in part because the South had employed a Jeffersonian device—withholding cotton to force England and France to recognize the CSA—with disastrous results: the British started cultivating cotton in Egypt and India), the South was left on its own, and eventually ran out of men, money, and matériel. With the planter aristocracy impoverished, Northern capital could transform the nation in its own image, ignoring both farmers and laborers in the Reconstruction of the nation. Only then did the United States emerge as an industrialized urban nation. What stood between it and the dependency that enveloped Latin American republics was the timing of independence, the peculiarities of the impact of the Napoleonic wars on its economy, and the narrow definition of citizenship adopted by the national state. Above all, however, U.S. dependency on Britain—especially the cotton economy—heightened sectional tensions between North and South, shattering the Jeffersonian alliance and destroying the foundations of the commercial, agrarian, dependent state he championed.[38]

Notes

1. John Agnew, *The United States in the World-Economy* (New York: Cambridge University Press, 1987), 11–47; J. Potter, "Atlantic Economy, 1815–1860: The U.S.A. and the Industrial Revolution in Britain," in *Essays in American Economic History,* ed. A. W. Coats and Ross M. Robertson (New York: Barnes and Noble, 1970), 14–48; Seymour Martin Lipset, *Continental Divide: The Values and Institutions of the United States and Canada* (Toronto: Canadian-American Committee, 1989), 1–18.

   Though I will not frame this article directly in the literature of postcolonialism, in part because so little has been written on the United States as a postcolonial state, I believe that it is essential to state here that the United States, because of its dependent economy, multiethnic and multiracial population, and the presence of a "creole" elite (I use this term loosely—it is usually applied to Latin America, but is necessary to enable comparison) had many features of post-colonial states elsewhere in the Americas. See Bill Ashcroft, Gareth Griffiths, and Helen Tiffin, *Key Concepts in Post-Colonial Studies* (New York: Routledge Press, 1998), 186–95.

2. Charles Sellers, *The Market Revolution: Jacksonian America, 1815–1846* (New York: Oxford University Press, 1991), 3–33; Louis Hartz, *The Liberal Tradition in America* (New York: Harcourt, Brace and World, 1955), 35–86; George M. Frederickson, "Comparative History," in *The Past before Us: Contemporary Historical Writing in the United States,* ed. Michael Kammen (Ithaca, N.Y.: Cornell University Press, 1980), 457–73; Carl N. Degler, "In Pursuit of American History," *American Historical Review* 92 (February 1987): 1–12; Ian Tyrrell, "American Exceptionalism in an Age of International History," *American Historical Review* 96 (October 1991): 1031–55.

3. Sean Wilentz, "Against Exceptionalism: Class Consciousness and the American Labor Movement, 1790–1920," *International Labor and Working Class History* 26 (fall 1984): 1–24; Marcel van der Linden,

"Transnationalizing American Labor History," *Journal of American History* 86 (December 1999): 1078–92; Richard S. Dunn, *Sugar and Slaves: The Rise of the Planter Class in the English West Indies, 1624–1713* (Chapel Hill: University of North Carolina Press, 1972); Carl N. Degler, *Neither Black nor White: Slavery and Race Relations in Brazil and the United States* (New York: Macmillan, 1971); Stanley L. Engerman and Eugene D. Genovese, eds., *Race and Slavery in the Western Hemisphere: Quantitative Studies* (Princeton, N.J.: Princeton University Press, 1975); Peter Kolchin, *Unfree Labor: American Slavery and Russian Serfdom* (Cambridge, Mass.: Belknap Press of Harvard University Press, 1987).

4. Nicholas Canny, "Writing Atlantic History; or, Reconfiguring the History of Colonial British America," *Journal of American History* 86 (December 1999): 1093–1114.

5. Anthony McFarlane, "Independence and Revolution in the Americas," *History Today* (March 1984): 40–49.

6. Lester D. Langley, *The Americas in the Age of Revolution, 1750–1850* (New Haven: Yale University Press, 1996), 1–10.

7. Peggy K. Liss, *Atlantic Empires: The Network of Trade and Revolution, 1713–1826* (Baltimore: Johns Hopkins University Press, 1983), 105–221; John H. Elliott, "Colonial Identity in the Atlantic World," in *Colonial Identity in the Atlantic World, 1500–1800,* ed. Nicholas Canny and Anthony Pagden (Princeton, N.J.: Princeton University Press, 1987), 3–13; Linda K. Salvucci, "Anglo-American Merchants and Stratagems for Success in Spanish Imperial Markets," in *The North American Role in the Spanish Imperial Economy,* ed. Jacques Barbier and Allan J. Kuethe (Manchester: Manchester University Press, 1984), 127–33. For a critique of Eurocentric models of historical change, see Gyan Prakash, "Subaltern Studies as Postcolonial Criticism," *American Historical Review* 99 (December 1994): 1475–90.

8. Tyrrell, "American Exceptionalism," 1031–55; Agnew, *United States,* 31–47; Howard Lamar, "From Bondage to Contract: Ethnic Labor in the American West, 1600–1890," in *The Countryside in the Age of Capitalist Transformation,* ed. Steven Hahn and Jonathan Prude (Chapel Hill: University of North Carolina Press, 1985), 293–324; William G. McLoughlin, *Cherokee Renascence in the New Republic* (Princeton, N.J.: Princeton University Press, 1986), 3–91; Jeremy Adelman and Stephen Aron, "From Borderlands to Empires, Nation-States, and the Peoples in Between in North American History," *American Historical Review* 104 (June 1999): 814–41.

9. Gordon S. Wood, *The Radicalism of the American Revolution* (New York: Vintage, 1991), 325–69; Joyce Appleby, *Capitalism and a New Social Order: The Republican Vision of the 1790s* (New York: New York University Press, 1984), 25–78; Robert Brenner, "The Origins of Capitalist Development: A Critique of Neo-Smithian Marxism," *New Left Review* 104 (July–August 1977), 25–93. Brenner provides a particularly good analysis of the difference between commerce and capitalism.

10. Eric Foner, *The Story of American Freedom* (New York: W. W. Norton, 1998), 3–28; idem, *Tom Paine and Revolutionary America* (New York: Oxford University Press, 1976), 71–106.

11. Foner, *American Freedom*, 29–37; Catherine M. Stock, *Rural Radicals: From Bacon's Rebellion to the Oklahoma City Bombing* (New York: Penguin, 1997), 15–54; Edward Countryman, "'Out of the Bounds of the Law': Northern Land Rioters in the Eighteenth Century," in *The American Revolution*, ed. Alfred Young (DeKalb: Northern Illinois University Press, 1976), 37–69; Rachel N. Klein, *Unification of a Slave State: The Rise of the Planter Class in the South Carolina Backcountry* (Chapel Hill: University of North Carolina Press, 1990), 78–108; Marvin L. M. Kay, "The North Carolina Regulation, 1766–1776: A Class Conflict," in Klein, *Unification of a Slave State*, 73–123; Staugton Lynd, *Anti-Federalism in Dutchess County, New York: A Study of Democracy and Class Conflict in the Revolutionary Era* (Chicago: Loyola University Press, 1962), 37–54; Michael A. McDonnell, "Popular Mobilization and Political Culture in Revolutionary Virginia: The Failure of the Minutemen and the Revolution from Below," *Journal of American History* 85 (December 1998), 946–81.

12. Daniel K. Richter, *The Ordeal of the Longhouse: The Peoples of the Iroquois League in the Era of Colonization* (Chapel Hill: University of North Carolina Press, 1992), 255–84; McLoughlin, *Cherokee Renascence*, 3–91; Gregory E. Dowd, *A Spirited Resistance: The North American Indian Struggle for Unity* (Baltimore: Johns Hopkins University Press, 1992), 47–89; Stephen Aron, "Pigs and Hunters: 'Rights to the Woods' on the Trans-Appalachian Frontier," in *Contact Points: American Frontiers from the Mohawk Valley to the Mississippi, 1750–1830*, ed. Andrew R. L. Cayton and Frederika Teute (Chapel Hill: University of North Carolina Press, 1998), 175–204; James T. Carson, "Native Americans, the Market Revolution, and Cultural Change: The Choctaw Cattle Economy, 1690–1830," *Agricultural History* 71 (winter 1997): 1–18; Richard White, *The Roots of Dependency: Subsistence, Environment, and Social Change among the Choctaws, Pawnees, and Navajos* (Lincoln: University of

Nebraska Press, 1983); Daniel H. Usner Jr., *Indians, Settlers, and Slaves in a Frontier Exchange Economy: The Lower Mississippi Valley before 1783* (Chapel Hill: University of North Carolina Press, 1992), 105–44, 244–75.

13. Peggy Liss, "Creoles, the North American Example, and the Spanish American Economy," in *Spanish Imperial Economy,* ed. Barbier and Kuethe, 13–25; Agnew, *United States,* 31–35; Stock, *Rural Radicals,* 33–54.

14. Carl Van Doren, *The Great Rehearsal: The Story of the Making and Ratifying of the Constitution of the United States* (New York: Viking, 1948), passim; John L. Brooke, "To the Quiet of the People: Revolutionary Settlements and Civil Unrest in Western Massachusetts, 1774–1789," *William and Mary Quarterly* 46, 3d. ser. (July 1989): 425–62; Stock, *Rural Radicals,* 33–54; Harry B. Yoshpe, *The Disposition of Loyalist Estates in the Southern District of the State of New York* (New York: Columbia University Press, 1939), 113–19.

15. Van Doren, *Great Rehearsal,* passim; Drew R. McCoy, *The Elusive Republic: Political Economy in Jeffersonian America* (New York: W. W. Norton, 1980), 105–35; Agnew, *United States,* 31–39; Appleby, *Capitalism and a New Social Order,* 25–78; T. H. Breen, "Ideology and Nationalism on the Eve of the American Revolution: Revisions *Once More* in Need of Revising," *American Historical Review* 84 (June 1997): 13–39.

16. McCoy, *Elusive Republic,* 120–35; Van Doren, *Great Rehearsal,* passim; Foner, *American Freedom,* 42–43.

17. Saul Cornell, *The Other Founders: Anti-Federalism and the Dissenting Tradition in America, 1788–1828* (Chapel Hill: North Carolina University Press, 1999), 1–15, 19–50; John L. Brooke, *The Heart of the Commonwealth: Society and Political Culture in Worcester County, Massachusetts, 1713–1861* (Amherst: University of Massachusetts Press, 1989), 189–229; Thomas Slaughter, *The Whiskey Rebellion: Frontier Epilogue to the American Revolution* (New York: Oxford University Press, 1986), 36–45; Agnew, *United States,* 34–35.

18. Richard Hofstadter, *The Idea of a Party System: The Rise of Legitimate Opposition in the United States, 1780–1840* (Berkeley: University of California Press, 1970), 1–73; James R. Sharp, *American Politics in the Early Republic: The Nation in Crisis* (New Haven: Yale University Press, 1993), 17–30; Charles S. Sydnor, *Gentlemen Freeholders* (Chapel Hill: University of North Carolina Press, 1952), 21–59.

19. Sharp, *American Politics,* 31–50; McCoy, *Elusive Republic,* 136–65; Hofstadter, *Idea of a Party System,* 74–121; Foner, *American Freedom,* 41–44.

20. Sharp, *American Politics*, 31–50; McCoy, *Elusive Republic*, 136–65; Cornell, *Other Founders*, 187–94; Hofstadter, *Idea of a Party System*, 74–121.

21. McCoy, *Elusive Republic*, 166–84; Sharp, *American Politics*, 53–84; Hofstadter, *Idea of a Party System*, 74–121; Slaughter, *Whiskey Rebellion*, 55–60, 75–89; Lynd, *Anti-Federalism*, 55–81; Alan Taylor, *William Cooper's Town: Power and Persuasion on the Frontier of the Early American Republic* (New York: Vintage, 1995), 86–114; Alan Taylor, *Liberty Men and Great Proprietors: The Revolutionary Settlement on the Maine Frontier, 1760–1820* (Chapel Hill: University of North Carolina Press, 1990), 89–121; Klein, *Unification of a Slave State*, 109–48; Stock, *Rural Radicals*, 33–54; David M. Ellis, *Landlords and Farmers in the Hudson-Mohawk Region, 1790–1850* (Ithaca, N.Y.: Cornell University Press, 1945), 16–64; Foner, *American Freedom*, 42–43; Dowd, *Spirited Resistance*, 90–115.

22. Cornell, *Other Founders*, 174–94, 230–43; Hofstadter, *Idea of a Party System*, 74–121; Michael Kammen, *Spheres of Liberty: Changing Perceptions of Liberty in American Culture* (Madison: University of Wisconsin Press, 1986), 48–52; Foner, *American Freedom*, 43; Slaughter, *Whiskey Rebellion*, 125–42.

23. McCoy, *Elusive Republic*, 185–235; Sharp, *American Politics*, 226–88; Agnew, *United States*, 36–39; Sellers, *Market Revolution*, 34–102.

24. Dowd, *Spirited Resistance*, 123–90; Adelman and Aron, "From Borderlands to Borders," 814–41.

25. Andrew R. L. Cayton, "'Noble Actors' upon 'the Theatre of Honor,'" in *Contact Points*, ed. Cayton and Teute, 235–69; Dowd, *Spirited Resistance*, 123–90; McLoughlin, *Cherokee Renascence*, 3–91; Daniel Feller, *The Public Lands in Jacksonian Politics* (Madison: University of Wisconsin Press, 1984), 3–13; Elliott J. Gorn, "'Gouge and Bite, Pull Hair and Scratch': The Social Significance of Fighting in the Southern Backcountry," *American Historical Review* 90 (February 1985): 18–43.

26. McLoughlin, *Cherokee Renascence*, 59–91; Daniel H. Usner Jr., "American Indians on the Cotton Frontier: Changing Economic Relations with Citizens and Slaves in the Mississippi Territory," *Journal of American History* 72 (September 1985): 297–98; Adelman and Aron, "From Borderlands to Borders," 814–41; Lamar, "Bondage to Contract," 293–324; Lucy Eldersveld Murphy, "To Live Among Us: Accommodation, Gender, and Conflict in the Western Great Lakes Region, 1760–1832," in *Contact Points*, ed. Cayton and Teute, 270–303.

27. Sellers, *Market Revolution*, 34–69; McCoy, *Elusive Republic*, 236–59; Agnew, *United States*, 36–39; Taylor, *Liberty Men*, 209–49; Stock, *Rural Radicals*, 33–54; Sean Wilentz, *Chants Democratic: New York City and the*

Rise of the American Working Class, 1788–1850 (New York: Oxford University Press, 1984), 23–103; Gerald W. Mullin, *Flight and Rebellion: Slave Resistance in Eighteenth-Century Virginia* (New York: Oxford University Press, 1972), 140–63.

28. Sellers, *Market Economy,* 76–102; Hofstadter, *Idea of a Party System,* 170–211; Agnew, *United States,* 41–47; Potter, "Atlantic Economy," 14–48.

29. Ibid.

30. Sellers, *Market Revolution,* 103–201; Wood, *Radicalism,* 271–305; Foner, *American Freedom,* 50–58; Carol Sheriff, *The Artificial River: The Erie Canal and the Paradox of Progress, 1817–1862* (New York: W. W. Norton, 1996), 27–51.

31. Harry L. Watson, *Liberty and Power: The Politics of Jacksonian America* (New York: Hill and Wang, 1990), 73–95; Dixon Ryan Fox, *The Decline of Aristocracy in the Politics of New York* (New York: Columbia University Press, 1919), 271–359; Thomas Skidmore, *The Rights of Man to Property!* (New York: Burt Franklin, n.d. [1829]), 125–44; Marvin Meyers, *The Jacksonian Persuasion: Politics and Belief* (Stanford, Calif.: Stanford University Press, 1957), 3–15; Arthur Schlesinger Jr., *The Age of Jackson* (Boston: Little, Brown and Company, 1945), 18–44; Richard P. McCormick, *The Second American Party System: Party Formation in the Jacksonian Era* (Chapel Hill: University of North Carolina Press, 1966), 329–56; Hofstadter, *Idea of a Party System,* 212–71; Sellers, *Market Revolution,* 269–300; Foner, *American Freedom,* 58–68.

32. John Ashworth, *Slavery, Capitalism, and Politics in the Antebellum Republic* (New York: Cambridge University Press, 1995), 113–97; Schlesinger, *Age of Jackson,* 103–89; Wilentz, *Chants Democratic,* 219–54; Paul E. Johnson, *A Shopkeeper's Millennium: Society and Revivals in Rochester, New York, 1815–1837* (New York: Hill and Wang, 1978), 79–135; Mary P. Ryan, *The Cradle of the Middle Class: The Family in Oneida County, New York, 1790–1865* (New York: Cambridge University Press, 1981), 145–242; Christine Stansell, *City of Women: Sex and Class in New York, 1789–1860* (Urbana: University of Illinois Press, 1985), 3–37.

33. Sidney L. Harring, *Crow Dog's Case: American Indian Sovereignty, Tribal Law, and United States Law in the Nineteenth Century* (New York: Cambridge University Press, 1994), 25–56; McLoughlin, *Cherokee Renascence,* 411–52; John Mack Faragher, "'More Motley than Mackinaw': From Ethnic Mixing to Ethnic Cleansing on the Frontier of the Lower Missouri, 1783–1833," in Cayton and Teute, *Contact*

Points, 304–26; Andrés Reséndez, "National Identity on a Shifting Border: Texas and New Mexico in the Age of Transition, 1821–1848," *Journal of American History* 86 (September 1999): 668–88; Stephen B. Oates, *The Fires of Jubilee: Nat Turner's Fierce Rebellion* (New York: Harper and Row, 1975), 129–54; Ashworth, *Slavery*, 197–223; Marcus Cunliffe, *Chattel Slavery and Wage Slavery: The Anglo-American Context, 1830–1860* (Athens: University of Georgia Press, 1979), 1–31; William W. Freehling, *Prelude to Civil War: The Nullification Crisis in South Carolina, 1816–1836* (New York: Harper and Row, 1965), 219–59.

34. Peter Temin, *The Jacksonian Economy* (New York: W. W. Norton, 1969), 59–112; Agnew, *United States*, 41–47; George R. Taylor, *The Transportation Revolution* (New York: Holt, Rinehart and Winston, 1951), 176–206, 324–51.

35. Temin, *Jacksonian Economy*, 113–47; Schlesinger, *Age of Jackson*, 190–226; Wilentz, *Chants Democratic*, 255–325; Amy Bridges, *A City in the Republic: Antebellum New York and the Origins of Machine Politics* (New York: Cambridge University Press, 1984), 18–38, 83–124; Ashworth, *Slavery*, 384–414; Lee Benson, *The Concept of Jacksonian Democracy: New York as a Test Case* (Princeton, N.J.: Princeton University Press, 1961), 86–109; Foner, *American Freedom*, 63; Ronald Walters, *The Antislavery Appeal: American Abolitionism after 1830* (New York: W. W. Norton, 1978), vii–xii; Sellers, *Market Revolution*, 364–95; James Fenimore Cooper, *The American Democrat* (New York: Alfred A. Knopf, 1931 [1838]), 91–128.

36. Ashworth, *Slavery*, 414–50; Temin, *Jacksonian Economy*, 148–77; Schlesinger, *Age of Jackson*, 434–83; Wilentz, *Chants Democratic*, 326–59; Ellis, *Landlords and Farmers*, 225–312; Charles E. Brooks, *Frontier Settlement and Market Revolution: The Holland Land Purchase* (Ithaca, N.Y.: Cornell University Press, 1996), 176–232.

37. Ashworth, *Slavery*, 228–38, 451–98; Foner, *American Freedom*, 95–100; Eric Foner, *Free Soil, Free Labor, Free Men: The Ideology of the Republican Party before the Civil War* (New York: Oxford University Press, 1970), 11–72; George Fitzhugh, *Cannibals All! or Slaves without Masters*, edited by C. Vann Woodward (Cambridge, Mass.: Harvard University Press, 1960), 71–84, 187–256.

38. James McPherson, *Battle Cry of Freedom: The Civil War Era* (New York: Oxford University Press, 1988), 234–307, 546–67; Eric Foner, *Reconstruction: America's Unfinished Revolution, 1863–1877* (New York: Harper and Row, 1988), 460–63.

"The Yoke of Improvement": Sir John Sinclair, John Young, and the Improvement of the Scotlands, New and Old

Daniel Samson

Sir John Sinclair (1754–1835), president of the British Board of Agriculture and author of *The Statistical Account of Scotland* (1791–93), is commonly credited as one of the principal architects of the Scottish enclosures of the late eighteenth and early nineteenth centuries.[1] In attempting to direct state policy toward specific programs—surveys and rational "improvement" of use—his were the guiding hands behind decades of reorganization in Lowland Scottish agriculture, as well as the enclosures and eviction of thousands from the Highlands after 1790. His vision of an "elevated" Scottish husbandry was to be effected by a combination of statistical knowledge, a sweeping and programmatic reorganization of agriculture and the fishery, and a strong dose of moral exhortation. While often critical of wholesale evictions, he boasted of the fantastic returns the Scottish people would receive when their traditional methods had been adapted to the needs of an international market.

One of Sinclair's assistants was a recent graduate of Glasgow University by the name of John Young (1773–1837). Young embraced Sinclair's ideals, but unlike the laird, he had no ambivalence regarding the correctness of the evictions. A decade later, Young emigrated to Nova Scotia, where he continued his mentor's crusade. His major work, *The Letters of Agricola* (1822), set out a program for the improvement of agriculture in Nova Scotia, a program by which the farmers of this corner of the empire might submit to "the yoke of improvement." Young's plan for agricultural societies and the creation of a rural gentry was an attempt to plant British-ness overseas. Wrapped around a core of what C. A. Bayly refers to as "agrarian patriotism," such plans were very attractive to the colonial state and local elites.[2] Young envisioned a program of government—a means by which the state might, through institutions of civil society, reach into the countryside and employ members of the emergent rural middle class as its agents of reform and bring order to a fragmented social body. In promoting improvement (that is, in posing a close relationship between what we would call economic development and liberal government), these writers offered a model for the government of individual economic actors—one led not by individuals themselves, but by an elite which posited order and progress as suitable means and ends: an elite which accepted some aspects of the emerging liberal order, but not all.

This essay has two components. The first compares Young's and Sinclair's visions of improvement and emphasizes the cultural component of what is typically viewed in an overly narrow political-economic context. While Young is often put forth as a colonial reformer and an intellectual of a nascent liberalism,[3] I wish to suggest that a broadening of the inquiry allows us to see the more complex makeup of Young's program. Young's alleged liberalism, much like his mentor's, demonstrated little engagement with the idea of markets, still less use of democratic ideals or liberty, and offered an older (and highly class- and gender-specific) vision of the role of elite men as social leaders—a very limited liberalism, indeed. The second part of the essay picks up the institutional form of a "Board of Agriculture" and examines its role and function in this conservative discursive context. Based on Sinclair's British model, and situated in Nova Scotia's weak structure of local government, Young's institutional arrangement allowed the Nova Scotia "Central Board of Agriculture," and especially its local societies, to play an unusually prominent role in the local politics. Agricultural societies were an important feature of civil society across the Anglo-

Atlantic world, but in Nova Scotia they pushed that boundary and came to assume an effective state role.

Britain's Board of Agriculture was one of those curious late-eighteenth-century hybrid bodies that manifested improvement's ambiguous, sometimes ambivalent, location in the shift from mercantilism to laissez-faire capitalism, and from paternalism to liberal self-regulation. It is most frequently cited as one of those bodies which broke the crust of custom: a body whose embrace of the new spirit of capitalist enterprise in part rationalized the enclosures of Britain's remaining commons.[4] This is, essentially, true; but in describing these reformers as laissez-faire modernizers, we miss their regulatory spirit—their clear sense not that the market would be determinant, but that a particular social order should prevail. When we read Sinclair—indeed, as we shall see, too, when we read Young—we are struck more by the spirit of regulation than by the spirit of freedom; we are struck by the sense that the improvers were compelled by a sense of duty to their nation, their class, and their manhood—much more so than by any faith in the invisible hand of the market. To miss the economic locus of all this is to reduce enclosures and the agricultural revolution to the banalities of better farming; but equally, to ignore the cultural context is to misunderstand how they perceived their mission.

Sinclair is remembered most of all as a statistician and an encloser—indeed, as a man who brought those two together in agrarian patriotism.[5] His life can be sketched quickly by describing him as the laird of a substantial estate at Caithness, in northeastern Scotland; as a parliamentarian (a weak supporter of Pitt, who abandoned the Whigs in 1795, sat as an independent until 1808, but who entered the cabinet in 1810); and as the founder and president of the Board of Agriculture from 1793 to 1798, and from 1805 until 1811. He was perhaps the leading spokesperson of his day for enclosure and improvement, but was best known as a compiler of "useful information" (most notably the immense [twenty-two-volume] and quite amazing *Statistical Account of Scotland*).[6]

But there was also so much more. Indeed, as his major biographer makes clear, even though he was a man of prodigious energy, enthusiasm, and capacity, he had his fingers in far too many pies. As estate owner, he took very seriously his charge to manage not only the estate itself, but also its people. At a time when population was rising, that was difficult, and much of his money and energy went into breeding sheep and improving the productivity of his farmlands without, as he claimed, displacing his tenantry. When it became clear that that would be only partly successful, he turned toward developing nonagricultural employments on his estate—cottage industries, as well as the fishery—and ensuring that all had access to crofts.[7] His duties as estate owner also gave him a command in the militia. No tepid patriot, Sinclair raised two battalions, personally outfitting them and taking one of them to help crush rebellion in Ireland in 1798. As an amateur scientist and patriot, he was a member of numerous scientific and quasi-scientific societies, such as the Royal Society, the British Fisheries Board, the British Wool Board, and, of course, the Board of Agriculture. He was a founding member of the Highland Society, and embraced both its program of economic change and its Ossian-inspired cultural program. Together with Sir Joseph Banks, he was one of the founders of the African Association, and helped finance Mungo Park's exploration of the Niger in 1788. This interest in colonial matters, which, as Bayly points out, was quite unusual for an agrarian patriot,[8] extended further, and among Sinclair's many designs were projects for Statistical Accounts of Ireland and India. He even offered himself as a candidate for secretary for Ireland (though, typically, he pleaded he was too busy when the prime minister actually appeared interested a year later). All of this, and still more, he achieved while dividing his time between Caithness, Edinburgh, and London, and while compiling and editing the *Statistical Account,* as well as four other major books (most, again typically, multivolume), writing literally hundreds of pamphlets (both under his own name and that of the Board's), and maintaining a correspondence with numerous writers across Britain, Europe, and America (including Sir Joseph Banks, Sir Henry Dundas [Lord Melville], Comte de Mirabeau, and even George Washington).

Labeling Sinclair's political-intellectual position is difficult. He combined the nation-centered self-interest of the mercantilist with the land-based beliefs of the physiocrats, and coated it with the liberals' emphasis on progress and innovation. Following C. A. Bayly, we can place Sinclair in the tradition of "agrarian patriotism," by which he means an integrative, national "moral community" composed of great landowners, yeomen farmers, and professionals. Adopting the high road, they put forth an agrarian-centered vision of the improved society as a patriotic centerpiece for their support of a nation at war.[9] The Board's three major reports on enclosure emphasized the ideals of agrarian patriotism, arguing that when the problem of wastelands and common fields was viewed "in a national point of view," it was obvious that the "improvement of the soil is the best source of national wealth," not colonial trade. Here, the argument was rooted in an isolationist position whereby independence and security of supply were fundamental. "[F]oreign commerce and distant possessions" created wealth, but it was "not [only] the addition to the rent, but to the produce of the country, that is to be taken into consideration." [10] More produce meant more food to sustain a growing population. While Britain fared better than the Continent in the late eighteenth century, poor crops in 1772, 1782, 1793, and 1794 all raised the specter of famine, higher food prices, and political instability. During the wars with France and America, agrarian patriots advanced their position by making the political link between the security of the nation and its independence of foreign trade, especially in foodstuffs, but also other vital basic goods such as wool, and of course more basic military goods such as men.

> The increase of population . . . merits to be particularly mentioned. His mind must be callous, who feels himself uninterested in measures . . . the object of which is to fill the desart [*sic*] with a hardy, laborious, and respectable race of inhabitants, the real strength of a country; because [it is] the fruitful nursery, not only of the husbandman, but also the fleets, the navies, and the artists of the nation.[11]

Sometimes, Sinclair pushed the point, as when he argued that the "inclosed country is perhaps, the strongest of any. Every hedge and ditch becomes a rampart . . . [and were] this kingdom completely inclosed . . . [Britain] should have little reason to apprehend the landing of any body of men."[12] Still, the obvious benefits were clear. Improvement and enclosure could raise capital; increase rents, produce, and the population; and even render the country more defensible. It was obvious, then, that the nation needed improvement, and those that would bring it, he concluded, were the "real statesmen, and true patriots."[13]

What gives unity to Sinclair's work is his drive toward rationalization. The *Statistical Account* is the most obvious manifestation of this. His account offered a means of comprehending what even a Highland laird knew to be incomprehensible unless systematically organized. His ultra-Baconian obsession with facts meant that some of his reordering was no more intelligible than it had been on the ground.[14] Yet, his various attempts at systematically collecting and digesting huge swaths of material into "Codes"—and what Sinclair rather fancifully termed his "Codean System of Knowledge"—display a fantastic zeal for ordered knowledge and its benefits.[15] In his life, Sinclair actually completed two such "codes"—the *Code of Health and Longevity* (four volumes, 1807), and the *Code of Agriculture* (1817)—and planned, but never completed, a "Code of Political Economy" (for which Sinclair conceived the *Statistical Account* as preliminary), a "Code of Natural and Revealed Religion," and—the ultimate—a "Code of Useful Knowledge," a summary of all his codifications.[16] But his sense of order and the imperative to rationalize went well beyond textual digests. In the 1790s—when his plate was already overflowing—he took on campaigns for the standardization of British weights and measures, and reforms to the monetary system; and the General Enclosure Bill, too, fits nicely within his broader program of rationalization and standardization.[17] The rational planner was also evident in his design for the improvement of his estate at Thurso. The plan acknowledged that some might suffer by his innovations, and like a good patriot, he feared that that might cause emigration and depopulation. He therefore set out a planned development of an entirely new town at Thurso, including cottage industries, improved fishing facilities, and housing, as well as allotments for his displaced tenants.[18] Envisioned as what might happen were enclosure carried out properly—according to a "system"—Thurso was to be a model post-enclosure Highland town, and he was to be the model encloser.

The allotments issue remained close to Sinclair's activities throughout the 1790s and 1800s—all through the time that he and the Board were attempting to obtain the General Enclosure Bill—and it was one of the few things he and Arthur Young ever agreed on. But this, too, was a rationalization: the reorganization of labor. Though seldom explicitly extolling the benefits of specialization, the *Statistical Account* endlessly detailed scenarios where specialized production brought greater returns. Sinclair's reorganization of Thurso was clearly premised on restricting tenants' laboring lives to single crafts, be they farming, fishing, or artisan work. The resulting specialization of labor would mean increased productivity, higher returns, and of course greater happiness for the people—or at least as much "as the imperfect condition of human nature will admit of."[19] The allotments were understood to be temporary: they would cushion the tenants during the transition; they were not to encourage a new way of life. At Wick, a fishing village in the northeast reorganized by the Highland Society, no such allotments were allowed; indeed, the entire plan was premised on creating a fishing center, not a village of farmer-fishers.[20] Sinclair would move slowly, but he would move.

Sinclair's conception of improvement as progress stemmed from his adoption of a peculiarly rigid formulation of the stadial thesis. Common amongst most writers of the Scottish Common Sense School, the stadial thesis took an anthropological view of social and economic development, arguing that human history was clearly divisible into relatively discrete stages, whose principal markers were based in production and trade. Its use is evident in almost all Sinclair's discussions of improvement, but is most evident in his short (by Sinclair's standards!) 1793 work: *Specimens of Statistical Reports; Exhibiting the Progress of Political Society from the Pastoral State, to that of Luxury and Refinement; Intended to Furnish Examples of the Proper Mode of Drawing Up Accounts, Either of Parochial, or of Other Districts, and of Collecting Facts, In Order to Ascertain, The Principles of Statistical Philosophy, and the Sources of National Improvement*. The full title reveals the close connection between the stadial thesis and the necessity of not only change, but also change directed through careful planning by those who best understood society's ways. This is a fascinating account that deserves some extended comment, but here I wish to draw attention to only two features. First, I wish quickly to point out how this work illustrates the stadial thesis, and how clearly it—and the entire *Statistical Account*—was linked to Sinclair's program. In 200-odd pages, Sinclair selected seven parish surveys that illustrated both how the surveys were completed, and how each parish represented a distinct stage in social improvement from pastoralism to agriculture, to industry, and finally to trade. Seven chapters, describing seven parishes, move successively through the stages from pastoral to agricultural, to "greater agricultural," to "where Manufactures have commenced," to "where Manufactures have been established," to a "District with Manufactures and Foreign Commerce," and finally to Edinburgh, a "Specimen of a large City, giving a view of the Progress of Arts, Luxury, and Refinement." The logic is obvious, and when one reads the individual accounts, it is clear that the work was intended to draw out the precise nature of the differences between the parishes, and of the manner in which advancements were made. Kingussie, the first parish, was fettered by "vexatious servitudes, that bane of industry and improvement"; relied on the ancient black cattle market; lacked a village, and therefore any division of labor; and its people received no instruction or direction in the correct course of action. But the problems were not merely material; they were also cultural. Though "obnoxious to poverty," these Highlanders were "brave, hospitable and polite," and though they had retained the Gaelic, they had "preserved but few traditions of their civil history; and these are scarcely worth the trouble of recording."[21] Morham, the second parish, was not much more advanced, but its fields were "almost entirely inclosed . . . [and its] agriculture is in a state of high improvement."[22] And so on. As the fields get fenced in, black cattle give way to breadcorns, agricultural productivity increases, manufactures develop to supply local needs, foreign trade grows, and luxury and refinement become available. Though the path is not certain—the discussion of the manufacturing center of Neilston makes clear the moral regulation necessary to maintain civility—the broad movement is clear. Certainty was possible, however, and the entire point of this work was to emphasize the necessity of wise guidance and correct actions—or "good police"—in achieving improvement. Rationalization was not the work of nature, but of rational men; there was no invisible hand here, only the wise, benevolent, and necessary guiding hand of the improver.

The second feature I wish to draw attention to is the endpoint, the final destination of the thesis: the stage of "luxury and refinement." As I have stressed in this paper, Sinclair's paternal concern for his tenants—and of tenants in general—was real, and grew from his experiences as a resident landholder, a parochial nationalist, and a self-described British patriot. Yet, this work—and indeed even the title alone—makes clear the limits of his plans, and especially of his audience. There is no sense in which the betterment of the lives of the mass of people is equated with, or even comprised in, the attainment of "luxury and refinement." His concern for tenants' well-being was genuine, but limited. A strong roof, a well-built fence, and a good supply of potato flour were all that he ever discussed. "Luxury and refinement" was not only a fashionable idea with quite legitimate intellectual integrity, but also an attractive idea to those who sought a lifestyle suitable to those of landed wealth; it was bait, intended to hook his fellow patriots—those who were perhaps less visionary than their self-appointed leader, but perhaps more desirous of the comforts of the British landed classes. We should not dismiss Sinclair's paternal care; nor, however, should we treat the laird as a progressive visionary. Ultimately, Sinclair was an encloser—a man of vision, but one who often knew not what he had brought about. In the summer of 1804, on seeing tenants from Inverness on the road to Perth—and thence America—Sinclair decried the loss of his countrymen, though most particularly the agrarian patriot decried "the martial part of the kingdom thus depopulating."[23] His agent, George Dempster—as enthusiastic an improver as the laird—recognized this limited perspective better than his employer. On learning of the loss of 138 former Caithness tenants in a shipwreck off Newfoundland in 1808,

Dempster reminded his employer that these tenants were lost before they boarded the ship, not after. "I fear we are star-gazers who know the motion of the Stars better than the miseries endured by our fellow subjects."[24] Nothing in any of Sinclair's voluminous public works comes close to such a frank admission of the limits of the improver.

The stadial thesis provided the organizational framework for planned change in British society. Thus, in its use of the stadial thesis, the *Statistical Account* offered the improver not only the specific and synoptic overview of where and what innovations were needed, but also proof of the value of innovation. Codified, tabulated, and presented in the form of a tendentious narrative, the information from surveys demonstrated clearly that improvement brought independence, wealth, and luxury where it was applied, and poverty, dependence, and moral decay where old habits were allowed to remain. Wastes and common lands were products of the past, "derived from that barbarous state of society, when men were strangers to any higher occupation than those of hunters or shepherds." But it was not just in the past, and these barbarous ways could be seen among "those who live in the neighborhood of great wastes [and who] are still an idle and lawless set of people."[25] Enclosure was not just about economic efficiency and bodies for the defense of the empire; it was about rational management, moral regulation, and the civilizing process. The ill-considered enclosure, too, had its own perils, and Sinclair was just as quick to attack those whose only plans were to "drive away the present inhabitants . . . [and] then to cover the mountains with flocks of wild, coarse wooled, and savage animals."[26] Such careless actions not only created unnecessary social problems, but the results offered no real advance in profits, or in methods. Sinclair was not alone in feeling both the tug of Highland tradition, and the push of capitalist innovation. Most contemporary observers at least paid lip service to the effects change was having on their tenants; but some, such as Sinclair and James Anderson, made it central to their writings on political economy. Indeed, as we shall see, it was ironic that John Young should have adopted Sinclair's methods and Anderson's pen name—"Agricola"—as the Nova Scotian was much less sympathetic to the "peasants" than were these Scots.[27]

Young's assessment of Nova Scotia's political-economic context, his recognition of the peculiar features of colonial and metropolitan policy, his attempts to grapple with the particulars of regional and colonial markets, and his optimistic but not wholly erroneous assessment of Nova Scotia's agricultural potential all mark *The Letters of Agricola* as no simple plagiarism of his mentor's principal tenets, and the work stands as a fairly sophisticated application of some of the key ideas of late-eighteenth-century British economic thought. This was not, however, the emergent mainstream of liberal political economy; it was, rather, the peculiarly physiocratic and regulationist program of the disciples of improvement. The colonial context is crucial. If, in Sinclair, we see admiration for the stalwart Scottish peasant—or sometimes even for the steady, if modest, improvements of the English smallholder—for Young, the New World brought new perils, and thus new, or at least revised prescriptions. Indeed, as we shall see, the primitive, poorly developed society of the settler colony, where anarchy was always already in place, meant that paternal-tutelar regulation would be even more necessary than in Britain. We know little of Young before he arrived in Nova Scotia, except that he attended Glasgow University, was a Glasgow cloth merchant, an officer of the city, and had an unspecified relationship with Sinclair. His one other published work, *An Inquiry into the Impolicy of Fixing Wages by Law* (1813), would seem to add further support to the image of Young as a liberal. [28] Yet, when we turn to his agrarian program, the influence of Sinclair is clear.

When Young's letters began to appear in a Halifax newspaper, the *Acadian Recorder*, in July 1817, Nova Scotia's economy and society were in the early days of a new era of nonmilitary development. The British conquered Acadia in 1710, and though forced to return Ile Royale (Cape Breton) they were awarded the mainland by the Treaty of Utrecht in 1713. Other than establishing a capital at Annapolis (Port Royal), the British did little until the founding of Halifax in 1749, and a half-hearted effort at colonization after expelling much of the Acadian population in 1755. The arrival of 20,000 loyalists following the American Revolution in 1783 jump-started the colony's development. But the renewal of war with revolutionary France in 1793, and the United States in 1812, meant that the colony had enjoyed only ten years of peace since 1776. For the military-mercantile elite of the capital, this was a good thing, and Halifax's reputation as the haunt of privateers and unsavory merchants—not to mention a good part of the city's early wealth—emerged here. [29] But the peace brought with it an economic downturn, and it would be a long peace.

The downturn was near-catastrophic for many of the colony's merchants, and the effects were felt across the countryside. Young himself almost went bankrupt, and his emergence as an important political intellectual was probably fortunate for his family's well-being. [30] Thus, not desiring "embarrassment" for himself or for his new homeland, *The Letters of Agricola* began on one of Sinclair's principal themes: independence.

Softened by the hothouse economy of the war, he maintained, Nova Scotia's farmers were ill prepared for the peace. Agricultural production had fallen behind, the price of labor was too high, and the "constant and unceasing drain on our specie for the purchase of American produce" threatened the colony's future. The province simply would not be economically viable were a better balance of payments not achieved. Against the view that Nova Scotia's agriculture was limited by nature, Young argued that Nova Scotia's crisis "may be traced to ignorance and inactivity, not to the niggardliness of nature, nor the want of physical capabilities." Nova Scotia's problem, he argued, was that it had "entirely reversed . . . [the] natural order" for the creation of national opulence. The "natural order," of course, was the order set out in the stadial thesis, and Young impressed upon his readers the necessity of reversing the ill-considered policy of colonial Nova Scotia. The "natural progress of opulence in every free state" was "first, the introduction of agriculture . . . next the erection and increase of towns . . . and last of all foreign trade." Nova Scotia's trade-centered economy was an unnatural form. "Let us reverse this general system of conduct, let return to the natural principles of national opulence . . . and our prosperity will forward with accelerated motion." [31]

The explanation of this reversal lay in two areas: a misguided government policy which encouraged towns and trade more than agricultural settlement, and the "stupid and contented indolence" of the bulk of the province's farmers. Given his largely elite audience, the first critique was made only implicitly, as above in discussions of the "natural"—that is, correct—order. It was also nonspecific. Towns had been built too soon (a decision, his elite audience could recall, some years ago, and of the imperial government); fisheries were given too much encouragement (that, too, was long-standing policy of the imperial government); and trade was too much favored (let us not forget the merchant marine's contribution to the war!). Vaguely contextualized concerns allowed Young to critique policy without pointing fingers at those whose support he needed. "Stupid" farmers, however, were easier targets. Most Nova Scotia farmers, Young continued, were unskilled in even the rudiments of good farming practices. The provincial farmer worked the land in a "sluggish torpor" and

> aspires to nothing more than the independence of poverty. He rears his miserable hovel . . . [and] plants a few potatoes to eke out a miserable existence. . . . His ambition rises not above the possession of a little herd . . . and a patch of ground where the energies of vegetation waste themselves in rank and poisonous weeds.

Traveling around the province (a doubtful claim), he questioned farmers on their knowledge of scientific farming, and on whether they read agricultural works, such as the Scottish *Farmers' Magazine,* but the "only answer I received was the broad and vacant stare of inanity."[32]

Young's emphasis on issues such as "natural order" and the quality of settlers points to the peculiar issues and concerns of the colonial context. By employing the language of the stadial thesis, Young could set up comparisons with "primitive" forms such as the "Arab in the desert," the "barbarian tribes around us," and "the savage life," and his British, largely middle-class audience could nod approvingly. The Nova Scotia settler, he implied—and his audience could know with him—was not far above that very low standard. It was not a society of "husbandmen"; it was a population of "emigrants," "mechanics," and others drawn from the "dregs of society." If they were to be husbandmen, these "people who live in the midst of woods and morasses" would have to be taught.[33] So, it was relatively simple: a country without well-trained farmers was ill equipped to supply its most basic needs, and that threatened its economic viability. But it is clear, too, that Young's economic theory, again much like his mentor's, was greatly shaped by cultural considerations—not the least of which was an utter disdain for the "peasants" who made up much of the province's rural population. "That colony must always be poor," he concluded in his first letter, "which buys its own bread and must be liable to many accidents. . . . That portion of the globe which cannot produce bread for its people is no place for the multiplication of the species, or for the expansion of dignified and independent sentiment."[34] The first part of this comment is unambiguously economic: Nova Scotia would be poor so long as it imported most of its flour. But, as the second part suggests, it was not simply economic issues which concerned Young. What was Young's vision of the improved society?

In *The Letters of Agricola,* Young argued that the advocates of the nation were the educated and public-spirited men who could impart—through emulation—the proper methods of science to an ignorant population. "Agriculture is not an *Art,*" he opined in his first letter, "which may be acquired like other mechanical trades by patient drudgery and plodding dullness." Colonial farmers' "ill-directed and unenlightened efforts may . . . obtain a stunted and ungenerous crop"; but lacking the "knowledge of soils, the application of composts and manures, the structure of implements, the habits of plants, and . . . [the] philosophical improvements to which husbandry has been indebted during the last century," they were doomed to "waste the profuse liberality of nature, and wait the menacing and sure approach of penury."[35] Young's methods, however, were hardly pure science.

Science offered a useful language by which Young might not only legitimize his approach to—and indeed his use of—political economy, but also by which he might imagine the refashioning of colonial society and government. In *The Letters of Agricola,* the discourse of science was also one of class, and thus much of the argument hinges on culture and social position. By demonstrating how much science (and of course men of science) could bring to the "ignorant and unlettered boor[s]" who made up most of the province's farmers, Young was arguing for the place of a class of educated and moderately wealthy men, and their role as social leaders. He was very clear in describing what characteristics marked this better class of men; and he was not at all above flattering his way into their good opinions. Scientific farming required the manner of a gallant, middle-class man. Nature, after all, was a woman, and the "ignorant and unlettered" farmer

> wants the talents and address to court vegetative nature in her coyer moods, to draw forth her latent beauties, and induce her to display the full luxuriance of her charms. These she reveals only to those ardent and scientific admirers, who penetrate her sequestered recesses, who study her in all the windings and mazes of vegetation, and labour to acquire the knowledge of soils, the application of composts and manures . . . [36]

Agricultural improvement—clearly, at least in this illustration, the domain of men—was much like seduction. Not to improve, he argued, "betrays a want of manly firmness." Yet, equally clearly, it was not simply a masculine sphere, but a cultured, educated, and middle-class masculine sphere.

This cultural particularity can also be seen in his patrician vision of the improved rural landscape. There are two senses to Young's use of the term *cultivation:* first (and more obviously) as the cultivation of the soil, and second as a signifier of advanced culture. When he discusses the cultivation of the soil, he sees more than fields of wheat. The imagined landscape of the improver featured the "verdant meadow . . . the cultured hill and the planted and ornamental woodland," a vision very much out of step for "a people who live in the midst of woods and morasses." [37]

The second use of cultivation—as an advanced cultural condition—situated people within this larger landscape. "Agricultural pursuits" and the "pleasures of the country life," he writes, were the stuff of poets, the

> relaxation of the nobleman and the retreat of the philosopher. The merchant or manufacturer whose mind has been broken down by the strain of

business, regards them as the solace and enjoyment of his summer years
. . . [there] he can escape the smoke of the city [and] inhale the fresh country air.

Young allowed that as a still immature colony, this form of country life
might be premature. But therein lay a potential future danger. The settler
was not "the improver"; indeed, with the unusually fertile conditions of
newly cleared land, the colonial farmer seldom needed to be better ac-
quainted with the techniques of British agriculture. Settlers had to "struggle [with the forest] for subsistence . . . [and were] not in a condition to
acquire a relish for convenience, far less for refinement." The provincial
farmer, mired in the "morasses" of the forest, needed to be taught this
"taste for convenience and refinement."[38] Young's vision of this better life
was clear. For him, the farm of the "improver" was not just a house and
fields, but the "ornamental pleasure-ground—the shrubbery, the lawn, the
tasteful villa, the substantial family seat"; it was not just cultivated fields,
but a cultivated lifestyle.

We might be tempted to describe Young as spokesperson for an emergent capitalist order. But this would be misleading. Profit and accumulation, for example, though frequently discussed, were clearly not to be the
primary motivations for improvement. "Our first great duty is to encourage
Agriculture" because it is "in every age and in every place . . . the prime
source of national prosperity and grandeur." Here the "patriotic undertaking" of improvement was the adoption of the high ground of moral leadership for a national wealth which the middle classes would define, and by
which they could undoubtedly profit.[39] But neither the leadership nor the
leaders' motivations could be understood to be unambiguously determined
by their relationship to economic matters. Young invoked the language of
civic humanism to convince colonial elites of their responsibilities. Though
improvers would achieve financial gains (and he was unapologetic on that
point), duty, not mere self-interest, propelled the improver. Indeed, rural
life served as a moderating force on the excesses of capitalist society, a
place where the potential rapaciousness of commercial affairs might be
tempered. And Young emphasized the capacity of country living to
"repress, or at least to moderate the strifes of ambition." Among the
"peaceful occupations," one does not find the

rivalships of business, the collision of commercial arrangements, the jeal-
ousies of capital, [or] the grasping selfishness of cupidity . . . which disturb
the harmony of society. . . . Among farmers there have never been . . . the

secrets of trade, concealments, distrusts and all that loathesome brood of passions which have raged in commerce since the first dawn of civilization.

The virtue that could be achieved through self-restraint played a crucial role in his political economy. There was no questioning the vital importance of a substantial and propertied middle class, but what mattered for Young was this historic vision, a vision which hinged on achieving that harmony between civic duty and elite prosperity.[40]

Improvement, for Young, meant the encouragement of "enterprise," but it did not mean simply freeing individuals to act "in obedience to the dictates of [their own] interest." Moderation, forbearance, and a genteel self-restraint were equally important; enterprise was critical, but unchecked ambition could cause "strife"; competition could be "honorable," but rivalry could cause "torment"; accumulation was necessary, but unrestrained "gain" was "cupidity." Finding the balance between these poles was one of the most important challenges for the improver, a challenge which would have to be taken up by leading men in the state and civil society as they directed the lives of others, as well as their own. For Young, improvement was still a duty, and was thus also a constituent part of civic virtue—of subordinating one's private interests to the public good. At the same time, as most everyone understood, much more than honor came to those who displayed such civic virtue.

Viewed through the lens of liberalism as an economic concept, Young's program might be seen to anticipate a late-nineteenth-century liberal political economy of development—but only in some ways. Young was advocating a type of modernization, but it was as much centered on imagining the proper government of people as on the creation of a correct economics. We might describe it as a curiously hybrid colonial form: a kind of patrician economic liberalism, reworked for the standards of the colonies. In bringing the weight of European practice upon a New World issue; in premising colonial-national prosperity on the ideas of Sir John Sinclair, the Board of Agriculture, and Scottish Common Sense economics; in articulating his plan as a program by which the rural elite might gain some control over the direction of their futures; and in situating all of this on the surety of science, Young offered something for an entire range of aspiring members of the elite and elite-led middle classes. It would be some men's claims to the capacity to control nature and to plan a civilized society which would in turn support their claim to dominion.

Like the Sovereign of the Creation, [the husbandman] commands, and . . . is obeyed; he speaks, and it is done. The weeds, which are the natural inmates of the soil, disappear at his bidding; the grasses spring up and form a carpet for his feet; the corns are subject to his power . . . the features of a rugged and forbidding territory are transmuted into the beautiful and sublime, and soften under the influence of his transforming smile.

The improver had a duty to perform, an obligation to contribute to the society in which one found oneself, and that duty brought with it a claim to power. One also had to learn to subordinate oneself to greater powers for the greater good; whether God or the "invisible hand," there were conditions acting on one's will which imposed important constraints. It was in this crucial location—between subordination and self-government, and between discipline and action—that the modern political subject could be seen to emerge. To discipline oneself in such a way as to be self-governing and yet governable was to become a liberal subject.[41] Young's virtuous citizens were demonstrating their capacity to be governed. But in this colonial context, it was even more important that some demonstrate they could govern—and govern both society and nature, and indeed themselves.

If we move our understanding of the meaning of improvement not only beyond the technical issues such as proper farming, but also beyond a narrowly understood "economy," we can begin to see how broadly situated the term was in this period. For Young, as for Sinclair, improvement was much more than an economic issue. It was also a matter of police, and of moral and social regulation. Improvement was about better farming, and it was about economic policy; but it was more about the necessary knowledge and conditions for proper government. It was, after all, the only way Young could conceive of a properly organized society; when one came from the center of the world, emulation made sense in so many ways. Transferred to the peculiar conditions of the New World, improvement became a justification for conquest, as well as a program for the refashioning of politics, for the maintenance of order, and for the reaffirmation of class rule.

The influence of agrarian patriotism, and of men like Sir John Sinclair in Nova Scotia, was less related to the broader application of surveys and techniques of surveillance and macromanagement than it was to the creation of bases for the emergence of civil society.[42] Compared with the New England model, Nova Scotia's constitution forged a heavily centralized government with a strong executive, a correspondingly weak Assembly, and virtually no town government.[43] The Nova Scotia model was created in reaction to what the colonial office saw as problematic in the earlier American colonies. It put great power in London and Halifax. Outside the capital, with no local government and only weak support for the state church, such a model allowed little scope for local control or the development of any of the institutions of civil society outside of Halifax. While the absence of an official church was filled quickly and readily by itinerant evangelicals, the gap in civil society was only slowly and partially filled by voluntary societies such as the Masonic Lodge and the North British Society.[44] These and other voluntary societies would develop in the decades after 1815, but none would have the success, or the influence, of the state-supported agricultural societies that Young precipitated with his letters.[45] Forged in this unusual political-constitutional context, and set up specifically to establish a bridge between the state and what might become civil society, Young's program, and in particular the local agricultural societies, were powerful influences in the making of liberal subjectivities in colonial Nova Scotia.

Of course, in Britain, the context was quite different. The organization of the British Board was unusual.[46] As one of the founding figures in the Highland Society, the British Fisheries Board, and British Wool Society, Sinclair knew the strengths and weaknesses of voluntary societies, and he wanted something stronger. And he got it. The "Board of Agriculture and Internal Improvement" was Sinclair's reward for his handling of the finance committee during the monetary crisis of 1793. The prime minister, William Pitt (the Younger), and Sinclair drew up the Board's constitution together. While it is not clear whether Sinclair wanted something as state-centered as the Board of Trade, or whether Pitt wanted something closer to a standard voluntary society, the result was something of a hybrid. The operating funds came from both government grants and subscriptions, and it was composed of both elected officials and others appointed from its voluntary membership. Unlike the Boards of Trade and Admiralty, however, it was not a Committee of Council, and therefore had no executive power. Thus, while the Treasury could not inspect its accounts, the presence of official members, appointed by the executive, meant that it was nonetheless subject to some public and even parliamentary scrutiny. This unusual structure gave it certain advantages (both guaranteeing operating funds and yet not being impeded by the scrutiny of bureaucrats, nor of either House), as well as offering certain problems (most notably that it was less powerful, but also that its status was then correspondingly lower). The final product was so unusual that its approval by the Lord Chancellor was not granted for over a year. Even at the height of the war, and even with Pitt's name on it, the executive was wary of approving an institution that so clearly muddled the line between public and private affairs.

The Board was divided into Ordinary and Honorary members. The former provided most of the energy and enthusiasm, while the latter—including the Lord Mayor of London, several bishops and an archbishop, Sir Joseph Banks (president of the Royal Society), and the Surveyors General of Woods and Forests and of Crown Lands—offered further political connections, as well as a certain prestige.[47] The ordinary members came from a broader background, but they were typically significant landholders and included a number of notable figures. Being practical, rather than "scientific" in its intentions, the Board appealed to men of more generalized interests than, say, the Royal Society or the Board of Trade. Most were landowners, interested in the practical issues of economic growth more than in academic investigation. Most of them, too, put themselves forth as men with broader visions and interests, and most saw a place for the state in the necessary reforms of the day. Among the active members were aristocrats and major landowners—such as Lord Egremont, the Dukes of Bedford and Grafton, and Lord Winchilsea (another enthusiast for allotments to the poor)—and some of Britain's leading bankers, including Sir John Call, Sir Robert Barclay (who used his wealth to advocate for improved working-class housing), and Robert Smith (who used his wealth to buy up boroughs and thus became Lord Carrington). And though Pitt did not allow his name to go forth on either list, his support was evident. As impressive as this was, with no members in the executive council the security of such support could never be expected. Sinclair also managed to convince Arthur Young to accept the job of secretary, and together the two men dominated the Board's activities for the next fifteen years.

The Board assumed a range of activities, though almost all centered on either agricultural research (essays, prize competitions for both practical and theoretical achievements), or lobbying for enclosure. The county surveys (1793–95) and the three reports on enclosures[48] constituted the major activities of the Board until 1812. In seeking political support, the surveys, like Sinclair's own work, were always pitched as directed toward securing the future of the nation against famine—especially, as then, in times of war. Writing to Pitt in 1795, Sinclair described the first general report as nothing less than "the basis of the future improvement of the country." This was particularly urgent in times of war, but the possibilities offered by the general reports would last much longer.

> At a time when the nation was on the brink of famine it is extremely desirable that the inquiries of the Board of Agriculture should be Speedily brought to a termination in order that every proper or possible measure may be taken to prevent the risk of scarcity in future.[49]

Here was material Parliament could work with—a plan whereby a positive state could ensure the future security of the country and the correct management of its resources. Though the plans never served the clear utilitarian purposes envisioned by its architects, the scientific program provided security for those who sought to improve the rural world.[50]

Like its British model, the constitution of Nova Scotia's board would be unusual. In December 1818, and in direct response to Young's "letters," a board was formed at Halifax to initiate a renewed effort toward agricultural improvement in Nova Scotia. The respectability of the institution was a reflection of its august membership.[51] The directors included much of the city's mercantile-political elite—the provincial administrator, the president of Council, the archbishop, and the governor—and they called upon the still anonymous "Agricola" to step forth and lead their efforts. Young was cautious, but not modest, and so he became president and secretary of the Central Board of Agriculture.

Like the British board, Nova Scotia's would be financed by a combination of voluntary subscriptions and an annual grant from the Assembly. Its function would be "to direct and watch over the agricultural interests of the entire province" by collecting and publishing information; assisting immigrants; offering premiums; introducing new machinery, seed, and livestock; and generally directing "the enterprize and emulation of the farmer into the channels most conducive to our prosperity." The Central Board members' views of what was necessary were much like Young's, though they occupied themselves much less with the uncomfortable issues of trade and the stadial thesis. Provincial agriculture, S. G. W. Archibald argued in introducing the resolutions, was in the hands of an "ignorant" people who, since Young's letters, had been "generally awakened from that state of inaction and inattention to their best interests." Now, continued Alexander Stewart, there were "a great many in our population, enlightened, opulent, and full of activity and zeal" who could forward the cause of improvement. Following the central emphasis on emulation and the organization of power, the Board was to "exercise a wholesome vigilance and control over the [local societies] . . . and this control was a circumstance which formed one of the most essential and important parts of their duty." Like Young, they believed Nova Scotia "was a country replete with natural resources and inhabited by a hardy peasantry."[52] Now, added Brenton Haliburton, "the peasants require only instruction." No clearer statements of the improvers' paternal design were possible.

Nova Scotia's rural elites fully embraced Young's program, and within the local societies we find similar emphases. While often despairing of their ability to attract a broader base of participation, the societies uniformly boasted of their attracting the "most respectable inhabitants of the country." In Amherst, Alexander Stewart announced the formation of a society, and ascribed its certain success to its prestigious membership, "comprising . . . the greater part of the wealth and respectability of the country."[53] But the respectability these men found in their communities might not have been so clear in the capital, and they were sometimes forced to strike a defensive pose against any suggestions which defamed their positions. J. S. Morse, the secretary of the Cumberland society and a member of the Legislative Assembly, wrote specifically to counter an unsigned newspaper report that attempted to "represent our Society to be composed of the lower order of the inhabitants." He included a current membership list that clearly demonstrated the opposite to be true: "it will be seen . . . that the 'Cumberland Agricultural Society' comprises a large portion of the Magistracy and of the respectability of this county."[54] Such claims were commonly made, and as Graeme Wynn's examination of the membership of several Pictou societies illustrates, the pattern of local elite domination continued through the reorganized societies of the 1840s and 1850s.[55]

Much like the many other fraternal societies springing up in the towns and villages of the region, they allowed rural men—and, to a much lesser extent, women—to meet, to discuss matters political and social, and to demonstrate their social rank. They provided a forum in which the aims and aspirations of local elites and the state could be brought together, and thus formed loci for rural politics and the contestation of political power and influence. In describing their societies, these local improvers give us a clear portrait of how they viewed both themselves and their functions. Most saw themselves as those who Richard John Uniacke believed understood "the true interests of this country," those who would "make every possible exertion to . . . keep alive the laudable and patriotic spirit" of agricultural improvement.[56]

Society members' correspondence also demonstrates, however, that they knew they had a mission: to change the behavior of those around them. And, again consistently, they stressed the same direction for change: "to induce the people to forego the unprofitable practices and modes of their ancestors," and to enter the modern world of agricultural improvement.[57] Most societies argued that their chief object was "to shake off [non-members'] prejudices and old Customs." Provincial farmers, the improvers continued, suffered under the weight of tradition and custom, whether learned from their "ancestors," or from years of "habit." Acadians and Highlanders seem to have been particularly burdened by tradition; they were not only "bigoted in the good old ways," and "their prejudices . . . deeply rooted," but also, another writer argued, "lazy."[58] These prejudices seem to have been rooted in the transference of Old World custom. And they were apparently persistent.

> Many of the worst principles of bad husbandry adopted by our forefathers are still in vogue. . . . the prejudices of former days remain in all their force . . . [and] scarce an appearance of improvement exists. It therefore becomes your society not to relax in their exertions, and it is the duty of every member to endeavour to extend the bounds of [the society's] usefulness as far as his opportunities in his private sphere will enable him to do.[59]

The local improvers remained confident and optimistic. Much like Young, they narrated a possible history: the errors of the past continued, but even within their communities stood the public-spirited who would lead them to a bright future. Changing these habits would take time, but the improvers believed history (and now economics) was on their side. Few farmers were assuming the responsibility of improving their own lives. Someone else had to.[60]

The local agricultural societies were, in effect, state agencies. Not only were they funded by and responsible to the state, they comprised in large part the very people who represented the state within the numerous communities of our area. In addition to the normal forms of patronage available from Halifax, the £40 to £60 made available to each society made a handsome pot for a broader, or deeper, distribution of funds. The 5s or 10s a society required as membership might be three or four days' work for a laborer or farmer in need of cash; but for the better capitalized, it represented access to better seed, imported breeding stock, and subsidized equipment. Here was an ample incentive to emulate. But it was a very small group, never representing more than 10 percent of the households in any one district, and most were already very closely associated with the state. A list of the 111 who served on the executive of twelve societies in northern Nova Scotia shows that in seventy-one cases, the man was also a member of the legislature, or a judge, a justice of the peace, a commissioner of roads, or some other appointed official. That these societies maintained some autonomy did not alter the fact that they were part of the fabric of rule. That they represented only a tiny segment of the population did not make them inconsequential. These were the same men who disbursed road monies every spring, and the same men who might (or might not) serve the court order that represented the end of a family's credit. Some were the same men for whom thousands of others voted in provincial and local elections. As such, these men may not have required either the possible material rewards of agricultural society membership, or the status such activities engendered, but they certainly felt they did. Here was a state body that offered local elites material rewards, enhanced status, and the warm glow of civic virtue.

But there was not enough patronage to supply everyone so well, and it is evident that the local societies were interested in much broader issues than manure, livestock, and seed. In praising their own efforts, the expansion of production was often mentioned, but no more than many other topics, such as the spiritedness of debate at the last meeting, the superiority of the English plough which ate up a third of their provincial grant, the straightness of fences in their community, the improved grooming of their horses, the respectability of their membership, the breaking of centuries-old habits, the correct tone established in a speech at the last meeting, and the proper deportment of their wives and daughters. All of these—and much, much more—speak to the centrality of these societies in establishing the proper conduct upon which the broader society should be governed. Their utter disdain for the unimproved, their willingness to point repeatedly to the poor, the Acadian, the Highlander, and indeed women as the sources of difficulty—and as the objects of improvement—speaks to concerns which relate to political culture much more than simple economics. The broader program was rooted in education, but the particular technique was emulation—"the inspiring influence of . . . example." Improvement would come when the "plodholes" saw the better methods of their social superiors. This sense of human-directed social change is vital. There is no sense of the liberating or growth-enhancing possibilities of either economic or political freedoms. The ancient habits of the ignorant Highlanders and their like would be broken by emulation, not the civilizing force of the market. Elite men, not *doux commerce*, would transform rural Nova Scotia society.

Was John Young a transatlantic agrarian radical? I certainly think he exemplifies one type within that broad category. And I think part of our understanding of why he was a radical lies in the enthusiasm with which his program was adopted, the influence these institutional forms continued to have for the next few decades, and the new role they were able to fill. To be sure, improvement was a much broader cultural movement, and thus much of what we see in Nova Scotia can be situated simply as part of the general transatlantic exchange of ideas and practices. Yet, Nova Scotia's culture of improvement was different from that found in Upper Canada— or, for that matter, Massachusetts or other similar locales. The reason, I maintain, is that a particular and powerful version of that broader culture was brought into a colony where a social and political vacuum offered it a nourishing environment. Moreover, as I hope I have shown, Sinclair's patrician vision of the place and technique of improvement can be traced, through Young, directly into the provincial countryside. At the same time, Nova Scotia's culture of improvement was also different from that in Scotland, as Sinclair's vision was reshaped in the transatlantic process. Such cultural-intellectual transfers are complex, and not easily reduced or particularized. But it is clear that the unusual, or perhaps simply different, features of state and society in colonial Nova Scotia both reshaped and were given shape by the praxis of Sir John Sinclair, as translated by John Young. Improvement was, as Bruce Curtis emphasizes, part of a global process, but it found different expression in different contexts.[61] The combined vision of elite-led voluntary societies, forging a new institutional relationship with the state, and the deployment of an agrarian patriotic understanding of progress gave shape and cultural meaning to an organizing civil society.

Young's conservative radicalism, like Sinclair's, looked backward as much as forward, invoking the Tory myth of stability, elite emulation, and a harmonious order, while at the same time urging innovation and "enterprise." Young, like many other enterprising individuals who arrived in the British North American colonies at this time,[62] envisioned a kind of gentry capitalism: it would put new men like himself in positions of wealth and power, but it would adopt the appearance, and much of the outlook, of a landed aristocracy. Though Sinclair's influence, and certainly his broader significance, was greater, both men attempted to alter the context of rural-national policy through the combined effects of their own intellectual interventions and the implementation of new practices and relationships between civil society and the state. Both fully believed in the benefits of improvement, and yet both also held to a certain caution concerning how much innovation they would encourage, and more particularly how much free activity they would accept as legitimate.

Recent work on Upper Canadian state formation, state education, and evangelical Christianity in Upper Canada has noted the important place of the "culture of improvement" in nurturing the development of the liberal self.[63] These works offer suggestive possibilities for further research, but have limited applicability in Nova Scotia. Evangelicalism was much less important, and the combination of much greater religious pluralism and a more centralized state delayed the introduction of normal schools and state education. In rural Nova Scotia, the culture of improvement also emphasized education and the development of the self, but it did so more through the channels of paternalistic voluntary societies. The most important of these were the agricultural societies. But their reliance on state support and guidance meant that this important component of civil society would operate only under constraints governed by elite-led, though fragmented, political considerations, a deeply conservative social milieu, and the illiberal legacy of men like Sir John Sinclair. In this context, metropolitan emulation encouraged local elites to embrace an older model of civic virtue—one based more on elite leadership. Political authority, both secular and religious, limited any emphasis on individual governance to those for whom such issues mattered—themselves. If, in some parts of the province, evangelicalism offered a point of organization and identity for dissent in rural society, the agricultural societies offered a pole for cohesion.[64] With civil society so completely linked with, and dependent upon, the colonial state, local politics in rural Nova Scotia remained an elite preserve, and weakened one avenue for the emergence of a broader popular democratic politics.

Notes

1. J. M. Neeson, *Commoners: Common Right, Enclosure and Social Change in England, 1700–1820* (Cambridge: Cambridge University Press, 1993),

30–1; J. M. Bumsted, *The People's Clearance: Highland Emigration to British North America* (Edinburgh: Edinburgh University Press, 1982), 19–20; and C. A. Bayly, *Imperial Meridian: The British Empire and the World, 1780–1830* (London: Longman, 1989), 121–25. For an interesting popular debate on Sinclair, see *http://www.mids.org/sinclair /who/jamie.html.* My thanks to Colin Duncan and Leslie Butler for comments.

2. Bayly, *Imperial Meridian,* esp. 100–32. A note on terminology: By "colonial state," I am referring to those institutions and practices associated with the government of Nova Scotia, while I use "British state" to refer to those associated with Great Britain, including the colonial apparatus. In a nineteenth-century settler colony, distinctions between one "state" and another are perilous, and sometimes meaningless. Clearly, the local government officials lacked complete autonomy, though the distinction remains specifically and contextually important.

3. Stanley MacMullin, "In Search of the Liberal Mind: Thomas McCulloch and the Impulse to Action," *Journal of Canadian Studies* 23, nos. 1–2 (1988): 68–85; D. C. Harvey, "The Intellectual Awakening of Nova Scotia," *Dalhousie Review* 13 (1933): 1–22; and D. A. Sutherland, "1810–1820: War and Peace," in *The Atlantic Region to Confederation: A History,* ed. Phillip A. Buckner and John G. Reid (Toronto: University of Toronto Press, 1994), 258–59.

4. J. L. Hammond and Barbara Hammond, *The Village Labourer, 1760–1832: A Study in the Government of England before the Reform Bill* (London: Longmans, 1919); E. P. Thompson, *Customs in Common: Studies in Traditional Popular Culture* (New York: New Press, 1993), 159–75; Bayly, *Imperial Meridian;* and Neeson, *Commoners.*

5. Ian Hacking, *The Taming of Chance* (Cambridge: Cambridge University Press, 1990), 26–28; Richards, *Agrarian Transformations,* 189–90 and 251–53; Neeson, *Commoners;* and Bayly, *Imperial Meridian,* 123–25.

6. Rosalind Mitchison, *Agricultural Sir John: The Life of Sir John Sinclair of Ulbster, 1754–1835* (London: Geoffrey Bles, 1962), passim.

7. Mitchison is largely uncritical on this point, fully accepting not only Sir John's good intentions, but also the complete program of the enclosures as short-term pain for long-term gain. Eric Richards, however, is no fan of the enclosures, and shares Mitchison's take on Sinclair. See his *Agrarian Transformation,* 252–53.

8. Bayly, *Imperial Meridian,* 125. Though an unusual mix, and therefore interesting, Sinclair was generally hostile toward colonialism, and

particularly investment in the overseas possessions, a point we will pursue below. See also Bumsted, *People's Clearances*, 47–51.

9. Bayly, *Imperial Meridian*, 80; and on improvement, war, and national integration, see Linda Colley, *Britons: Forging the Nation, 1707–1837* (London: Pimlico, 1992). For examples of the war-inspired patriotic programs, see Sir John Sinclair, *Report of the Committee of the Board of Agriculture . . . Concerning the Culture and Use of Potatoes* (London: Bulmer, 1795), v; and *Account of Experiments tried by the Board of Agriculture in the Composition of Various Sorts of Bread* (London: Nicol, 1795).

10. Sir John Sinclair, *Report of the Committee of the Board of Agriculture to Take into Consideration the State of the Waste Lands and Common Fields of this Kingdom* (London: n.p., 1795), 35.

11. Ibid., 39.

12. Ibid., 40.

13. Sir John Sinclair, *Specimens of Statistical Reports; Exhibiting the Progress of Political Society* (London, 1793), xi.

14. Later works explicitly made the claim to Baconian ideals. See Sir John Sinclair, *Analysis of the Statistical Account of Scotland* (Edinburgh: Constable, 1825), 59–60.

15. Sir John Sinclair, *Prospectus Explaining the Nature and Superior Advantages of the Codean System of Knowledge* (London, 1819). See also James C. Scott, *Seeing Like a State: How Certain Schemes to Improve the Human Condition Have Failed* (New Haven, Yale University Press, 1998).

16. Mitchison, *Agricultural Sir John*, 216–24; the connection between the Code of Political Economy and the Statistical Account is discussed in the preface to his *Analysis of the Statistical Account of Scotland* (Edinburgh, 1825). Both published works were very popular, running to four English editions and being translated into French and German.

17. Mitchison, *Agricultural Sir John*, 154, 184–85.

18. See the plate in Mitchison, *Agricultural Sir John*, between pages 186 and 187. See also T. C. Smout, "The Landowner and the Planned Village in Scotland, 1730–1830," in *Scotland in the Age of Improvement*, ed. N. T. Phillipson and Rosalind Mitchison (Edinburgh: Edinburgh University Press, 1970), 83–85.

19. Sir John Sinclair, *Specimens of Statistical Reports; Exhibiting the Progress of Political Society* (London, 1793), vii.

20. Sinclair was involved in these plans, but played no major role. Mitchison, *Agricultural Sir John*, 196–97.

21. Sinclair, *Specimens of Statistical Accounts*, 4–5, 9.

22. Ibid., 16–17.

23. Sinclair to Dundas (Lord Melville), 4 August 1804, as cited in Mitchison, *Agricultural Sir John*, 194.

24. George Dempster to Sinclair, 11 January 1808, as cited in Mitchison, *Agricultural Sir John*, 199. This is also one of the few occasions when Mitchison allows that Sinclair's plans were possibly not in the tenants' best interests.

25. Sinclair, *Waste Lands*, 4.

26. Sir John Sinclair, *Address to the British Wool Society* (London: n.p., 1791), 11.

27. James Anderson, *Observations on the Means of Exciting a National Industry* (Edinburgh: n.p., 1777).

28. John Young, *An Inquiry into the Impolicy of Fixing Wages by Law* (Glasgow: R. Chapman, 1813). The connection to Sinclair is made in J. S. Martell, "The Achievements of Agricola and the Agricultural Societies, 1818–1825," *Bulletin of the Public Archives of Nova Scotia* 2, no. 2 (Halifax, Public Archives of Nova Scotia, 1940), 9; [John Young, Secretary], *Report of the Provincial Agricultural Society* (Halifax, 1823), 11. See also D. C. Harvey, "Pre-Agricola John Young, or a Compact Family in Search of a Fortune," *Collections of the Nova Scotia Historical Society* 32 (1959): 125–59; and R. A. MacLean, "John Young," *Dictionary of National Biography* [Canada], 5:930–35. My thanks to John MacLeod of the Public Archives of Nova Scotia for assistance in tracking down this text.

29. D. A. Sutherland, "War and Peace," in *The Atlantic Region to Confederation: A History*, ed. Phillip A. Buckner and John G. Reid (Toronto: University of Toronto Press, 1994), 235–42.

30. Harvey, "Pre-Agricola John Young"; MacLean, "John Young," 932.

31. Young, *The Letters of Agricola*, 454.

32. Ibid., 18.

33. Ibid., 23, 25, and 447.

34. Ibid., 20–21.

35. Ibid., 18 [original emphasis].

36. Ibid.

37. Ibid., 60 and 447.

38. Ibid., 444–47.

39. Ibid., 60.

40. Ibid., 28 and 447.

41. Michel Foucault, "On Governmentality," in *The Foucault Effect: Studies in Governmentality*, ed. Graham Burchell, Colin Gordon, and Peter Miller (Chicago: University of Chicago Press, 1991), 87–104.

42. An obvious exception to this comment is Thomas Chandler Halibur-ton's *Historical and Statistical Account of Nova Scotia* (Halifax: J. Howe, 1829). Haliburton's title, and his method, was very clearly drawn from Sinclair's model, though certainly by this period that model was very well known.

43. Elizabeth Mancke, "Early Modern Imperial Governance and the Origins of Canadian Political Culture," *Canadian Journal of Political Science* 32, no. 1 (1999): 3–20; and "Two Patterns of New England Transformation: Machias, Maine and Liverpool, Nova Scotia, 1760–1820" (Ph.D. diss., Johns Hopkins University, 1989).

44. G. A. Rawlyk, *The Canada Fire: Radical Evangelicalism in British North America, 1775–1812* (Kingston and Montreal: McGill-Queen's University Press, 1994), 124–40.

45. I examine this broader development in colonial civil society in my manuscript in progress: "The Spirit of Industry and Improvement: Liberal Government and Rural-Industrial Society, Northern Nova Scotia, 1790–1867."

46. My description draws heavily on Mitchison, *Agricultural Sir John*, 138–53.

47. Ibid., 142.

48. Arthur Young, comp., *General Report on Enclosures. Drawn up by Order of the Board of Agriculture, with an Introduction. by Sir John Sinclair* (London, 1805).

49. Sinclair to Pitt, 5 September 1795, as cited in Mitchison, *Agricultural Sir John*, 154.

50. W. E. Minchinton, "Agricultural Returns and the Government During the Napoleonic Wars," *Agricultural History Review* 1 (1953): 130–40; W. E. Mingay, *Parliamentary Enclosure in England: An Introduction to its Cause, Incidence, and Impact, 1750–1850* (London: Longman, 1997), 29–31.

51. *Acadian Recorder*, 19 December 1818, reprinted in John Young, *The Letters of Agricola on the Principles of Vegetation and Tillage* (Halifax: John Howe, 1822), 206–13. The letters had begun in July.

52. All quotations from the report of the first meeting as recorded in the *Acadian Recorder*, 19 December 1819, and reprinted in *Letters of Agricola*, 206–13.

53. William McKeen to John Young, Mabou, 10 March 1821, no. 121, vol. 7, RG8, Public Archives of Nova Scotia [hereafter PANS].

54. J. S. Morse to Young, Amherst, 7 January 1819, reprinted in Young, *Letters of Agricola*, 257–58. See also Alexander Stewart to John Young,

Amherst, 2 January 1821, no. 175, vol. 6, RG8, PANS. Young echoed these descriptions on the respectability of the members of the local societies; *Letters of Agricola,* 256, 261.

55. J. S. Morse to Young, 7 January 1819, reprinted in Young, *Letters of Agricola,* 257–58; Reverend Thomas Trotter to Young, 20 January 1819, Dorchester [Antigonish], reprinted in Young, *Letters of Agricola,* 283–84; and Graeme Wynn, "Exciting a Spirit of Emulation Among the 'Plodholes': Agricultural Reform in Pre-Confederation Nova Scotia," *Acadiensis* 20, no. 1 (1990): 36–38, 49.

56. Uniacke to Young, 29 February 1820, no. 62, vol. 2, RG8, PANS.

57. James MacGregor to Young, 20 October 1820, no. 141, vol. 6, RG8, PANS.

58. James Jenks to Caleb Lewis, Cumberland Agricultural Society, 2 January 1821, no. 174, vol. 6, RG8, PANS; Stephen Oxley to John Young, 16 December 1818, reprinted in *Letters of Agricola,* 224–27; John McLennan to Central Board, Middle River, 12 December 1854, no. 221, vol. 16, RG8, PANS; Report of the River John Agricultural Society, 1842, no. 111, vol. 18, RG8, PANS; and Report of the Pictou Agricultural Society, 1843, no. 1, volume 22, RG8, PANS.

59. Provincial Agricultural Society, Report for 1843. See also the report of the Maxwelton Society for 1849, no. 153, vol. 18, RG8, PANS; and the Report of the River John Agricultural Society, 1844, no. 122, vol. 18, RG8, PANS.

60. Report of the River John Agricultural Society, 1844, no. 122, vol. 18, RG8, PANS; and McKeen to Young, 1 August 1821, no. 126, vol. 7, RG8, PANS.

61. Bruce Curtis, *True Government by Choice Men: Inspection, Education, and State Formation in Canada West* (Toronto: University of Toronto Press, 1992), 14. See also Sean Cadigan, *Hope and Deception in Conception Bay: Merchant-Settler Relations in Newfoundland, 1785–1855* (Toronto: University of Toronto Press, 1995); and Ranajit Guha, *The Rule of Property in Bengal: An Essay on the Idea of Permanent Settlement* (Paris: Mouton, 1963), 167–73.

62. Daniel Samson, "Industrial Colonization: The Colonial Context of the General Mining Association, Nova Scotia, 1825–1842," *Acadiensis* 29, no. 1 (1999): 1–26.

63. Curtis, *True Government by Choice Men;* and Michael Gauvreau, "The Empire of Evangelicalism: Varieties of Common Sense in Scotland, Canada, and the United States," in *Evangelicalism: Comparative Studies of Popular Protestantism in North America, the British Isles, and Beyond,*

1700–1900, ed. Mark A. Noll, David W. Bebbington, and George A. Rawlyk (New York: Oxford University Press, 1994).

64. Mancke, "Two Patterns of New England Transformation"; and Rawlyk, *Canada Fire.*

Threatening *Pardos: Pardo* Republicanism in Colombia, 1811–1830

Marixa Lasso

In 1825 Simón Bolívar wrote to Vice President Francisco de Paula Santander, "Legal equality is not sufficient for the people, who want absolute equality, public and domestic; and later will want *pardocracy* (rule of blacks and mulattos), which is their natural inclination, and to exterminate the privileged classes later on." Bolívar had good reasons for worrying. Between 1811 (the first year of independence) and 1831, the Magdalena River basin (extending roughly from Cartagena to Honda) witnessed at least eleven alleged racial conspiracies, three of which became urban riots.[1] In the distant towns of Guayaquil and Angostura, other racial conspiracies echoed their sentiments.

The mere language used in these conspiracies was threatening enough. Runaway slaves from Hacienda La Egipcia in Honda were heard singing, "Blacks over, whites down."[2] In a similar tone, an anonymous broadside in Mompox threatened: "the damn whites . . . will all be f——d because blood will run like in Saint-Domingue."[3] These conspiracies reveal that during the first two decades of the republican era, the notion of race war had become an integral part of pardos'[4] political imaginary. This was true not only in Venezuela, the better known case, but in other regions such as the coast

of Colombia, the Magdalena River basin, and the port of Guayaquil—
regions where they not only constituted a significant demographic sector,
but had also played a crucial political and military role in the Wars of
Independence.

Elite racial fears—in particular, Bolívar's constant reference to
pardocracy—are well known to historians. We are also familiar with the
main reasons behind these fears. Although white patriots had won blacks'
decisive military support with promises of equality, they feared the military
power that blacks and mulattos had gained during the war.[5] White creoles
also resented the prestige and power of *pardo* military officers, and worried
that the independence war could escalate into a race war along Haitian
lines. In contrast to historians' awareness about elite racial fears, little is
known about who were these dangerous *pardos,* how they read the republican promise of freedom and equality, and to what extent the language of
race war had permeated their political aspirations.[6]

This chapter builds on criminal cases in which *pardos* were accused of
promoting racial enmity to provide a glimpse into the lives of Afro-Colom-
bians during this period, and how they understood and lived their changing times. In the cases here examined, race-war rumors emerged from the
political activities of concrete *pardos,* whose names, professions, and words
have come down to us. Some of these cases focus on *pardos* who had
achieved considerable power during the wars, and who enjoyed a degree
of power that was unimagined in colonial society for men of their racial
category. Of those whose occupation is provided by the documents, two
were generals, one was a colonel, and two were literate artisans. Moreover,
the *pardos* that were sent to trial for sedition all had in common their literacy. Even the one slave analyzed here was a literate man who, according to
his owner, had become a leader because of the "natural influence that people who know how to read and write enjoy over those who are ignorant of
it."[7] These men were eager to use their writing and reading skills to seek
legal justice or to express their political views.

It is crucial to note that blacks' political claims emerged in a changing
system, a revolutionary situation. Both white and black creoles agreed over
the fact that colonial social structures had irrevocably changed: they publicly acknowledged legal equality between blacks and whites, as well as
their shared Colombian citizenship, and despised previous racial distinctions as part of a despotic colonial past. In this context, racial threats did
not emerge from a desire to challenge a political system, reverse a social
order, or reestablish lost rights.[8] What made the threats of race war

analyzed here different and special is that they derived from a struggle about the extent and nature of the revolution.[9] They thus provide an insight into blacks' diverging interpretation of the meanings and consequences of revolutionary change.[10]

On 13 February 1811, Buenaventura Pérez landed in jail. He was a *zambo* (half Indian, half black) artisan, and had been accused by a fellow *pardo* artisan, blacksmith Vicente Castro, of conspiring to create a *juntica* against local whites to support the revolutionaries of nearby Ambalema.[11] Moreover, Castro charged, Buenaventura had complained loudly about the lack of justice in his town, and had cursed the illustrious town council of Honda (*"se cagaba en el ilustre cabildo"*). According to the testimony of other artisans, Buenaventura had invited a group of them to join him outside the city with a purpose that would only be revealed at the meeting. When interrogated by the *cabildo* officers, Buenaventura denied all charges. Yet he reaffirmed his conviction that, indeed, "there was not justice in his town." This only won him an additional charge for contempt. Although we will never know whether Buenaventura actually tried to conspire against the whites or not, his trial is revealing of conflicts between *pardos* and the elite over who would control local justice (and how) after the revolution.

This judiciary case exposes a long conflict between Buenaventura and the Honda elite over the administration of justice. The local elite was tired of Buenaventura's habit of using the law to complain to the central government about them. The tradition of seeking arbitration from the central government was a legacy of earlier colonial procedures, when the king was seen as the source of justice in confronting the arbitrariness of "evil" local authorities—a notion that was an ancient and intrinsic part of colonial legitimacy. Humble people, including slaves, used this strategy, often with success.[12] Following this tendency, Buenaventura tried to appeal to the viceroy against local abuses, an action that earned him the public humiliation of being struck by a town officer. All of this was to no avail, because the mayor broke into his house and stole his petition to the viceroy.

The traditional aspiration of expecting justice from the central government only heightened during the Wars of Independence. Buenaventura, like other patriot *pardos*, believed that the new era would bring an end to this type of local despotism. Fully immersed in the patriot rhetoric of liberty against despotism, he reminded the new republican magistrate: "you [the magistrate] have been sent by the supreme government of Santa Fé . . . to administer justice to all the patriots oppressed by their mandarin despots."[13] In concrete terms, justice meant for Buenaventura that he would get paid for his work, and that local bosses would not jail and strike him for resorting to the law to pressure them to comply with their monetary obligations. Buenaventura was not alone in his belief that the new system would curb elite abuses; it was a recurrent motif among the *pardos* that joined the patriot side. For the people in the town of Camarones, the *patria* meant that peoples' backs would have a rest from the blows of their local bosses.[14] For *pardos* from Mompox, it meant that the traditional elite that had controlled corruption and contraband could not use its power to withhold the money that they owed to the troops. They applauded the attempts of the local intendant, who was a *pardo* like them, to curb elite corruption.[15] In all these cases, a new patriotic language reshaped an old demand for justice from the central government, which now, *pardos* believed, the new republican era could finally completely fulfill.

Buenaventura's criminal accusation, like other accusations of racial conspiracies, emerged at a critical revolutionary point. It was February 1811, a moment when Colombian cities abounded with revolutionary juntas (cabinets of government), through which the creole elite sought to replace colonial authorities and govern themselves in the name of the king. In this political conjuncture, Buenaventura tried to gather the support of other *pardo* artisans to form a *juntica* (small junta) against local whites.[16] Apparently, Buenaventura sought to replace the elite of Honda, which had a reputation of being pro-Spanish, with a *pardo* junta, and to ally with the revolutionaries from the nearby town of Ambalema. The patriots from Ambalema, with the support of local *pardos* like himself, would establish republican justice against local despots.[17] In the words of Buenaventura, if they (*pardos*) did not take charge, whites "would ruin it all."[18] Regardless of whether he was conspiring against the whites or was only attempting to create an alternative artisan junta against the pro-Spanish Honda elite, the instability of the moment may have made him believe that it was possible for *pardos* to take control from the traditional elite into their hands.

The Honda elite likely also felt the precariousness of the new times and its potential danger to their traditional supremacy. Only a few months earlier, a junta had overthrown the viceroy in Santa Fé, and with him three hundred years of Spanish rule. Now everything seemed possible, even the formation of *pardo*-artisan juntas.[19] Under these critical circumstances, it was imperative for the elite to control figures like Buenaventura. They saw his attempts to use the law against the powerful as a sign of "his usual pretentious character." They called his suit libelous and argued that, if he was "not stopped in time," he would "continue insulting the people of honor."[20] Yet, legal arguments against "pretentious" *pardos* needed to be adapted to the new times. The revolutionary courts could find accusations of insolence against town council members to be an insufficient cause for condemnation. Still less would they deny Buenaventura's rights to seek justice from Bogotá. Quite different was an accusation of race war, which was an appalling seditious and unconstitutional act. It was the most effective way to delegitimize Buenaventura's political grievances.

Buenaventura's hopes that the central government in Bogotá would support his rightful attempts to end local despotism were partially fulfilled. The new republican authorities set him free, with the argument that legal irregularities voided the town council's legal procedures. Once freed, Buenaventura continued undeterred with his legal habits and filed a suit with the central republican government against the local authorities, asking for monetary compensation for the losses that he had endured while unfairly imprisoned.

If for some free *pardos* the Wars of Independence represented the possibility of fulfilling an old desire for justice, for many slaves the wars opened new avenues to achieve their freedom. Some slaves took advantage of the similar policies of the royalist and patriot armies to free the slaves who joined them; others took advantage of contemporary political chaos to run away.[21] To succeed, slaves had to adapt their tactics to the changing times and ideologies. The case of the slave Tomas Aguirre, alias "Tomasico," shows how the Wars of Independence had altered power relations between slaves and their owners, and forced them to adapt their political strategies to the new revolutionary times.[22]

From the beginning of the independence conflict, Tomasico's political behavior was determined by his desire for freedom. During the turmoil caused by the wars, he revolted with the slaves from his hacienda and ran away to the mountains nearby.[23] He then allied himself with the royalist troops, and in 1816 he took the city of Honda by surprise, capturing two patriot captains, whom he delivered to the royalist army. The Spanish rewarded Tomasico with his freedom.[24] Like many other slaves from New Granada, having to choose between the king's troops and the creole forces, he sided with the king.[25] This was a quite understandable strategy, considering that the king was traditionally seen as a source of justice vis-à-vis local slave owners. Moreover, during the first years of the wars, it likely made more sense to slaves to trust the ability of the king to free them, rather than that of the insurgent army. Throughout the rest of the wars,

Tomasico and the slaves from his hacienda remained in the nearby mountains, aloof from political developments. They never supported the patriot army. Yet, the patriot victory involved political changes that Tomasico could not ignore.

The establishment of a new republican system radically affected the ways Tomasico understood the notion of freedom. While fighting for the king, Tomasico saw the possibility of freedom either as a special reward for his services, or as the de facto result of running away from the hacienda. This was freedom within a slave society. However, the new republican era changed this concept radically. Now, the dominant abolitionist political discourse considered slavery to be a momentary but necessary evil, incompatible with a modern and civilized nation such as Colombia, and soon doomed to end.[26] In his petition to Congress, Tomasico (or his lawyer) took full advantage of this new language. In addition, he denounced the fact that he was taken prisoner by the military for running away as an affront to his personal guarantees as a citizen and a free man.[27] His petition rejected the rights of owners to take the law into their own hands, and the differences between *libertos* (freed slaves) and white men. This rhetoric proved successful with the congressional commission that examined his case, which decided his owner's arbitrary acts had transgressed his rights as a citizen.[28]

Not only had the political discourse changed to the advantage of Tomasico,[29] but also the instability brought by the long years of war gave him considerable weapons of negotiation with the new owner of his hacienda. The new owner bought cheaply a worthless hacienda with insubordinate slaves, who, according to local opinion, "besides being evil, in their expressions they do not cease to show their hatred and enmity to the whites."[30] They were heard singing "Blacks over, whites down," and had never served anyone willingly. The recognized leader of these slaves was Tomasico. Both he and his new owner were fully aware of the crucial importance of their initial steps toward each other and the other slaves. These steps would determine who would dominate the hacienda. Tomasico's new owner tried to gain the favor of his slaves with philanthropic tactics. He summoned all the slaves from his hacienda and held a lottery contest among them, the two winners receiving their freedom. Tomasico refused to attend this ceremony. To do so would have entailed recognizing the authority of his owner, and renouncing the freedom he had gained while fighting for the Spanish. He decided to negotiate individually his own freedom. In contrast to the conciliatory liberal and nationalist language that he used with the government, he requested that his owner recognize his free-dom with a machete in his hands. Cunningly, his owner neither accepted nor refused. He wrote Tomasico a certificate of freedom that the overseer would give him if he behaved faithfully and peacefully for one year. A clever tactic, since having Tomasico, the acknowledged leader, behave faithfully would reestablish order and discipline in his hacienda. However, Tomasico did not comply with the pact. He continued to encourage acts of disobedience among the slaves and stole the certificate of freedom from the overseer, an act which eventually sent him to jail.[31] In one of his trips to Honda, the governor of Mariquita imprisoned him in the military garrison.

His wife, a free woman, took his cause to court.[32] As we saw, Tomasico's lawyers argued in defense of his rights as a citizen, and demanded that the central government stand by its principles of liberty and equality. Since Tomasico's owner could not openly oppose this liberal philanthropic rheto-ric, he chose a different strategy. He asked respectable citizens to testify to Tomasico's well-known rebellious character and enmity toward whites. One after the other, elite members of his region testified to Tomasico's infa-mous behavior.[33] We do not know whether this strategy proved to be suc-cessful. The congressional commission in charge of Tomasico's case upheld his demand, but the documents are silent about the final outcome since the case ends with the congressional decision to send the case back to the Supreme Court. Yet, the conflict itself shows the extent to which the wars disrupted power relations. The elite capacity of coercion had greatly dimin-ished, and a new liberal ideology had shaken the traditional legitimacy of their authority. Power relations had to be renegotiated, and nobody knew with certainty how and with what outcome.

The political and social ambitions of the *pardos*, who had achieved an unprecedented degree of social mobility during the wars, were one of the most intense sources of conflicts between them and the local elite. The legal barriers for *pardos'* access to prestigious positions had been completely abolished, and through the army, they had risen to the highest positions of military and political power. The question was how much further these changes would go. The two most renowned and dramatic racial conspira-cies in Gran Colombia—the 1817 revolt of General Píar in Angostura, and the 1828 revolt of General Padilla in Cartagena—were stirred by *pardos'* ex-pectation to have the same access to political power as their white counter-parts. Even if Píar and Padilla had reached some of the highest positions of power in society, they felt discriminated against because of their color.

Píar was the most terrible rival of Bolívar himself in the crucial year of 1817, when the patriots had just begun to consolidate their offensive. It was a moment when the question of the nature of the patriot army was open to contestation. Píar led the opposition to Bolívar's scheme to monopolize the control of the army, and eventually openly defied Bolívar's power.[34] In his fight against Bolívar, he stirred racial conflicts between *pardo* and white soldiers. Píar courted several black and mulatto officers, trying to convince them that he was persecuted by the government simply for being mulatto. He claimed that as long as the *mantuanos* (the Venezuelan white elite) remained in control, *pardos* would never enjoy power and representation, and that their freedom and happiness could only be achieved if they eliminated Bolívar and all the whites who wanted to command them from Caracas.[35] Ten years later, similar events took place in the city of Cartagena. The city's two most powerful men, the *pardo* general Padilla (a national hero since his victory in the battle of Maracaibo) and the white general Montilla, struggled for control over the city. During the debates over whether or not to replace the 1821 Constitution with Bolívar's new conservative Bolivian one, they took opposite sides. Padilla favored the more liberal constitution of 1821.[36] Padilla's attempt to gain popular support against Montilla ended in a popular riot that declared him the city's general commandant. Like Píar, Padilla used racial grievances to gain the support of local *pardos*, trying to galvanize them with the argument that they were not receiving the promotions they deserved because of their color.[37] Bolívar's response to both conspiracies was swift. Neither their rank and crucial role in the Wars of Independence, nor their enormous popularity with the troops could save their lives. Their crime was too dangerous and deserved no mercy. They were both executed as traitors to the republican cause.

As contemporaries were well aware, events surrounding *pardo* generals like Padilla or Píar had enormous symbolic weight. They represented the possibilities and limits to *pardo* aspirations offered by the new regime. Another alleged *pardo* conspiracy, this time in Guayaquil, was framed around the figure of a *pardo* general, José Laurencio Silva, who never participated in it, but became a source of public discussion about the continuity of racial hierarchies under the republic.[38] In September 1826, General Silva was on everybody's mind. In a social gathering, Ignacio de Icaza commented that Silva "could be a general but never a noble."[39] De Icaza also commented on the excessive pride of *pardos*—a recurrent theme during this period—and expressed his hopes that that the new centralist Bolivian constitution would put a reign on *pardo* pride, establishing a real difference between *pardos* and nobles. Presbyter Hidalgo repeated these comments to Oyarbide, a local *pardo,* who soon wrote and published a dialogue between a pigmy and his partners to satirize creole wishes that a new conservative constitution would restore the difference between *pardos* and nobles.[40]

According to Bolívar, 1826 Guayaquil was rife with conflicts between whites and *pardos.* "It had much of *Republiqueta* and much of *Pardocracy,*" he wrote.[41] For this reason, when he sent José Laurencio Silva to take charge of Guayaquil's military garrison, he warned him of exciting hatred between different sections of Guayaquil's people, and recommended that he provide sound advice and maintain public peace.[42] Indeed, in January the provincial government of Guayaquil wanted to contain "a few pernicious *pardos*" who were promoting ideas against the whites among their class.[43] For this, they asked the Interior Ministry to send 500 veterans, with the request that they not include any *pardo* officer.[44] In that tense environment, Oyarbide's satire could only stir up local spirits. One of his collaborators was accused of saying, "the time for *pardos* to rule and f——k all the whites had arrived." Groups of *pardos* were seen discussing the pamphlet, deciding whether or not they should sign it. And the authorities began a trial for sedition against him and his closest collaborators. They were accused of fomenting discord between different classes (an ambivalent term that often referred to race). According to the reading of local authorities, Oyarbide's publication contained seditious statements against the government and showed a dangerous hostility toward whites. They sent Oyarbide and his collaborators to Bolívar's headquarters with the request that they never be allowed to come back to Guayaquil.[45]

The conflict between Oyarbide and de Icaza revolved around the question of whether prominent *pardos* would be considered social equals to the white elite. *Pardos* like Oyarbide not only expected to have the same access to political power as their white counterparts, but they also hoped that white creoles would recognize them as their social equals, which involved access to the codes of honor that until then had been the sole prerogative of the white elite. As a patriot *zambo* sergeant from Ocaña said, *zambos* also had honor.[46] Similarly, the discontent of Arcia, the mayor of Majagual, was not based on any limits posed to his political ambition. As a mayor in his town, he had obtained the highest available local political position. To Arcia's complaint that *pardos* were not yet treated as equals, local whites asked what else they could possibly want than to have a *pardo* mayor. However, Arcia was unsatisfied. He complained about the difficulties he confronted as a humble craftsman made mayor: his poverty prompted people to accuse him of charging the fees attached to his position with unusual exactitude. He took offense when the white ladies highlighted his humble origins, denying him the politeness appropriate to a gentleman, and he strongly resented challenges to his political authority by the male members of the white elite.[47]

Unlike what would characterize future race relations in Latin America, successful *pardos* were not incorporated into the local elite and thus severed from *pardos* from the lower classes. They were a source of pride for other *pardos* and of discontent for creoles. It was not clear whether this would continue to be the case. Tellingly, along with the rumored statement by de Icaza that Silva "could be a general but never a noble,"[48] there circulated another version, according to which he had asked if Silva would "recognize his class" now that the new constitution had abolished classes. These contradictory versions are quite telling about the fluidity and uncertainty of racial hierarchies at the time. In both versions, de Icaza vigorously opposed lower class *pardos'* yearning for equality, which was what stirred Oyarbide's indignation. Yet, in the first version, all *pardos* would continue as a separate, lower class, while in the second, certain *pardos* would be incorporated into the elite and removed from their "class."

Although the local governments of both Cartagena and Guayaquil filed suits against Padilla and Oyarbide with accusations of sedition and enmity toward whites, a closer examination of these cases casts serious doubts about *pardos'* intentions of finishing off white rule. Even though I was not able to find a copy of Oyarbide's pamphlet against de Icaza, everything leads to the conclusion that it did not contain any outcry against whites. Oyarbide was found innocent in his first trial because the judge considered his pamphlet devoid of any manifestations against Bolívar, or any other seditious comments. For this sentence, the *cabildo* sent the judge to jail until he repented for not having seen the seditious nature of the pamphlet. Moreover, Oyarbide refuted having attacked the Liberator. He had only challenged what he considered to be the retrograde comments of people who wanted to reinstate odious racial divisions. Similarly, none of the testimonies against Padilla indicates that he had pronounced any desire to eliminate the whites. He had merely denounced discrimination against *pardo* officers in military promotions, and criticized the conservative nature of the Bolivian constitution.

However, an analysis of the political circumstances surrounding these trials reveals the enormous political significance of these race-war rumors.

It was no chance that they coincided with major local debates over the convenience of adopting the Bolivian constitution in Colombia. Oyarbide's trial began shortly after the town's formal pronouncements in favor of the Bolivian constitution, the 1826 *Actas de Guayaquil*.[49] And Padilla's revolt emerged from a dispute over whether the military should support the Bolivian constitution or not. In his defense of the Bolivian constitution, Bolívar argued that a lifelong president with the power to appoint his successor would bring to a halt elections, a situation "which [would] result in that great scourge of republics—anarchy, which is the handmaiden of tyranny, the most imminent and terrible peril of popular government."[50] What anarchy meant for him becomes apparent in his use of *pardos'* racial threat to convince Vice-President Santander about the virtues of conservative government.[51] He could well remember when in 1814 *pardos* and *zambos* closed the Congress of Cartagena after the election of an aristocratic president, and imposed their own leader in the presidency.[52] Padilla saw it in similar but less-virtuous terms. He told his supporters that the conservative Bolivian Constitution "provides no advantages to the second class, who had fought on the battlefield to suppress tyranny."[53]

It is not far-fetched to suppose that critical political conjunctures not only promoted fervent discussions over the meaning and extent of racial equality but also unleashed race-war rumors. Even if Padilla did not pronounce any racial threats, two days after the populace declared him Cartagena's general commandant, rumors about massacring the whites spread. One witness overheard somebody in a group of five to six persons saying that "this would be a good night to finish off the whites."[54] On the same day, another witness overheard two corporals saying, "It's getting necessary to finish off the whites."[55] A Venezuelan *pardo* officer, Captain Ibarra, stated that "he feared that people would turn to the last resort of declaring war on the whites."[56] Similarly, words about dangerous gatherings of blacks and *zambos* ran through Guayaquil. These rumors found receptive ears among the white elite, who saw confirmed their deepest racial fears. Besides, transforming politically active *pardos* such as Padilla and Oyarbide into racial conspirators had obvious advantages for the local elite. With this strategy, Guayaquil's town council banished Oyarbide and four other men from the region, freeing local politics from the intervention of outspoken *pardos* who had demonstrated their readiness to fight for their rights. Similarly, one of Montilla's first steps after regaining control of Cartagena was to initiate criminal procedures that were clearly aimed at demonstrating the dangerous racial overtones of Padilla's revolt. Although it is not clear what influence this report had on Padilla's execution—he was also tried for participating in the 28 September famous conspiracy to assassinate Bolívar—Montilla thought it would be compelling against his powerful rival.

It would be a mistake, however, to attribute elite accusations to mere Machiavellian tactics. All seems to indicate that the notion of race war was on everybody's mind. One testimony after the other mentioned *pardos* talking of finishing up the whites, threats that sometimes appeared on city walls as anonymous broadsides. The elite repeated them in personal letters, official accounts, and even in the secret sessions of Congress.[57] In spite of the frequency of racial threats, or talk of racial threats, the question remains as to what extent *pardos* and whites thought a race war was a real possibility. They had very good motives for such a belief in the nearby example of Haiti and in *pardos'* unprecedented degree of power, which was matched with a new liberal ideology that heightened their aspirations.

In two of the cases examined here, Haiti was explicitly mentioned. In Mompox, an anonymous broadside threatened that "blood will run like in Saint Domingue."[58] In the town of Majagual, Mayor Arcia was accused of having said, "a new and bloodier war against the whites will start, just as it had in Guarico [Cap-Français]."[59] The use of Haitian images by local *pardos* should not be surprising, considering the close ties between Haiti and the coast of Colombia. Traditionally a crossroad between Spanish America and the Caribbean, the province of Cartagena had been in close contact with Haiti. As the work of Julius Scott has revealed, slaves moving with their owners played a crucial role in disseminating news about the Haitian revolution among the Caribbean slave population.[60] In 1799, the city of Cartagena was shaken by a slave conspiracy between Haitian slaves and local African slaves to take the city and kill all the whites. Although the alleged conspiracy was stopped in time, thanks to the denunciation of a member of the *pardo* militia, a group of slaves did manage to run away and burn a few nearby haciendas, leaving the local elite with a new source of anxiety in their already problematic relations with local blacks.[61] Lower-class Colombians from the coast could also establish contact with the revolutionary era through some other rather odd events. In 1795, the colonial authorities witnessed with surprise the arrival of French privateers on the coast of Rio Hacha. The privateers not only arrived with a tricolor flag, which they intended to raise in the city fortress after the plunder, but also their ship itself was named "Mulatto's Fantasy" (*Fantasía de un mulato*).[62] A few years later, another French flag arrived on the Colombia coast, this time legally. In 1804, the Spanish authorities discussed what to do about two French government commissioners from Saint-Domingue and Martinique, who had proudly displayed the tricolor flag in the house they occupied in Cartagena's lower-class neighborhood of Getsemaní.[63] Contacts between Cartagena and Haiti increased during the revolutionary wars. During the short-lived Republic of Cartagena, when, in desperate need of funds, the government transformed the city into a haven for Caribbean corsairs in 1812, French and Haitian sailors became a common sight in the city.[64] Haitian sailors helped defend Cartagena against the Spanish siege,[65] and after the patriot defeat, a significant number of residents left the port, finding refuge in Pétion's Haiti.[66] By the end of the revolutionary wars, most inhabitants of the coast must have been fully aware of the nearby presence of an independent black country, which soon became an appealing image for expressing local grievances and aspirations.[67]

Another crucial factor in making racial threats believable was the war itself: *pardos* had been a decisive factor in the patriot victory, and held considerable power in the army. Moreover, those *pardos* who served as soldiers heard multiple patriotic speeches that emphasized their protagonism in the construction of the fatherland. Again and again, conspiracies echoed the feelings of two soldiers from Cartagena who stated that "they themselves had created the fatherland, they were its founders, but without destroying the whites, they would never enjoy their freedom."[68] The war had also created symbols of black resistance. In 1822, Calisto Noguera, described by Cartagena authorities as "an unknown son of the fatherland," was accused of being a "seditious enemy of the whites." He had expressed his discontent with the government, resorting to the image of General Píar, the *pardo* Venezuelan general who was executed by Bolívar in 1817 for fomenting racial war. Noguera had said that although Píar had died, there would be no lack of other Piares in Cartagena. It is quite suggestive that a Cartagenero used the image of Píar five years after his death. It shows that *pardos* were aware of important *pardo* figures and racial conflicts from other regions, which should not be surprising considering the extent to which the revolutionary army moved *pardos* back and forth between Venezuela, Colombia, Peru, and Ecuador. News about *pardo* heroes and conspiracies may have traveled with them. The experience of having fought a long and bloody war that overturned a three-hundred-year-old government probably made believable the possibility of continuing the Wars of Independence to the point of abolishing white rule.

For many *pardos*, the Wars of Independence opened the possibility of challenging traditional racial hierarchies. Seeking to unify Americans of all colors in their struggle against the Spanish, the patriot camp had developed a powerful rhetoric of equality, which *pardos* actively used to fight for full racial and political equality. Slaves skillfully used the new rhetoric of freedom to challenge their enslavement, while free blacks and mulattos drew on the notion of equality to gain access to social and political spaces that had, until then, been the exclusive domain of the elite. *Pardos* had good reasons for believing their struggle would be successful. They not only constituted a demographic majority in the coastal regions of Colombia, but they had gained new military strength and political power through their participation in the wars. Moreover, the nearby island of Haiti provided a close and recent example of how far black political and military power could go. While the military power of *pardos* and the Haitian example were a source of empowerment for *pardos*, they were a source of constant worry for the elite. Race-war rumors reflected this ambivalence. They tell us that the colonial racial legacy did not go unchallenged, and that *pardo* republican politics during the revolutionary era were crucial to the emergence of modern racial constructs in Spanish America.

Notes

1. I have found nine alleged conspiracies in the Magdalena River region in twenty years (one in 1811, one in 1814, one in 1822, two in 1823, one in 1828, and three in 1831). There were probably many more because the analysis of this region unfortunately must be limited to what has survived in the central government archives in Bogotá. Venezuela is well known for its nineteenth-century racial conflicts, but I will only analyze Píar's famous case. I will also examine a case from Guayaquil that came to the attention of the Ministry of Interior in Bogotá. Research in Ecuadorian archives would probably bring to light additional cases.
2. Archivo del Congreso, Colombia, Cámara-Informes de Comisiones, 48, fols. 223–52.
3. Archivo Histórico Nacional de Colombia (hereafter AHNC), República, Archivos Criminales, AC, 66, fols. 804–11.
4. Although the term *pardo* literally means mulatto, it was often used to name any free person of African descent.
5. For the pervasiveness of racial fears among the elite, see John Lynch, *The Spanish American Revolutions*, 190–227; Frank Safford, "Race, Integration, and Progress: Elite Attitudes and the Indian in Colombia,

1750–1870," *Hispanic American Historical Review* 71, no. 1 (1991): 1–33; Robin Blackburn, *The Overthrow of Colonial Slavery, 1776–1848* (London: Verso, 1988), 340–60; Winthrop Wright, *Café con Leche: Race, Class, and National Image in Venezuela,* (Austin: University of Texas Press, 1990), 23–34; and Gerhard Masur, *Simon Bolívar* (Caracas: Grijalbo, 1987). For the elite antagonism against black military officers, see Anthony Maingot, "Social Structure, Social Status, and Civil Military Conflict in Urban Colombia, 1810–1858," in *Nineteenth Century Cities: Essays in New Urban History,* ed. Stephen Thernston and Richard Sennett (New Haven: Yale University Press, 1969).

6. The historical understanding of Spanish-American blacks and mulattos during the Age of Revolution has greatly benefited from the literature on slavery, which has highlighted the importance of lower-class, geographically mobile men and women in disseminating news concerning the Haitian Revolution and abolitionist politics among the Caribbean slave population. See Julius S. Scott, "The Common Wind: Currents of Afro-American Communication in the Era of the Haitian Revolution" (Ph.D. diss., Duke University, 1986); D. B. Gaspar and D. P. Geggus, eds., *A Turbulent Time: The French Revolution and the Greater Caribbean* (Bloomington: Indiana University Press, 1997). The pioneer work of Alfonso Múnera has rescued *pardos'* crucial participation in Cartagena's independence movement; see his "Failing to Construct the Colombian Nation: Race and Class in the Andean-Caribbean Conflict, 1717–1816" (Ph.D. diss., University of Connecticut, 1995). See also Aline Helg, "The Limits of Equality: Free People of Colour and Slaves during the First Independence of Cartagena, Colombia, 1810–15," *Slavery and Abolition* 20, no. 3 (1999): 1–30; Marixa Lasso, "Revisiting Independence Day: Afro-Colombian Politics and Creole Patriot Narratives, Cartenga, 1809–1815," in Andrés Guerrero and Mark Thurner (eds.) *After Spanish Rule: Postcolonial Predicaments of the Americas* (Durham, N.C.: Duke University Press, December 2003).

7. Archivo del Congreso, Colombia, Cámara-Informes de Comisiones, 48, fol. 243.

8. Amidst the vast literature on rebellions, I have found particularly useful the following analyses of lower-class ideology during festivals, carnivals, and rebellions: Natalie Z. Davis, *Society and Culture in Early Modern Europe* (Stanford, Calif.: Stanford University Press, 1975); Ranajit Guha, *Elementary Aspects of Peasant Insurgency in Colonial India* (Delhi: Oxford University Press, 1983); and James C. Scott, *Domination and the Arts of Resistance: Hidden Transcripts* (New Haven: Yale

University Press, 1990). For Caribbean slaves' use of insurgency language during festivals, see Robert Dirks, *Black Saturnalia: Conflict and Its Ritual Expression on British West Indian Slave Plantations* (Gainesville: University Presses of Florida, 1987).

9. A comparable situation can be observed in the Mexican Revolution, when the state and the lower classes agreed on the necessity of radical change, but not necessarily on the nature of this change. Gilbert M. Joseph and Daniel Nugent, *Everyday Forms of State Formation: Revolution and the Negotiation of Rule in Modern Mexico* (Durham: Duke University Press, 1994).

10. AHCN, República, Secretaría de Guerra y Marina, T. 14, fols. 115–16.

11. The following discussion about Buenaventura is taken from AHNC, Anexo, Secretaría de Guerra y Marina, 106, fols. 443–77. For an extended analysis of this and the following cases, see Marixa Lasso, "Race and Republicanism in the Age of Revolution: Cartagena, 1795–1831" (Ph.D. diss., University of Florida, 2002).

12. For an analysis of colonial state legitimacy in New Granada, see John Leddy Phelan, *The People and the King: The Comunero Revolution in Colombia, 1781* (Madison: University of Wisconsin Press, 1978); Anthony McFarlane, "Cimarrones and Palenques: Runaways and Resistance in Colonial Columbia," in *Out of the House of Bondage: Runaways, Resistance and Marronage in Africa and the New World,* ed. Gad Heuman (London: Cass, 1986), 146–148.

13. AHNC, Anexo, Secretaría de Guerra y Marina, 106, fol. 460.

14. AGI, Cuba, 890B, "Testimonio de la Causa Criminal contra Juan José Mexias," 1819, fol. 4.

15. AHNC, República, AC, 66, fols. 804–11. AHNC, República, Secretaría de Guerra y Marina, 30, fols. 342–50, 368–69, 564, 616–20.

16. AHNC, Anexo, Secretaría de Guerra y Marina, 106, fol. 445.

17. For the conflicts between Ambalema and Honda, and the latter's reputation of being pro-Spanish, see Roberto Velandia, *La Villa de San Bartolomé de Honda;* and Jose Manuel Restrepo, *Historia de la Revolución de la República de Colombia* (Medellín: Editorial Bedout, 1974), 1:164.

18. AHNC, Anexo, Secretaría de Guerra y Marina, 106, fol. 445.

19. The Santa Fé Junta was created on 20 July 1810. For the details of this revolutionary movement, see Jose Manuel Restrepo, *Historia de la Revolución,* 1:131–36.

20. AHNC, Anexo, Secretaría de Guerra y Marina, 106, fol. 462.

21. Robin Blackburn, *The Overthrow of Colonial Slavery;* John Lynch, *The Spanish American Revolutions.*

22. Archivo del Congreso, Colombia, Cámara-Informe de Comisiones, 48, fols. 223–52.

23. Ibid., fol. 445.

24. Ibid., fol. 233.

25. Francisco Zuluaga, "Clientelismo y Guerrilla en el Valle del Patía, 1536–1811," in *La Independencia: Ensayos de Historia Social,* ed. Germán Colmenares (Bogotá: Instituto Colombiano de Cultura, 1986), 111–36.

26. Jaime Jaramillo Uribe, "La controversia jurídica y filosófica librada en la Nueva Granada en torno a la liberación de los esclavos y la importancia económica y social de la esclavitud en el siglo XIX," *Anuario de Historia Social y de la Cultura* (Bogotá), no. 4 (1969): 63–86.

27. Archivo del Congreso, Colombia, Cámara-Informe de Comisiones, 48, fols. 223–24.

28. Ibid., fols. 250–51.

29. Of course, slavery was not yet abolished in Colombia, but changes were immense. Legal equality between free blacks and whites was firmly established, and not even the most recalcitrant slave owners dared defend slavery publicly as a permanent and necessary institution.

30. Archivo del Congreso, Colombia, Cámara-Informe de Comisiones, 48, fol. 232.

31. Ibid., fols. 243–44.

32. AHNC, República, AC, 66, fols. 745–46.

33. Archivo del Congreso, Colombia, Cámara-Informe de Comisiones, 48, fols. 231–35.

34. José Manuel Restrepo, *Historia de la Revolución de Colombia* (Medellín: Editorial Bedout, n.d.) 3:358–64; John Lynch, *The Spanish American Revolutions,* 210–12; and "Bolívar and the Caudillos," *Hispanic American Historical Review* 63, no. 1 (1983): 3–35.

35. "Proceso a Píar," in *Memorias del General O'Leary,* ed. Simón O'Leary, vol. 15, documentos 351–423. Asdrubal González, *Manuel Píar* (Caracas: Vedell Hermanos Editores, 1979), 189.

36. For a description of liberal-conservative conflicts, see David Bushnell, *The Santander Regime in Gran Colombia* (Westport, Conn.: Greenwood Press, 1970). For the details of Padilla's life, see Enrique Otero D'Costa, *Vida del Almirante José Padilla, 1778–1828* (Colombia: Imprenta y Litografía de las Fuerzas Militares, 1973).

37. AHNC, República, AC, 44, fols. 86–118. For more detailed analysis of this documentation, see Marixa Lasso, "Haiti as an Image of Popular

Republicanism in Caribbean Colombia: Cartagena Province, 1811–1828," in *The International Impact of the Haitian Revolution,* ed. David Geggus (Columbia: University of South Carolina Press, 2000). For a different, and more recent, interpretation of the same trial, see Aline Helg, "Simón Bolívar and the Specter of *Pardocracia*: José Padilla in Post-Independence Cartagena," *Journal of Latin American Studies* 35, no. 3 (2003): 447–471.

38. For a biography of José Laurencio Silva, see José Carrillo Moreno, *José Laurencio Silva: Paradigma de Lealtad* (Caracas: Edición de la Presidencia de la República, 1973).

39. AHNC, Colombia, República, Historia, leg. 4, fols. 561 and 564.

40. Ibid., fol. 561.

41. "Bolívar to Santander," Guayaquil, 19 September 1826, *Obras Completas,* ed. Vicente Lecuna (Havana: Editorial Lex, 1950), 473.

42. "Bolívar to Laurencio Silva," Magdalena, 18 May 1826, cited by Jose Carrillo Moreno, *José Laurencio Silva,* 78.

43. AHNC, República, Secretaría de Guerra y Marina, 106, fol. 165. Also, Senado-Consultas, 59, fol. 182.

44. Ibid.

45. AHNC, Colombia, República, Historia, leg. 4, fols. 555–67.

46. AGI, Cuba, 719 A, "Sumaria instruida contra los Individuos que se manifiestan en las tres relaciones que van por cabeza, acusados de infidencia en los sucesos ocurridos en dicha ciudad." Ocaña, 1819, fol. 43.

47. AHNC, República, AC, 61, fols. 1143–1209.

48. Ibid., fols. 561 and 564.

49. For a political narrative of the 1826 pronouncements in favor of the Bolivian constitution, see Mariano Fazio Fernández, *El Guayaquil Colombiano, 1822–1830* (Guayaquil: Banco Central del Ecuador, 1988), 87–102.

50. Simón Bolívar, "Message to the Congress of Bolivia," in *Selected Writings of Bolivar,* comp. Vicente Lecuna, ed. Harold Bierck Jr., trans. Lewis Bertrand (New York: The Colonial Press, 1951), 2:601.

51. "Carta a Santander," 8 August 1826; "Carta a Santander," 4 July 1825, and 7 August 1826, in *Obras Completas de Bolívar,* comp. Vicente Lecuna.

52. M. E. Corrales, *Efemérides y Anales del Estado de Bolívar* (Casa Editorial de J. J. Perez, 1889), 2:162–95.

53. M. Lasso, "Haiti as an Image of Popular Republicanism," 184–86.

54. Ibid.

55. Ibid.

56. Ibid.

57. José Manuel Restrepo, *Memoria que le secretario de estado y del despacho del interior presentó al Congreso de Colombia sobre los negocios de su departamento. Año de 1823–13*, Bogotá, Por Espinosa, 1823–13. Biblioteca Nacional de Colombia, Miscelanea, no 1.160, "Letter from Bernabé Noguera to Manuel Pardo," Mompox, 4 June 1823. AHNC, República, Historia, 1, fol. 168.

58. AHNC, República, AC, 66, fols. 804–11.

59. M. Lasso, "Haiti as an Image of Popular Republicanism," 179–80.

60. Julius S. Scott, "The Common Wind."

61. AGI, Estado, 53, no. 77 (1 and 2). Allan Kuethe, *Military Reform and Society in New Granada, 1773–1808* (Gainesville: University Presses of Florida, 1978), 141–43.

62. Archivo General de Simancas (Hereafter AGS), Secretaría de Guerra, 7064, Exp. 33 (1).

63. AHNC-C, Colonia, Milicias y Marina, 113, fols. 76–87.

64. Paul Verna, *Petión y Bolívar: Cuarenta años de relaciones haitiano-venezolanas y su aporte a la emancipación de Hispanoamérica* (Caracas: Imprenta Nacional, 1969), 316, 337.

65. Manuel Corrales, comp., *Documentos para la historia de la Provincia de Cartagena de Indias, hoy Estado Soberano de Bolívar, en la Unión Colombiana* (Bogotá: Imprenta Medardo Rivas, 1883), 183.

66. Paul Verna, *Petión y Bolívar,* 334.

67. Marixa Lasso, "Haiti as an Image of Popular Republicanism."

68. AHNC, República, AC, 44, fols. 86–118.

Multiple Crossings: Thomas Ainge Devyr and Transatlantic Land Reform

Reeve Huston

O ne of the most colorful characters to make his appearance in the nineteenth-century Atlantic world was the globe-trotting reformer. Those transnational radicals who are well known to late-twentieth-century historians—Garibaldi, Byron, Bolívar—represented a tiny minority of this social type. A long list of developments—widespread economic dislocation in the Old World and economic growth in the New, the repression of reform and revolutionary movements in much of Europe, the emergence of cheap and rapid transportation, the explosion of print media—facilitated the movement of reformers and their ideas across international boundaries, making the eclectic stew of movements known as "Reform" a genuinely cosmopolitan affair on both sides of the Atlantic. Since the 1970s, several historians have offered comparative analyses of transatlantic reform movements, while others have traced the movement of nineteenth-century reformers across international boundaries. These works have broken down the national boundaries that once arbitrarily divided up the history of reform into separate national stories, providing a clear view of the international character of reform movements and the ways in which different national movements cross-fertilized. But most pay little attention to the *transmission* of ideas across international boundaries, instead treating reform movements as single international entities, or simply comparing two or more national movements. A handful of historians do trace the transplantation of reform programs and ideologies, but most of these stress continuity over change, depicting reform ideas as arriving unchanged from their point of origin.[1]

This article offers a brief political and intellectual biography of the land reformer Thomas Ainge Devyr, tracing the development of his reform message as he moved from northwestern Ireland to northern England and to the United States. His story contradicts many historians' belief that reform ideas moved unchanged across and between continents. Instead, his peripatetic career suggests that in the nineteenth century, land reform made multiple crossings, in two senses. First, Devyr's reform creed developed incrementally and dialectically in three different national contexts, changing with each crossing of national boundaries as the Irishman confronted new political and social circumstances, new allies, and new constituencies. Second, the transatlantic movement of English agrarianism was fragmented and uneven, journeying across international boundaries with multiple individuals, and with innumerable books, newspapers, and pamphlets. That tradition thus informed Devyr's brand of land reform not in Britain, but in the cosmopolitan reform culture of the United States. In addition to tracing Devyr's evolving land-reform ideas, this essay examines the reception of those ideas, especially by the people whom Devyr devoted much of his life to liberating: the tenants of Ireland and of New York State. Their reception of his ideas, as well as the response of politicians and other reformers, determined the fate of those ideas.

Thomas Devyr was born in 1805 in Donegal, a market village on the shore of Donegal county in Ireland's far northwest. There was no land-reform movement in Ireland during Devyr's youth. The only such movement in the entire empire was a small movement of the followers of Thomas Spence in and around London. Between the 1780s and the second decade of the nineteenth century, Spence published a series of pamphlets in which he denounced private property in land as a violation of natural right. The land in any country, he argued, "belongs at all times to the living inhabitants of the said country in an equal manner." Beginning in the 1810s, Spence's ideas won a devoted following in London, where weekly meetings and scores of pamphlets and broadsides broadcast the message that all of England's land was "the People's farm." But the Spenceans' influence did not reach beyond London city limits until the early 1840s, after Devyr had left for the United States.[2] Devyr's early agrarianism was largely self-created, and was shaped by four influences: the agrarian crisis that engulfed County Donegal during his youth, popular agrarian violence in Donegal, the radical Enlightenment, and the Irish movement for Catholic emancipation.

Devyr grew up surrounded by a countryside in crisis. Until the 1830s, most Donegal tenants farmed under the rundale system, in which land was held collectively in kinship groups known as *clachans*. Individual households were allocated several small strips of land for cultivation, while all members of the clachan grazed their cattle on an unfenced outfield. During the half-century leading up to Devyr's birth, this system underwent enormous strain. Rapid population growth led tenants to subdivide their holdings, resulting in crowded clachans, overgrazed outfields, and increasingly small, fragmented, and depleted plots of cropland for each household. At the same time, landlords began a century of dramatic rent increases; many replaced long-term leases with short ones, or "tenancy at will." Many also began a campaign to destroy the rundale system, evicting tenants to consolidate tenant holdings into large, individually held, well-hedged farms. Pressed by evictions, overcrowding, increasing rents, and decreasing farm output, Donegal tenants suffered from "extreme poverty" from the eighteenth century on. Large populations of cottiers and landless laborers grew up around the estates. Both tenants and the landless who lived on the coast supplemented their diminishing incomes through fishing and harvesting kelp for fertilizer; those away from the coast turned to linen production. But the linen trade collapsed and herring populations gave out in the 1820s, causing widespread distress. In the mid-1820s, a rector of the Church of Ireland wrote that the average landholding was "barely sufficient to supply the family with necessaries." Demands for rent, tithe, and cess took a significant portion of this paltry subsistence, reducing the diet and clothing of Donegal tenants to "the very lowest state."[3]

County Donegal's rural poor did not quietly submit to landlords' new exactions, or indeed to the older demands of the Church of Ireland. Peasant resistance in the north was never as widespread as in southwestern counties like Limerick or Tipperary, but it was widespread enough during the early nineteenth century to win Donegal a reputation for lawlessness and violence. In some areas of the county, resistance to rent, tithe, and cess collection was so fierce as to require landlords' agents and tax men to bring armed bands on their rounds. Poaching was rampant, and gangs of young men skirmished with the landlords' wardens to defend their access to fish and game. Secret societies were active throughout the county. These societies, like those elsewhere in Ireland, sought to protect the subsistence of the local poor by enforcing popular standards of behavior on landlords and local authorities. They passed "laws" at secret meetings that set limits to rents or tithes, prohibited practices like the impounding of tenants' livestock for nonpayment of taxes, or set maximum prices for foodstuffs during times of dearth. Transgressors of these laws received anonymous letters, threatening violent retribution unless the regulations were honored. If the transgressors failed to comply, they were attacked. During the famine of 1836–37, secret societies burned the outbuildings, crops, and turf stacks of men who violated the "laws" governing the price of potatoes. Devyr recalled that during his youth, a local secret society "carded" a local merchant, scraping and scarring his back with the combs used for carding wool, in a successful attempt to compel him to reduce his price for grain.[4]

The aims and grievances of these rural resisters were limited and particularistic. They sought to set limits on rents, tithes, and food prices, and to defend common rights to fish and game, not to rid the world of landlords and tax collectors. Nowhere in the agrarian resistance of the Donegal poor—or indeed of the Irish poor—was there articulated a vision of a world transformed. Still, as Michael Beames has observed for Irish secret societies in general, their behavior bespoke a clear sense of class conflict. The rural poor of Donegal shared a sense of landlords and the representatives of the colonial church and state as enemies, and many participated in a dedicated effort to enforce local, popular codes of behavior and of economic justice in the face of those powerful enemies.[5]

It is not clear to what extent Devyr shared in the misery of his neighbors, or whether he joined with them in resisting the demands of landlords and tax collectors. The only information we have about Devyr's early life comes from his autobiography, written when the author was in his late seventies. He may have, like many other British labor reformers, given in to the temptation to exaggerate or even fabricate his plebeian origins. Devyr's parents were bakers, and he described his family as "very poor." According to his account, he and his siblings went without shoes during his youth, even in winter, and the children were sent away to work for wages when they reached their mid-teens. He worked as a potato digger as a boy and, at age sixteen, emigrated to northern England in search of work. This description is consistent with what we know about the material conditions of Irish artisans, who tended to fare about as well as tenants with small or moderate landholdings. But by Devyr's own account, his family was spared the extreme want and dislocation suffered by nearby tenants and laborers. The Devyrs sent their children to school through their childhood and early teens—a far longer period than most tenants and laborers could afford. And after he failed to find work in Liverpool, Devyr began a career as an itinerant peddler—a job at which he succeeded "tolerably well," earning enough to open his own store after a few years.[6]

Devyr claimed to have shared not only in his neighbors' poverty, but also in their resistance to landlords and tax collectors. Devyr wrote that he and the "crowd of boys" with whom he spent his evenings illegally "redeemed our share" of the fish from Lough Eske, a local lake owned by the Earl of Arran. When the Earl's water keepers exhibited a new aggressiveness in apprehending poachers, the boys marched on them with rifles, forcing them to retreat. Devyr also claimed to have tussled with the local lord's "custom man" when the latter tried to collect the lord's tax on local exchanges. When the custom man impounded several traders' merchandise for evading the tax, Devyr and the other peddlers broke into the lord's storehouse and reclaimed their goods. Devyr did not join any secret societies, but wrote that he applauded their actions. Devyr's depiction of himself as a rural resister is certainly plausible. Local artisans and petty traders frequently participated in agrarian violence, and Devyr's depiction of his gang's and the secret societies' grievances, aims, and actions is entirely consistent with what we know about agrarian resistance in Ireland and Donegal.[7] But we simply cannot be sure that his claims are true—especially since his later agrarian thinking contradicted the thinking of rural rebels. We can, however, be certain that Devyr knew the aims and grievances behind agrarian violence, as well as the specific methods of the resisters. This knowledge formed a clear backdrop to Devyr's early agrarian thought.

Whether or not he shared fully in the poverty and infrapolitics of his poorer neighbors, it is clear that Devyr participated in another cultural world which his poorer neighbors could not enter: the virtual community bounded by the printed word. Reading and writing skills were relatively widespread throughout northern Ireland in Devyr's day, but most students of the Irish "hedge schools" learned a bare, functional literacy. At a young age, Devyr developed a passion for reading, especially chivalric novels like *Parismus* and *Don Bellianis*. For him, reading offered transcendence beyond a dreary, parochial life, and the material for a new self-fashioning. The boy thrilled to the exploits of the knights-errant he read about, and came to model his actions and manners on "the contempt of danger, the toils, the vigilance, the honor of those brave men vindicating right and striking down wrong and oppression." He altered his style of speaking to match that of the characters he read. In remaking himself, however, Devyr recalled that he distanced himself from his poorer compatriots. "My language taking shape from my thoughts," he later wrote, "often exposed me to the ridicule of those around me, all very poor and wholly illiterate." Taunted by his fellow potato-diggers for refusing to fight another young boy, Devyr haughtily replied: "I'll let you know I *read* books of knight errantry." By his early twenties, his literacy and his growing success as a trader provided him entry into the associational life of the local middle class. On some evenings in his late teens or early twenties, Devyr began attending the gatherings of an informal oratorical and literary society, whose members included a druggist, a bookseller, a chapel schoolmaster, a young man preparing for college, and a merchant and smuggler.[8]

Along with chivalric fantasies and an entry into middle-class associational life, Devyr gained another important benefit from his readings: the ideas of the radical Enlightenment. From his readings—and most probably from Tom Paine—Devyr learned the theory of natural rights, with all its axioms: that government and society were governed by laws as concrete and immutable as Newton's laws of physics; that all social misery resulted from violations of natural law; that perfect human happiness could be achieved by conforming to natural law; and that natural law could be discovered by observation and reason. Devyr may have read Tome Paine's application of natural-law inquiry to the land question, *Agrarian Justice*. Reasoning from the labor theory of value, Paine argued that land, "in its natural, uncultivated state," was the creation of God, not the work of human hands. Therefore, it was *"the common property of the human race."* But human improvements on land—plowing, fertilization, houses, barns, hedges—were the product of human labor and could be claimed as individual property. The problem, as Paine saw it, was that proprietors claimed ownership to the soil as well as to the improvements upon it—a violation of natural law and the source of unnatural inequality and human misery. To correct this wrong, Paine proposed that "every proprietor . . . of cultivated land" pay a modest ground rent in the form of an inheritance tax "to the community . . . for the land which he holds." That rent would be pooled into "a national fund" which would pay for pensions for the aged and disabled and provide a one-time payment of £15 sterling to all citizens who reached the age of twenty-one.[9]

It is possible, but unlikely, that Devyr read Thomas Spence, an even more radical land reformer in the Enlightenment tradition. Spence was a prolific but quite obscure writer—most of his pamphlets, written between the 1770s and the second decade of the nineteenth century, never made it to a second edition. Still, the parallels between Spence's ideas and Devyr's later work raise the possibility that Devyr had read him. Spence agreed with Paine that land was the common property of the inhabitants of a community, but made no distinction between raw land and improvements. To him, both "belong[ed] at all times to the living inhabitants of the . . . country in an equal manner." Rather than calling for a mere tax on the land, Spence called for each parish to seize all real estate for itself. This seizure would usher in a decentralized, democratic utopia based on a community of landed property. Each parish would become the perpetual owner of the land and buildings, and would be responsible for their maintenance. All would be free to use the land and the improvements thereon, paying rent for the privilege. These rents would be used to pay national taxes, provide for the maintenance of the poor and the support of the unemployed, fund public works and encourage agricultural and other innovations, "and, in a word, in doing whatever the people think properly, and not, as formerly, to support and spread luxury, pride, and all manner of vice." This utopia would also be marked by universal male suffrage, a citizen army, dramatic political autonomy for each parish, and a complete absence of tolls or taxes, as all public expenses would be funded by rent. Even less likely than Devyr's reading Spence is his coming upon the writings of even more obscure British agrarian theorists of the late eighteenth and early nineteenth centuries: William Ogilvie and Charles Hall.[10]

If Devyr read Spence's and Paine's agrarian tracts, they seem not to have made an immediate impression upon him. When he was initiated into the world of reform, he focused not on the land, but on the liberal project of establishing religious toleration and civic equality. At the age of sixteen or eighteen, Devyr became a subscriber to Daniel O'Connell's Catholic Association, an organization that aimed at Catholic emancipation—the granting of full political representation and the right to hold office to Catholics. O'Connell's was the first movement in Irish history that brought together the middle class and the rural and village poor. Led by the Catholic middle class and clergy, and combining the liberal politics of the emerging Irish middle class with a new strategy of democratic mobilization, Catholic Association brought hundreds of thousands of Ireland's poor into politics, raising over £20,000 through its penny-a-month "Catholic Rent," dispensing legal and other aid to subscribers, and conducting mass petition campaigns. In 1826, the Association successfully mobilized the votes of hundreds of

thousands of "forty-shilling" tenants to defeat their landlords' political interests. In this movement, Devyr had his first experience in mass politics.
In the process, he found a real-world outlet for his chivalrous fantasies: as
a Reformer, he learned to see himself as acting on the courage, the self-
sacrifice, the passion for righting wrongs and protecting the weak that he
had long admired in his fictional knights-errant. Late in life, he wrote that
"my faith in Dan was such that I only wished he would call us to some glo-
rious battlefield, and let us conquer, or let us die, for the cause which he
represented."[11]

As a member of the Catholic Association, Devyr probably absorbed
O'Connell's ideas concerning the land question. O'Connell did not offer a
coherent program for land reform until 1845, but he did consistently advocate a few general propositions. His guiding principle was that landlords
had an obligation to promote the economic well-being of their tenants.
This conviction came from the Catholic Church's conservative and paternalistic social teachings, which stressed the reciprocal obligations of the
rich and the poor, and impressed upon the rich the duty of charity. These
teachings were reinforced by O'Connell's own experience as a minor landlord, in which capacity he proved conservative, non-improving, and thoroughly paternalistic. His paternalism led O'Connell to encourage landlords
to reside among their tenants; as a member of the House of Commons
from 1827 on, he repeatedly advocated imposing a punitive tax on nonres-
ident landlords. And it led him to defend passionately tenants' right to security of tenure. In 1830, he began a public campaign and proposed
legislation for repeal of the Sub-Letting Act, which made it easier for Irish
landlords to clear their estates and consolidate landholdings. He denounced
the supporters of the Act as "heartless and unfeeling men, who thought it
better to support upon an estate a great many beasts and very few human
beings, than a large population. . . . it was not . . . the part of a considerate
and humane Government to make itself the auxiliary of the landlord."[12]

By the time he came of age, Thomas Devyr was thus exposed to three
distinct political cultures: the infrapolitics of the rural and village poor, a
new politics of mass mobilization, and the printed politics of the radical Enlightenment. All three of these cultures would inform his early scheme for
land reform. Devyr's dedication to the land question followed hard on the
heels of the achievement of Catholic emancipation and his subsequent dis-
illusionment with the movement and its leader. The Parliamentary bill that
enacted Catholic emancipation in 1829 included a provision that raised the
landholding requirements for the Irish vote to match those for English

tenants—from forty shillings to ten pounds. In addition to disfranchising over four-fifths of Ireland's voters, this enactment led landlords to consolidate their tenant farms in an effort to maximize the number of voters under their control. The result was widespread evictions. Devyr later recalled witnessing "the long lines of miserable men," largely former forty-shilling tenants, "darkening the highways" in search of work. Soon thereafter, Devyr concluded that O'Connell and other Association leaders pocketed high fees from the Catholic Rent for the letters of advice they sent to subscribers, while poorly-paid employees actually wrote and sent those letters. With this realization, "my faith in Mr. O'Connell departed forever."[13]

The chivalric passion for reform which Catholic emancipation had awakened in Devyr survived his disillusion with that cause. With the achievement of Catholic emancipation, Irish politics took a sectarian turn; Devyr, a religious skeptic from a mixed Methodist and Catholic family, found little in mainstream politics to occupy his energies. Instead, he turned toward reforming Ireland's land system. His new commitment was no doubt inspired in part by own witness to the misery of his neighbors and by the wave of evictions that followed Catholic emancipation. Even more influential, probably, was the famine of 1831. After poor harvests in 1829 and 1830, in 1831 the potato crop rotted in the ground. Severe food shortages followed, and the price of provisions skyrocketed. Throughout Donegal and much of the rest of Ireland, tenants and laborers sold their tools, clothes, beds, and blankets for food. The yearly stream of migrants searching for work in Scotland and northern England reached flood stage, and thousands took to begging in the roads and villages. Although some landlords devoted substantial amounts to buying food in London for distribution to the local poor, most spent only token sums. Their charity quickly dried up, leaving the poor to their own devices. In Devyr's home town of Donegal, notices were posted calling a meeting "for the purpose of crying down rents and tithes," but the assembly seems not to have been held. An unknown number of people perished from starvation and disease.[14]

In the wake of the famine, Devyr began debating Ireland's land system with his customers and neighbors. By 1833, he was habitually steering every conversation toward "the foundation question of the ownership of the soil." In 1836, he published a pamphlet containing his thoughts on land reform: *Our Natural Rights*.[15] The pamphlet began by applying the natural-law philosophy, which Devyr had learned from reading Enlightenment radicals, to the Irish land system. That system, he wrote, created enormous wealth, luxury, "ease and sloth" on the one hand, and poverty, ignorance, and "continuous toil" on the other. It also led to the impoverishment of the soil, as landlords left potentially productive land as wastes, and as tenants neglected to make improvements on their farms because landlords would raise the rent to reflect the value of such improvements. The problem, Devyr argued, was that the current system of "absolute ownership" of the soil violated natural law. "The land was indisputable [*sic*] given to supply the natural wants of man"; no one had a right to "deprive the people of the *means* given by God for their supply." To demonstrate this truth, Devyr drew on the labor theory of value and the Bible. The source of all rightful property, he argued, was labor. Anything created by human labor belonged absolutely to its creator. But land was "produced by the Almighty Power," and no human could claim ownership. Biblical precedent also confirmed that God, not humans, owned the land. Quoting God's statement in Leviticus 25 that "the land is MINE, for ye are strangers and sojourners with me," he reminded his readers that God had prohibited the Israelites from selling land for more than fifty years. Though a family might lose its property through sale or debt for a time, the land was to be returned on the Day of Jubilee. In claiming absolute property in land, Devyr concluded, every landlord committed the double sin of blasphemy and idolatry, for he denied the Divine Word and sought to "make us strangers and sojourners with him" (that is, with the landlord), rather than with God.[16]

In its analysis of the land question, *Our Natural Rights* restated Tom Paine's and Thomas Spence's main ideas, providing a fuller and more elaborate justification for those ideas than Paine or Spence had offered. Devyr affirmed both writers' assertion that land was the common property of all humanity, and echoed their appeal to the labor theory of value in justifying that assertion. But once Devyr moved from analysis to proposing reforms, the similarities ended. Like Spence's analysis, *Our Natural Rights* seemed to point logically toward an abolition of private property in land and a redistribution of the soil. But Devyr was less faithful to his own logic than was Spence. In his proposals, he drew not on Spence or even Paine, but O'Connell and Catholic social teachings. Rather than denying the validity of large landholdings or of private property in land, he called for "limited ownership"—a form of proprietorship that made landlords stewards of the land in the interests of the entire community. Landlords were to provide all tenants with perpetual leases and limit rents to "a sufficiency for [the landlord's] reasonable wants." Each landlord was to take up residence among his tenants, and earn their rents by "stimulating their industry by his advice and encouragement, and civilizing and *refining* them by his intercourse." Such beneficence could be coercive; Devyr suggested that landlords might require their tenants to manure their fields and improve their cottages. To prevent new inequalities from springing up among tenants, limits would be set on the amount of land an individual farmer could rent, and subleasing would be prohibited. These reforms, Devyr believed, would end the "barrenness and desolation" that reigned over Ireland's soil, as each tenant, "undrained by heartless extortion," would "render his field fruitful, and his cottage comfortable." Poverty in the cities would be ended as well. The flood of impoverished peasants to the cities would cease, ending the downward pressure on wages; tenants would increase their output, their trade, and their consumption, thus augmenting the income of merchants and artisans.[17]

Our Natural Rights was deeply contradictory, both in its reasoning and its social message. The Enlightenment reasoning that informed Devyr's critique of property in land disappeared in the Irishman's proposals. In the process, his radical, rights-based analysis of property in land gave way to a marked paternalism. Devyr did not offer a natural-law justification for his embrace of landlords' superior social power. Instead, his proposed reform rested on notions of social duty and, implicitly, an organic vision of society. "Like every member of society," Devyr wrote, the landlord "has a duty to perform, . . . and to the non-performance of that duty society owes much of its crime, more of its ignorance, and almost the sum-total of its misery." Behind this notion of patrician duty lay a deep ambivalence about Ireland's rural poor. On the one hand, Devyr described the principles behind secret societies' resistance to landlords as "springing out of common sense and common justice," indicating trust for the common sense and good principles of the poor. On the other, he regarded the lower orders as lawless, violent, and "uncivilized." Devyr was confident of their capacity to "become another and a better people." But he insisted "fearlessly and emphatically" that "the people can never be civilized . . . by any other than the landlord's agency."[18]

Devyr's proposals bore an ambiguous relationship to the aspirations and struggles of Donegal's poor. Like his neighbors, Devyr aimed not at getting rid of landlords, but at forcing them to respect the subsistence needs of their tenants. But he rejected their hatred of landlords and their belief in an implacable conflict between the rich and the poor, embracing instead the Church's vision of mutual obligations and reciprocal duties. Devyr's strategy for accomplishing reform rejected the anonymous violence practiced by his neighbors, drawing instead on the strategies of Catholic emancipation: mass education and agitation. He called for the establishment of newspapers and voluntary associations devoted to limited ownership in "every townland in the empire." With "the public mind" thus aroused, "that *great spirit*" whose "waking start" had already forced tyrants to abolish Catholic political proscription and rotten boroughs "would spring into active and vigorous life, and establish . . . the long troddendown rights of mankind."[19]

There is no indication that Devyr had any impact on Irish politics or his Donegal neighbors. By his own account, his neighbors rejected his belief that enlightened landlords could do justice to the rural poor. They looked to the reprisals of the poor to keep landlords' rapaciousness in check. After hearing one of Devyr's monologues on the land question, a blacksmith in Donegal exclaimed, "Landlords! . . . If one of them attempted to put another shilling on the land in this part of the world we'd pay him the difference with a few inches of cold steel. The scoundrels!" "Every acre" of local land, the blacksmith confided, "is under the shield of Tommy Downshire"—the local secret society.[20]

Within a year of writing *Our Natural Rights,* Devyr left with his family for London, where he found work editing the Irish Department of the *Constitutional,* a radical weekly. Although the followers of Thomas Spence held weekly meetings in London and kept up a steady stream of publications, Devyr seems not to have had any contact with them. Instead, he continued as a prophet in the wilderness, using the pages of the *Constitutional* to disseminate his views about land reform. But he quit in a dispute over editorial policy and, after several month's unemployment and an unhappy stint working for Scotland Yard, signed on as associate editor of the *Liberator* of Newcastle-upon-Tyne. That newspaper was allied with the emerging Chartist movement—a campaign among industrial workers and petty proprietors that demanded universal manhood suffrage, annual parliaments, a secret ballot, and the equalization of parliamentary representation. Devyr arrived in early 1838, in the midst of a severe industrial depression and just before the initial publication of the People's Charter. Soon after his arrival, he was elected corresponding secretary of the Northern Political Union, the main organization of the Newcastle Chartists.[21]

At the *Liberator* and in the Northern Political Union, Devyr found a familiar intellectual environment. Like him, Chartist activists were steeped in the radical Enlightenment tradition of Paine. Like him, they saw gross disparities of wealth and power as symptoms of natural laws violated, and sought to search out and correct the transgression. This new political community was far less receptive to Devyr's paternalism, however. Chartists demanded the political enfranchisement of smallholders and the propertyless, and they relied on what activists called "political Methodism"— collective *self*-education, *self*-uplift, and *self*-mobilization—to accomplish this goal. No audience could have been more hostile to the notion that the poor needed to be "civilized" by the class that oppressed them.[22]

In this new environment, Devyr abandoned his earlier paternalism. Among Chartist activists, Devyr witnessed something new: workers, many of them quite poor, who read deeply, debated ideas intelligently, and practiced the political "chivalry" to which Devyr had begun to devote his own life. Late in life, Devyr recalled the political commitment of these activists: "At six o'clock, throwing down their implements of toil, those true—not mock—noblemen would hasten home, lunch bread and cheese, and a glass of ale, and off on foot to a meeting, generally one or two, sometimes six or seven, miles off." Through the Chartists' "political Methodism," he recalled, "tens of thousands of men in England" learned "the rights and duties of men, in rational, civilized communities," and began their acquirement of "taste, refinement, and the truest and highest development and enjoyment of life." Devyr became a fervent convert to the Chartists' brand of democratic mutualism; never again would he insist that "the people" needed their betters to raise them from ignorance and degradation.[23]

Devyr's new outlook was reflected in the very few paragraphs he wrote on the land question. Rather than looking to landlords to uplift the tenantry, Devyr began to embrace a vision of landlords as the enemies of humanity, and to imply that the poor could take care of themselves. In July 1839, he proposed that the vast uninhabited lands of Ireland be turned over to the unemployed. And he denounced "the blasphemous aristocracy" for refusing to "let the people reclaim the soil, except upon the condition that all its enhanced value shall go to the accursed rent roll, leaving the people still at the old level of rags and famine." Such exclamations were few. His employers at the *Liberator* forbade him from publishing pieces on land reform. That issue, they argued, would, along with all others, be resolved by a democratically elected Parliament once the Charter had been granted. As a consequence, Devyr did not find the opportunity to systematically rethink his ideas about land reform in accordance with his newfound mutualism and egalitarianism.[24]

. Though frustrated with his employers' editorial policy, Devyr's dedication to the Chartist cause grew. As he took on an ever-greater role in the movement, the Irishman abandoned his earlier faith that "moral force" could force reform on a resistant elite. Faced with violent repression at the hands of the magistrates from August 1838 on, Chartists throughout the North of England began to call for armed resistance to what they saw as the authorities' unlawful use of force. Militants in and around Newcastle stockpiled 60,000 iron pikes, as well as numerous firearms. In late 1839, Chartists in several northern cities laid plans for an armed uprising, to take place on 12 January 1840. Devyr helped lead the effort, coordinating the manufacture and distribution of arms, overseeing rebel drill, and laying plans for battle. But on the night of 12 January, only seventy of the seven hundred men who had sworn to join the uprising assembled, and Devyr spent the night chasing after his rump army to prevent them from torching the city. To complete this debacle, the local magistrates soon got wind of Devyr's leadership in the conspiracy. A sympathetic local official sent word that Devyr was about to be arrested. The Irishman gathered his family and caught a ship to the United States.[25]

Devyr arrived in New York City determined to continue his work of reform—and chose the unlikely vehicle of the Democratic Party. With financial backing from local party leaders, Devyr founded a Democratic newspaper in Williamsburg, a tiny village in Brooklyn, New York. The Irishman accepted at face value Democratic leaders' claim that their party was the champion of popular rights in the United States. As editor of the Williamsburg *Democrat*, he brought his chivalric brand of reform to the service of the Democratic Party. Local Democrats were not pleased. Although he skewered the 1840 Whigs' Log Cabin and Hard Cider campaign in hilarious verse, the editor would not be held to party discipline. In his first three years, he lambasted the Jacksonians' opposition to a protective tariff (a centerpiece of their program); denounced Daniel O'Connell's Irish Repeal Association, despite the fact that it had already won the passionate support of his fellow Irish immigrants and was being courted by local Democratic leaders; condemned the efforts of Irish-born Democrats to create an Adopted Citizens' Democratic Association as a dangerous introduction of sectarianism and ethnicity into politics; praised the main political rival of his partner and financial backer; and called for public ownership of the railroads, despite the Jacksonians' laissez-faire economic policy. Not surprisingly, his tenure as editor was spent struggling to keep the paper afloat in the face of an advertising boycott, a libel suit, and multiple conspiracies and public meetings that aimed at shutting it down. By 1844, Devyr was on the lookout for another job.[26]

While he fought with his fellow Democrats, Devyr found a second outlet for his reform energies: the Anti-Rent movement of upstate New York. The upper Hudson Valley, the Catskill piedmont, and the Susquehanna and Mohawk valleys were home to a score of leasehold estates—tracts of leased farms and town lots on which tenants held long-term leases. Together, these estates comprised about two million acres, and were home to some 260,000 people—about a twelfth of the state's population. In 1839, tenants on the 750,000-acre manor of Rensselaerwyck began organizing to resist their landlord's demands. Over the next five years, the movement spread to estates in eleven counties, claiming between 25,000 and 60,000 supporters in 1845. The movement's demands expanded to include the breakup of leasehold estates and their distribution among the people who farmed them.[27] In 1842, Devyr began writing for the anti-rent *Helderberg Advocate* and speaking at movement events.

For the second time, Devyr joined with a potential mass constituency for his land-reform scheme. But he did not at first try to link the Anti-Rent movement to a broader program. Of his writings during the early years of the movement that have survived, none offered a critique of absolute property in land, or called for the sort of systematic reform that he had advocated in *Our Natural Rights*. Instead, Devyr reiterated the complaints of most tenants: that landlords' titles were fraudulent, that they had obtained tenants' consent to their leases through fraud and coercion, and that they "prey[ed] upon the produce of others' toil." Devyr's reticence apparently did not result from his publisher's refusal to publish pieces on land reform, as it had in Newcastle. Instead, it grew out of an anomaly in his thinking. Now a devotee of popular rule, Devyr nonetheless had not hit upon a solution to land monopoly to replace his earlier emphasis on patrician duty. He simply had no solutions of his own to offer the anti-renters.[28]

Devyr's intellectual impasse came to an end in 1844, when two men dropped by the offices of the *Williamsburg Democrat*. One of these men was George Henry Evans, an English-born printer and journalist. Evans had edited and published the *Working Man's Advocate*, arguably the most important labor newspaper in the antebellum United States, covering and championing the Workingmen's Party and the early Trades Union movement. As a workingmen's advocate, Evans had been an ally of Thomas Skidmore, a radical agrarian who advocated an equal division of all property. But Evans did not endorse those ideas, or any other scheme to equalize property. The journal collapsed after the Panic of 1837, and Evans had retired to a market farm in New Jersey, where he had read Tom Paine's *Agrarian Justice* and the utopian socialists Charles Fourier and St. Simon. But the writer who most influenced Evans was Thomas Spence, the English agrarian. Like Spence (and several others), Evans concluded that land was the common inheritance of all humanity. But where Spence called for all land to be held collectively and rented out to individuals, Evans worked out a different implication, more attuned to the American context: that every man had a right to own and occupy as much as he and his family could till. Evans expressed these ideas in the language of American republicanism, arguing that if human beings had a right to "life, liberty, and the pursuit of happiness," they had a natural right to enough land to sustain life and enjoy liberty. Although he saw private property in land as a violation of natural right, he never advocated the redistribution of present landholdings. Instead, he called for a prospective legal limitation on the amount of land anyone could own; the exemption of a minimum acreage from seizure for debt; and the distribution of the federal lands, free of charge, to actual settlers, and the prohibition of anyone accumulating more than a prescribed amount—usually 160 acres. Beginning in 1841, he began broadcasting these ideas in a series of journals.[29]

Evans and his companion, the printer and reformer John Windt, had come to recruit Devyr into a new land-reform organization, the National Reform Association. Devyr agreed. He quickly threw himself into the work of the movement, speaking at the association's weekly meetings in Manhattan, serving as a delegate to labor conventions, and reprinting *Our Natural Rights* with a new appendix, addressed to Americans, that embraced Evans's ideas and program. But Devyr's greatest service to the cause was among the anti-renters. He continued to speak at anti-rent functions and helped organize support in New York City. In the spring of 1845, he was hired as editor of the tenant movement's first statewide journal, the *Albany Freeholder*.[30]

Devyr's conversion to National Reform exemplified the scattered and uneven transmission of English agrarianism to the United States. Though British-born, he either had not encountered the ideas of Spence, Paine, or the other English agrarian theorists, or had rejected them in favor of the organic social thought of Daniel O'Connell and the Catholic Church. He had worked out his ideas on his own, and his thought displayed the eclecticism and contradictions of an autodidact's musings. Devyr's conversion to English agrarianism came, ironically, in the United States, through the agency of a fellow British immigrant who had learned Spencean thought in the New World, compounded it with the ideas of American thinkers, and translated it into a distinctly American idiom.

To compound the irony, Devyr's conversion to Spencean agrarianism came at the very moment that his former radical colleagues in England, who had forbidden him to write about the land question, embraced agrarian reform as well. In 1843, the year before Devyr joined the National Reform Association, Feargus O'Connor began campaigning for land reform through the pages of the *Northern Star*, the leading Chartist newspaper. O'Connor's efforts spread the land question far beyond the circle of Spence's followers in London. In 1845, O'Connor and his allies formed the Chartist Co-Operative Land Company, which sought to buy land for distribution in small, independent farms by pooling modest payments from numerous subscribers. Over the next three years, tens of thousands of British workers sent in subscriptions, enabling the company to buy six estates. At its peak in 1847, the Land Company boasted 247 branches and tens of thousands of subscribers. Although they seem to have done so independently, the company's promoters endorsed virtually the same ideas that Evans had pioneered—most notably that every man had a natural right to a small portion of land, and that the distribution of land in small plots would end the overcrowding of urban labor markets, resulting in higher wages and forcing employers to respect the dignity of their workers.[31] After years of frustration and silence on the land question, Devyr witnessed his Chartist allies embrace land reform—from across the Atlantic.

The influence of Spence, through Evans, did not teach Devyr an entirely new social vision. Rather, it resolved the contradictions in his earlier thought, enabling him to replace his former paternalism with a democratic vision of land reform that was fully grounded in natural-rights philosophy. In the pages of the *Freeholder*, Devyr took his long-standing Enlightenment investigation of private property in land to a logical conclusion—and one that was consistent with his new democratic commitments. Echoing his argument in *Our Natural Rights*, he wrote that Nature had supplied all people "with the wants of humanity" and "the hands of humanity to win for themselves a lodging and a bed and board . . . *Here* is the hungry belly, and the arm willing to work. *There* is the soil, mutely courting the hand of cultivation." But where before he had argued only for a natural right to *access* to the soil (which could legitimately be mediated through a landlord), now he insisted that "the Law of Nature and Nature's God" bequeathed to "every man who comes into this world . . . an equal right to the soil" itself.

Similarly, Devyr again drew upon Leviticus and the labor theory of value to challenge current practices of holding property in land. But where before he had argued only for "limited ownership" of the soil in the form of stewardship by landlords, now he insisted that land was not a commodity. Human beings, he maintained, had only a usufruct right to the soil; none had a right to buy it or sell it. Devyr thus abandoned his paternalist, land-lord-centered vision of land reform, urging Americans to "chase out of the Republic . . . the thief who has hitherto stood at God's store-house door—shutting man out from his free bounty or making that store-house a prison in which every man . . . was condemned to *hard labor for life*."[32]

Treating land as a commodity broke a link in nature's "circular chain of harmonies," creating endless human misery. Like his radical Enlighten-ment forebears and his former Democratic allies, Devyr subscribed to Adam Smith's belief that an unregulated market was the best arbiter of re-lations among producers. "The law of demand and supply," he insisted, "is a most harmonious *and regulating* law, provided man has the option of 'supplying' his wants from the soil." Private property in land made a mock-ery of this promise of social harmony, for it inevitably led to Land Monop-oly, from which sprung all the evils to which humanity was heir. Those who worked the land were compelled to pay tribute to its nominal owners, supporting those proprietors in idleness and luxury while they themselves lived in poverty and ignorance. Destitution and overwork inevitably took its toll in crime, immorality, and insanity. Other members of the property-less class flocked to the cities, where they flooded labor markets, driving wages to starvation levels. These emigrants, too, lived lives "much more toilsome and joyless than those of the lower animals"; they, too, paid the price in crime, debauchery, and mental illness. Such degradation endan-gered republican government by creating a servile and ignorant citizenry. At the same time, the power, wealth, and superior learning of the great landowners gave them excessive influence in government, resulting in "monopoly of Legislation." To Devyr, the experience of England and the Continent warned Americans of the impending consequences of land mo-nopoly in their own country:

> What has raised the accursed thrones of the old world? . . . Monopoly of the Soil sustains . . . Aristocracy . . . Monarchy is the central head of that mon-ster . . . *all* the anarchy, *all* the wars, all the hunger, nakedness, and desola-tion of heart—*all* the sterility of human intellect—*all* the social crime that has, up to this day, turned God's fair earth into a human hell, *all, all* had their deep rank root in Land Monopoly.[33]

Restoring humanity to its natural right to land, Devyr predicted, would usher in a new utopia. Nature's bounty would ensure that every family lived in "cleanliness and comfort." With the means of production available to all, the law of supply and demand would be "freed of the Anti-human influences that are at work upon it"; market exchange would turn society into "one vast system of cooperation" from which all producers would benefit. Universal access to land would create a new race of free and independent yeomen who would "guarantee the power—the prosperity—and the undying stability of the Republic." And it would free all people from incessant toil, providing producers with the leisure they needed to free themselves from ignorance. The result would be an era of unprecedented progress and enlightenment.[34]

Like his mentor Evans, however, Devyr never proposed a wholesale redistribution of land. At his most radical, the Irishman gave his readers and listeners mixed messages. He sometimes insisted that "degradation, crime, and human agony must continue, and grow more intense . . . or the rights of property must be invaded." But he explicitly disavowed any desire "to disturb . . . the *present* ownership of land." In his specific proposals, he clung to Evan's program for land reform: a legal limit on all future accumulation of land, laws exempting homesteads from seizure for debt, and the distribution of federal lands in small, inalienable lots to settlers, free of charge.[35]

No anti-rent leader enjoyed more influence and goodwill among the anti-renters than Thomas Devyr. But his message engendered enormous controversy. Devyr's vision of a republic made up entirely of small landholders resonated powerfully with the anti-renters' own belief that freedom could only be obtained when all men had a claim to land. "In all free governments," the Delaware County insurgents declared, "it is essential that the people themselves be free. They cannot be free unless independent. . . . To be completely sovereign, they must individually be the lords of the soil they occupy, and hold it freely, subject to no superior but the people themselves."

But tenant insurgents divided bitterly over Devyr's attack on private property in land. The Irishman's conviction that land belonged to everyone as a matter of right appealed to older notions of property rights, which were under attack but had not disappeared from New York's estates. Since the early settlement of the estates, tenants had subscribed to a widespread notion that wilderness land rightfully belonged to those who "improved" it by clearing trees, breaking cropland, and constructing houses, fences, and barns. They believed that independent proprietorship was the natural status of free men, and that as long as unimproved land existed, everyone willing to improve it had a claim to a portion of it. Earlier generations of tenant insurgents had marshaled these beliefs into an attack on landlords' claim to the soil. The rebels on Claverack Manor in 1766, for example, declared that "the land belongs to its bona fide tillers." The majority of tenants who remained loyal to their landlords cherished similar ideas. Eighteenth- and early-nineteenth-century tenants and squatters all agreed that improvements on the land belonged to the person who made them. They regularly paid for such improvements, even to squatters who had no claim to the soil, and they strove to force landlords to respect their property in their improvements. Tenants and squatters also made extensive use of unimproved estate lands for hunting, fishing, grazing, and timber cutting. They believed that resources on "common lands" were rightly the property of any local resident willing to expend the labor to get them.[36] Although tenants never attacked private property in land, they did offer alternatives to the notion that such property derived exclusively from paper title. They subscribed to the notion that property rights derived from labor and occupation, rather than (or in addition to) purchase or inheritance. As such, they had much in common with Devyr's attack on paper titles.

These beliefs came under attack from the 1820s on, however. As estate populations grew and unimproved soil went under the plow, many tenants bought timber lots to ensure themselves a supply of wood. Such lots were by definition unimproved, and their legal owners engaged in persistent low-level conflict with neighbors who exercised their customary right of cutting timber on them. More dramatically, town meetings became the scene of protracted battles between the advocates of free-ranging livestock and those who wished to prohibit animals from running on the commons. By the late 1820s, many—but not all—towns had prohibited all animals from grazing on common lands. Those who promoted these changes rejected older ideas that rooted property rights at least partly in the labor of the proprietor, embracing instead the belief that natural resources were subject to the exclusive use of those who held paper title to them. Just as important, the number of landless and land-poor estate residents grew, while their more prosperous neighbors increasingly hired them for wages or subleased part of their land to them. In this context, any claim that occupation and improvement gave a person a right to the soil might expose the divisions between the proponents and opponents of common right, and lead to conflicts between the landed and the landless.[37]

Thus, although anti-renters embraced earlier rebels' belief that only individual proprietorship could guarantee freedom, most were now eschewing the notions of property rights that had once gone along with that belief. Instead, they simply claimed that landlords' titles were fraudulent.[38] Devyr's insistence that all men had a natural right to land gave expression, in new terms, to older beliefs that property rights grew out of manual labor. But it went against the trend among most tenants, which was to abandon those beliefs in favor of regarding legal title as the sole legitimate marker of property.

A second problem for Devyr was that his rivals for leadership of the Anti-Rent movement bitterly opposed his brand of land reform. These leaders were activists from the Whig and Democratic parties. Like Devyr, they embraced a vision of universal landownership, but they insisted that it would come about not through "agrarian" measures, but through economic competition, social mobility, and the laws of the market. Ira Harris, an Albany County Whig, argued that land was not the common inheritance of humanity, but "an article of the market" which served as "the reward to successful industry." The leasehold system destroyed the prosperity of the communities it touched, not by violating a natural right to land, but by retarding its sale. The fees that landlords charged tenants who sold their farms, Harris declared, created "a blight upon the prosperity of those counties where such tenures prevail." Harris embraced the anti-renters' belief that republican freedom was best guaranteed by widespread landownership, and he sought to use the power of the state to destroy the leasehold system. But he insisted that in a healthy economy, land would be unevenly distributed. "The real estate of a country," he declared, should be left free to center . . . in the hands of the industrious and prudent. Every attempt to interrupt this natural course of things is contrary to the true interests of a *republican* community."[39]

Devyr and his Whig and Democratic rivals coexisted peacefully until May 1845, when Devyr began efforts to organize an electoral alliance between the anti-renters and the National Reformers. Devyr's rivals reacted quickly. Robert Watson, an Albany County Democrat, warned the anti-renters to eschew "agrarian, levelling doctrines." Charles F. Bouton, the Democratic owner of the *Albany Freeholder*, fired Devyr as the paper's editor. Devyr moved down the street and opened the *Anti-Renter*, a journal openly allied with the National Reformers. In its pages, the Irishman carried on a vitriolic campaign against the "Freeholder gents"—a small clique of "political quacks" who, he warned, sought to take over the Anti-Rent movement and to turn it into a vehicle for advancing their parties and their careers.[40]

The controversy between Devyr and his rivals opened up bitter divisions among the anti-renters. "A.D.C.," a National Reform sympathizer from Delaware County, wrote in mid-1846 that "land monopoly is the all absorbing topic of discussion in almost all of our private and public assemblies." Dozens of local movement leaders—and hundreds, perhaps thousands of ordinary tenants—became converts to National Reform. Devyr's new paper enjoyed a circulation of two thousand. Scores of letters poured into the offices of the *Anti-Renter* and George Henry Evans's *Young America*, endorsing the notion that each citizen had a natural right to land. Over a dozen local anti-rent associations held meetings to support the *Anti-Renter* and call for the freedom of the public lands. In the hill towns of Albany County, anti-rent activists created chapters of a new organization, called "the National Reform and Anti-Rent Vanguard Association," which merged the two movements into one.[41]

Other insurgents denounced their neighbors' challenge to existing definitions of property rights. Some followed Harris's belief that property in land was the reward to successful labor. "William Tell" of Rensselaer County declared, correctly, that the majority of anti-renters supported the right of a man to hold any amount of property "accumulated through his own honest industry." Most, however, gave no theoretical defense of their beliefs, and saw no reason to do so. That land was a commodity was simply common sense; to challenge this belief was outside the bounds of civilized discourse. Most anti-renters thus challenged landlords' dominion over their estates on the basis that their paper titles were fraudulent. "Clermont" of Columbia County insisted that although large landed estates "tend . . . to make the many . . . serfs and vassals of the few," the tenants "do not ask for a division of the lands. They say if the lords do, in fact, *own* the lands they claim, they alone have a right to dispose of them."[42]

Most anti-rent activists, however, refused to take sides in the struggle between Devyr and his rivals. L. W. Ryckman, a National Reform lecturer, wrote from a tour of Albany and Rensselaer counties that "I find no opposition to our principles, except from the Old Hunkers, and Commercial and Land speculators." Still, he found "a great unwillingness to agitate or discuss any thing outside of their local affairs." When broad principles and alliances threatened to divide their movement, most anti-renters stuck to immediate, unifying demands. And they fought their leaders' attempts to force them to choose sides. The anti-renters of North Blenheim made this clear when they declared that God had created the land for all humanity, then passed a resolution praising Ira Harris, Devyr's most prominent factional rival, for his service to the anti-rent cause. From late 1845 on, anti-rent associations throughout the leasehold district called unity meetings, in which they forced their quarreling leaders to share the podium.[43]

These debates reveal much about the place that members of the rural middle class sought in the emerging capitalist order. The activists who supported Devyr and the National Reformers did not differ significantly in age, occupation, or wealth from the activists who opposed them. Both were mature, prosperous, property-owning heads of household. Rather than pitting class against class, the conflict over the nature of property and the distribution of land split the rural middle class, and may have divided other classes as well.[44] Whether they supported Devyr, opposed him, or refused to take sides, these activists had for twenty years or more sought to increase their market production, and many, if not all, celebrated their integration into a broader, diversified economy. But they divided bitterly over whether the rules of capitalist political economy should apply to the central means of production in their communities—land. A majority believed that the rules of the market, when fairly applied, rewarded labor fairly, or they instinctively accepted those rules as common sense. A significant minority, however, challenged those rules. These radicals rejected neither markets nor diversified economic development; instead, they embraced a vision of development in which independent proprietorship was guaranteed as a natural right, not subject to the laws of the market. They revived, in a new form, the beliefs and aspirations of their frontier agrarian forebears. Most, however, refused to address the issue: social change and factional struggle brought, above all, ambivalence about property rights.

Devyr lost his struggle with his rivals. His defeat resulted partly from the ambivalence of his constituents, but mostly from the superior resources of his opponents. Activists with ties to the major parties controlled the *Albany Freeholder* and had access to money and powerful organizations; most importantly, they could promise access to the state itself. Devyr and his supporters had no such advantages. In 1846, the Whig and Democratic allies of the anti-renters mounted a powerful campaign to win the anti-rent nomination for John Young, the Whigs' choice for governor. Led by Ira Harris, they railroaded the critical Albany County convention, illegally but successfully nominating delegates loyal to Harris to the state convention. Harris's forces won control of the state convention and got the nomination for Young. Several National Reformers bolted the convention and, sixteen days later, held a convention for a new "Free Soil" party. Devyr won a nomination for the state legislature and championed the new party in the pages of the *Anti-Renter*. But the Free Soilers had no money, and only twelve days to campaign. When election day came, the anti-renters voted overwhelmingly for John Young, giving him the margin of victory. The Free Soilers garnered only a few hundred votes. Devyr, broke and despairing, closed the doors of the *Anti-Renter* and returned to Williamsburg. His relationship with the Anti-Rent movement was over.[45]

Devyr's relationship to the anti-renters bears witness to the ambiguous, problematic, and sometimes contentious relationship that could prevail between mobile and cosmopolitan reformers in the nineteenth century, and the far more locally oriented people whom they proposed to lead. Devyr served as the bearer of a transatlantic culture of land reform to the anti-renters, and their reception of him was mixed. To the extent that he radicalized the thinking of his constituents, his success depended on his loyal work on behalf of their local aims, and on the extent to which the fundamentals of his thinking—his appeals to the labor theory of value and the Bible; above all, his wholehearted advocacy of universal landownership—paralleled cherished ideas in their culture. Devyr offered a radical reformulation of a waning notion of property in tenant culture, one that still appealed to numerous tenants: the idea that the land belonged to those who worked it. Some embraced his ideas, while some explicitly rejected them; most, however, refused to engage in the debate, sticking unreflectingly to a relatively new "common sense" that held that the sole basis of property rights was legal title.

Ironically, the success that Devyr met with in winning the hearts and minds of New York tenants was largely the result of his conversion to a brand of land reform with roots in England—a conversion that took place in the United States. Before he wholeheartedly embraced the Spencean tradition, he won no supporters at all. The ideas that allowed him to win some supporters were forged in three countries through his efforts to build movements in specific local circumstances, with different local allies, and among different local constituencies. Devyr's career makes clear the transatlantic character of nineteenth-century land reform, and the multiple avenues by which reform ideas and programs crossed the Atlantic. It also suggests that the transmission of those ideas and programs is only the beginning of the story of land reform; those ideas and programs met with success or failure, or an ambiguous mix of both, when reformers confronted specific local constituencies.

Notes

1. Historians who treat reform movements as single transatlantic movements include David Brion Davis, *The Problem of Slavery in the Age of Revolution* (Ithaca, N.Y.: Cornell University Press, 1976); Robin Blackburn, *The Overthrow of Colonial Slavery, 1776–1848* (London: Verso, 1988); and Eric Foner, *Tom Paine and Revolutionary America* (New York: Oxford University Press, 1976). For an analysis that compares national reform movements without specifying the reasons for their similarities, see Jamie Bronstein, *Land Reform and Working-Class Experience in Britain and the United States, 1800–1862* (Stanford, Calif.: Stanford University Press, 1999). For works that trace the transatlantic movement of reform programs and ideas and depict them as arriving in a new environment essentially unchanged, see Foner, *Tom Paine;* Drury, *Transatlantic Radicals and the Early American Republic* (Lawrence: University Press of Kansas, 1997); R. J. M. Blackett, *Building an Antislavery Wall: Black Americans in the Atlantic Abolitionist Movement, 1830–1860* (Baton Rouge: Louisiana State University Press, 1983); Ray Boston, *British Chartists in America* (Manchester: Manchester University Press, 1971); Stanley Nadel, "From the Barricades of Paris to the Sidewalks of New York: German Artisans and the European Roots of American Labor Radicalism," *Labor History* 30 (1989): 47–75; and Paul Avrich, *Anarchist Portraits* (Princeton, N.J.: Princeton University Press, 1988). Three works break out of the pattern I describe here, offering superb analyses of the ways in which reform ideas were transformed in new national environments: Bruce Levine, *The Spirit of Forty-Eight: German Immigrants, Labor Conflict, and the Coming of the Civil War* (Urbana: University of Illinois Press, 1992); Carl J. Guarneri, *The Utopian Alternative: Fourierism in Nineteenth-Century America* (Ithaca, N.Y.: Cornell University Press, 1991); and Eric Foner, "Class, Ethnicity, and Radicalism in the Gilded Age: The Land League and Irish-America," in Foner, *Politics and Ideology in the Age of the Civil War* (New York: Oxford University Press, 1980), 150–200.

2. Malcolm Chase, *The People's Farm: English Radical Agrarianism, 1775–1840* (Oxford: Oxford University Press, 1988), 27–44, 50–67, 78–177.

3. James Anderson, "Rundale, Rural Economy, and Agrarian Revolution: Tirhugh, 1715–1855," in *Donegal: History and Society: Interdisciplinary Essays on the History of an Irish County,* ed. William Nolan, Liam Ronayne, and Mairead Dunlevy (Dublin: Geography Publications, 1995), 448–50, 456–57; David Dickson, "Derry's Backyard: The

Barony of Inishowen, 1650–1800," in *Donegal,* ed. Nolan, Ronayne, and Dunlevy, 421–23; Breamdán Mac Suibhne and David Dickson, "Introduction" to Hugh Dorian, *The Outer Edge of Ulster: A Memoir of Social Life in Nineteenth-Century Donegal* (Dublin: Lilliput Press, 2000), 10–11; Dermot James, *John Hamilton of Donegal: This Recklessly Generous Landlord* (Dublin: Woodfield Press, 1998), 25–27.

4. Mac Suibhne and Dickson, "Introduction," 2–3, 5, 10; Thomas Ainge Devyr, *The Odd Book of the Nineteenth Century, or, "Chivalry" in Modern Days, A personal Record of Reform—Chiefly Land Reform, for the Last Fifty Years* (Greenpoint, N.Y.: the author, 1882), Irish and English section, 32, 84–87, 91, 93. On agrarian secret societies throughout Ireland in the early nineteenth century, see Michael Beames, *Peasants and Power: The Whiteboy Movements and their Control in Pre-Famine Ireland* (New York: St. Martin's Press, 1983), 42–101.

5. Beames, *Peasants and Power,* 89–97.

6. Devyr, *Odd Book,* Irish and English section, 36, 37, 39, 40, 45–46, 51, 53. On the tendency of British labor reformers to exaggerate or fabricate their plebeian origins, see Patrick Joyce, *Visions of the People: Industrial England and the Question of Class, 1840–1914* (Cambridge: Cambridge University Press, 1991). On the material conditions of Irish rural artisans, see Beames, *Peasants and Power,* 55–57, 60, 62.

7. Devyr, *Odd Book,* Irish and English section, 32, 57–58, 60–64, 84–87, 91, 93, 106–7; Beames, *Peasants and Power,* 55, 57, 60, 62, 71–88, 93–94.

8. Devyr, *Odd Book,* Irish and English section, 36–38, 40–41, 99.

9. Tom Paine, *Agrarian Justice,* in *The Life and Works of Thomas Paine,* ed. William M. Van der Weyde, 12 vols. (New Rochelle, N.Y.: Thomas Paine National Historical Association, 1925), 10:9–37. For evidence of the Enlightenment's influence on Devyr, see Thomas Ainge Devyr, *Our Natural Rights: A Pamphlet for the People, by One of Themselves* (1836; American ed.: n.p., n.d.), 19–20, 24–26.

10. Thomas Spence, "The Rights of Man," in *Pig's Meat: The Selected Writings of Thomas Spence, Radical and Pioneer Land Reformer,* ed. G. I. Gallup (Nottingham: Spokesman, 1982), 59–66. The remainder of Spence's writings through 1810 were an elaboration upon the ideas in this pamphlet. See Gallup, ed., *Pig's Meat,* 67–185, passim. For discussions of Spence and his influence, see Chase, *People's Farm;* and Bronstein, *Land Reform,* 30–35. For a discussion of the ideas of Ogilvie and Chase, see Bronstein, *Land Reform,* 26–29.

11. Bronstein, *Land Reform,* 59, 67–68. On the Catholic Association, see McDonagh, *The Hereditary Bondsman: Daniel O'Connell, 1775–1829* (London: Weidenfeld and Nicolson, 1988), 232–80; Fergus O'Ferrall, *Daniel O'Connell* (Dublin: Gill and MacMillan, 1981), 41–67; Fergus O'Ferrall, *Catholic Emancipation: Daniel O'Connell and the Birth of Irish Democracy, 1820–30* (Dublin: Gill and MacMillan, 1985); Foster, *Modern Ireland,* 296–302.

12. O'Ferrell, *Daniel O'Connell,* 73–74, 79, 94–98; MacDonagh, *The Emancipationist: Daniel O'Connell, 1830–1847* (London: Weidenfeld and Nicholson, 1989), 18–19, 26–27; Joseph Lee, "The Social and Economic Ideas of O'Connell," in *Daniel O'Connell: Portrait of a Radical,* ed. Kevin B. Nowlan and Maurice R. O'Connell (Belfast: Appletree Press, 1984), 71–74.

13. Devyr, *Odd Book,* Irish and English section, 66–68; Foster, Modern Ireland, 301–2.

14. Foster, *Modern Ireland,* 306–7; James, *John Hammond,* 68, 72–75.

15. Devyr, *Odd Book,* Irish and English section, 101, 108.

16. Devyr, *Our Natural Rights,* 19–20, 24–26.

17. Ibid., 21, 29–30. On Spence's ideas and the ideas and activities of his followers, see Chase, *People's Farm,* 27–44, 50–67, 78–177.

18. Devyr, *Our Natural Rights,* 29, 33, 34.

19. Ibid., 23–24, 26–27, 31, 37.

20. Ibid., 101.

21. Ibid., 136, 140–44, 157. On the Chartists, see Dorothy Thompson, *The Chartists* (London: Temple Smith, 1984); J. T. Ward, *Chartism* (New York: Harper and Row, 1973).

22. Thompson, *Chartists;* Ward, *Chartism;* Eileen Yeo, "Some Practices and Problems of Chartist Democracy," in *The Chartist Experience: Studies in Working-Class Radicalism and Culture, 1830–60,* ed. James Epstein and Dorothy Thompson (London: Macmillan, 1982), 345–74; Peter Cadogan, *Early Radical Newcastle* (Durham: Sagittarius Press, 1975), 112–31.

23. Devyr, *Odd Book,* Irish and English section, 159, 161–62.

24. *Northern Liberator,* 27 July 1839, quoted in Jamie Bronstein, *Land Reform and Working-Class Experience in Britain and the United States, 1800–1862* (Stanford, Calif.: Stanford University Press, 1999), 287n. 64; Devyr, *Odd Book,* Irish and English section, 161.

25. Devyr, *Odd Book,* Irish and English section, 177–82, 200–5, 208–9; Thompson, *Chartists,* 77–87; Ward, *Chartism,* 119–42; Cadogan, *Early Radical Newcastle,* 120–31.

26. Devyr, *Odd Book,* Irish and English section, 186, American section, 25–26, 28–30, 33–39.

27. For an overview of the leasehold system and the Anti-Rent movement, see Reeve Huston, *Land and Freedom: Rural Society, Popular Protest, and Party Politics in Antebellum New York* (New York: Oxford University Press, 2000); Charles McCurdy, *The Anti-Rent Era in New York Law and Politics* (Chapel Hill: University of North Carolina Press, 2001); David Maldwyn Ellis, *Landlords and Farmers in the Hudson-Mohawk Region* (1945; reprint, New York: Octagon Books, 1967); Henry Christman, *Tin Horns and Calico: A Decisive Episode in the Emergence of Democracy* (1945; reprint, Cornwallville, N.Y.: Hope Farm Press, 1978).

28. Devyr, *Our Natural Rights,* appendix to the American edition, 52–55; Devyr, *Odd Book,* American section, 42–43.

29. *Radical* (New York City); *Man* (New York City); *Young America* (New York City); Helene Zahler, *Eastern Workingmen and National Land Policy, 1829–1862* (New York: Columbia University Press, 1941); Bronstein, *Land Reform,* 32–33, 42–43, 119–22.

    Jamie L. Bronstein argues that Spence's influence upon Evans's thought has been greatly exaggerated, pointing instead to Thomas Skidmore as the main influence. It is true that Evans was an admirer and an ally of Skidmore, even as he disagreed with most of his specific proposals. But unlike Evans, Skidmore was not preoccupied with land reform per se, but with equally dividing all property, both real and moveable. He posited not a natural right to land, but a natural right to an equal share of all existing property. Furthermore, Evans did not embrace land reform when he read and worked with Skidmore, but when he read Spence and Paine, who did posit a natural right to land and proposed schemes to honor that right. Finally, Evans himself traced the origins of the Workingmen's movement (in which he and Skidmore were allies) and the National Reform Association to Spence's writings. See *Working Man's Advocate,* 8 June 1844, quoted in Bronstein, *Land Reform,* 33.

30. Devyr, *Odd Book,* American section, 41–42; *Albany Freeholder,* 1845.

31. Bronstein, *Land Reform,* 9–15, 52–86; Thompson, *Chartists,* 299–306; Ward, *Chartism,* 173–95.

32. *Freeholder,* 14 May, 4 June, 11 June 1845.

33. *Freeholder,* 23 April, 30 April, 7 May, 4 June 1845; Devyr, *Our Natural Rights,* 56–60.

34. *Freeholder,* 30 April, 4 June 1845; Devyr, *Our Natural Rights,* 56–60.

35. Devyr, *Our Natural Rights,* 56–60; *Freeholder,* 14 May 1845. See also *Freeholder,* 7 May, 21 May, 18 June 1845; *Anti-Renter,* 31 January 1846.

36. "The Case of the Inhabitants of New Canaan," New York Land Papers, quoted in Kim, *Landlord and Tenant,* 358. See also the petition of Petrus Luver and others, reprinted in E. B. O'Callaghan, ed., *Documentary History of the State of New York* (Albany: Weed and Parsons, 1850), 3:501; *Hudson Bee,* 6 August 1811. For a fuller discussion of popular ideas and practices concerning property rights on the estates, see Huston, *Land and Freedom,* 33, 42–43. For discussions of such ideas and practices in other contexts, see William Cronon, *Changes in the Land: Indians, Colonists, and the Ecology of New England* (New York: Hill and Wang, 1983), 56–57, 73, 77; Alan Taylor, "Agrarian Independence," 222–25; Taylor, *Liberty Men and Great Proprietors,* 101–14.

37. For a discussion of economic and demographic change and the decline of the tradition of the commons in the leasehold towns, see Huston, *Land and Freedom,* 47–56.

38. Ibid., 114–16.

39. Ira Harris, *Abolition of Distress for Rent: Remarks of Mr. Ira Harris of Albany, upon the Bill to Abolish Distress for Rent* (Albany: Freeholder, 1846), 3–7, 20; idem., *Speech of Mr. Harris of Albany, in Committee of the Whole upon the Anti-Rent Question* (Albany: Freeholder, n.d.), 18–19. For a wider discussion of the anti-renters' Whig and Democratic allies, see Huston, *Land and Freedom,* 140–46.

40. *Freeholder,* 9 July, 6 August 1845; *Young America* (New York City), 2 August, 9 August, 16 August, 23 August, 30 August, 6 September, 13 September, 8 November 1845, *Anti-Renter* (Albany), 31 January, 6 June 1846.

41. *Young America,* 10 May, 14 June, 9 August, 23 August, 6 September 1845, 21 February, 28 February, 7 March 1846, and passim, 1845–46; *Freeholder,* 17 September 1845, 21 January, 25 February, 26 August 1846, 27 October 1847, 8 March 1848; *Equal Rights Advocate* (Hudson, N.Y.), 15 July, 19 August 1846. *Anti-Renter,* 14 February, 21 February, 6 June 1846, and passim.

42. *Freeholder,* 27 August, 17 September, 5 November 1845.

43. *Young America,* 7 March 1846; *Anti-Renter,* 13 September 1845, 28 February 1846; *Freeholder,* 3 September, 10 September, 17 September 1845, 25 February, 8 April, 14 October 1846.

44. Of the thirty-three supporters of Devyr and the National Reformers who could be identified, twenty-six, or 79 percent, had played a leading role in at least one association meeting. Over half had done so

more than once, and at least a quarter served as officers in their local anti-rent associations. A table correlating anti-rent activists' factional affiliation with their occupation resulted in a Pearson chi-square of 9.286 with a probability of 0.098, indicating a likelihood of 10 percent that the relationship was random. The table correlating the factional affiliations to landholdings of farmers yielded a Pearson chi-square of 3.929, with a whopping probability of .686, indicating a likelihood of 69 percent that the relationship was random. When factional affiliation was converted to a dummy variable, simple linear regressions linking leaders' landholdings and age in 1845 yielded paltry $R2$'s of .001 and .006 respectively. In other words, activist's landed wealth accounts for only one-tenth of a percent of the variation in their factional affiliation, while their age accounts for six-tenths of a percent of that variation.

I located anti-renters who supported the National Reformers through the lists of officers and speakers at meetings that explicitly endorsed the National Reform Association or helped collect funds for the *Anti-Renter*, through a list of men who served as agents for Devyr's newspaper, and through scattered instances of anti-rent leaders attending National Reform conventions or publicly declaring themselves supporters of National Reform. These were all in the *Anti-Renter*, 17 January, 14 February, 21 February, 6 June 1846; *Young America*, 17 May, 12 July, 30 August, 28 November 1845; *Freeholder*, 26 August, 9 September 1846. I have excluded from this group those who participated in meetings that endorsed part of the National Reform program without declaring their allegiance to the organization, since many town associations did so without supporting Devyr against his Whig and Democratic rivals. My aim is to count as National Reform supporters only those who explicitly sided with Devyr and his allies when the movement split into factions.

For my methods in locating association activists and in tracing them and the National Reform supporters through the 1850 census, the Westerlo tax list, and Whig and Democratic conventions, see Huston, *Land and Freedom*, 260n. 4.

45. Huston, *Land and Freedom*, 168–72.

"Primitive Christianity" and "Modern Socialism": Thomas W. Woodrow and Agrarian Socialism

David A. Y. O. Chang

In May 1914, the first issue of *Woodrow's Monthly Journal of Radical Thought on Political, Social and Religious Lines* was published in Hobart, Oklahoma. The editor of the fledgling magazine, Universalist minister Thomas W. Woodrow, promised his readers that his magazine would present "Socialism from the standpoint of Christianity" and "Christianity from the standpoint of Socialism." The content of the first issue indicated what Woodrow meant by such a statement. Although he quoted repeatedly from Marx's *Capital,* Woodrow proclaimed that he could "use more violently revolutionary language simply by quoting scriptures than was ever used by Marks [*sic*], Engles, Lasalle, Bebel, Kautsky or any Socialist that ever wrote or spoke." In fact, asserted Woodrow, "Primitive Christianity" and "Modern Socialism" proposed the identical "Scheme of Redemption." Salvation would come in this world, not in the next, he argued. Woodrow proclaimed that humanity would only reach spiritual freedom once humankind had broken "free from Economic masters"—that is, once it had achieved socialism.[1]

Historians of the early-twentieth-century United States expect to find vigorous socialist movements where heavy industries and sweatshops attracted radicalized immigrant proletarians, and where leftist labor unions could politicize workers. Hobart boasted neither heavy industry nor immigrant masses, nor labor unions. A town of 3,843, Hobart was the county seat of rural Kiowa County.[2] Like other such towns in other such counties, Hobart existed to serve, govern, and profit from nearby farmers. General stores, implement dealers, grain and cotton mills, banks, even the county courthouse—ultimately, all depended on farmers for their trade. A railroad station provided passenger and freight service, but residents of Hobart were far from the big city, let alone centers of American socialism such as Milwaukee or New York.[3]

How can we explain the emergence of *Woodrow's Monthly* and its editor from such an anomalous setting? This article takes that problem as its task. It begins with an examination of the religious and political movements (Quakerism, Universalism, and the Oklahoma Boomer movement) in which Woodrow took part prior to becoming a Socialist. It then traces the transformation of rural land ownership in Woodrow's adopted state of Oklahoma. The article describes the political movements, including socialism, that tried to protect the interests of small farmers in that transformation. Finally, it considers Woodrow's role in Oklahoma socialism and agrarianism.

The significance of Woodrow for the history of agrarianism and socialism in the United States springs from the fact that despite his relative isolation, he manifested an interest in and familiarity with insurgent movements abroad that were unusual for an agrarian socialist of his day and region. Historians have debated the relative importance of Marxism and Jeffersonian agrarianism on the American agrarian socialists of the early twentieth century.[4] This article therefore dedicates particular attention to considering to what degree transatlantic movements affected Woodrow's socialism. It concludes that Woodrow's local engagement with Oklahoma socialism, rooted in his religious beliefs, led him to consider events and ideas from overseas. Although ideas from abroad affected his own idiosyncratic brand of socialism, that socialism ultimately took its shape from Woodrow's local context, and especially from his religious beliefs.

Woodrow: Quaker, Universalist, and Oklahoma "Boomer"

It is unfortunate, for one peering into Woodrow's past in search of the roots of his political thought, that historians know little of his early life. Thomas W. Woodrow was born around 1850 and was reared a Quaker in

Iowa.[5] By 1881, Woodrow had left the Society of Friends and organized a Universalist church in Hutchinson, Kansas. The thirty-one-year-old established himself as pastor of the group.[6] By 1890, preaching took Woodrow and his wife, Emma, back to Iowa, where he traveled from small town to small town as an evangelist. [7] In 1902, he and Emma settled in the town of Speed in Oklahoma Territory. Until the year before, Speed had lain within the bounds of the Kiowa Indian reservation. In 1901, however, the United States had "opened" the area to new settlement, and a flood of white immigration ensued.[8] The Woodrows were part of that settler tide. This was not, however, Woodrow's first encounter with the lands that would become the state of Oklahoma. In the 1880s, Woodrow reportedly presided as minister over opening ceremonies of a colony of settlers that demanded that Washington allow them to take up Indian lands in Oklahoma. Known as "Boomers," they went so far as to invade Indian lands, forcing the federal government to evict them.[9]

By the time he settled in Oklahoma Territory in 1902, then, Thomas W. Woodrow had been immersed in three religious and political movements that would profoundly affect his political thought: Quakerism, Universalism, and the agrarian expansionism of the Boomers. It is worthwhile to examine the ideas of all three of these important movements in order to later evaluate their impact on Woodrow's thought.

Egalitarianism marked Woodrow's religious background. Quakers espoused the doctrine of the Inner Light, the notion that all souls had access to direct contact with the divine. Hierarchy was, of course, not unknown in American Quaker communities or Quaker thinking, but a strong dedication to equality marked the group's theology and worship.[10] This same emphasis on the equality of all souls was strongly evident in Universalism, the religion that Woodrow adopted and evangelized. American Universalism emerged out of dissident movements in eighteenth-century Britain, Ireland, and New England. Working against the Calvinist notion that in the last days God would redeem only a minority of sinful humanity, Universalists argued that God would redeem all souls; that is, salvation would in the end be universal. Universalists of the late nineteenth and early twentieth centuries retained from their insurgent roots a profound belief in the equality of all humanity.[11] In their political activism, Quakers and Universalists of the nineteenth century worked for an equality in society commensurate with the equality of souls. Members of both groups occupied prominent places in the abolitionist, woman suffrage, temperance, and other reform movements. The two denominations that most influenced

Woodrow, Quakerism and Universalism, thus embraced activism as a way of making their egalitarian ideals a social reality.[12]

Woodrow brought these ideals to the expansionist agrarianism of the Boomer movement in the 1880s. Beginning in 1879, whites from Kansas, Missouri, and other states began to gather in the towns along the Kansas border with Indian Territory. (Indian Territory constituted the bulk of the future state of Oklahoma.) These would-be homesteaders and speculators, known as Boomers, began by claiming that post–Civil War treaties entitled them to settle a section of Indian Territory known as the Unassigned Lands. Over the course of a decade, many Boomers would come to argue that Washington should open the entire Indian Territory to white settlement. Not content to lobby and pamphlet in favor of their cause, the Boomers embarked on a series of invasions of the Unassigned Lands, beginning in 1881. Led by David L. Payne, hundreds of Boomers repeatedly ventured into Indian Territory, only to be ousted by federal troops in what Danney Goble has termed "an elaborate choreography of invasion, expulsion, and reinvasion."[13] It is unclear whether Woodrow participated in these invasions or not, but his association with the Boomers would lead historians to remember him as "Oklahoma's first preacher."[14]

The movement drew its members (though not its leaders) and its agrarianism mostly from "modest farm families." Most of the Boomers joined Payne in hopes of obtaining 160 acres of tillable land, the cherished dream of so many westering farm families in the nineteenth century.[15] They brought to the movement the agrarianism that was their heritage, and the suspicions of railroads that would motivate much of the populist revolt in coming years.

"Agrarianism," in this context, refers to political movements based on the belief that farmers by rights are independent producers, and that their independence derives in large part from owning their own land. Rooted in Jeffersonianism and fed by the United States' conquest of a continent in the nineteenth century, this agrarianism was crucial to the creation of Oklahoma and the development of insurgent farmer politics there. W. H. Miller expressed this Jeffersonian agrarianism when he wrote to the secretary of the interior in 1882 to complain on behalf of the Boomers that "we are houn'd down by the Soldiers as though we were criminals." Miller complained that the eviction of "the actual settler" was particularly galling, given that the federal government was promising a grant of Indian Territory land to a railroad as a reward for laying track through the territory.[16] Such a policy ran counter to the republican and agrarian egalitarianism of the Boomers. That the federal government should dedicate its energies to keeping farmers off land it intended to grant to a large business was contrary to the notion that land belonged in the hands of farmers.

The Boomers' call for the opening of Indian Territory also revealed a hostility to Indians owning land. Miller made this clear when he told the secretary of the interior that "this land does not belong to any Indian tribe or nation but to the United States. . . ."[17] Like Boomer leader David W. Payne, Miller argued that these lands were "part of the public domain," belonged "to the people," and American citizens were thus entitled to settle there. Further erasing indigenous claims to the land, Payne and the Boomers often insisted on referring to it as "Oklahoma," rather than "Indian Territory."[18] Not all advocates of opening Indian Territory expressed the same racial anxiety as the one who wrote to President Rutherford B. Hayes to warn him that, in order to obtain land, white men were marrying "squaws" and "filling the country with lawless half breeds."[19] But the movement that Woodrow took part in was premised not only on an agrarian belief in distributing land to farmers, but also on dispossessing Indians of their lands.

Woodrow seems not to have stayed long with the Boomers on the Kansas-Indian Territory border. Whereas the Boomer movement remained active there through most of the 1880s, Woodrow founded his church in Hutchinson, in central Kansas, in 1881. He traveled widely to preach in towns in Kansas and Arkansas, expounding upon such topics of religious and social interest as "One Fatherhood, One Brotherhood, and One Destiny."[20] In 1890, his wife Emma bore a son. The boy died the following year, motivating Emma to study medicine (she practiced as an osteopath), first at Drake University in Des Moines, Iowa, and then in Kansas City.[21] In the meantime, the Boomer movement contributed to the political effort that led to the opening of the Unassigned Lands in Indian Territory, to new settlement in 1889, and to the transfer of the bulk of the rest of the territory to white settlement by 1903.

Oklahoma, 1889–1910: Agrarianism Betrayed

That year, Thomas and Emma settled in Speed (later renamed Hobart), Oklahoma Territory. Emma set up her medical practice there. Thomas's activities and profession are more obscure, though the 1910 census enumerated him as a traveling evangelist.[22] Until 1914, Woodrow stayed out of the historical record.

The period was one of rapid political and social change in Oklahoma. To understand the socialist politics that Woodrow embraced in coming years, we must take time to understand the transformation in politics and land tenure in the region between 1889, when the federal government began the transfer of land to new white settlers, and 1914, when Woodrow emerged as a socialist editor and activist. The dream of creating a rural society of small landowning farmers motivated the Boomers and many others who came to Oklahoma. Although neither allotment nor statehood happened simply to satisfy the demands of poor whites for land and political rights (powerful corporate interests and federal officials' beliefs in expansion were important here), white leaders constantly invoked the vision of a republic of white landowners to justify white settlement and Oklahoma statehood, which came in 1907. Agrarianism permeated discourse throughout Oklahoma: Democrats, the Populist Party, and the "dirt farmer" faction in the Farmers' Union all trumpeted this same hope.[23]

There was reason to imagine that Oklahoma might offer a haven for the small farmer. The land openings of the 1880s and 1890s made it possible for tens of thousands of American families to obtain 160 acres of land. In the eastern part of the state, lands that Indian nations had previously held in common were distributed as individual plots to tribal members. As Indians sold their allotments (often as the result of trickery), even more land became available. This newly available land became a powerful magnet for those who hoped to establish themselves as independent farmers.

Rapid land concentration and the growth of a tenant-based farming economy, however, dashed those hopes in the first decade of the twentieth century. By 1910, the farm tenancy rate in most of Oklahoma's cotton-growing counties exceeded 70 percent. In counties with a more mixed crop base of corn, wheat, oats, and cotton, tenancy rates were lower, but even there they often exceeded 50 percent. Such was the case in Woodrow's home of Kiowa County, where more than half of the farmers were tenants in 1910. Most paid part of their harvest as rent on land and a cabin. Small farm owners did not fare much better, as they depended on credit to finance planting and harvesting. Soon, many found themselves heavily mortgaged. In Oklahoma, the agrarian dream of a vast yeomanry of independent farmers quickly gave way to frustration at widespread farm tenancy and indebtedness.[24]

The Enduring Politics of Agrarianism, 1890–1910

These frustrations would give an insurgent, agrarian flavor to political movements in Oklahoma that stretched from the Populists in the 1890s, through the Farmers Union in the first years of the twentieth century, to the progressive Democratic Party politics of the early statehood period, culminating in the remarkably successful Socialist Party of the second decade of the twentieth century. Agrarianism literally left its mark on the map of Oklahoma. Travelers along the Red River, which constitutes the border between Oklahoma and Texas, pass alongside the Oklahoma counties of Jefferson, Jackson, Bryan, and Tillman. When the men who transformed the Indian Territory into the state of Oklahoma drew boundaries on the land, they inscribed it with the names of major American agrarian politicians—Thomas Jefferson, Andrew Jackson, William Jennings Bryan, and Ben Tillman. It is hardly surprising, then, that the Populist movement enjoyed considerable success in Oklahoma. As early as 1892, the People's Party was active in Oklahoma Territory, and in 1894 one out of three voters there lent their support to the party's candidate for territorial congressional delegate. As was true elsewhere, the party reached its greatest success—and the beginning of the end of its political viability—when it embraced fusion (the nomination of one candidate by two parties) with the Democratic Party in 1896. That year, Oklahoma sent a joint Democrat-Populist delegate to Congress. Populist political fortunes waned thereafter.[25]

The impulse for structural change did not die, however. From that point on, former Populists threw their efforts into cooperative marketing and purchasing under the aegis of the Farmers Union. Beginning in 1903, Farmers Union organizers from the neighboring states of Texas and Kansas crisscrossed the Indian and Oklahoma territories. Immediately, they and local populists set to trying to push up sagging cotton prices by withholding crops, i.e., voluntarily keeping their crops off the market to boost prices. The move may have contributed to a rise in cotton prices between 1903 and 1906.[26] By 1907, however, the Farmers Union in the territories had crumbled under the weight of harassment by hostile officials, dissension among members, and the financial panic of 1907. As Oklahoma became a state, then, neither the People's Party nor the Farmers Union remained viable vehicles of agrarianism in Oklahoma. Both organizations, however, had done much to propagandize both general agrarian principles (particularly the notion that farmers should own the land they tilled) and specific strategies of rural action, such as cooperative marketing. These ideas reached further and lasted longer than the People's Party or the Farmers Union. Agrarianism and the farmers that espoused it played a prominent role in the Democratic Party in the state's early years. The progressive wing of that party, which united poor farmers with urban workers, miners, and educated reformers, steered the party and the state constitution leftward. The Oklahoma constitution provided for initiatives and referendums, outlawed trusts and monopolies, and "mandated tax equity on real property"—a central concern of farmers.[27]

Soon, however, a landlord elite came to dominate politics in the new state of Oklahoma. Men like Robert Lee Williams turned landed wealth into political domination of the state. A white attorney, Williams used his legal skills to turn limited capital into an empire of tenant farms in southeastern Oklahoma, building a political career that won him the posts of state supreme-court chief justice and governor. What a few men like Williams did at the state level was repeated a hundred times by locally prominent men like C. Guy Cutlip, whose family's land speculation laid the basis for his career as a judge and Democratic Party leader in Seminole County.[28] Though they themselves were landlords, men like Williams and Cutlip paid homage to agrarianism in their speeches and pronouncements.

In the years following statehood and preceding U.S. entry into World War I, poor farmers became a restive force in Oklahoma politics. Tenants and embattled small farmers pushed Oklahoma's politicians to endorse a slew of policies that farmers thought would save them from disaster. A progressive land tax, relief from usurious interest rates, lower rail-shipping rates, government supervision of farm rental contracts, government crop warehousing and price supports—Oklahoma farmers pushed for all of these policies and more in the first decade of statehood.[29] Most of these measures, of course, ran counter to the interests of the wealthiest and most powerful leaders of the dominant Democratic Party. Democratic politicians did institute some palliative measures, such as a limited farm-loan program, and an anti-usury law that was rarely enforced.[30] These did little, however, to allay the anxieties of Oklahoma's farmers.

Agrarian Socialism in Oklahoma, 1908–1914

The Socialist Party more vigorously responded to the demands of poor farmers, making strong statements against widespread tenancy and for cooperative marketing.[31] As the Democratic Party moved right, more and more farmers and workers migrated into the Socialist Party. Whereas the party had won fewer than 10,000 votes statewide in 1907, it claimed over 21,000 in 1908, almost 25,000 in 1910, and over 41,000 in 1912. In five years' time, then, the party more than quadrupled its votes, winning seats for a number of local and state officials and legislators. The Socialist Party in Oklahoma had a larger membership than any other state branch of the party, measured both in absolute numbers and as a percentage of the electorate.[32] The Socialist Party appealed to Woodrow and to others because it represented the rural poor, who came to constitute its base. Studies of election returns demonstrate that those counties that voted Socialist were those with high tenancy rates, low farm values, and extensive indebtedness. Tenants who grew cotton on share-rental agreements joined with landowners who farmed wheat with borrowed money to build one of the most successful Socialist parties in American history.[33]

Working together, farmers and supporters like Woodrow joined agrarian ideals to class analysis. State party leaders in Oklahoma City initially hewed to Marxist orthodoxy, contending that because land was part of the means of production, and under socialism the means of production must be in the hands of the state, individual land tenure must be abolished.[34] Although this position was consistent with Marxist theory, it ran counter to the agrarian dream of small farmers. The call for communal land tenure therefore acted as a brake on the growth of the party. Jim Bissett persuasively argues that the turning point for the party came when the rural rank and file forced it, in 1912, to endorse the notion that all farmers should own their own land. In Oklahoma, the Socialist Party grew into a viable party because it sacrificed theoretical consistency to embrace this central tenet of agrarianism.[35]

Socialist newspapers and lecturers spread the party's message throughout the Oklahoma countryside. The most prestigious of the Socialist newspapers that were available in Oklahoma was *The Appeal to Reason,* which would greatly influence Woodrow's thought and activism. The Oklahoma edition of this Kansas newspaper covered events in the state, across the nation, and abroad that were of interest to socialists. With its mix of news and opinion, it claimed over 44,000 readers in 1915. Socialists throughout the state also started local papers to win new party members and rally the faithful to the cause. In the decade from 1910 to 1920, small-town papers with such titles as the *Otter Valley Socialist,* the *Sentinel Sword of Truth,* and the *Okemah Sledge Hammer* provided readers with a Socialist viewpoint on events of the day.[36] Traveling stump speakers also raised awareness of the party.

Prominent among these speakers were ministers who often spoke in churches. The rhetoric of such evangelists intensified the religious over-tones of the events. Frequently making reference to scripture and touching upon prophetic themes of justice, socialist speakers, whether ministers or laypeople, championed socialism in the context of religion.[37] The fervor of socialist evangelists and their audiences at times lent the tone of evangeli-cal camp meetings to socialist encampments. An observer described a 1914 meeting attended by about 1,500 people as follows:

> They opened with a prayer. We had the finest singing you ever heard. I saw old men and women weep like children. They shouted for joy for the com-ing victories through cooperation.[38]

Woodrow and Oklahoma Socialism, 1903–1916

Thomas W. Woodrow was one of Oklahoma's socialist editors and evangel-ists. As early as 1903, he was delivering "sermons openly socialistic in con-tent."[39] He brought with him the religious and social ideals of his Quaker youth and Universalist adulthood. To these, he added a broad familiarity with European socialist ideas and agrarian movements in Mexico and Eu-rope. As befitted the state where he lived and the tenant base of the Okla-homa Socialist Party, Woodrow emphasized the need for land reform, and socialism as a means to achieve it. As the Socialist Party faltered in 1915 and 1916, however, Woodrow began to turn away from political socialism, embracing instead a more utopian Christian communitarianism. When he did so, the impact of other agrarian and socialist movements abroad on Woodrow's thinking lessened considerably, and he grew more distant from farmers' politics.

Woodrow's editorials demonstrated a familiarity with socialist thought from abroad, not just the general progressive and agrarian ideas that were common currency in Oklahoma. He sprinkled the issues of his magazine with quotations from and mentions of European leftists such as Emma Goldman, Jean Jaurès, and Karl Marx, as well as Americans such as Henry George.[40] For the most part, however, Woodrow did not engage these ideas at length in his magazine. Most of his extended theoretical discus-sions were theological rather than political. Nonetheless, Woodrow's mag-azine demonstrated that its editor was conscious of and influenced by European socialism, and aimed to share its ideas with his readers.

Not surprisingly, given the central role land tenure played in the Okla-homa socialist movement, Woodrow paid particular attention to land politics abroad. He informed his readers about landlord-tenant relations in England and a rent strike by French peasants.[41] The area that he dedicated the most attention to, however, was Mexico. In issue after issue, Woodrow argued that Mexican land tenure was particularly instructive for Americans, because as in the United States, Mexican land ownership was heavily concentrated. Woodrow argued that whereas dictator Porfirio Diaz had "illegally robbed" the Mexican people of their "lands, mines, public functions and social rights," the American people had been "legally robbed" of the same things in their own nation. The difference was, he argued, that the Mexican constitution protected the people's access to "lands, titles, and franchises," but the American constitution did not.[42] In response to Woodrow Wilson's claim that Mexico needed land reform, Thomas Woodrow replied that the United States needed a strong dose of the same medicine.[43] Using an extended quote from *Capital*, he warned that if farmers were deprived of land, they would be forced into vagabondage, and ultimately into the wage system.[44]

The *Appeal to Reason*, the Kansas Socialist newspaper, brought these sorts of ideas and events to the attention of Woodrow and Oklahoma socialists in general, demonstrating the role the press played in the spread of radical ideas. It published news of socialist, agrarian, and left-wing movements in the United States and abroad. Woodrow and other socialists in the state could learn in the *Appeal* that the Socialist Party had declared its opposition to United States intervention in civil war in Mexico, and that the central issue in that conflict was land tenure.[45] They could read about the ideas and the assassination of France's Socialist president, Jean Jaurès. The *Appeal* brought Oklahoma readers news of efforts to reform finance and land distribution in the United States and abroad.[46] Woodrow dedicated considerable attention to these issues in his magazine, and filled a scrapbook with clippings from the *Appeal* and other publications on such topics as events in Russia, the labor movement in New Zealand, and French socialism.[47] Clearly, international news influenced his socialism.

The *Appeal* also provided Woodrow information on European and American socialist and agrarian theorists. Woodrow clipped and saved articles on Marx, Edward Bellamy, and other socialist writers, and incorporated information on them into his magazine. The *Appeal* frequently supplied its readers with excerpts or articles on the ideas of Marx, Robert Owens, Kautsky, and others.[48] The newspaper also offered the chance to learn more by purchasing socialist classics or pamphlets on such topics as "Socialism: A Historical Sketch," and "Socialism and the Farmer."[49] The

Appeal thus disseminated news and ideas from the socialist movement worldwide to editors like Woodrow, who interpreted the information for their own readers and interspersed it with statements of their own socialist beliefs.

For Woodrow, these beliefs come sharply into focus in his version of "The Landlord's Prayer." Various versions of the prayer, which satirized what a landlord might pray, circulated in radical circles in the late nineteenth and early twentieth centuries.[50] In an undated manuscript, Woodrow presented his own:

> Our father which art in Washington,
> Plutocracy be thy name.
> Thy kingdom continues
> Thy will be done in the United States as it is in Europe, specially in Russia.
> Give us this day our daily plunder
> and forgive us our tricks as we forgive those who trick us.
> And lead us not into cooperation,
> but deliver us from Socialism.
> For thine is the land, and the capital, forever. Ah-men.

First and foremost, the title "The Landlord's Prayer" and its references to land make clear the importance of land tenure to Woodrow's agrarian socialism. Second, the fact that the landlord addresses his petition and praises to the "father which art in Washington" underline Woodrow's belief that state power existed to serve the capital-owning class. Third, the reference to Russia reveals his awareness that the socialist and agrarian struggle was international in scope, pitting capitalism against "cooperation" and socialism.

Perhaps most revealing, however, was the form the satire took: that of a prayer. Woodrow's religion was the foundation of his political thought. Some historians have implied that evangelists of socialism such as Woodrow used Christianity as a "medium" or "vehicle" to deliver their true message of socialism. These historians note that the rural poor to whom Woodrow and his colleagues addressed their message were immersed in evangelical religion. Because themes of justice and redemption permeated evangelical Christianity, and because socialists could readily adopt the camp-meeting format to political propagandizing, evangelical religion proved invaluable to spreading "the gospel of socialism."[51] Undoubtedly, all of these advantages encouraged Socialist speakers in Oklahoma to convey their message in an evangelical language.

Judging from Woodrow's case, however, religion gave shape to the political ideas and action of socialist evangelists. It was not a mere vehicle to deliver the more important content of socialism. In most issues of his monthly, Woodrow dedicated considerably more than half of his space to discussions of religion and theology. Woodrow claimed to hearken back to a "primitive Christianity" that appeared startlingly "modern" by the standards of his day.[52] Woodrow's Christianity was not the revivalist evangelical religion that was so prominent in the Oklahoma countryside, but a latitudinarian and intellectualized faith that was willing to engage with spiritualism and other heterodox movements of the day.[53] He eschewed displays of religious fervor for reasoned discourse, and favored discussion of social progress in the here and now over emphasis on otherworldly individual salvation.[54] In the early issues of the magazine, Woodrow went to particular pains to demonstrate that his kind of "primitive Christianity" was identical to socialism. The "plan of primitive Christianity," he wrote, was "Cooperation in living, with Economic Mutuality and Equality," and ultimately "Government in the hands of workers." This, he argued, was identical to "the Program of Social Democracy." Woodrow maintained that it was only because of the corrupting influence of "paganized Christianity" (in which he included most all organized churches) that men and women remained blinded to the socialist message of Christianity. Once the church was purified of all such ecclesiastical "tomfoolery," Woodrow wrote, above its pulpit would be emblazoned the socialist battle cry, "Workers of the World Unite, You Have Nothing to Lose But Your Chains. You Have a World to Gain." For Woodrow, Christianity and socialism were one and the same.[55]

Woodrow did not believe, however, that Americans would build socialism merely by being good or enlightened Christians. By 1914, Woodrow had thrown his energies into the political support of the Socialist Party. He traveled to towns around Oklahoma to lecture on socialism. Not content merely to give speeches, Woodrow began publishing his magazine in May 1914. The magazine took on a partisan tone. In anticipation of the election of 1914, for example, he urged his readers to forsake the Democrats and back the Socialist Party. "Vote with your class," Woodrow entreated Oklahomans, "not with your economic enemies."[56] Later that year, Woodrow made the leap from propagandizing for the Socialist Party to running for office as the Socialist candidate for state insurance commissioner. The party that year aimed to take the gains of previous elections and build on them to transform politics in Oklahoma. The Socialists succeeded to a remarkable extent. Oklahomans voted five Socialists into the state house of representatives and one into the state senate; more than one hundred Socialists won local and county offices. In the race for governor, the Socialists carried three counties, surpassing the Republican vote to come in second to the Democrats in twenty-five other counties, and polling over 20 percent of Oklahomans' votes.[57] Woodrow did not win his race, although he garnered 21 percent of votes statewide.[58] As a propagandist and as a candidate, Woodrow was playing a part in a movement that threatened the future of the state's Democratic Party and inspired Socialists nationwide.

Woodrow: From Socialism to the Cooperative Commonwealth, 1915–1919

Woodrow chose this moment of triumph to distance himself from Socialist politics. Already in March 1915, Woodrow was announcing that his magazine was a "Socialist religious" publication rather than a "Socialist political" one.[59] Although he retained his membership in the Socialist Party in 1915, he informed his readers that they should vote however they wanted, if they chose to vote at all. He was working, he stated, not for the Socialist Party, but for "the religion of socialism," which he defined as "religious ideals of life here and life hereafter that accord with the ethics of social science."[60] At a time when the Socialist Party in Oklahoma was enjoying the peak of its prestige and power, Woodrow's magazine dedicated less space to the politics of land reform and more to religious issues, such as the immortality of the soul and the promise of salvation for all humanity.

Woodrow's gradual distancing from Socialist politics mirrored a softening of political support for the party in Oklahoma. Historians have speculated that the agricultural boom of the latter part of the decade between 1910 and 1920 lessened the Socialist appeal at a time when party activists were already exhausted from their efforts in 1914. With prices up for commodities, especially cotton, the kinds of farmers who had supported the Socialist Party may have felt less urgently the need to effect radical social change. Furthermore, Oklahoma Socialists had spent much political fervor and energy to build an insurgent party in 1914.[61] In such a context, it is not surprising that in 1915 Woodrow remained in the party, but lessened his efforts on its behalf.

In 1916, Socialist fortunes began to sour in the state. In that year's elections, the Democrats routed the Socialists. The Socialists' declining returns reflected both a weakening of support for the party and the fact that in

1916 the Democratic-controlled legislature instituted restrictions on voter registration that worked against the kind of poorly educated and highly mobile men who were so crucial to the Socialist vote.[62] The Socialist Party lost all of its seats in the state house of representatives.[63] In 1914 it had been possible to believe that the Socialist Party would continue to grow until socialism was achieved in Oklahoma. In 1916, although the party still enjoyed levels of support in the state that would have been impressive elsewhere, results disappointed Oklahoma Socialists.

In the aftermath of the election, Woodrow decisively abandoned Socialist politics. He announced to his readers that the campaign "cured the author of the reputation of being a PARTY socialist."[64] He argued that electoral politics was ultimately a futile way to try to emancipate humanity. The travails of electoral struggle, Woodrow claimed, had led other Socialists to give up their activism, and had even driven the editor of the *Appeal to Reason* to suicide. Woodrow boasted that he had abandoned Socialist political action before these others. Whereas in the past, he had drawn on scripture to support the Socialist political cause, in 1916 he summoned biblical authority in his appeal to other Socialists to follow him out of politics: "Come out of her, my people, that ye be not partakers of her sins, and that ye receive not of her plagues."[65]

Although Woodrow abandoned Socialist politics, he did not forsake hopes of a socialist future. Already in the very first issue of his *Monthly*, Woodrow had emphasized that cooperatives were "the right hand of the socialist movement and constitute[d] its most important part." His enthusiasm for cooperation had made up part of a vigorous engagement with Socialist politics. By late 1916, Woodrow had moved away from this balance and toward an exclusive focus on cooperation. He argued that reorganization of economic production must precede socialist victory in politics. For his source, he drew on socialist scripture, the Communist Manifesto, which maintained that the political system of any epoch reflected the "prevailing mode of economic production and exchange." Woodrow thus reasoned that the organization of the economy along cooperative lines would inevitably lead to the victory of socialism. The pursuit of Socialist electoral victory in the context of a capitalist economy, he told his readers, was folly and "contrary to the teachings of the great founders of the [socialist] movement."[66]

Woodrow's endorsement of a "Cooperative Commonwealth" helps to situate him in the history of socialism in America. The utopian tone of Woodrow's call to cooperation placed him as part of an important stream of

American communitarian dissent that had its roots in the first half of the nineteenth century. From Robert Owen to Edward Bellamy, and from New Harmony to Brook Farm, Americans had posited that cooperation must supplant competition to build a just society. Such movements, like Woodrow after 1916, tended to reject class conflict and the political pursuit of socialism in favor of the effort to begin building socialism by building cooperative society.[67]

The apolitical, utopian, cooperative, Christian socialism that Woodrow had arrived at in 1916 placed him ideologically apart from the Oklahoma farmers of the day. Certainly, many of them were dedicated to cooperation. Cooperative marketing and purchasing had figured prominently in the efforts of the Farmers Union prior to statehood, and farmers large and small endeavored to build cooperatives for decades thereafter. These farmers did not, however, by and large see grand "Cooperation" as the means to build a noncompetitive society. Rather, they hoped to use unassuming cooperatives to maximize the price they received for their crops and minimize the costs they paid for their inputs.[68] They accepted that competition was inherent to capitalism and sought to compete more effectively. In his years as a partisan Socialist, Woodrow had agreed, and held that Oklahomans should vote their class to create a system in which they could better compete. After 1916, the editor portrayed competition and class conflict as something society must move beyond through cooperation. When Woodrow did so, he differed from the farmer majority around him.

Woodrow also moved away from the central interest of Oklahoma's poor farmers: the broad distribution of land ownership. The argument that every farmer should own a farm had played a crucial role in founding the state of Oklahoma and building the Socialist Party in the state. In 1914, Woodrow had supported this position when he published statements calling for land reform in the United States. In 1917, however, Woodrow repeatedly maintained that private land ownership, like private ownership of wealth in general, was wrong. All land, he argued, should be communally owned.[69] Woodrow kept one foot planted in mundane farm politics when he celebrated the passage of the Federal Farm Loan Act of 1916. He dedicated greater energy, however, to his contention that "[t]he opportunity of all to the free and equal use of the land, supplemented by the opportunity to the free and equal use of all machinery . . . , will abolish the injustice and inequality in the social condition of mankind."[70] The statement ran diametrically opposite to a central tenet of Oklahoma agrarian politics, socialist or otherwise. From the Boomer movement to the People's Party, to the Farmers Union, to the Socialist Party in the triumphant year of 1914, Oklahoma agrarians had aimed to help small farmers obtain and keep their own land. Woodrow long fit within the mainstream of Oklahoma agrarianism on the issue of land ownership, though his religious and political thought was unorthodox. By late 1917, he had abandoned the political position that arguably meant most to Oklahoma's farm tenants and small landowners.

At the same time that Woodrow distanced himself from political socialism and the agrarian call for "land to the tiller," he ceased engaging with socialist and agrarian movements and thinkers abroad. With the single exception of Mexico, which he continued to cover, Woodrow increasingly referred only in passing to movements abroad. When he did, he was more likely to mention the cooperative movement in England than land tenure there.[71] Correspondingly, after 1915, Woodrow rarely drew on thinkers that had influenced the transatlantic socialist or agrarian movements. When he referred to Marx, for example, it was either in passing, or in order to take Marx's ideas in a direction the founder of modern socialism had not intended—for example, to argue that the building of cooperatives should take primacy over socialist political struggle.[72] Woodrow's engagement with socialist and agrarian movements abroad had never been profound, but he had demonstrated more interest in them at the height of his involvement in Socialist politics, especially in 1914. As he drew away from the Socialist Party and from the notion that all farmers should own their own land, he also drew away from transatlantic socialism and agrarianism. Woodrow's attention to these movements first waxed and then waned with his dedication to Socialist politics in Oklahoma.

Questions and Conclusions

This fact leaves open the question of influence: Had his interest in movements abroad driven his political activism, or was it the other way around? It would be implausible to argue that Woodrow's knowledge of agrarian and socialist movements in Europe and Mexico had motivated his political activism. Even at the height of his involvement in the Socialist Party, those movements had never commanded the bulk of his attention in his writing or sermons. Although Woodrow sprinkled his pages with quotes from Marx, Kautsky, and Goldman, and references to French tenant farmers and German socialism, he did not dedicate sustained discussion or analysis to them. Rather, the tremendous success of the Socialist Party in Oklahoma from statehood to 1914 encouraged in Woodrow an international vision and hope. When his optimism for political socialism faded, so did his interest in socialism and agrarianism abroad.

They had, however, left some mark on his thinking and politics. The most vivid evidence of this lies in the fact that when Woodrow switched his focus from socialism to cooperation, he legitimated the change in terms of a central tenet of Marxism—that relations of production drive politics. Woodrow did not turn his back on socialism. He continued to insist that only a cooperative economy could build political socialism. The last surviving issue of *Woodrow's Monthly* was published in 1917, and is largely dedicated to championing cooperation as the basis of socialism. Two years later, in 1919, Woodrow died, just as the Red Scare and repression of the interwar period threatened to banish even the memory of the Socialist hopes of the decade from 1910–1920.[73]

It was local events that decided the level of Woodrow's engagement with international issues, and with which international issues he engaged. When Woodrow changed his focus from political socialism to cooperation, he shifted his attention abroad away from socialists and agrarians and onto the cooperative movement in England.[74] For Woodrow, local issues and conditions drove international interest, not the other way around.

Throughout these changes, Woodrow's religion remained at the heart of his politics. In the 1880s, Woodrow's memorable contribution to the Boomer movement was to preside as minister over an opening ceremony for a Boomer settlement. In his early political sermons, Woodrow wed his critique of "landlordism" to his call to return to "Primitive Christianity." In the early, partisan issues of his *Monthly,* he argued that it was in political struggle that humanity would achieve the redemption Christ promised. Finally, after he shifted his energies to calling for a nonpartisan effort to build the Cooperative Commonwealth, Woodrow told his readers that in this effort, they would be returning to the purity of the early Christian church. Woodrow declared himself an advocate of "Primitive Christianity" and proclaimed that this religion shared the same social vision as "Modern Socialism." Historians would be tempted to turn this formula on its head and say that his was a modern Christianity by the standards of his community, and a primitive socialism by the standards of Marxists of his day. His liberal Protestantism formed the basis of a utopian socialist vision. From start to finish, Woodrow's politics drew its sustenance from his religion.

It is to this taproot, ultimately, that historians must look in order to place agrarians such as Woodrow in their transatlantic context. Woodrow's political beliefs were based in churches that grew out of dissident movements in Protestantism. Those religious beliefs crossed the Atlantic with settlers, continued to evolve in an American context, and informed the political choices of believers such as Woodrow. Mediated by local conditions and historical contingencies, they shaped American politics, including American agrarianism and socialism. The dissident nature of Woodrow's Quaker and Universalist background makes it particularly easy to discern the impact that the egalitarianism and activism of these faiths had on his politics. For this reason, Woodrow's politics suggests that those who seek the transatlantic dimension of American radical politics would do well to seek its religious roots.

Notes

1. "Pronunciamento," *Woodrow's Monthly* 1, no. 1 (May 1914): n.p.; "Woodrow's Magazine," *Woodrow's Monthly* 1, no. 1 (May 1914): 3.
2. U.S. Bureau of the Census, *Thirteenth Census of the United States: Supplement for Oklahoma* (Washington, D.C.: Government Printing Office, 1913), 581.
3. On early twentieth-century Hobart, see "Historical Program Booklet: Shortgrass Saga, 50th Anniversary, Kiowa County, 2–6 August, Hobart, Oklahoma, 1901–1951" (n.p.: n.d., 1951).
4. For the debate on this issue among historians of Oklahoma, see John Thompson, *Closing the Frontier: Radical Response in Oklahoma, 1889–1923* (Norman: University of Oklahoma Press, 1986), 87, 138–39; Jim Bissett, *Agrarian Socialism in America: Marx, Jefferson, and Jesus in the Oklahoma Countryside, 1904–1920* (Norman: University of Oklahoma Press, 1999), xiv-xvi; James R. Green, *Grass-Roots Socialism: Radical Movements in the Southwest, 1895–1943* (Baton Rouge: Louisiana State University Press, 1978), 134; Garin Burbank, *When Farmers Voted Red: The Gospel of Socialism in the Oklahoma Countryside, 1910–1924,* Contributions in American History, no. 53 (Westport, Conn.: Greenwood Press, 1976), xiv–xvi.
5. There is disagreement in the sources as to Woodrow's place of birth. On the one hand, he wrote that he grew up in Iowa. This makes sense, given that Iowa contained important centers of Quakerism. On the other hand, the manuscript census of 1910, the only census enumeration of Woodrow I was able to locate, lists his place of birth as Missouri. This may, however, be inaccurate, as the same census gives Emma Woodrow's birthplace as Missouri also, whereas other sources

indicate she was born in Iowa. Furthermore, the census enumerator hardly seems trustworthy, given that he recorded Woodrow's first name as "William." "Coming," *Woodrow's Monthly* 1, no. 6 (November–December 1916): 30; *U.S. Census Population Schedule, 1910,* microcopy no. T624 (Washington, D.C.: National Archives, n.d.), Oklahoma, Kiowa County, Hobart Township, Sheet 19A. For other sources on Emma Woodrow's place of birth, see "Death Ends Colorful Career of Pioneer Woman Doctor," (Hobart) *Kiowa County Star-Review,* 25 May 1950, copy in finding aid of Rev. Thomas W. Woodrow Collection, Western History Collections, University of Oklahoma, Norman, Oklahoma (hereafter, Woodrow Collection, WHC). For Woodrow's Quaker upbringing, see Roger Horne, "The Christian Socialism of Thomas W. Woodrow, 'Oklahoma's First Preacher,'" *Chronicles of Oklahoma* 69 (1991): 80. On Quakers in nineteenth-century Iowa, see Errol T. Elliot, *Quakers on the American Frontier: A History of the Westward Migrations, Settlements, and Development of Friends on the American Continent* (Richmond, Ind.: Friends United Press, 1969), 115–30.

6. William G. Cutler, *History of the State of Kansas* (1883; reprint, Topeka: Kansas State Historical Society, 1976), 2:1372.

7. On Universalism in Iowa, see Elva Louise Tucker, "The History of the Universalist Church in Iowa, 1843–1943" (Master's thesis, University of Iowa, 1944); Dorothy S. Grant, *Universalism in Iowa, 1830–1963,* Discussions on Religious Liberalism, no. 4 (n.p.: Prairie State Universalist Association, 1964).

8. Arrell M. Gibson, *A History of Five Centuries* (Norman, Okla.: Harlow Publishing, 1965), 302–3.

9. Horne, 85.

10. Sidney E. Ahlstrom, *A Religious History of the American People* (New Haven: Yale University Press, 1972), 176–78; Thomas D. Hamm, *The Transformation of American Quakerism: Orthodox Friends, 1800–1907* (Bloomington: Indiana University Press, 1988), 10.

11. Paul K. Conkin, *American Originals: Homemade Varieties of Christianity* (Chapel Hill: University of North Carolina Press, 1997), 95–97; Elmo Arnold Robinson, *American Universalism: Its Origins, Organization and Heritage* (New York: Exposition Press, 1970), 5–6, 88–93, 123–25.

12. Margaret H. Bacon, *The Quiet Rebels: The Story of the Quakers in America* (New York and London: Basic Books, 1969); Robinson, 88–93.

13. Danney Goble, *Progressive Oklahoma: The Making of a New Kind of State* (Norman: University of Oklahoma Press, 1980), 7.

14. Horne, 78, 85.

15. Payne was a speculator and may have had ties to railroad companies interested in Indian Territory lands. Carl Coke Rister, *Land Hunger: David L. Payne and the Oklahoma Boomers* (Norman: University of Oklahoma Press, 1942), 37, 71–75. On the social background of the Boomers, see Thompson, 48.

16. W. H. Miller to Hon. G. H. Orth, 22 January 1882, letter M178, box 64, Special Case no. 78: Settlement of Indian Territory, Entry 102: Special Cases, RG 75: Bureau of Indian Affairs, National Archives (hereafter NA), Washington, D.C.

17. Miller to Orth, 22 January 1882.

18. David W. Payne to Lieut. Pardee, 16 July 1880, letter W1669, box 85, Special Case no. 111: Invasion of Indian Territory, Entry 102: Special Cases, RG 75, NA.

19. "Biased Braves," clipping attached to W. E. Savage to the Secretary of the Interior, envelope S412, box 64, Special Case no. 78: Settlement of Indian Territory, Entry 102: Special Cases, RG 75, NA.

20. See, for example, *Arkansas City Republican,* 7 November 1886; *Arkansas City Republican,* 24 July 1886; Horne, 81–82.

21. "Death Ends Colorful Career of Pioneer Woman Doctor."

22. Horne, 84–85; *U.S. Census Population Schedule, 1910,* microcopy no. T624 (Washington, D.C.: National Archives, n.d.), Oklahoma, Kiowa County, Hobart Township, Sheet 19A.

23. Thompson, 81–82; Green, 7–10; James R. Scales and Danney Goble, *Oklahoma Politics: A History* (Norman: University of Oklahoma Press, 1982), 11.

24. *Thirteenth Census of the United States, Supplement for Oklahoma,* 523–24, 645.

25. Bissett, 24; Thompson, 72–74.

26. Bissett, 23–30.

27. Scales and Goble, 16.

28. R. L. Williams, "Graduated Land License Tax Report," folder 1, box 14, Robert Lee Williams Collection, Accession no. 82.115, Oklahoma Historical Society, Manuscripts Division, Oklahoma City (n.d. circa 1914). Sammah and Halia Harjo to Amo B. Cutlip, Warranty Deed with Relinquishment of Dower, 2 February 1907; Mary Fixico to Amo B. Cutlip, Warranty Deed with Relinquishment of Dower, 9 February 1907; Robert Johnson to Amo B. Cutlip, Warranty Deed with Relinquishment of Dower, 12 February 1907; Jacksey Watko to Amo B. Cutlip, Warranty Deed with Relinquishment of Dower, 12 February

1907; Sally and John Hulwa to Amo B. Cutlip, Warranty Deed with Relinquishment of Dower, 16 February 1907; A. W. and Mollie Butts to Amo B. Cutlip, Quit Claim Deed, 11 March 1907; George Hulbutta to Amo B. Cutlip, Warranty Deed with Relinquishment of Dower, 22 March 1907; Wesley Chupco to Amo B. Cutlip, Warranty Deed, 7 April 1909; J. Wesley to Amo B. Cutlip, Warranty Deed with Relinquishment of Dower, 20 April 1907; Thomas F. and Lillian Robertson to Amo B. Cutlip, Quit Claim Deed with Relinquishment of Dower, 25 March 1909. All of these deeds are located in folder 17, box 9, C. Guy Cutlip Collection, WHC. Thompson, 36–38.

29. Green, 66–72; Burbank, 44–48; Scales and Goble, 41–43.
30. On progressive and agrarian Democrats in this period, see Goble, 20–40.
31. Thompson, 142–45.
32. Scales and Goble, 64.
33. Ibid., 67.
34. The 1910 state Socialist platform, for example, declared the party's intention to "bring into collective property the land" in the state. "Socialist Party State Platform," 1910, folder 40, box 12, Fred Barde Collection, Manuscripts Division, Oklahoma Historical Society, Oklahoma City (hereafter OHS).
35. Bissett, 61–69; Burbank, 44–51. State Platform, Socialist Party of Oklahoma, folder 1, box 1, Socialist Party Collection, OHS. See especially "Renters' and Farmers' Platform," 8–9.
36. "44,030," *Appeal to Reason,* 13 November 1915.
37. Burbank, 14–40; Green, 151–53.
38. Quoted in Burbank, 19.
39. Horne, 84.
40. "Anarchism by an Anarchist," *Woodrow's Monthly* 1, no. 4 (March 1915): 23; "Socialism and Religion," *Woodrow's Monthly* 1, no. 4 (March 1915): 5. For Woodrow's discussion of and quotation from Marx, see among others "The United People's Church," *Woodrow's Monthly* 1, no. 4 (March 1915): 12; "From the Communist Manifesto," *Woodrow's Monthly* 1, no. 5 (September 1915): 4–5.
41. "The Only Practical Method," *Woodrow's Monthly* 1, no. 4 (March 1915): 8; "France in Hard Straits," *Woodrow's Monthly* 1, no. 4 (March 1915): 8.
42. "The Mexican Situation and the United States," *Woodrow's Monthly* 1, no. 1 (May 1914). For other references to Mexico, see, for example, "Corroborative Comments," *Woodrow's Monthly* 1, no. 2 (August

1914): 28; "Conquest, Not Intervention," *Woodrow's Magazine* 1, no. 6 (1916): 15; "Towards Single Tax in Mexico," *Woodrow's Magazine* 1, no. 7 (January–February [1917]): n.p.

43. "Concentration of Land Ownership in the United States," *Woodrow's Monthly* 1, no. 2 (August 1914): 22.

44. He quoted, "Thus were the agricultural people, first forcibly expropriated from the soil, driven back from their homes, turned into vagabonds, and then whipped, branded, tortured by laws grotesquely terrible, into the discipline necessary to the wage system." "The Dague Industrial Army Bill," *Woodrow's Monthly* 1, no. 1 (May 1914): 12–13.

45. "Socialist Party Declares Against Mexican War," *Appeal to Reason,* 2 May 1914, p. 1.

46. "Real 'Jeffersonian Democracy,'" *Appeal to Reason,* 27 June 1914, p. 2; "Socialism and Money," *Appeal to Reason,* 22 August 1914, p. 2; "A Public Ownership Land," *Appeal to Reason,* 20 January 1917, p. 4.

47. Scrapbook, box 2, Woodrow Collection, WHC.

48. "Beginnings of Socialism," *Appeal to Reason,* 20 June 1914; "The Owen Colonies," *Appeal to Reason,* 20 May 1914; "Socialism Only Hope," *Appeal to Reason,* 18 July 1914; "Owen and Marx," *Appeal to Reason,* 8 August 1914, p. 3.

49. "Says Appeal Classics are Big Source of Information," *Appeal to Reason,* 3 February 1917, p. 3; "Books on Socialism," *Appeal to Reason,* 4 August 1917, p. 4; "Appeal Socialist Classics!" *Appeal to Reason,* 11 August 1917, p. 4.

50. Untitled and undated manuscript, box 2, Woodrow Collection, WHC. Horne dates this manuscript entry as 1904. Horne, 85.

51. Thompson, 144; Bissett, 87. James R. Green takes the political power of Socialists' religious beliefs more seriously than most scholars. Green, 151–75.

52. Henry Warner Bowden notes that a wide variety of reformers and dissidents, from Pentecostalists to Anglican defenders of High Church tradition, claimed as their own the impulse to return to the principles and practices of the apostolic church. Henry Warner Bowden, "Perplexity over a Protean Principle: A Response," in *The American Quest for the Primitive Church,* ed. Richard T. Hughes (Urbana: University of Illinois Press, 1988), 172.

53. Daniel W. Hull, "The Philosophy of 'Magnetic Healing,'" *Woodrow's Monthly* 1, no. 4 (March 1915): 16–19; "Spirit Mediumship and Immortality," *Woodrow's Monthly* 1, no. 5 (September 1915): 21.

54. "Other World—Salvation-ism," *Woodrow's Monthly* 1, no. 2 (August 1914): 4; "Despotism of Otherworldism," *Woodrow's Monthly* 1, no. 6 (November–December 1916): 6; "Believing without Thinking a Curse to the Mind," *Woodrow's Monthly* 1, no. 6 (November–December 1916): 8–9; "The Church That Is to Be," *Woodrow's Monthly* 1, no. 1 (May 1914): 9; R. A. Dague, "Philosopher and God," *Woodrow's Monthly* 1, no. 4 (March 1915): 13–14; William A. Prosser, "The Rev. William A. Sunday, Evangelist: A False Prophet," *Woodrow's Monthly* 1, no. 1 (May 1914): 16–19.

55. "Pronunciamento," *Woodrow's Monthly* 1, no. 1 (May 1914): n.p.; "Joining Church for Salvation," *Woodrow's Monthly* 1, no. 1 (May 1914): 11.

56. "Good Political 'Dope,'" *Woodrow's Monthly* 1, no. 2 (August 1914): 27.

57. Scales and Goble, 76; Green, 291–93.

58. Horne, 79.

59. "Not a Socialist Political, But Socialist Religious Journal," *Woodrow's Monthly* 1, no. 4 (March 1915): 3.

60. "Non-Partisan, Non-Sectarian," *Woodrow's Monthly* 1, no. 5 (September 1915): 26.

61. Burbank, 108–9.

62. Bissett, 132–36.

63. Thompson, 130–31.

64. "Cured at Last," *Woodrow's Magazine* 1, no. 6 (November–December 1916): 32.

65. "Futility of Politics as Means of Human Emancipation," *Woodrow's Magazine* 1, no. 6 (November–December 1916): 28.

66. "The Dispensation of Socialism," *Woodrow's Monthly* 1, no. 1 (May 1914): 14–15; "Which First, Industrial or Political," *Woodrow's Magazine* 1, no. 6 (November–December 1916): 4; "Dispensation of Socialism," *Woodrow's Magazine* 1, no. 6 (November–December 1916): 16–17, a reprint of the same article in *Woodrow's Monthly* 1, no. 1 (May 1914): 14–15.

67. Edward K. Spann, *Brotherly Tomorrows: Movements for a Cooperative Society in America, 1820–1920* (New York: Columbia University Press, 1989), 226–42; Carl J. Guarneri, *The Utopian Alternative: Fourierism in Nineteenth-Century America* (Ithaca, N.Y.: Cornell University Press, 1991), 6–7.

68. Bissett, 28–29.

69. "Concentration of Land Ownership in the United States," *Woodrow's Monthly* 1, no. 2 (August 1914): 21–22; "Early Christianity

Communistic," *Woodrow's Magazine* 1, no. 6 (November–December 1916): 22–23.

70. Ibid; also, "Inalienable Rights of Man," *Woodrow's Magazine* 1, no. 6 (November–December 1916): 24–25.

71. "Conquest, Not Intervention," *Woodrow's Magazine* 1, no. 6 (November–December 1916): 15; "Towards Single Tax in Mexico," *Woodrow's Magazine* 1, no. 7 (January–February [1917]): n.p.; Untitled, *Woodrow's Magazine* 1, no. 6 (November–December 1916): 29; "Dispensation of Socialism," *Woodrow's Magazine* 1, no. 6 (November–December 1916): 16, a reprint of the same article in *Woodrow's Monthly* 1, no. 1 (May 1914): 14.

72. "Which First, Industrial or Political," *Woodrow's Magazine* 1, no. 6 (November–December 1916): 4; "Not For or Against Any Party," *Woodrow's Magazine* 1, no. 6 (November–December 1916): 4.

73. Horne, 89.

74. "Dispensation of Socialism," *Woodrow's Magazine* 1, no. 6 (November–December 1916): 16–17, a reprint of the same article in *Woodrow's Monthly* 1, no. 1 (May 1914): 14–15.

Radical Rhetoric, Repressive Rule: *Sindicato* Power in the Atlixco (Mexico) Countryside in the Early Twentieth Century

Gregory S. Crider

"Transatlantic" ideas, rhetoric, and practices have shaped the politics of the Mexican countryside for many generations. As liberal dictator Porfirio Díaz sought to modernize Mexico with private agriculture, diverse industry, national railroads, and European cultural values during his prolonged regime (1876–1911), peasants and workers relied on both "traditional" and "modern" responses to the dramatic social changes they experienced. In the revolutionary and postrevolutionary struggles of the period from 1910 to 1930, transatlantic philosophies and practices of anarchism, communism, and liberalism influenced distinctly modern forms of political organization (trade unions, peasant leagues, political parties). In the 1930s, President Lázaro Cárdenas encouraged and relied on mobilization of these popular political forms to support construction of the "institutions" that would deliver on some of the radical promises of the Revolution, including agrarian reform, pro-labor legislation, expropriation of foreign oil companies, and socialist education.

In the rural region of Atlixco in the state of Puebla, new political brokers emerged over the first half of the twentieth century, deriving power from revolutionary labor laws, alliances with state and national political forces, and mobilization of popular support. The most powerful of these new brokers were textile *sindicato* leaders, or trade-union bosses, in Atlixco's seven *fábrica* communities. At the height of Cardenista reformism and "institutionalization," these bosses—or *"patrones"* as workers came to refer to them—consolidated vast domains of influence in both the mill communities and the surrounding agrarian regions (from where virtually all of the textile workers originated, and where most maintained close family and land connections). Empowered with the exclusive right to hire and fire workers, these bosses leveraged this right and access to other resources not only to dominate shop-floor activities but also to assert control over local housing, markets, justice, social events, education, religion, and political positions. Their influence extended to peasant communities through *municipio* appointments, granting of mill jobs, and distribution of agricultural resources. *Sindicato* power—cloaked in Marxist, class-based, progressive, modern rhetoric, and decorated with red and black banners—became so pervasive that one mill community, Metepec, came to be called *"la Rusia chiquita"* ("the little Russia").

While this intriguing case bears on numerous political and social issues of the postrevolutionary era, this essay focuses attention on how the new *patrones* of Atlixco encouraged a political culture in which they could effectively promote, protect, and prolong their positions of power. The *sindicato* bosses of the 1930s and later, I argue, selectively drew language, images, and symbols, as well as practices and strategies, from two potentially contradictory sources of political culture. On the one hand, anarchist and Marxist labor organizers and political activists had played crucial roles between 1910 and 1930 in mobilizing regional workers, and ultimately in leveraging union recognition, closed-shop collective contracts, and other labor rights. Once these "radical" leaders had been effectively removed from the region by the 1930s, the new, more politically moderate *sindicato* bosses eagerly embraced "radical" ideas and icons, applying class-oriented and revolutionary rhetoric to establish legitimacy with state-level and national political leaders, and also to appeal to the laboring masses to struggle against the oppressive forces of capital, capitalism, and cronyism. From this angle, the new *sindicatos* represented rational, modern, and nationally integrated structures that supplanted more "traditional" political and social relations in the countryside and protected the vulnerable masses from selfish factory owners, landlords, and corrupt politicians. Language, symbols, and ideas appropriated by these *sindicatos* reflected transatlantic influences of Marxism, socialism, and, more broadly, modernity.

But the new bosses, on the other hand, also borrowed heavily from more traditional notions of patron-client relations associated with the Mexican countryside. Of course, the very term *patrón* had a history of designating the landlord, the military cacique, and even the factory owner, and the new bosses used this legacy to construct their own personal domains over obligated subjects, demanding (and enforcing) personal deference, submission, loyalty, and service in return for limited privileges and protections. Reproduction of this pattern of patronal rule is evident in the self-images and values crafted by bosses in their communities, in the demands and rites imposed upon workers and peasants, and in the language chosen to articulate *sindicato* needs. Ultimately, these tools—drawn from both radical, modern influences and patronal traditions—provided significant utility to the bosses in building their own new revolutionary patron-client networks of power.

Textileros received the mixed images and practices of *sindicato* bosses with corresponding complexity. *Sindicato* triumph resulted in a significant structural inversion of power. In addition to controlling key municipal government positions, the union—not the government, landlord, or mill owner—occupied each community's grandest and most elaborate building, serving as the focal point for resolving local conflicts, addressing quotidian personal needs, and gaining access to the state. In material terms, the *sindicato* delivered electricity, communal bathing facilities, health and dental clinics, athletic fields, and clock towers—as well as better wages, more paid vacations, and safety protections. Further, the unions' use of radical rhetoric validated the class identities and demands of both mill workers and peasants. At the same time, however, the network of power claimed by the new bosses left little room for challenge or negotiation with local residents. Personal deals struck with *patrones* were always conditional, limited, temporal, and subject to dramatic change. Workers who stepped over the lines of *sindicato*-imposed "discipline" faced fines, work suspension, forced exile, physical abuse, and—in hundreds of cases—murder.

While reinforcing local and regional domains of power, the *sindicato* boss regime also came to mediate between Atlixco's residents and national state-formation. Unions and their leaders came to control access to the institutions of the emerging revolutionary state. From the perspectives of workers and their families, this power meant that *sindicato* bosses were the most immediate and essentially exclusive representatives of the state. In

Atlixco, the *sindicatos* clearly played a significant intermediary role in the social and cultural transformations associated with Mexican state-formation.

To explore the sources of local political culture and their role with national state-formation processes, I have organized this essay in three sections: radical influences in the *sindicatos* of Atlixco, patronal political culture, and working-class responses and political culture.

Radical Influences in the Sindicatos of Atlixco

Throughout the nineteenth century, capitalist industrial investment poured into the state of Puebla, conveniently located between the port of Veracruz and the major markets of Mexico City. By the end of the century, when the modernizing authoritarian military regime of Porfirio Díaz expanded railroads to connect domestic markets, extended favorable tax and credit policies, and enforced anti-labor standards, foreign and domestic investors had begun to transform the rural economy of Puebla into a major hub of textile production. In Atlixco, owners of La Concepción and La Carolina upgraded the technology of their mills in the 1890s, and between 1898 and 1902, investors constructed and opened five new factories on former agricultural estates, including El Volcán, El León, San Agustín (Los Molinos), El Carmen, and Metepec. Metepec, on the outskirts of the town of Atlixco, became the largest textile mill in the state, and one of the three largest in Mexico. With the seven factories of Atlixco producing the bulk of cotton textiles, the state of Puebla became the most important textile-producing state in the nation.[1]

The mills employed numerous paternalistic strategies to attempt to control their labor force, but workers responded in ways to protect their interests and resist this control. In the tradition of Manchester and Lynn, factory owners maintained company housing complexes under the 24-hour vigilance of private guards, established company stores to monopolize trade of most food staples and alcohol, controlled local rail cars and buses, provided the only medical services, and extended credit and collected debts directly from weekly pay.[2] The Porfirian state backed mill owners with coercion and legal support, but even after the Revolution, the owners continued their strategies of control and repression, including the formation of *sindicatos blancos* or company unions.

Atlixco's *textileros* drew from a variety of ideological and political sources—from anarchists and revolutionary sindicalists to liberals and

Catholics—to organize themselves and challenge the owners' control efforts. In the final years leading to the overthrow of the Porfirian regime, Atlixco's workers had begun large-scale organization in collaboration with the radical Gran Círculo de Obreros Libres from Orizaba, initiating strikes during the fall of 1906 in each of the seven *fábricas,* and demanding better wages, shorter hours, and more autonomy on the shop floor and in the company housing complexes.[3] Federal troops aided company forces to repress these actions, but *textileros* continued to organize and seek recognition; a general strike, initiated at El León and involving more than 8,000 textile workers statewide, contributed to the Zapatista victory in Atlixco in May 1911.[4] During the years of the armed conflict of the Revolution (1910–1920), workers continued to challenge mill owners, initiating numerous actions and enduring lockouts and repression. In 1918, a variety of workers' resistance groups—including anarchists, supporters of the "Red battalions" that supported General Alvaro Obregón's revolutionary forces, and the reform-oriented *"laboristas"*—banded together to form the Confederación Sindicalista del Estado de Puebla (CSEP). The "Sindicalista" would participate in 1918 in founding the national Confederación Regional Obrera Mexicana (CROM), a moderate national labor organization that aided General Alvaro Obregón's efforts to defeat the counterrevolutionary Delahuertistas in exchange for political support and eventual political appointments (once Obregón became president in 1920).[5] The appointment of one national CROM organizer as interim governor, Vicente Lombardo Toledano, would lead to anti-scab protections and other pro-labor measures in the state of Puebla.[6]

Radical leftist activists played an important role in organizing new work sites and peasant communities, developing strategies of direct collective action, and defining class-oriented goals, language, and symbols. Leaders of the Confederación General de Trabajadores (CGT), founded by anarchists and communists in 1921 to promote *"Revolución Social pro Comunismo"* through direct action, had cautiously agreed to work with reformists under the CROM umbrella with the ultimate aim of gaining control of the dominant labor organization's ideological and political direction.[7] In Atlixco, local Partido Comunista de México (PCM) organizers irritated state and national CROM leaders by forming autonomous committees and political discussion groups throughout the region.[8] In April 1925, a local strike of El Volcán workers and a statewide teacher strike for better pay both violated orders from the CROM national Central Committee, with the latter action resulting in an intervention of thousands of federal troops and the execution of the statewide CSEP leader. National CROM leaders became increasingly alarmed by the rising presence of Communist and leftist influences in the CSEP and among the people of the countryside of Atlixco.[9] According to PCM activist Julio Ramírez, the party's major campaigns to organize the Atlixco *fábricas* began in September 1926.[10] All came to recognize Metepec as "*rojo*" headquarters.

The growing influence of leftist organizers alienated both moderate CROM leaders and mill owners. Between December 1926 and April 1928, owners of all seven mills engaged strategies to neutralize the nascent labor unions, including extensive layoffs and even plant closings.[11] At the same time, the collective contract emerging from the national Convención Industrial Obrera del Ramo Textil (1925–27) and signed into law granted exclusive collective-bargaining rights to only one signatory organization for each shift of workers at a given factory.[12] This legal development opened the door for a historic compromise that would shape local social relations for decades. The terms of the agreement were never explicated officially, but the understanding was clear: in exchange for ousting radical leftist influences from their ranks and guaranteeing a reliable source of labor, CROM leaders attained exclusive recognition, as well as some material and political concessions.[13] Subsequently, the CROM formed a new statewide Central Committee in August 1928, expelling communists and other dissidents, and forcing workers and local leaders to choose one side or the other. Dramatic conflict followed this formal split and resulted in more expulsions, arrests, and murders. By the middle of 1929, CROM violence and terror overwhelmed the PCM activists and forced them to abandon the Atlixco region.[14]

In the decades that followed, local CROM leaders, who organized as the Cámara del Trabajo (CDT) in Atlixco, took credit for all working-class gains and also appropriated some of the symbols of their departed radical rivals. Once the CGT was effectively vanquished, CDT-CROM leaders claimed responsibility for the shorter work week of 48 hours, a raise in wages, and standardization of the pay scale in the collective contract. After all, the CDT-CROM was the only signatory of the legal document.[15] But Cámara leaders, as they assumed many duties and roles formerly administered by mill owners or managers, also became the providers of the most important municipal services, including transportation, water distribution, and postal delivery. The *sindicatos* soon controlled local sales of tortillas and baked goods, and even took over the company stores, converting them to *sindicato* consumer cooperatives. Through the 1930s and 1940s, the *sindicatos* constructed sports fields, public parks, cinemas, and sanatoriums, and expanded electricity, potable water, and medical services. In Metepec, the community most remote from the town's center, the *sindicato,* under the leadership of rising star and strongman Antonio J. Hernández, constructed a new housing complex architecturally designed to facilitate *sindicato* vigilance and control.[16]

As the CDT-CROM *sindicatos* expanded services and erected new buildings, leaders made certain to attach their own names, ideas, and symbols to these projects. The most glaring example of this practice is the *sindicato* headquarters. Adorned with brightly painted images of the Revolution, prominent displays of the CROM acronym, and even sculptures of hard-working, muscular *textileros,* these buildings appeared as shrines to the *sindicatos* and their historic missions. All who entered the isolated mill community of El León, for example, passed through a gold-painted, lion-mounted, imposing archway marking the boundary of the territory of the Sindicato "Obreros Perseverantes" ("Persevering Workers") of the CROM. Once inside, residents and visitors would notice painted signs and forged plaques recognizing individual *sindicato* bosses and the CROM for their efforts in bringing the community schools, parks, sports facilities, medical and dental clinics.[17] Further, *sindicato* leaders even commissioned local writers to pen hagiographic testimonies to their personalities. Jesús Cerrillo, a teacher from the Escuela del Sindicato de la Colonia Obrera de "El León," wrote the heroic tale of a hard-working, dedicated *textilero,* Agustín Pérez Caballero, who struggled valiantly within the ranks of the confederation and educated himself to rise to the position of *sindicato* boss and respected local politician. His public works projects, Cerrillo wrote, showed Pérez's commitment to local residents.

> The Emergency Clinic of the Sindicato de Obreros Perseverantes [de El León], the "30 de abril" Zócalo [town square] with its beautiful and symbolic monuments built to [display] workers' spirit, the "Héroes de Chapultepec" Children's Park, the "7 de enero" *frontón* courts, the addition to the "José Ma. Morelos" School, and the Monumental Arch [gateway to the community]—these works are true reflections of his efforts to achieve social welfare and to make his community a pleasant and peaceful place. All of its residents dedicated to work, forging their future with a harmonious and hopeful plan.[18]

No doubt, Cerrillo and other *patrón*-dependent teachers promoted these images to their students as well.

Though they formally denounced the CGT and communists as fraudulent class traitors, CDT-CROM bosses also appropriated many symbols and discursive references from the departed anarchists and communists. Even the names of Atlixco unions reflected these earlier radical influences. For instance, in Metepec, the organizational title was "Sindicato de Obreros Revolucionarios de Metepec" (Sindicato of Revolutionary Workers of Metepec); and in Los Molinos, the title was "Sindicato de Obreros Emancipación Proletaria . . ." (Proletarian Emancipation Sindicato of Workers).[19] The CDT-CROM continued to attach the motto "Salud y Revolución Social" (Health and Social Revolution) to its letterhead and other printed materials, and used mill owners as foils in *sindicato* propaganda. Even as some *sindicatos* splintered from the CDT-CROM in the 1930s, they retained similar slogans, such as "Por la Revolución Social" (For Social Revolution) and "Por una Sociedad Sin Clases" (For a Society Without Classes).[20] Voluminous evidence from *sindicato* and municipal archives illustrates the class-oriented, revolutionary discourse engaged by *patrones* during the 1930s, but a sampling of CDT-CROM posters and leaflets gives readers a sense of the language. A 1933 poster calls workers of the region to unite against political opponents to achieve "manumission of the Universal Proletariat." A 1934 recruiting circular invited "the working-class masses" to join their "class brothers" in the Cámara to fight for "mutual class goals." A 1939 broadside accused rival leaders of colluding with owners, selling out working-class interests, and being "bourgeois."[21] Of course, irony dripped from these claims and charges, but *sindicato* bosses continued to publicly endorse revolutionary change through class solidarity and activism.

A walk through the textile workers' eco-museum, housed in a refurbished wing of the now-defunct factory at Metepec, exposes one to the day-to-day sights and sounds of factory and community life, as well as the political relics of a century's struggles. Although the artifacts from the 1930s and after do not include hammers and sickles or other direct references to communism or anarchism, red and black *sindicato* silk banners advocating "social revolution"; photos of thousands of union members attending public assemblies, and of workers whose lives were sacrificed to political violence; and posters connecting local labor struggles to national and international causes and calling for *textileros* to defend their class rights—all serve as reminders of the *sindicatos'* radical roots.[22] In using these revolutionary, radical symbols and language, Atlixco's regional *sindicato* bosses sought to accomplish two goals. In terms of the national political discourse of the "Revolution," they wanted to connect to this language and gain legitimacy among national political brokers, especially the Cardenistas in the 1930s. Further, the new *patrones* thought, on some level, that these words and symbols would appeal to and influence the region's peasants and wage workers.

Patronal Political Culture

"Patron-client" relations can be traced back through the social histories of many regions and cultures of the world, and through many periods. Typically, these relationships involve a "patron" who controls access to a key resource (such as land, water, political privilege, or means of violence), and "clients" who are essentially forced to give labor, tribute, and/or loyalty to the boss in exchange for access to the resource, other material necessities, and protection. These very personalized vertical relations are generally unequal, exploitative, and ultimately coerced. In colonial and postcolonial Mexico, the paradigm of patronage was the *hacendado*. During the generalized fighting and dislocation of the Revolutionary years, numerous military caciques in regions throughout Mexico, including southern Puebla, built new patronage networks based on their ability to control the means of violence and provide personal safety and material necessities (food, supplies, weapons, ammunition) to *campesinos* in exchange for political support. The "modernizing" tendencies of the postrevolutionary state-building regimes of Obregón, Calles, and Cárdenas (collectively, 1920–1940) did not erase the practice of patronage; many regional power brokers, in fact, endured or evolved from postrevolutionary political institutions.[23] Patronage, in one form or another, was solidly linked to the postrevolutionary state.

The union *patrones* of Atlixco, however, were not military leaders, bandits, landlords, factory owners, or old-school oligarchs; these leaders had emerged from the rank and file of *textileros* (some with peasant roots), struggled through the labor wars for recognition, and ultimately wrested power from the monopoly formerly controlled by mill owners. Through the collective contract and other postrevolutionary laws, institutions, and protections, labor unions gained collective bargaining rights, closed-shop representation, sanction to hire and fire factory workers, and control over former company stores and housing. While these changes reflected the collective strength of textile workers, the new bosses used their new powers to replicate social patterns of *patrón* rule. Controlling access to the key resource of jobs (as well as housing, education, and other services), *sindicato* bosses demanded personal service, political loyalty, and work in the mills from their client-workers. Further, the new bosses employed violence to reinforce the bonds of obligation.

This is not to say that patron-client relations were precisely the same as they had been in earlier times, in different economic modes, under older political regimes, or in other geographic circumstances. Any number of events and processes in the first four decades of the century were changing the parameters for the exercise of political authority. The turmoil of the Revolution had uprooted millions of Mexicans from their homes, separating them from jobs and means of subsistence, and breaking or weakening earlier patronal ties. In a process that began well before the Revolution as peasants moved to work for wages in industrial enterprises, even those in rural settings such as Atlixco, their material needs and roles as consumers changed significantly and, no doubt, altered particular expectations of new bosses. Further, as political leaders asserting competing national projects and representing opposing economic classes and geographic interests vied for control of the reins to govern the republic—frequently exchanging power and even leaving apparent "vacuums" at moments—local and regional politics also took on new dynamics. The creation and enforcement of new laws and institutions at national and state levels resulted in changes in local priorities, privileges, and points of political leverage. In Atlixco, for example, the *cláusula de exclusión* (the "exclusionary clause" that authorized a single *sindicato* with the closed-shop right to hire and fire a factory's workers) empowered workers with more negotiating leverage with owners, but also established an essential base for construction of the *sindicato* patronage system. The practice of patronage over the years, then, was not smooth and seamless, but ruptured, patched, and remade.

But the continuities of patron-client relations are striking. The personalistic nature of these relations meant that each *patrón* made and enforced demands in his own idiosyncratic style. Through rewards and punishments, however, the collective actions of *sindicato* bosses created a clearly understood code of social values that reached from shop floor to cantina, from marketplace to *caserío*, from *zócalo* to household. The chain of *sindicato* patronage began with the *textilero* from Metepec who, by the late 1930s, emerged as the CDT-CROM *jefe máximo* of the region: Antonio J. Hernández. Leaders from each of the *fábrica* communities gave Don Antonio personal loyalty, and delivered political and armed support in exchange for the rights to oversee each community. In turn, these *sindicato* bosses distributed rewards, such as favorable shop-floor positions and access to preferred housing, to those who would serve them most loyally and could offer special services—especially informants and *pistoleros,* but also baseball players and musicians. Even though the personal styles of *sindicato* bosses ranged from the "nice" *patrón* who cultivated the image of the respectable, formal, imposing patriarch to the "tough" *patrón* who flaunted powers of coercion and personal excess, the system as a whole effectively established hierarchies and competition, and was even stronger because of the contrasting styles.[24] Further, shop-floor hierarchies of *"superiores"*and *"inferiores"*extended from supervisors to spinners and weavers, but also from these permanent workers to the *ayudantes* (assistants) whom they often hired, but who were not formal *sindicato* members (and thus were not paid collective contract wages). These assistants were usually the young (most were preteen) and vulnerable sons, nephews, and *hijos adoptivos* of permanent workers.

Throughout the *sindicato* system, bosses at every level demanded submission and deference. Patronal behavior encouraged one-to-one relationships with inferiors that emphasized individual favors and personal obligations. *Sindicato* bosses distributed jobs in ways to promote competition and mistrust among workers, and exploited the division of tasks in shop-floor production as well as the fast pace and loud noise of the mill to further isolate workers. The standard use of spies in the mills' production sections also inhibited trust and communication. The inter-*sindicato* wars of the 1930s strengthened practices of vigilance and violence, resulting in even more fear and mistrust. For example, bosses formed "vigilance committees" to screen applicants, issue *sindicato* credentials, and investigate potential offences. *Patrones* enforced local discipline by ordering job suspensions, firings, fines, withdrawal of favors, forced exiles from the region, assaults, and murders against those suspected of challenging or betraying them, disrupting local order, or not fulfilling the expectations of patron-client reciprocity.[25] The same politics of domination and submission also affected generational and gender relations in the household.

Mexican elites, of course, for centuries have invented and reinvented rituals and public ceremonies intended to reinforce social hierarchy and legitimate institutions of power.[26] In Atlixco, the ceremony of patronal domination was practiced in numerous community events, such as grand openings of new services and facilities, political rallies for regional and statewide candidates, May Day parades, holiday celebrations, musical concerts, baseball games, and fiestas to mark the *patrón*'s birthday or saint's day. Whether the *patrón* was speaking, performing, being feted, or simply attending, these public events served to magnify his beneficence and power while reinforcing the dependence of the workers and other local denizens. Typically, the *patrón*—surrounded by an entourage of lieutenants, aides, and armed bodyguards—sat center-stage, as a variety of musicians and other entertainers on the *sindicato* payroll performed before him and the crowd of residents. Even those leaders not gifted with great oratory skills used the opportunity to remind workers of *sindicato* achievements, announce new *sindicato* projects and services, and denounce political challengers and opponents; the more threatening these opponents, the more valuable the protection offered by the *sindicatos*.[27]

Behind closed doors, other important ceremonies also took place. Though personal meetings with the *patrón* were private and (for most) infrequent, virtually every male resident had gone through the experience and indelibly marked the ritual in his memory. A comprehensive analysis of all public and private ceremonies is not necessary in this space, but a brief description of the initial, formal encounter between the newcomer asking the *patrón* for *sindicato* membership and privileges illustrates some essential dynamics. In an earlier work, I described a typical initial interview from the late 1920s and 1930s:

> Through personal contacts, job applicants made appointments several days or weeks in advance of their interviews. Entering the sindicato building already aware of the vast and threatening power of the organization and its *patrón*, a prospective worker often had to sit or stand in the reception room along with dozens of others seeking jobs and other favors from the *patrón*. After waiting several hours or even days, the applicant finally made his way into the *patrón*'s office and typically had only a few minutes to explain his situation, his need to work, and his commitment to the sindicato. Though each *patrón* had his own style of rule, former workers recall that the customary presence of armed *allegados* [hired associates] with the sindicato leaders could be intimidating. As these thugs watched over, the leader observed the supplicant's demeanor, explained the general terms of employment, and outlined the sindicato's expectations of the new worker. While the leader considered the individual's particular circumstances and abilities, the worker generally could only plead his case, and rarely had much leverage to negotiate job arrangements in this face-to-face meeting. The deal sealed with a handshake, this meeting formally introduced the worker to the sindicato, to work in the *fábrica*, and to life in the sindicato-dominated community.[28]

The *patrón*'s intention in this initiation process was to establish the foundation of the relations of power that would persist throughout the new worker's stay in the community.

Despite some significant economic and political changes over the second half of the century, the personalistic relations and the initial interview ceremony remained central to patronal authority. In a study of labor relations in the *fábrica* La Concepción, anthropologist Francisco Javier Gómez Carpinteiro described a potential worker's first encounter with the *sindicato* boss in the late 1980s:

> One can observe long lines of people, all with previous appointments ('arranged a week before'), . . . in search of work or a solution to a labor conflict. The applicants are sons and daughters, nieces and nephews, and sons and daughters-in-law of a worker, of a widow, or of a *compadre* of the sindicato boss. Each applicant waits his/her turn to enter. Once inside, the boss greets the sponsor of the possible worker and asks, generally, about the state of the family, about the job situation in the *fábrica*. . . . [The] worker traditionally says [in appreciation], "As I may serve you." . . . We could only reconstruct, based on conversations with those who once were applicants, how they stated their cases: "the money is not enough to sustain our family," "my son, or son-in-law, needs to take care of his woman," "my nephew would like to continue his studies." In few words, the job was needed.[29]

These interviews were important rituals to enforce the patterns of domination and submission. As Gilbert Joseph and Daniel Nugent have written in assessing cultural aspects of domination, "Subjects were repeatedly reminded of their subjected identities via rituals and media of moral regulation, and not only through their manifest, concrete oppression."[30] Atlixco's residents could not escape these reminders.

Working-Class Responses and Political Culture

We can consider the case study of Atlixco in light of three significant issues pertaining to the nature of political rule in early-twentieth-century Mexico: the role and significance of radical or revolutionary language, the ability or inability of non-elites to mobilize this language, and the impact of popular struggles on state-formation.

I have posited in this essay that radical, revolutionary words and symbols became the semi-official public lexicon of the *sindicato* bosses in Atlixco. Once the CDT-CROM had eliminated the real political threat of anarchist and communist organizers, local Cámara leaders were freer to expropriate and exploit the class-based, militant-solidarity language and imagery of their antagonists. This use was intended, at least in part, to appeal to (or to appease) the postrevolutionary national state-builders, most notably the Cardenistas, and would prove necessary in the Cámara's eventual incorporation into the dominant national political apparatus. This was not a predictable or inevitable development. In fact, the Confederación de Trabajadores de México (CTM; Confederation of Workers of Mexico), the national broad-front unification of most major labor groups forged in 1936, was closely allied with the Cardenistas on a national level and had launched aggressive recruiting efforts and affiliated with numerous unions throughout the state of Puebla in the mid-1930s.[31] In the mills of Atlixco, some of the smaller textile unions indeed broke ranks from the CROM, aligned with the statewide affiliate of the CTM, and engaged Cámara forces in a bitter, bloody, deadly, protracted war for control of the region before being violently defeated and forced to accept the terms of a resolution dictated by Antonio J. Hernández and the CDT-CROM.[32] While the CROM withered to a very small national presence by the 1930s, the CTM was ascendent, quickly becoming the dominant national voice and body of organized labor and remaining a powerful political force for the rest of the century. In contrast with the national landscape, the CDT-CROM remained the predominant power in the Atlixco countryside, and was brought into the fold of the Revolutionary state. Accepting the language and ideology of the "Revolutionary" state, Cámara leaders could use the national state (and, eventually, the political apparatus of the Partido Revolucionario Institucional) to legitimate and maintain local power, while the state benefited from Atlixco's incorporation and support. Cámara strongman Hernández first attained the political position of federal deputy in 1943 and, as one scholar noted, "repeated as a federal deputy more times since 1943 than almost any other Mexican public figure."[33]

But presumably, all of the pro-worker words, solidarity symbols, calls for social revolution, and militant anti-capital intonations were also intended to speak for, enchant, or at least strike a chord of legitimacy with the working-class and peasant masses of the Atlixco countryside. Did they succeed? No, not really. Interviews and other primary accounts of workers and other residents suggest that responses to *sindicato* power and rhetoric covered a range of perspectives. Some claimed political apathy, while others, declaring deep personal commitment to their *patrones,* also deferred to their bosses on political matters. Some, many years later, expressed their disdain for the bosses, their affiliations, and political leaders in general, but of course were never able to express their thoughts within the confines of the *fábrica* communities and the terror of the *sindicatos.* Still other workers referred to the CROM's opponents as "fascists," "Communists," or "enemies of the working class," echoing the same labels applied by their *sindicato* bosses. The closest that workers came to embracing the *sindicato*'s images and messages was to express appreciation for the jobs, the public improvements, and other material gains.[34] Longtime *textilero* Juan Osorio, for example, concluded that " . . . to say Antonio I. Hernández is to say tranquility, peace, and work."[35] But these qualities are more closely identified with expectations of a good *patrón* than with "revolutionary" aims. *Sindicato* bosses relied more on their distribution of jobs and resources and use of extreme violence than they did on rhetoric to ensure their base of client-workers.

Did the *sindicato* bosses' use of language that formally called for the collective empowerment of peasants and workers then create opportunities for these non-elites to leverage these words and ideas for their actual empowerment? Was "discursive negation"—or the non-elite use of elite words, symbols, and logic in order to resist, challenge, or limit elite power—a weapon for the workers of Atlixco?[36] Several conditions appeared favorable for this practice. Not only did the *patrones* engage a language that validated workers' identity and rights, but the *sindicato* bosses depended on members to labor in the mills, to fight against challengers, to maintain community peace, and to support political candidates and causes identified by the bosses. Their ability to command these services from residents is what gave them such bargaining power with mill owners and national political brokers, but it also created a dependency on the residents' loyalty and compliance. Further, once the unions consolidated local authority, the inter-*sindicato* conflicts created potential vulnerabilities in pitting *patrones* against one another.

But ultimately, other factors negated or overpowered the possibilities created by these conditions, and worker and peasant options for active engagement of discursive negation remained limited. *Patrón* need for an obedient, supportive labor force, for example, was counteracted by the abundance of peasants desperate for wage-paying jobs throughout the regional countryside. Rural poverty, loss of landholdings, and growing needs for currency resulted in a steady in-migration of peasants, providing the vulnerable labor force that the bosses needed. For instance, sociologist Wilbert E. Moore recounted a time in the 1920s when some three hundred workers from the same village of Santa Ana Xalmimilulco were fired en masse from Metepec, but were soon replaced by other wage-seeking peasants. Moore documents the steady inflow of peasants through the 1940s.[37] The aggressive expansion of the CDT-CROM into the villages of the surrounding countryside, organizing peasant leagues and small vendor associations, also generated access to new laborers. The ready supply of available labor afforded the *sindicato* bosses greater license to enforce strictly their notions of *"disciplina"* by firing, exiling, or killing workers who presented intractable problems. The extensive *sindicato* systems of surveillance, vigilance, and police and military operations demanded a compliant behavior, magnified paranoia, and quickly snuffed potential threats to security. The intense inter-*sindicato* conflict may have allowed the rare bold individual with special knowledge (such as access to inner workings of rival *sindicatos*) or abilities (such as thuggery or gunslinging) to bargain for privileges (though this carried some obvious big risks), but it also drove *patrones* to intensify vigilance and violence and to clamp down on threats of challenge, dissent, or disorder.[38]

We know, however, that even during these times of greater direct use of coercion, workers actively engaged in independent thinking, and employed what James Scott has called "weapons of the weak" as defense against their employers and *sindicatos*. On the shop floor, for example, *textileros* developed personal bonds to warn one another about the arrival of a supervisor, played tricks on those suspected of pushing the work pace, created a nonverbal language of hand signals and body gestures to communicate through the factory din, learned to hide materials or debilitate equipment in order to create break times, protected one another when sneaking a sandwich or drink, and taught new workers to never be left alone with a *sindicato* supervisor, snitch on co-workers, or forget about the omnipresence of *sindicato* spies.[39] These practices, intended to be secret from the *sindicato* bosses and supervisors, reflected a collective awareness of the way that things should really be done—an awareness distinct from the rules imposed by the *sindicatos*. Further, when residents referred to Metepec as *"la Rusia chiquita,"* they were alluding to the *sindicato*'s expansive authoritarian rule in the region, control over all public services, unrelenting and stifling surveillance, strict enforcement of town discipline as well as its class-based official ideology, the "public transcript" of how *sindicato* power served workers' needs and interests. Their reference was a not-so-secret critique of *sindicato* power (and perhaps ideology), a "hidden transcript" of how power should work in Atlixco.[40]

This case is unsettling. All of the evidence leads me to agree that *sindicato* rule was not just stagnantly but increasingly authoritarian, repressive, coercive, and like a "little Russia." But (this is the troubling part), these patrons were workers who had wrested power from the landlords and company bosses and who had converted this power into, among other things, numerous material advances for workers and peasants. One might even argue that, following the Revolution and the triumph in local labor wars for recognition, several aspects of *previous* "hidden transcripts"—those critiquing the public discourse of rule by factory owners and landlords— had been uncovered and realized in the material and legal gains. Moreover, the emergent system was not the result of top-down, Soviet-style imposition of a "revolutionary" blueprint of ideology and structure, but was a homegrown network of domination that had rejected the attempts by outsiders, namely communists and the Cardenista state, to control the region. Though they would depend on external forces, such as federal labor law and political alliances, all of Atlixco's *patrones sindicales* had worked their way up through the ranks of factory work and *sindicato* service. Some were first-generation mill workers with agrarian roots; most continued to live in the modest dwellings of the *caserío*. They had close family who continued to labor in the mills.[41] These elites did not have to learn non-elite language or culture, nor adopt working-class deportment, because they were of this culture and behavior.

This fact certainly may have strengthened patronal rule in Atlixco, because the *sindicato* bosses were more adept at discerning the nature of residents' concerns, identifying subtle signs of resistance, and reading the hidden transcripts of the community. Historian Marjorie Becker has written about the Cardenistas' failed attempts to bring land-reform programs and socialist education to the state of Michoacán, and about local resistance, expressed largely through religious and cultural terms, to these outside influences. Though peasants effectively applied "weapons-of-the-weak" strategies, prolonged engagement in the *campesino* vs. Cardenista conflict led the state-makers to learn enough local culture to consolidate political rule there.[42] Similarly, the Cristero War of the 1920s had presented a conservative, religious discourse to defend local issues and challenge revolutionary hegemony.[43] Unlike areas where a conservative or reactionary language represented a grass-roots oppositional stance to the revolutionary state, the homegrown leaders of Atlixco activated a radical discourse to assert local autonomy, and *then* to integrate to national political structures.

This political integration informs our understanding of a third issue: the impact of popular struggles on state-formation. In their introductory essay to *Everyday Forms of State Formation*, Joseph and Nugent argue that state-formation is an ongoing, conflicted, negotiated "*cultural* process with manifest consequences in the material world," and, responding to the ideas of James Scott and others, emphasize the "processual nature" of popular culture that develops in the context of unequal power.[44] These ideas help us understand the Atlixco case in some ways. Local labor leaders negotiated the terms of their integration to the national state, battling with rival organizers and defeating CTM plans to take over the region. In the end, the Cardenistas had to accede to recognizing and working with these local leaders, and national political elites felt the repercussions of the negotiations. Puebla's governor in the late 1930s, Maximino Avila Camacho, had negotiated a mutual support deal with Don Antonio and other statewide CROM leaders, a deal that paved the way for Maximino's brother Manuel to rise in prominence and succeed Cárdenas as president of the republic in 1940. The conservative, often repressive *avilacamachista* political machine, in fact, retained control of the governorship from 1937 to 1959, and generated important national political players as well, including President Gustavo Díaz Ordaz (1964–70).[45] The ascendency of *avilacamachismo,* and the working relationship that the CDT-CROM had forged with these politicians ensured that Don Antonio and his cohorts would have access to state resources and power, including political positions. This access was a crucial force in allowing the Cámara to continue to consolidate and expand its domination in the region. The relationship forged between Atlixco's *sindicato* leaders and the national political apparatus, then, might be considered a "bottom-up" process of integration to the national state.

"Bottom-up" pressures no doubt influenced state-formation processes in postrevolutionary Mexico; but the relative strength of the Atlixco bosses represented neither a national pattern nor a unique case. As already mentioned in this essay, numerous regional *patrones* and caciques had adapted to the postrevolutionary political apparatus, negotiating the terms of their integration while shaping the meaning of the state.[46] From a top-down perspective, just as the Romans found different ways for colonies to adhere to the Empire, Cardenista statemakers implemented multifaceted, multi-textured, sometimes even contradictory strategies and solutions to patch together the fabric of a national state. Scott is correct, I think, in asserting, "The postrevolutionary Mexican state, though surely a child of the Enlightenment and of nineteenth-century views of scientific progress, was far less determined, it seems, than was Lenin to force a high-modernist, centralized, utopian grid on society at no matter what cost."[47] In the Mexican case, regional resistance and pressure had forced this approach on the state in numerous ways.

The meaning of the state, the terms of regional conflicts, and the relevance of radical symbolism were all dynamic forces, adapting and changing in response to one another, and to other developments over time. When the federal government moved decidedly to the right with Manuel Avila Camacho's presidency, the currency of leftist and radical language would seem to have fallen in value with national political brokers. Indeed, Communist Party officials and left-leaning labor leaders did face increasing persecution and isolation in the 1940s. The CTM, clearly in the state's favor during the Cárdenas administration, now faced exclusion from previous privileges, increasing pressure for political moderation, and renewed competition from rival confederations (including the national CROM) as the *avilacamachista* state engaged a "divide-and-rule" approach to labor.[48] Yet class-oriented language and symbols did not lose all meaning in this new political context. Though clearly conservative, and repressive of those considered "extremist," President Avila Camacho continued to make rhetorical overtures to political moderates and to the Mexican people. In Atlixco in the 1940s, CDT-CROM *sindicato* bosses suddenly found themselves in alliance with the conservative leadership of both statewide and national governments, yet continued to use revolutionary phrases and trademarks in their correspondence, announcements, and public oratory. This practice did little to scare off the *avilacamachistas,* who were well aware of the *sindicato* bosses' political pragmatism and commitment to maintaining local hegemony. It is highly unlikely that Atlixco's *sindicato* leaders used this radical, class-oriented language (unless in sarcasm) when communicating in private with *avilacamachista* politicians. Circumstances led the local bosses to a dual strategy of private discussions of political moderation with state and federal-level politicians, and continued public use of class-oriented references.[49]

At the same time that local and regional bosses were negotiating with the state, they were also negotiating—bashing, bending, nurturing, rigging, cajoling, pressuring, fixing, intimidating—a relationship with the workers and peasants of Atlixco. As presented in this essay, Atlixco's residents may have had independent thoughts, alternative notions of power, and cultural defense mechanisms, but the suffocating and violent enforcement of patronal expectations severely limited public or collective expression. Violators of patronal code were stifled, banished, or killed. For peasants, would-be workers, and veteran *textileros* and their families, there was very little room to "negotiate" or to bargain, even though the bosses were "pro-worker." This case is important for understanding state-formation because it tells us that these "middle" brokers, the *patrones sindicales* between the subalterns and the national statemakers, were central both in applying pressure upward to shape the terms of state-formation, and in pressing downward to exercise control and domination over the rural communities. These middle brokers were key to holding the state together, and gave real, everyday meaning to the state.

In many regards, from the point of view of the workers, peasants, and vulnerable in Atlixco, the *sindicato* functioned as the state. The postrevolutionary union had come to control the key institutions of public life in the region: government offices, entry to markets, police and military forces, public utilities and services, civic associations, as well as access to employment opportunities. There was no viable way to sidestep the *sindicato* and deal directly with statewide or national political brokers. Even when dissident *sindicato* bosses split from the CDT-CROM, they maintained very similar repressive relations with residents with parallel structures and ceremonies of power. These practices gave meaning to the state at this local level. Anecdotally, when I interviewed veteran workers who had experienced the years of *sindicato* formation and the inter-*sindicato* wars, it is not surprising that they could fill an ear with information and stories about Antonio J. Hernández and the leaders of their particular unions, but had little to say about statewide or national politicians. When I asked one worker his opinion of Lázaro Cárdenas, for example, he replied, "Was he one of the generals?" Though the practices, ideas, and language of the Cardenistas and other national politicians touched the lives of local residents, they did so only through the interpretation, manipulation, and practice of the middle brokers. Workers and peasants found meaning in the "state" through these brokers.

Notes

I thank Peter Beattie, David Cook, Timothy Henderson, David LaFrance, Debra O'Neal and Thomas Summerhill for their comments during the writing of this essay, as well as Florencia Mallon, Steve Stern, and the Latin American Labor History Conference collective for their ongoing engagement with and support for my work. Support from the James L. and Christine McMillan Spivey Endowed Instructorship at Wingate University aided in the writing of this essay. Errors are my own.

1. Much of the information and analysis of this section of this article draws from Gregory S. Crider, "Material Struggles: Workers' Strategies

during the 'Institutionalization of the Revolution' in Atlixco, Puebla, Mexico" (Ph.D. diss., University of Wisconsin-Madison, History, 1996), chap. 2. On textile production in Puebla, see Leticia Gamboa Ojeda, *Los empresarios de ayer: El grupo dominante en la industria textil de Puebla, 1906–1929* (Puebla: UAP, 1985), 25–34; Wil Pansters, *Politics and Power in Puebla: The Political History of a Mexican State, 1937–1987* (Amsterdam: CEDLA/Centro de Estudios y Documentación latinoamericanos, 1990), 36; Samuel Malpica, *Atlixco: Historia de la clase obrera* (Puebla: UAP, 1989), 50–56, 96–98; Dawn Keremitsis, *The Cotton Industry in Porfiriato Mexico, 1870–1910* (New York: Garland, 1987), 104; Juan Carlos Grosso, *Estructura productiva y fuerza de trabajo: Puebla, 1830–1890* (Puebla: UAP, 1984); and J. Francisco Javier Rodríguez Salazar and Vicente Carrera Alvarez, "Crisis y reestructuración en el ciclo fabril de algodón: Puebla/Atlixco, 1955–1976" (Tesis Mae., Economía, UAP, 1987), 37–60. See also Jan Bazant, "Evolución de la industria textil poblana (1554–1845)," *Historia mexicana* 13, no. 4 (1964): esp. 501–12; Guy P. C. Thomson, "Protectionism and Industrialization in Mexico, 1821–1854: The Case of Puebla," in *Latin America, Economic Imperialism and the State: The Political Economy of the External Connection from Independence to the Present,* ed. Christopher Abel and Colin M. Lewis (London: Athlone, 1985), 125–46.

2. Several authors liken "paternalistic" styles of *fábrica* owners to those of landlords. Keremitsis 1987, 186–200; Alan Knight, "The Working Class and the Mexican Revolution, c. 1900–1920," *Journal of Latin American Studies* 16, no. 1 (1984): 58–59; Rodney D. Anderson, *Outcasts in Their Own Land: Mexican Industrial Workers, 1906–1911* (Dekalb: Northern Illinois University Press, 1976), 76. See also Crider, "Material Struggles," 26–29. On the company housing complexes, see Rey Sánchez Cuamatzi, Emilio Sánchez Flores, Julio Sánchez Gracida, Evelio Rodríguez Jiménez, Andres A. Sánchez Hernández, José A. Morales López, and F. Faustino Salas Velasco, "Recuperación del Caserío obrero histórico de Metepec Atlixco Puebla" (Tesis Lic., Arquitectura, UAP, 1988), 38–42; "Reglamento de las casas del pueblo de la fábrica de Metepec" [CIASA], in Sánchez Cuamatzi et al., 40–41; Kilian Popp and Konrad Tyrakowski, "El Caserío Metepec/Atlixco: Sobre el desarrollo de una temprana instalación industrial en México," *Comunicaciones* (Puebla: Fundación Alemana para la Investigación Científica) 13 (1976): 33–34; S. Malpica, *Atlixco,* 59–60, 105–8, 128.

3. Gamboa, "La huelga textil de 1906–1907 en Atlixco," paper presented at VI Encuentro sobre el Desarrollo del Capitalismo en México

(CIHS-COMECSO, October 1987); S. Malpica, *Atlixco*, 61. On the labor-capital conflicts in Río Blanco and Cananea, see John M. Hart, *Anarchism and the Mexican Working Class, 1860–1911* (1978; reprint, Austin: University of Texas Press, 1987), 90–98; Bernardo García Díaz, *Un pueblo fabril del porfiriato: Santa Rosa, Veracruz* (Méx.: SEP/80; Fondo de Cultura Económica, 1981), esp. 87–155.

4. David G. LaFrance, *The Mexican Revolution in Puebla, 1908–1913: The Maderista Movement and the Failure of Liberal Reform* (Wilmington: Scholarly Resources, 1989), 79–81, 121–23; S. Malpica, *Atlixco*, 38–44, 73; John Womack Jr., *Zapata and the Mexican Revolution* (New York: Vintage, 1968), 85–86; Knight, "The Working Class," 66.

5. Nicolás R. Coca Cabrera, interviewed by Ma. Teresa Ventura Rodríguez, 14 January 1980, in *Boletín de Investigación del Movimiento Obrero* (*BIMO*) 10 (December 1987), 163–66; S. Malpica, *Atlixco*, 70–78; Favio Barbosa Cano, *La C.R.O.M. de Luis N. Morones a Antonio J. Hernández* (Pue: UAP, 1980), 9–12; Barry Carr, *El movimiento obrero y la política en México, 1910–1929* (1976; reprint, Méx.: Era, 1981), 88–93; Ma. Teresa Ventura Rodríguez, "Una central obrera de vanguardia en la región: La Confederación Sindicalista de obreros y campesinos del Estado de Puebla," *BIMO* 9 (February 1986): 117. See also CROM, "Declaración de principios y programa de la CROM," May 1918, Saltillo, Coah., in Barbosa Cano, 93–111; CROM, "Actas de las sesiones del tercer Congreso Obrero nacional efectuado en Saltillo, Coah., en el que se fundó la CROM," Saltillo, 1–12 May 1918, in Barbosa Cano, 113–34; and Alvaro Obregón, Luis N. Morones et al., "Pacto secreto entre Alvaro Obregón y los líderes de la CROM-PLM," Méx., 6 August 1919, in Barbosa Cano, 187–88.

6. See Crider, "Material Struggles," 39–41; Barbosa Cano, 25–28; S. Malpica, *Atlixco* 1980, 85–87.

7. Rafael Carrillo, interviewed by María Eugenia de Lara, 16 July 1979, Ciudad de México, Archivo de la Palabra del Instituto Mora, PHO/4/105, pp. 11–111; Donald C. Hodges, *Mexican Anarchism after the Revolution* (Austin: University of Texas Press, 1995), 22; Barbosa Cano, 15–18; S. Malpica, *Atlixco*, 164–65; Ventura Rodríguez, "Una central obrera," 117.

8. Some of these organizing efforts in Puebla and Veracruz during the early 1920s are chronicled in Arnoldo Martínez Verdugo, "Hacia el movimiento de masas," in *Historia del Comunismo en México*, ed. Martínez Verdugo (México, D.F.: Grijalbo, 1985), 65–89.

9. Historian Samuel Malpica notes that, beginning in late 1926 and through 1928, Lombardo Toledano and other CROM leaders visited Atlixco to expel opponents from the Confederación and to ban communist newspapers. S. Malpica, *Atlixco*, 142–65; Julio Gómez (Ramírez-Rosovski), interview with Arnoldo Martínez Verdugo, 1978, excerpted in "Testimonio de un dirigente comunista," *Memoria: Boletín del CEMOS* 10 (May–June 1985): 241; "La obra de los rompehuelgas en los estados de Puebla y Tlaxcala," *El Machete* (PCM), no. 37, 18 May 1925, in Barbosa Cano, 285–87; Estela Munguía Escamilla, "La situación económica del magisterio poblano en los años 20," *BIMO* 11 (March 1988): 49–53; Ventura Rodríguez, "Una central obrera," 117–18; S. Malpica, *Atlixco*, 152–53; Barbosa Cano, 31–32. See also Estela Munguía, "Acerca de la Confederación Sindicalista del Estado de Puebla (CSEP-CROM)," *BIMO* 4 (August 1982): 137–38.

10. Julio Ramírez, "La actividad de los comunistas durante 1926–1928," *BIMO* 11 (March 1988): 144–48; Ramírez, "Autobiografía de Julio Gómez (Ramírez)" [8 October 1984] in *BIMO* 8 (March 1985): 171–74; Ramírez, interviewed by Ma. Teresa Ventura Rodríguez, 13 December 1979, in "Entrevista al Compañero Julio Ramírez," *BIMO* 9 (February 1986): 139–40; S. Malpica, *Atlixco*, 143–54. See also Jesús Márquez Carrillo, "Los orígenes del avilacamachismo. Una arqueología de fuerzas en la constitución de un poder regional: El Estado de Puebla (1929–1941)" (Tesis Lic., Historia, UAP, 1983), 217–18.

11. See Crider, "Material Struggles," 44–46; M. T. de la Peña, *La industria textil de algodón: Crisis, salarios, contratación* (Méx.: Sindicato Nacional de Economistas, 1938), 22–24.

12. De la Peña, 22–24.

13. See Nicolás R. Coca, interviewed by Ma. Teresa Ventura Rodríguez, 14 January 1980, in "Entrevista al Sr. Nicolás R. Coca." *BIMO* 10 (December 1987): 173; Barbosa Cano, 31–37; Lucia Alvarez Mosso and Ma. Luisa González Marin, *Industria Textil, Tecnología y Trabajo* (Méx.: Instituto de Investigaciones Económicas, UNAM, 1987), 127; Crider, "Material Struggles," 46–48.

14. Julio Gómez (Ramírez) interview, 1978 [1985], 242–46; Ramírez interview, 1979 [1986], 142–43; Ventura Rodríguez, "Una central obrera," 118–19; S. Malpica, *Atlixco*, 154–58; Hodges, 23. See also N. Coca interview 1980 [1987], 171; Barbosa Cano, 40.

15. Sánchez Cuamatzi et al., 42; De la Peña, 35–50.

16. Juan Cuautle Benítez, "El caserío obrero en Metepec, su fábrica y su sindicato (Un homenaje a los compañeros que dejaron su vida al pie

de la máquina)," in Luis Felipe Crespo Oviedo (Coord.), *"Los días eran nuestros . . .": Vida y Trabajo Entre los Obreros Textiles de Atlixco: Relatos obreros* (Pue.: Secretaría de Educación Pública, Dirección General de Culturas Populares/UAP/IMSS, 1988), 31–37; "Bases que regirán a la Colonia Obrera 'Guadalupe Victoria,' Fábrica de Metepec 1936" in Sánchez Cuamatzi et al., 44–45; Author's interview with Delfino S., Metepec, 2 June 1989. See also Popp and Tyrakowski, 34–35; Sánchez Cuamatzi et al., 42–45, 72–74, 120.

17. See Crider, "Material Struggles," 56–59.

18. Jesús Cerrillo H., "Actitud y Pensamiento: Ensayo Biográfico (Sindicato de Obreros Perseverantes de la Fábrica 'El León')," in *Los días . . .* , 251–65. All translations are by the author.

19. Mexican *sindicatos* typically chose names to represent some central ideal or organizing concept. Other *sindicatos* of textile workers in the state of Puebla named themselves for "Social Emancipation," "Labor and Justice," "Unity Creates Power," "Socialist Workers," "First of May," "Sindicato Democracy," and for historical heroes, such as the Chicago Martyrs, the Martyrs of January 7 (Orizaba radical labor organizers killed by Porfirian troops), Ricardo Flores Magón (the radical anti-Porfirian journalist and activist), and Aquiles Serdán (revolutionary martyr from Puebla). For a sampling of the names of many of the *sindicatos* across the republic, see "Sindicato de la industria textil," Archivo General de la Nación (AGN), Presidentes/Manuel Avila Camacho, exp. 151/7 [1942] published in *Boletín del AGN* 12 (1980): 42–50.

20. Some local *sindicatos* broke away from the Cámara in the early 1930s and challenged the CDT-CROM control of the region until reunification was achieved in the 1940s, formally in 1948. In another work, I examine this conflict closely and argue that, in essence, this struggle was about *sindicato* bosses fighting for "turf," and not over ideological issues. The inter-*sindicato* conflict then resulted in an intensification of repression of workers and peasants, not in an opportunity for workers to play these *sindicato* elites off one another. See Crider, "Material Struggles," especially chapters 5 and 6.

21. Archivo Municipal de Atlixco (AMA), Caja Presidencia: Margarito Hidalgo (SG) et al., CDT-CROM manifesto (s.n.), Atlixco, June 1933; Comisión de Orientación Social de CDT-CROM, "Invitación" (s.n.), Atlixco, December 1934; CDT-CROM manifesto (s.n.), Atlixco, May 1939.

22. Short of actually visiting the museum, one may consult the catalog to study some of its features. Luis Felipe Crespo Oviedo (Coord.), *"Los días eran nuestros . . ." Vida y Trabajo Entre los Obreros Textiles de Atlixco: Catálogo del museo obrero de Metepec* (Pue.: Secretaría de Educación Pública, Dirección General de Culturas Populares/UAP/IMSS, 1988).

23. For a few examples of the variety of regional patronage systems that survived and/or flourished during this period, see Mark Wasserman, *Persistent Oligarchs: Elites and Politics in Chihuahua, Mexico, 1910–1940* (Durham, N.C.: Duke University Press, 1993); Dudley Ankerson, *Agrarian Warlord: Saturnino Cedillo and the Mexican Revolution in San Luis Potosí* (DeKalb: Northern Illinois University Press, 1984), esp. 139–42; Wil Pansters, *Politics and Power in Puebla: The Political History of a Mexican State, 1937–1987* (Amsterdam: CEDLA, 1990), esp. 40–45; Heather Fowler-Salamini, "Revolutionary Caudillos in the 1920s: Francisco Múgica and Alberto Tejeda," in *Caudillo and Peasant in the Mexican Revolution,* ed. David Brading (Cambridge: Cambridge University Press, 1980), 169–92, esp. 190–92; Ramona Falcón, "Military *Caciques* in Magnificence and Decline: San Luis Potosí in the Mexican Revolution," in *Region, State and Capitalism in Mexico: Nineteenth and Twentieth Centuries,* ed. Wil Pansters and Arij Ouweneel (Amsterdam: CEDLA/Centre for Latin American Research and Documentation, 1989), 91–109; Carlos Martínez Assad, "La rebelión cedillista o el ocaso del poder tradicional," *Revista Mexicana de Sociología* 41, no. 3 (1979): 709–28; Raymond Buve, "Peasant Movements, Caudillos and Land Reform during the Revolution in Tlaxcala, Mexico (1910–1917)," *Boletín de Estudios Latinoamericanos y del Caribe* 18 (1975): 112–52.

24. I have written about the political impact of contrasting *sindicato* boss styles more extensively in Crider, "Good *Patrón* and Bad *Patrón*: Tracing the Origins of Political Authority in the Textile Mill Communities of Revolutionary Mexico," paper presented to Conference on Latin American History, Seattle, January 1998.

25. Issues of *sindicato* discipline as well as shop-floor organization and social relations are discussed in Crider, "Material Struggles," chap. 3.

26. For a broader, historical analysis of these rituals, see William H. Beezley, Cheryl English Martin, and William E. French, "Introduction: Constructing Consent, Inciting Conflict" in *Rituals of Rule, Rituals of Resistance: Public Celebrations and Popular Culture in Mexico,* ed. Beezley, Martin, and French (Wilmington: Scholarly Resources, 1994), xiii–xxxii.

27. This general description of the public ceremony of patronal domination draws from previously cited interviews, as well as from the photographs and reports published in the *sindicato*-friendly, statewide
daily newspaper *La Opinión,* during the years 1934–1940. See, for examples, the paper's coverage of May Day events: *La Opinión,* 3 May
1934, 3 May 1935, 3 May 1936, 3 May 1937, 3 May 1938.

28. Crider, "Material Struggles," 77–78. The meeting description is com-
piled from author's interview with Pedro H., 17 September 1989; author's interview with Delfino S., 2 June 1989; author's interview with
Willehado E. C., 30 May 1989, Metepec; author's interview with
Manuel C., 5 February 1990, Los Molinos, Atlixco, Pue.; Dante del
Moral F. (Marcos Lezama), "Había una vez un hombre," in *Los días
. . . ,* 184–88; José Solís Moreno, "Tienen fama los del Carmen," *Los
días . . . ,* 14–16. See also Francisco Javier Gómez Carpinteiro, "Proceso
de trabajo y sindicato en una fábrica textil en Atlixco" (Thesis, Anthropology, UAP, 1988), 210–13; and Emanuel Orozco Núñez, "La
Comuna de Atlixco: La comunidad sindical, composición e interac-
ción de sus campose sociales integradores" (Thesis, Social Anthropology, UAP, [1989?]), 117–21.

29. Gómez, 210–11. Author's translation.

30. Gilbert M. Joseph and Daniel Nugent, "Popular Culture and State
Formation in Revolutionary Mexico," in *Everyday Forms of State Formation: Revolution and the Negotiation of Rule in Modern Mexico,* ed. Joseph
and Nugent (Durham, N.C.: Duke University Press, 1994), 20.

31. On the formation of the CTM and its relationship to Cardenismo, see
Kevin J. Middlebrook, *The Paradox of Revolution: Labor, the State, and
Authoritarianism in Mexico* (Baltimore: Johns Hopkins University Press,
1995), 74–90; Arnaldo Córdova, *En una época de crisis (1928–1934),* 5th
ed. (México: Siglo XXI, 1989 [1980]), 38–43, 171–74; Barry Carr, *El
movimiento obrero y la política en México, 1910–1929* (México: Era, 1981
[1976]), 241–65; Carr, *Marxism and Communism in Twentieth-Century
Mexico* (Lincoln: University of Nebraska Press, 1992), 43–49; Alicia
Hernández Chávez, *Historia de la Revolución Mexicana, 1934–1940: La
mecánica cardenista* (México: El Colegio de México, 1981), 123–27;
Samuel León and Ignacio Marván, *En el cardenismo, 1934–1940* (México: Siglo XXI, 1985), 162–70; Virginia López Villegas-Manjarrez, *La
CTM vs. otras organizaciones obreras* (México: El Caballito, 1983), 20–22.

32. On the local inter-*sindicato* conflict, see Crider "*La División:* Beginning
to Assess the Multiple Meanings and Strategies for Dealing with the
Intersindicato Conflict in Atlixco, Mexico, 1920–1948," paper

presented to Latin American Labor History Conference, Duke University, 1997.

33. Roderic Ai Camp, *Mexican Political Biographies, 1935–1993*, 3d ed. (Austin: University of Texas Press, 1995), 348. See also Barbosa Cano, 56–88.

34. The responses are drawn from interviews that I conducted, and from the first-hand interviews and stories collected in *Los días*. . . . The responses are documented in Crider, "Material Struggles," esp. 345–66.

35. Osorio unexplainedly uses "I" for Hernández's middle initial throughout the story. Juan Osorio in *Los días* . . . , 285.

36. This discussion clearly draws from James C. Scott, *Weapons of the Weak: Everyday Forms of Peasant Resistance* (New Haven: Yale University Press, 1985), esp. chaps. 7 and 8. For example, Scott argues, "The dominant ideology can be turned against its privileged beneficiaries not only because subordinate groups develop their own interpretations, understandings, and readings of its ambiguous terms, but also because of the promises that the dominant classes must make to propagate it in the first place" (338).

37. Wilbert E. Moore, *Industrialization and Labor: Social Aspects of Economic Development* (Ithaca, N.Y.: Cornell University Press, 1951), 272–81.

38. Crider, "Material Struggles," chap. 3.

39. Ibid., esp. 133–39; Orozco, 110–11, 171–80; Gómez, 118–53.

40. Scott, *Domination and the Arts of Resistance: Hidden Transcripts* (New Haven: Yale University Press, 1990). The "*Rusia chiquita*" reference also reversed the official discourse of the *sindicato* leaders, who, as the Cold War progressed, blamed more problems on Communist influences. For example, in 1954, official CDT-CROM literature blamed disturbances in the Atlixco countryside on the prominent national leader of the Communist party, Valentín Campa, and his attempts "to implant soviet doctrines in the region." *Memoria de los trabajos ejecutados por el Comité Central de la CROM, 1953–1955* (México: CROM, 1955), 183–84.

41. Antonio J. Hernández's brother Cándido, for instance, perhaps enjoyed some privileges not accessible to those residents unrelated to the CDT-CROM boss, but he lived and worked in Metepec for most of his adult life. Author's interview with Cándido Hernández, Metepec, 7 June 1989.

42. Becker addresses Scott's analytical tools directly. Marjorie Becker, "Cardenistas, Campesinos, and the Weapons of the Weak: The Limits of Everyday Resistance in Michoacán, Mexico, 1934–1940," *Peasant*

Studies 16, no. 4 (1989): 233–50. See also Becker, "Torching La Purísima, Dancing at the Altar: The Construction of Revolutionary Hegemony in Michoacán, 1934–1940," in *Everyday Forms*, ed. Joseph and Nugent, 247–64; Becker, *Setting the Virgin on Fire: Lázaro Cárdenas, Michoacán Peasants, and the Redemption of the Mexican Revolution* (Berkeley: University of California Press, 1995).

43. The Cristero War, 1926–29, was a multiclass, conservative, cleric-led uprising that challenged the revolutionary state's authority to impose land reform and socialist education. Alan Knight assesses the Cristero War in the broader context of popular culture and peasant resistance. See Knight, "Weapons and Arches in the Mexican Revolutionary Landscape," in *Everyday Forms*, ed. Joseph and Nugent, 47–53.

44. Joseph and Nugent, "Popular Culture," *Everyday Forms*, ed. Joseph and Nugent, 13–22 [emphasis in the original]. On state-formation, the authors are specifically drawing from analysis in Philip Corrigan and Derek Sayer, *The Great Arch: English State Formation as Cultural Revolution* (Oxford: Basil Blackwell, 1985).

45. Pansters, 51–52; Stephen R. Niblo, *Mexico in the 1940s: Modernity, Politics, and Corruption* (Wilmington: Scholarly Resources, 1999), 76–79.

46. The essays in Joseph and Nugent's volume document a wide range of ways that regional forces shaped state-formation. Regional and "bottom-up" perspectives have complicated previous understandings of the so-called "corporatist" practices of the Mexican state.

47. Scott, "Foreword," in *Everyday Forms*, ed. Joseph and Nugent, x.

48. Niblo, 96–103.

49. David LaFrance suggested in personal correspondence that I consider the possibility of this dual (and duplicitous) strategy once the conservative *avilacamachista* regime came to power in the 1940s. See also Niblo, chap. 2, "Avila Camacho's Moderation."

Seeds of Subversion?
A New-World Plant and Agrarian Change in
Two Peasant-Based Empires, 1500–1999

James C. McCann

The opening of sustained contact across the Atlantic Ocean at the end of the fifteenth century set in train a number of significant exchanges in political economy and ecology, as well as the conceptual reframing of cultural universes throughout the greater Atlantic world. The Mediterranean "lake" of the classical world quickly lost its pivotal position and became a part of a periphery marginalized in both economic and intellectual terms. Part of the fallout from that change was a *weltanschauung* that had to accommodate a conceptual New World and material life wrought by the transfer of new configurations of political ecology on opposite sides of the Atlantic basin and beyond. The notion of "Transatlantic Radicals" thus needs to be defined broadly. It comprised, at least in part, a conglomeration of new ideas, new economies of labor, and the new possibilities based in the adoption of new foods, new crops, and their transformation of Old World agrarian systems. If the struggles were human, the weapons were often technology in the form of seeds and new forms of agronomy.

The purpose of this article is to examine comparatively the responses of two Old World agrarian empire systems to the effects of a singular New World stimulus, the food crop *Zea mays* (maize or corn). How did Old World peasant farmers respond to this new food source, and how did overarching empire states set the terms of their response to it in the critical two centuries following Columbus? The two empire systems posed here are the *terraferma* territories of northeast Italy's Venetian Republic, and the Ethiopian Solomonic Empire located in the northern highlands of the Ethiopian region of northeast Africa.

On the surface, these two agrarian empires appear quite different. Venice had its base in a commercial empire, but was returning to sink new roots in its agricultural hinterland. Ethiopia's foundations were embedded within highland dryland farming and extractions of exotic goods from its neighboring lowland zones in the south and west. But both systems shared a base in smallholder agriculture dependent on the oxen-drawn plow. The two imperial systems lay at opposite ends of the pre-Columbian Mediterranean world, and reflected the economic and spiritual influence of a Roman trade hegemony and the intellectual legacy of Eastern Christendom.[1] While radically different in terms of ecology, forms of social property, commercial context, and political culture, these two systems nonetheless shared an economic base in smallholder agriculture and the social milieu of peasant households. Maize adoption offers an interesting comparative lens.

My intent in this article is to suggest some terms of comparison to explore the relevant historical sources, rather than to be definitive, dogmatic, or reductionist in a theoretical sense. Examining the adoption of and response to maize as a crop and potential food source within the elite and peasant cultures of these two imperial systems may bring into sharp relief some fundamental historical truths about the broader terms of change in agrarian social and economic systems. In this case, the comparison will focus on conceptions of property, state relations to rural production, ideal conceptions of family and inheritance, and the links between past patterns and twentieth-century agrarian life. The historical records are limited in scope, and to a degree the poverty of the sources shapes the directions of the inquiry itself. This paper thus seeks to open a historical inquiry and to reconstruct the arrival of maize. It also will use that encounter as a lens from which to examine the changing world of these agrarian empires.

Radical Change in the Old World

The sixteenth and seventeenth centuries brought changes in economic and intellectual domains in the wider Mediterranean world that required responses from both peasant farmers and elite classes. The responses to maize by elite cultures emerge in historical sources in terms that are aesthetic, pragmatic, and sublime. But the symbols of the *mundus novus* also expressed themselves quite differently in the world of the cultivator, the part-time merchant, and the local cleric. The miller's gate, the brewer's hut, or bustling regional marketplaces were locations for the exchange of ideas— places that Carlo Ginzburg metaphorically describes as including "the soft ground muddied by the piss of the village mules." This evocative agrarian image suggests terms of comparison in peasant culture that pertain as much to the ambiance of my fieldwork interviews and participant observation in rural Ethiopia as they do to the archived traces of life in sixteenth-century Italy. In such muddied places, peasant intellectuals like Ginzburg's irascible miller, Menocchio, "must have talked about many things."[2] Though the paucity of historical sources leaves much to our imagination, these "things" must have included the exchange of news between neighbors and kinsmen about new crops, as well as new ideas about the extent of God's universe, the properties of curious new seeds, the excessive intervention of landlords into farmer business. It seems likely that farmers in Italy and in Ethiopia alike may have been curious about the new food crop and experimented with it out of sight of their elite overlords. The results were in one case almost immediate adoption, and in the other case a long-delayed but no less radical outcome.

Maize as a Transatlantic Radical

The Old World in general was, for maize, a *tabula rasa*. The importation of maize seeds into particular countries in the Eastern Hemisphere generally went unremarked, though it certainly was not unremarkable. Maize arrived in both northeast Italy and Ethiopia shortly after 1500 as part of the massive global ecological and demographic transformation that historian Alfred Crosby called the "Columbian Exchange."[3] There is, however, little documentary evidence of what must have been a conscious process of Europeans and Africans introducing this botanical curiosity to elite gardens or to peasant farmers' fields. Those who either assume a peasant agency or expect patrician innovation will, equally, find little to document their assertions.

Luckily, we can surmise a likely chronology for the first arrival of maize seeds into particular Old World farming systems, describe the nature of the farms' political ecology, and offer educated guesses about the agronomic personality of the maize types that first presented themselves as an economic option. Maize expresses its own history in its genetic makeup, its varieties and land races, its agronomic imperatives, its qualities as food, and its own peculiar symbiosis with its human hosts and the land they inhabit. If its documentary historical record is often maddeningly elusive, it is evident nonetheless that maize is extraordinarily versatile, both shaping and taking the shape of the farms and societies that cultivate it. By knowing the plant's genetic endowments and agronomic idiosyncrasies, we can read nuances (and even describe the evidence of dramatic historical shifts) into the disappointingly bare formal historical record.

As a food plant, maize has a split personality, appearing in diets in some times and places as a vegetable crop in the garden, and at other historical venues cultivated in the field as a grain. On a farm, it can be either or both. As a household garden crop, farmers can eat maize fresh at its green, milky stage; as dried kernels soaked, then boiled as a snack; or roasted on the cob. As a field crop, farmers broadcast seeds onto prepared plots and harvest dried ears; wives, young women, or the village miller then grind its kernels for flour.

In a strict nutritional and physiological sense, maize is a vegetable rather than a grain, offering vitamins A, C, and E (one of the ways in which a vegetable is defined nutritionally), but lacking the lower B vitamins that characterize a true grain such as sorghum, barley, or wheat. Corn is high in carbohydrates but low in useable protein, especially vital amino acids lysine and tryptophan; its leucine blocks absorption of niacin, a vitamin whose absence causes protein deficiency.[4] When sown as a field crop, however, maize deceptively takes the mantle of a grain, often replacing true grains like wheat, rice, sorghum, or millet in smallholder farming systems.

As a grain crop, maize yields more food per unit of land and labor than any other. Yet, to those Old World farmers seduced by maize's obvious virtues in yield, corn has also revealed a darker side. It is highly sensitive to deprivation of water, sunlight, and nitrogen; it rots easily in tropical storage. Even a few days of drought at its time of tasseling can halve the crop's yield. Thus, maize crops are extremely vulnerable to environmental shocks, especially drought, and may impoverish the bodies of those who depend too heavily on it for food, resulting in protein deficiency diseases such as pellagra and kwashiorkor. The end result is that when they plant maize, commercial farmers and peasant families alike walk a slender tightrope of risk.

Plant biology gives distinctive insights into maize's agronomic and historical personality. Like house mice, English sparrows, and *Anopheles gambiae* mosquitoes, maize requires human presence to survive. Unlike self-pollinating grain equivalents, such as wheat and rice, maize must cross-pollinate, and depends on humans to collect, select, and sow its seeds. By type, the first maize seeds that reached Old World farmers were generally Caribbean "flint" maizes, characterized by their hard starches, relatively longer storage capacity, and early maturity. Like most maize types, flint maizes also varied by the color of the kernels, height of the plant, and the shape of its husks. Flint maizes also generally were hardier than other types, and were the types first to adapt to colder North American sites, such as New England and the Midwest, or to the new ecological niches of highland Ethiopia and northeast Italy.

The Venetian Agrarian World

In the year 1500, the Venetian geographer Amerigo Vespucci used the title *mundus novus* (New World) in a treatise describing the new lands of the Western hemisphere reported to Europe by the Genovese sailor Christophe Colombo. Vespucci's intended reference was not merely to geography; he sought to invoke a metaphor connoting abundance, the sublime, and endless possibilities. To the more perceptive of Venice's patricians and mercantile class, the term had a special ring of irony. As perhaps the world's most globally aware merchants, Venetians must also have been the first to recognize that the opening of the Atlantic and Indian oceans to European commerce sounded the death knell of their own knowledge-based prosperity.[5]

Over the epoch from the sixteenth to the eighteenth century, Venice progressively lost its international grasp with the loss of the grain trade and the decline of its Eastern trade hegemony to the Dutch and the Portuguese respectively. With its declining mercantile monopoly within the eastern Mediterranean, its increasingly unprofitable industrial/artisanal economy, and a collapse of prices in the grain trade, Venice turned inward to its own *terraferma* in Veneto, Friuli, and Lombardy as the site for conservative investment in landed estates, where Venetians rediscovered a peasant economy they could exploit to serve as a tax base and as a guarantee of their own food supply.[6]

The political ecology of agriculture in northern Italy in the sixteenth century, however, held within itself an essential disequilibrium. Its property systems pitted estate owners' interests in controlling landholdings and rights of income against peasants' struggles for security of subsistence and tenure. Moreover, the agronomy of the cereal staple wheat was unstable as a food and taxable commodity. One of the New World's most profound agents of change in northeastern Italy in this epoch was a new plant that appeared initially here and there in Venetian gardens, herbaria, and in frescoes in hunting lodges and ducal palaces. Maize emerged in the New World first as a curiosity sown singly in household gardens in Venice and hinterland, but by the eighteenth century had become a staple crop overwhelmingly occupying pride of place in Lombardy and Veneto agricultural fields. The farms of northeastern Italy at the opening of the sixteenth century were to be the locus of significant agronomic change in the next two hundred years.

Before 1500, the agriculture of northeast Italy stood foursquare within the European political economy of winter wheat, supplemented by *"biade minute"* (minor cereal crops such as rye, sorghum, and millet) that fit awkwardly into crop rotations with winter wheat and local food needs. Wheat was king among the Europe's food crops, and the wheat bread made from northern Europe's soft winter wheat counted as the symbol ("daily bread") as well as the substance (wheat bread was the primary foodstuff in the region) of well-being. In most of Europe, soft bread wheat was the primary grain, though the bread of Italian towns by the seventeenth century was often blackened by imported Baltic rye when wheat crops failed. For the peasants of northern Italy, wheat was also a symbol of authority that served as the required medium for in-kind tax remittances to the state and rent payments to the landlord.[7]

The tyranny of wheat as the principal grain also lay in its precarious agronomy. Planted in October/November and harvested in late spring/summer, winter wheat was highly sensitive to fluctuations in temperature and moisture. The minor cereal crops—the *biade minute*—could not challenge wheat's dominant role either agriculturally or symbolically. Rye was an alternative and agronomically safer cold-climate cereal crop, but had too low a yield and fetched too unrewarding a price to attract farmers or their landlords to cultivate it extensively. Summer crops of

African origin, like sorghum and millet, could not reach maturity within the few months between wheat's spring harvest and fall sowing, or double cropping, and thus could not easily fit a regular crop-rotation pattern. Both crops were highly vulnerable to bird damage; millets were primarily livestock forage. Moreover, in Italy's Po Valley, wheat was restricted to the limited cropland immune to the spring flooding of the region's low-lying plains. Some of the seasonally flooded alluvial soils had already been given over to northern Italy's distinctive rice cultivation.

Agriculture in northeast Italy—especially in the Po River valley—was a historically dynamic system linked to both urban markets and estate management, but constrained by a fundamental bottleneck of crop-livestock integration. Most seasonally flooded land provided only a single harvest, after which the plot served as summer pasture and a limited source of hay for winter stall-feeding of cattle.[8] Because winter wheat occupied land that might otherwise serve as winter pasture for livestock (both draft animals and dairy herds), farmers had to transfer livestock to winter pasture in Alpine foothills. Thus, Po Valley farms annually lost a quarter of their precious manure. Farms in the plains of Lombardia, the coastal flood plains of Veneto, and upland zones around the Alto Adige subalpine region each had to deal with the vicious cycle of poor feed for livestock, the shortage of manure to maintain soil fertility, and the need to produce marketable cereal crops, especially wheat. At the same time, annual crop production had to provide the food and economic sustenance needed to support investment in perennial non-staple crops—such as wine grapes, mulberry leaves (for silk production), olives, and fruit trees—that helped sustain upland area economies.

At the center of this production paradox was a simultaneous need for human food and livestock forage. Breaking this cycle required an expansion of livestock forage and the utilization of seasonally flooded lands that could not support wheat production. The systematic harnessing of water and the transformation of lowland wetlands from seasonal flood plains to arable fields was one key to the cultivation of both winter wheat and summer crops. As early as the twelfth century, the systematic harvesting and management of water had begun on a small scale by Cistercian monks in the western Po Valley, south and east of Milan. By the sixteenth century, large portions of the low plain were irrigated, and seasonally flooded lands were under flood-control schemes designed and financed by urban capital and civil engineers. This technological change and economic investment combined urban capital, rural labor, and specialized engineering expertise to transform the relationship between nature and human economy. The use of urban commercial capital to create, in effect, new cropland under direct control of the urban investors increased landlord leverage over peasants who depended on contract terms for their access to land.

Over the course of the sixteenth- to nineteenth-century epoch, an increasing percentage of such reclaimed land moved into the regional agricultural economy, converting it to an integrated agricultural system of annual cereals (wheat, rice), livestock, perennial vineyards, and tree crops. The early practice of stall-feeding of livestock in Lombardy and Veneto also fostered local markets for livestock forage. Yet, demographic pressure simultaneously pushed agriculture onto marginal lands that required early-maturing crops (to avoid spring floods) and an increasing availability of fertilizer (manure from domestic livestock).[9] Peasants surmised much more quickly than complacent, conservative estate holders that the adoption of maize would cut this Gordian knot and offer some radical alternatives to the structure of the agrarian economy.

Maize in the Garden:
The Sublime and the Pragmatic

The opening of the New World constituted something of a spiritual and economic apotheosis for the northern Mediterranean and its heart at Venice. The news of the New World had showed literate Venetians the figurative handwriting on the wall. Patrician families in Venice thus began to launch new investments in rural holdings on the Italian mainland that seemed safer than mercantile voyages. Those investments consisted of water management and rural estates that extended Venetian control over rural lands and opened new year-round production.

Italy's Po Valley occupies a plain that extends north and south of 45 degrees North latitude—i.e., the same latitude as the U.S. corn belt. Moisture—the usual "limiting factor" for maize cultivation—is not an issue in the Po Valley, because the presence of the Alps and Piedmont to the north creates high humidity as well as a source of water for riverine and canal irrigation. The temperature range of both the plains and the hills of the regions of the *terraferma* falls well within the range suitable to maize.

Evidence of maize's first arrival in Italy is sketchy at best. In his compendium volume on maize in Italy, *Il mais e la vita rurale Italiana*, Luigi Messedaglia states that a certain Venetian diplomat, Andrea Navagero, visited a Spanish botanist, Giambattisi Ramusio, in the 1520s and saw maize cultivated. On his return to Venice, Navagero carried some maize seeds, most probably some of the Cuban Caribbean red flint that Columbus had first brought to Seville after his second voyage. This maize was cultivated in Polesine (southwest of Venice) by 1554.[10]

Maize formed part of a new economic beginning that had representations in the aesthetic world of the late Renaissance even before it appeared in its gardens and on its farm tables. As early as 1515, Giovanni della Robbia's terra cotta sculpture "Tentazione di Adamo" depicted a scene at the moment of Adam's fall in a imaginative Garden of Eden that contains images of maize plants within an exotic Eden. At the geographic and spiritual heart of Venice, the Palazzo Ducale in Piazza San Marco, the marble decorations on the canal portal constructed c. 1550 (directly below the "Bridge of Sighs") contain several ears of maize sculpted among the overall cornucopial theme of familiar fruits and vegetables. Finally, among the bucolic frescoes (c. 1540) decorating the walls of the hunting lodge of the Emo Capitilista family in the Colli Euganei (Euganean Hills, Venice's rural hinterland) are several ears of green maize, placed among images of fruits and vegetables decorating an internal doorway.[11] The early presence of maize as an iconographic symbol of abundance and exoticism suggests an expanding world view within the Venetian consciousness, at the same time as it asserts the elites' myopic view of maize as an exotic vegetable, rather than the dietary staple cereal it was to become.

A deeper and more profound indication of the cognitive adoption of maize within Italy is the variety and subtlety of regional and dialectal names used historically for the plant and its food products. We can read these names for insights into peasant perceptions of maize, in direct contrast to the esoteric elite views of maize in representational art. As in other world areas, the names ascribed to maize reflect some combination of its resemblance to known crops—especially sorghum (*sorgo*) or wheat (*frumento* or *grano*)—with perceptions of its provenance (*turco, moriscu, Indie, moro, Sicilia, saraceno*) or its appearance (*rosso, zalla,* i.e., red and yellow). One agricultural dictionary cited by Messedaglia offers a motley lexicon of names for maize: *formentone, frumentone, granoturco, sorgo turco, grano d'India, grano siciliano, grano di Roma, melgone, melicone melica, meliga, miglio zaburro, formentazzo, melgotto, melicotto, carlone, madonnino, polenta.* He also lists the words for maize in seventy-four regional dialects, including the Venetian dialect's *zalla* (i.e., *giallo*, yellow); *soturco* (from *sorgo turco* or Turkish sorghum); and *strepolin.*[12] The standard modern Italian generic terms for maize, *granoturco* and *mais,* are today dominant, though local dialectal terms for different varieties are still quite common.

Along with the historical value of the naming of maize by its peasant hosts, there is considerable historical insight derived from understanding the personality and characteristics of the maize itself. What arrived in Veneto and the Po Valley in the early sixteenth century was a maize type that reflected the ecological history of New World maize and the nature of the trade network that linked the eastern Caribbean to the Mediterranean—i.e., a Caribbean red flint maize type descended from the seeds brought by Columbus to Seville. Flint maize behaves in a way quite distinct from the more common modern "dent" varieties in that it has a shorter growing season, and has a harder starch endosperm that meant longer storage capacity and a higher milling fraction (more flour per unit under hand-milling) than other varieties. In Italy, the classic flint corns were the ancestors of the maize used still for polenta (i.e., human consumption), and which predated the modern hybrid "dent" varieties that arrived in the late 1940s and serve primarily as livestock feed (see below).

Northeast Italy's historical varieties of maize were all flints distinguished by their early maturity and hardiness. *"Cinquentino"* was the most common descendant of the Caribbean flint imports, named because of its 50-day maturity.[13] *"Quarantino"* was another classic flint variety that matured, reportedly, in only 40 days. *Marano* (a version of *cinquentino*) had distinctive red kernels that produced an orange-tinged polenta that was the staple of many generations of Veneto *contadini*, and may have been the type of maize that peasants originally called *"sorgo rosso."*[14]

In addition to its cultural and symbolic roles, maize moved steadily in its first hundred years from a minor curiosity to a major field crop and source of rural food in the late sixteenth and early seventeenth century. Though only obliquely appearing in historical records, this transformation of the cropping system and food-ways of peasant farmers was an important struggle played out within the agrarian political ecology of northeast Italy. Extant tenant contracts in the Venetian empire make it clear that landlords had extensive records of each landholding, including the exact surface, dimensions, soil type, and anticipated yield. Fassina describes just such an explicit contract in Vicenza that detailed exactly the condition of the fields at the beginning of the five-year contract, the crops to be sown in each year, and the condition the fields were to be left in at the contract's end.[15] As property owners, landlords had the legal right to alienate land and terminate tenant usufruct access. Tenant contracts specified in formal terms exactly the condition of the fields at the beginning of the contract, the pre-scribed crop rotation to be followed, areas to be left for pasture, and terms of rent collection.[16]

The preference for rent payment in wheat and direct control over culti-vation/management was a source of both subtle and overt struggle be-tween cultivators and landlords. Land tenure allowed landlords to set the terms of peasant access, while population growth over the sixteenth and seventeenth centuries generally increased landlord leverage over their cul-tivators. These terms favored wheat at the expense of security or tenure and peasants' own household food supply. Tenants, for their part, struggled to impart their own sense of entitlement to land as familial property that was heritable, partible, and a resource to guarantee subsistence.

In the first years of its adoption on peasant landholdings, landlords ap-parently allowed peasants to cultivate maize as a *biada minute* (secondary crop), a category to which landlords paid little heed as it comprised their tenants' own food supply and did not affect their rent payments in wheat. Across the region, however, it became apparent in the late sixteenth and early seventeenth centuries that maize's yield and perfect fit into the sum-mer crop rotational mix had revolutionized both the tenants' food supply and cultivation habits, supplanting rye, sorghum, and millet almost en-tirely. Maize allowed peasant farmers to put into summer cultivation plots flooded in spring that had heretofore been simply seasonal pasture. More-over, it also became clear that maize served a dual role as human food, and in the form of silage and stover filled the gap in livestock forage that al-lowed winter stall-feeding, thus expanding manure supplies and on-farm dairy production.[17]

Maize as a fodder crop also complemented the expansion of water con-trol in Veneto, converting seasonally flooded pasture into cropland culti-vated year-round in a wheat/maize rotation. During this initial expansion, maize crossed the threshold from subsistence food to a market crop, with local and then regional export. Such off-farm sales suggest an increasing urban consumption. Peasant smallholders accomplished this transition by expanding their own plantings and exploring maize's agronomic limits.

Most of maize's early entry into peasant plot rotations and into tenant/landlord disputes over plantings falls outside of the view of the written historical record. But a sketchy chronology is nonetheless possible. The first official estate record of maize is a 1582 *polizza de estimo* (estate es-timate) from landlord Pier Maria Contarini that indicates maize (*"formenton zalo"*) was grown by tenants on a seasonally waterlogged plot on his family's estate at Vighizzolo vinico Este. But it must have been expanding informally on tenant holdings for several years prior to that because in 1584 maize appears in the postmortem farm inventory of a peasant in a Vicenza village, and four years later maize made up part of a gift by a peasant farmer to the monastery of St. Bartholomew of Rovigo. By 1601 an official document from Venice's Rialto market states that maize was "bought by the most impoverished and miserable persons, for whom it is a source of sustenance with a good market."[18]

Historian Michele Fassina argues that by the early seventeenth century, maize had become a staple that appeared in every province of the Venetian republic. In the year 1618, the state itself recognized the agrarian constituency's insistence on the crop by officially accepting maize for the payment of taxes—a symbol reckoning the end of a much longer agrarian conflict. The year before, the major estate of the influential Contarini family at Piazzola sul Brenta had, for the first time, accepted land rent payments in maize. And during the 1630 Venetian plague, maize made up a large portion of the food sent by the state into that quarantined city, haunted by the carnival images of death. [19] Fassina's study of Polesine farm records from a single holding from the years 1718–64 indicates that maize, by those years, had become firmly established as the major crop in the region, accounting for over half of all farm income, and in some years as much as 70 percent of the total.[20]

Thus, the initiative to adopt maize derived from farm-level decisions by a peasant population chafing under restrictive property law and tenuous access to land. The chronology of maize's appearance in official records and its recognition by both landlords and the state was largely a response forced by peasant initiative and the *force majeur* of the crop's success on the farm itself. This initiative resulted partially from the weakness of the cropping system that had privileged elite preference for wheat, a crop poorly suited to Veneto's agro-ecological setting. But it also reflected peasants' choice of maize production as an avenue of resistance to their poor position of access to land, and elite efforts to maintain control over farm management. The adoption of maize opened new farm-level options in crop-livestock integration, as well as establishing new terms of sumptuary class divisions and rural-urban differentiation. Maize thus was both the symbol and the substance of peasant response to their plight. The Venetian peasant-led maize revolution was perhaps an example of agrarian radicalism, but one driven as much by agronomic needs as by a conscious political agenda. Peasant monocropping, and the domination of maize as the primary food source, had its most serious consequences only in the nineteenth century with the emergence of endemic pellagra among rural maize eaters, an affliction that came to symbolize their poverty.

Maize and the Solomonic Empire

The Venetian elites' appropriation of maize as a symbol of New World natural abundance and their own worldly opulence stands in sharp contrast to the silence of maize's reception in Ethiopia. *Zea mays*'s first unmistakable appearance in the historical records is Caspar Bauchin's 1623 observation of it; but it is likely that Portuguese Jesuits brought maize seeds with them in the early years of the seventeenth century as part of their program to broaden the new brotherhood's ecclesiastical ties in the lands of Prester John. Semitic-speaking Ethiopians called the new crop *"Yabahar mashela"* (lit. "the sea's sorghum"), reflecting its arrival from across the water.[21]

The oft repeated story goes that the Jesuits brought maize seeds with them from their mission outpost at Goa (off the coast of the Indian subcontinent) or directly from Iberia. Maize would have been for them a tropical food crop that they imagined would bring innovation and sustenance to a new community of believers and their mission base. After all, initial Jesuit successes in Ethiopia (Abyssinia) had included receiving a land grant at Fremona in Tigray from the grateful emperor. Indeed, there is circumstantial evidence that suggests that the maize that reached Ethiopia in those early years was probably the same red Caribbean flint maize that had moved from Spain to northeast Italy and thence into the Mediterranean and Near East in the mid-to-late sixteenth century. The Jesuit missionaries' success in their spiritual mission seemed assured in 1612, when the imperial court of Emperor Susenyos (1607–32) secretly converted from Ethiopian Orthodox Christianity to Roman Catholicism. The emperor's open proclamation of his conversion in 1622 brought on a violent but successful reaction among peasants and elite alike based in conservative rural areas, which may well have feared that the introduction of a foreign ideology portended a wider reform of property law and land-tenure practice. The 1632 abdication of the Catholic emperor, expulsion of the Jesuits, and the martyrdom of many reflected a deep-seated conservatism over both religious and social practices shared by rural elite and cultivators alike.[22] That maize arrived on the Ethiopian rural scene during this turmoil was no coincidence; the new crop was part and parcel of the expansion of world trade and the spread of new ideas about property, ideology, and material life.

Unlike the aesthetic evidence in the Venetian case, however, there is no reference to maize in any of the Ethiopian royal chronicles, or in any iconography from the period, despite the significant evidence of the Portuguese (and other European) success in influencing architectural style and iconography (the conversion of Emperor Susenyos and the imperial court to Roman Catholicism was part of that process). Indeed, the anti-Jesuit counterrevolution of 1632 rejected symbolically and with violence precisely the externally generated modernity associated with the Jesuits. The temporary conversion, and the quick and successful counterreformation led by Susenyos' son Fasiladas were, in fact, broadly reflective of a regional intellectual and social conflict over rationalism in religious and commercial life in the Nile Valley in the seventeenth century.[23]

Can we deduce from this a conservative peasant response to maize as a crop symbolic of dangerous outside influence? It is difficult to say. Unfortunately, the historical records from Ethiopia in the period offer no insights into whether maize had a value to elites as either a symbol or a food source. Equally, there is little or no evidence that Ethiopian highland farmers treated maize as anything more than a minor vegetable kitchen crop and agronomic curiosity; its adoption as a grain field crop had to wait several centuries. Even if the historical record is virtually silent on this issue, the agronomic exigencies for this long delay in maize adoption are worth examining.

Maize in the Agrarian System in the Solomonic Empire

Ethiopia's highlands have historically displayed a remarkable stability of technology in its evolution of a farming system and the building of its repertoire of food crops. Deep soils, dedicated farmers, and a distinctive African technology—the single-tine scratch plow called the *maresha*—allowed early innovation in cereal crops and agronomic strategies deployed within the highlands' kaleidoscope of micro-ecologies created by the highlands' range of elevations, soils, and rainfall shadows. By 1500 the plow, a classic battery of endemic cereal cultivars (barley, teff, wheat, sorghum, eleusine, etc.), and an annual cropping regime had existed for a millennium or more among a wide variety of local polities, ethnicities, and ecological frontiers.

Highland Ethiopian agriculture was finely tuned to the "limiting" factor of elevation and its effects on both temperature and rainfall. Crops, rotational systems, and seasonal rhythms of planting, harvest, and seedbed preparation fit a bimodal rainfall regime that had evolved over many generations. Ambilineal, partible patterns of property and the exigencies of micro-ecologies of soil and elevation meant that farmers generally controlled a series of small plots spread across several agro-ecological zones, each planted in its own rotational scheme. Ethiopian women did not plow, and had little control over plot management, but they nevertheless enjoyed direct influence over the processing of food and the garden crops (*gwaro*) grown in fertile soils around the house itself. There, herbs, vegetables, and condiment crops complemented the grains and pulses of the farm's main plots. Thus, maize may have begun in Ethiopia as a woman's crop.

What accounts for northern Ethiopian peasants' conservatism compared to Italy? In contrast to northeast Italy, crop choices—e.g., planting teff versus wheat, or sorghum versus eleusine—reflected a finely tuned judgment controlled only by the farmer himself. The farmers' adage *"maret ende mert"* ("do as the plot chooses") states that crop choice was decidedly local. It suggests the subtlety of local plot conditions, but also the historical fact that elites who held the bundle of income rights (*gult*) that included a tithe and rights to corvée labor (*hudad*) from rural cultivators had no such rights over farm-level management, choices of crops, or the distribution of land among those who had claims to usufruct rights (*rist*).[24] There were few sumptuary laws or status culture to separate rural social classes, though the facts of poverty meant that the elite ate more teff and more protein than those from whom they claimed labor and payments of rural product.[25]

At the opening of the seventeenth century, the political ecology of agriculture in highland Ethiopia was highly elaborated both in its agronomic and its political practice, resulting in a rural producers' adherence to a conservatism in both religious practice and in property rights. Elite rights of collection (*gult*) held within them an implicit recognition of peasant claims on inheritable rights of land use (*rist*). These entitlements were embedded within a system that also accepted a set of vertical relations of power in which the political and ecclesiastical elite occupied the highest point.[26] Smallholder rights to farm-level management and claims of usufruct cemented a sense of conservatism among farmers over changes in the hierarchy of authority, resulting in a strong sense of farmer entitlement over access to land and farm management. The circumstantial evidence suggests that in highland Ethiopia, maize had little effect on diet and farming systems. It remained nestled in the farming system as a garden vegetable crop cultivated by women and consumed green before the major cereal harvest, or as a field crop that occupied a narrow altitude niche between wheat and sorghum.

Maize in Ethiopia: Delayed Effects

Maize's arrival on the highlands in the late sixteenth or early seventeenth century caused little stir in and of itself.[27] Like their counterparts elsewhere in Africa, Ethiopian farmers who encountered the new crop appear to have added it unceremoniously to their complex crop mix. Maize first appeared as a grain in historical records of the early nineteenth century. In 1805 traveler Henry Salt noticed in Tigray a well-established field of "*e bahr mashella*" (lit. "the sea's sorghum"), which he glossed as Indian corn. He described a valley "well cropped, especially with Indian corn, which is usually more forward in this climate than any other grain," identifying maize by its most salient behavior, early maturity.[28] Other nineteenth-century travelers also found it here and there across the highlands, but never as the dominant grain crop it became in Veneto almost 200 years later. Most of these descriptions make it clear that what they saw in Ethiopia was a yellow flint maize with a low yield, a plant height "that does not exceed 1.25 meters and has ears of 10 rows of small grain."[29] As a flint maize, one could speculate that it was favored by women, not because of any yield advantage over other grains, but because of its suitability for hand-milling and its early maturity. Never dominant in either area planted or in the peasant diet, maize had difficulty, until the modern period, supplanting any of the diverse range of crops that made up the highland repertoire, or farmer dedication to the range of locally adapted crops.

Maize in Modern Ethiopia: The Southern Highlands

Maize's role as a dominant field crop began along the southern periphery of the Ethiopian highland kingdom among Cushitic-speaking farmers, rather than among the classic cereal-based farms of the northern highlands. By the middle third of the twentieth century, a new export economy of coffee in Ethiopia's southwest created a conflict between labor, land use, and the agricultural cycle of traditional annual cereal crops. Instead of collecting wild coffee from the forest, farmers began to propagate coffee seedlings and to integrate coffee- cultivation into their farm production. Maize, already cultivated here and there in southern cropping systems by the late nineteenth century, proved an ideal complement to the demands coffee made on farm labor. What evolved in the period after World War II was a widespread coffee-maize complex that paired coffee as a cash crop with maize as an early-maturing, low-labor (in sowing and harvest) food crop that provided sustenance before the coffee income in the fall. Those farmers who did not produce coffee benefited from off-farm cash income as coffee laborers, and still could sow maize on their own plots. By the 1950s this cropping system was well entrenched and increasingly included improved dent-type maize introduced by the early agricultural-extension programs sponsored by foreign donors.

The coffee-maize complex in southern Ethiopia—in some places also tying into the culture of *ensete ventricosum* (false banana)—expanded and matured over much of the southwestern highlands in the 1950–75 period and into the early years of the Ethiopian Revolution's socialist development policies (1974–91). Agricultural marketing policies formed by urban technocrats, however, squeezed local coffee-farm profits by price controls on coffee and most cereal crops (excluding maize, the cheapest and least marketable of food crops).

This state intervention, unprecedented in Ethiopian history, brought a decisive response from coffee farmers that paralleled Veneto's peasant strategies. By 1980, state-manipulated coffee prices and rising food costs had undermined the balance of the coffee-maize complex. Coffee farmers began to cut coffee bushes and broadcast maize into those plots to avoid state control over coffee marketing. In the half-decade from 1986 to 1991, maize as a percentage of total national crop production rose from 32 percent to 48 percent.[30] Government policies to resettle drought-affected farmers, force labor for road construction, and control marketable food crops provided further incentives for farmers to shift to the short-term exigencies of maize. What had been an agrarian production system seemingly immune from the attractions of maize suddenly rushed to embrace it.

Maize production also had a perverse appeal for peasant farmers outside of coffee-growing regions, including the agronomically conservative north. Unlike traditional crops—sorghum, teff, wheat, pulses—maize offered expediency and higher yields on plots that were increasingly smaller under the pressure of population growth. Farmers under pressure from forced labor for government projects or military conscription could broadcast maize seed after only one plowing, compared to four plowings for other cereals. Little weeding was necessary for local maize types; it grew well on newly deforested land; and its quick maturity and relatively high yields to labor and land (compared to teff or wheat) meant that there was at least one source of food to sustain families hard-pressed by shrinking plot sizes and growing population pressure. The rapid rise in maize production nationally in the years of the revolution (1974–91) showed the result of farmers' perceptions of both a demographic crisis and an oppressive national government. In 1970–71, maize made up 15.3 percent of the national cereal production (fourth among all cereals); in 1983–84, at the height of a famine and ten years of socialist agrarian policy, maize made up 28.3 percent, first place among all cereals.[31] Maize's percentage of the nation's overall cereal production has increased steadily since.

Despite the fall of the military government in 1991, international aid and agricultural-extension policies of the new government have dramatically expanded cultivation of improved and hybrid maize among farmers across the highlands, with the distribution of "minimum" packages of fertilizer and seed. Successes in yield improvement have been quick in coming, but may be unstable. During my 1998 visit to maize project areas in the southwest, I observed that row planting has become widespread, as has use of improved open-pollinated (dent) seed and nitrogen fertilizer. There is evidence, however, that farmers who have had success with hybrid seed are "recycling" it for seed corn for the next planting (with major losses in yield a likely result), or are choosing to return to traditional methods to avoid harming the soil.[32]

Sadly, surplus maize production in Ethiopia has few places to go. Regional markets are either unstable or uneconomical, storage and transport costs cannot cope with increased levels of production, and domestic urban markets have not yet fully accepted maize as a grain staple. It remains largely as quick-fix emergency food. Moreover, Ethiopia currently has no industrial capacity to process maize's constituent parts, and farmers have become increasingly dependent on external inputs (chemical fertilizer, herbicides, improved seeds) and market infrastructure to sustain their livelihoods. Still, in Ethiopia, maize cultivation continues to spread from plots in broadleaf forest to highland plateaus, and from remote lowland villages to urban vacant lots. Moreover, Africa—including Ethiopia—is distinctive among world regions in that 95 percent of its maize is consumed by humans, rather than used as livestock feed.[33]

Conclusion: Seeds of Subversion, Seeds of Industry

Ethiopia and Italy have traveled distinctive paths in their domination by maize in the late twentieth century. In sixteenth-century Italy, peasant farmers seized the moment early to embrace maize as a source of food, and as a crop that helped break the control of elite classes over agricultural practice. By the mid-nineteenth century, sumptuary habits of rural folk so depended on maize that pellagra and its protein deficiency (lack of niacin and key amino acids) came to symbolize this dietary monopoly, and lamentably equated maize with poverty. The apotheosis of maize production in northeast Italy in the mid-twentieth century ironically spelled the end of maize as a peasant crop that had sustained smallholder production and served as the linchpin of a peasant challenge to elite control. In the years from 1947 to 1950, and into the 1960s, maize expanded directly with the importation and development of new types of hybrid seeds that derived from international markets and post–World War II aid programs, led by the "transatlantic radicals" who preached the gospel of agricultural modernization. Under this revolution of agro-industrial empiricism, productivity increased on Italian maize farms from 1.55 metric tons per hectare in 1950 (1,924,3000 metric tons total production) to 3.21 metric tons per hectare (3,815,600 metric tons total production) in 1960.[34] In other words, though the total area planted in maize declined slightly, the total annual crop doubled (see figure 1). Thus, by 1990, Italy annually produced 6.4 million metric tons on 0.82 million hectares, with an average yield of 7.8 tons/ha. In this new configuration of maize production, only 15 percent of the product (i.e. flint maize for polenta) produced was for human consumption. Polenta (maize porridge, the old peasant staple) has become, ironically, an elite food and one of Italy's contributions to international haute cuisine, a far cry from its past as a peasant gruel and "transatlantic radical."

Yet, by the early 1990s, Italy had become the world's thirteenth leading maize producer; its total production is just below South Africa's (6.7) and just above Canada's (6.3). It has a modern seed industry, though operated by U.S.-based Pioneer Hybrid Seed Corporation. Only 15 percent of its maize is flint variety intended for human consumption.

Ethiopia, by contrast, ranks far down the global list in maize production, but ranks twenty-third in the world in calories relative to total human diet (fourteen of the top twenty-three are in Africa); 95 percent of all Ethiopia's maize serves human consumers. Ethiopia's highland producers initially had resisted maize's use as a field grain crop, choosing rather from among the wide range of local grains and leaving maize as a complementary garden crop until the mid-twentieth century. The conservatism of Ethiopia's smallholders derived from a shared ideology with the rural elite that sustained elite control over rural income, but secured peasant access to land. Thus Ethiopia's maize revolution has come late, and has been part of a decline toward a precarious subsistence and an increasing control by the state that now seeks to break traditional cropping patterns.

In both cases, however, the long-term result has been the globalization of maize into an industrial economy that requires inputs (hybrid seed, fertilizer, pesticides), and a market infrastructure that links farm production directly to global markets, rather than smallholder prerogatives. Radical seeds from the *novus mundus* thus ultimately transformed Old World political ecology in ways that are quite divergent.

Notes

1. Ethiopia's links in material culture and ideology to the Mediterranean world have been recently confirmed by the joint archaeological project at Aksum involving Boston University, the University of Naples, and the Ethiopian Ministry of Culture.

2. Carlo Ginzburg, *The Cheese and the Worms: The Cosmos of a Sixteenth-Century Miller* (New York: Penguin Books, 1982), 119–20.

3. See Alfred Crosby, *The Columbian Exchange: Biological and Cultural Consequences of 1492* (Westport, Conn.: Greenwood Press, 1972). A few scholars have claimed that maize in the Old World predated 1492, citing early Portuguese references to *milho zaburro* on the West African coast. See M. D. W. Jeffreys, "The History of Maize in Africa," *South African Journal of Science* (March 1954): 197–200, and idem, "The Origin of the Portuguese Word Zaburro as Their Name for Maize." *Bulletin de L'Institut Français de l'Afrique Noire*, series B, *Sciences Humaines* 19, nos. 1–2 (1957): 111–36.

4. I am grateful to Prof. Vincent Knapp for information on the chemistry of vegetables. For maize chemistry, see "Quality Protein Maize," *CIMMYT Today* 1 (1975): 1–12.

5. Carlo Ginsburg, *The Cheese and the Worms: The Cosmos of a Sixteenth-Century Miller* (Baltimore: Johns Hopkins University Press, 1982), 82–86. Ginzburg argues that the miller Menocchio's view of the news of a new world that filtered down to the village was as a wider metaphor

for a new spiritual and social world to unfold, rather than new lands for commercial exploitation.

6. Jan DeVries, *The Economy of Europe in an Age of Crisis: 1600–1750* (Cambridge: Cambridge University Press, 1976), 53–55; Ginzburg, *Cheese and Worms*, 15; Peter Musgrave, *Land and Economy in Baroque Italy: Valpolicella, 1630–1797* (Leicester: Leicester University Press, 1992), 3–5.

7. See Vincent Knapp, "What Europeans Ate in Agricultural Times: Eighteenth-Century Levels of Food Consumption and Nutrition," paper presented to the Seminar in Agarian Studies, Yale University, 22 January 1999, 2–6. For import of Baltic rye, see Musgrave, *Land and Economy*, 18.

8. Domenico Sella, *Crisis and Continuity: The Economy of Spanish Lombardy in the Seventeenth Century* (Cambridge: Cambridge University Press, 1979), 6–7.

9. For the most thorough description of water management in northern Italy, see Salvatore Ciriacono, "Investimenti capitalistici e colture irrigue la congiuntura agricola nella terrafirma veneta (secoli XVI e XVII), *Atti del Convegno Venezia e la Terraferma attraverso le Relazione dei Rettori*, 1980, 123–28. Ciriacono attributes early water management in Lombardy to Arab-Hispanic influences. See Salvatore Ciriacono, "Introduction," in *Land Drainage and Irrigation*, ed. Salvatore Ciriacono (Aldershot: Ashgate Publishing Limited, 1998), xx.

10. Around that time, as well, Giovanni Lamo, a Venetian, sent some seeds to the Duke of Florence, inviting him to plant them. Luigi Messedaglia, *Il mais e la vita rurale Italiana: Saggio di storia agraria* (Piacenza: Federazione Italiana dei Consorzi Agrari, 1927), 178.

11. Michele Fassina, "Il mais nel Veneto nel cinquecento: Testimonianze Iconografiche e prime esperienze colturali," in *L'Impatto della scoperta dell'America nella cultura veneziana* (Rome: Bulzone Editore, n.d.), 86. The plants depicted in the Tentazione de Adamo bas-relief may actually be sorghum rather than maize, given the early date (1515) and the difficulty of distinguishing the two crops in their early growth.

12. Messedaglia, *Il mais*, 29–39. Not in Messedaglia's list is *sorgo rosso*, a common term for maize in current Venetian dialect. See Michele Fassina, "Elementi ed aspetti della presenza del mais nel Vicentino: Con particulare riferimento a Lisiera e alla zona attraversata dal fiume Tesina," in *Lisiera: Immagini, documenti per la storia e cultura di una communità veneta-strutture, congiunture, episodi* (Lisiera: Edizioni Parrocchia

de Lisiera, 1981), 314–16. Interview with Anna DeGuio, 29 June 1999, Montecchia.

13. Christopher Dowswell, R. L. Paliswal, and Ronald P. Cantrell, *Maize in the Third World* (Boulder, Colo.: Westview Press, 1996), 18. Dowswell suggests that the seed was yellow Caribbean flint, though other evidence suggests the variety was a red flint. See Portières, "L'Introduction de Mais en Afrique." *Journal de'Agriculture Tropicale et de Botanique Appliquée* 2, nos. 5–6 (May-June 1955): 221–31.

14. Lit. "red sorghum," a name still used for maize in the Venetian dialect, and a variety that also became the first maize appearing in Egypt under local Arabic names signifying red color (*baladi hamra*, lit. "red sorghum."

15. See Michele Fassina, "Elementi ed aspetti," 321.

16. For examples of Venetian land surveys, see Silvestro Camerini, *La possidenza borghese in Transpadana* (Padova: Università di Padova, 1991), 119–94.

17. For a description of stall-feeding of cattle and draft animals, see Piero Rizzolatti, "La stalla e il governo degli animali," in Giovan Battista Pellegrini, ed., *I lavori dei contadini* (Vicenza: Nera Pozza Editore, 1997), 333–84. A beautiful illustration of the role of the stall on northern Italian peasant estates is found in the film "Tree of the Wooden Clogs."

18. Michele Fassina, "L'introduzione della coltura del mais nelle campagne venete," *Società e storia* 15 (1982): 36, 39.

19. Michele Fassina, "Il mais nel Veneto nel cinquecento," 91.

20. Michele Fassina, "Aspetti economici e sociale in una grande azienda agricola polesana nel corso del XVII secolo," *Uomini, Terra e Acque, Atti del XIV Convegno di Studi Sorici organizzato in collaborazione con l'Accademia del Concordi* (Rovigo: Associazione Culturale Minelliana Editrice, 1990), 229.

21. This name suggests a northern provenance, while the other common word for maize, *baqolo*, may be of Cushitic origin and suggests a second line of introduction from the south, perhaps via the Nile valley from East Africa. *Baqolo* is used more commonly in Amharic today.

22. For a fuller treatment of Jesuit activities in seventeenth-century Ethiopia, see Donald Crummey, *Land and Society in the Christian Kingdom of Ethiopia: From the Thirteenth to the Twentieth Century* (Urbana: University of Illinois Press, 2000), 67–72.

23. For a general summary of this period in Ethiopia, see Harold G. Marcus, *A History of Ethiopia* (Berkeley: University of California Press,

1994), 39–41. For similar, more lasting changes in ideology and social structure in the Nile Valley Sennar kingdom, see Jay Spaulding, *The Heroic Age of Sinnar* (East Lansing: African Studies Center, Michigan State University, 1982).

24. See McCann, *People of the Plow: An Agricultural History of Ethiopia, 1800–1990* (Madison: University of Wisconsin Press, 1995), 42–44, on issues of crop choice and farm management.

25. See debate on rural class compared in Donald Crummey, *Land and Society*, 127–29, in contrast to Donald Donham, "Old Abyssinia and the New Ethiopian Empire: Themes in Social History," in *The Southern Marches of Imperial Ethiopia. Essays in History and Social Anthropology*, ed. Donald Donham and Wendy James (Cambridge: Cambridge University Press, 1986), 3–48.

26. For an insightful comparison of northern European and highland Ethiopian family and property systems, see Allan Hoben, "Family, Land, and Class in Northwest Europe and Northern Highland Ethiopia," in *Proceedings of the First United States Conference on Ethiopian Studies*, 1973 (East Lansing: African Studies Center, Michigan State University, 1975), 157–70.

27. There is no record of maize's first arrival, but Portuguese Jesuit F. Paes often receives credit. The Jesuits established a farm at Fremona in Tigray to experiment and sustain their small community. See McCann, *People of the Plow*, 52.

28. Henry Salt, quoted in George Annesley Valentia, *Voyages and Travels to India, Ceylon, and the Red Sea, Abyssinia, and Egypt in the Years 1802, 1803, 1804, 1805, and 1806*, 3 vols. (London: William Miller: 1809), 3:5.

29. Antonio Cecchi, *Da Zeila alle frontiere del Caffa*, 2 vols. (Rome: Ermanno Loescher, 1886), 2:278.

30. See Kassahun Seyoum, Hailu Tafesse, and Steven Franzel, *The Profitability of Coffee and Maize among Smallholders: A Case Study of Limu Awraja, Ilubabor Region*, Research Report No. 10 (Addis Ababa, 1990), 10–22; McCann, *People of the Plow*, 184–86.

31. Ian Watt, "Regional Patterns of Cereal Production and Consumption," in Zein Ahmed Zein and Helmut Kloos, eds., *The Ecology of Health and Disease in Ethiopia* (Addis Ababa: Ministry of Health, 1988), 121.

32. The government's major emphasis on maize packages derived from the Global 2000 model begun in 1994. I am grateful to Ato Tekele Gebru for his help in my field work. For row planting as first "improvement" adopted by farmers, see Gerhart, *The Diffusion of Hybrid Maize*, 29–30. For early evidence of hybrid-seed recycling, I thank

agricultural economist Wilfred Mwangi, personal communication, May 1998; for fears of fertilizer sapping soil nutrients, interview with farmer Gali Abba Gojjam, Bonga District, May 1998.

33. Worldwide, the figure for human consumption is 34 percent (the bulk being fed to livestock). Byerlee and Eicher, *Maize Revolution,* 16; Dowswell et al., *Maize in the Third World,* 27.

34. L. Fenaroli, *Mais, 1946–67* (Bergamo: Fondazione Tito Vezio Zapparoli), 17–19; 55–57. Also personal information from Alberto Vederio and Marco Bertolini from the Instituto per la Cerealicoltura, Bergamo.

Transatlantic Travails: German Experiment Stations and the Transformation of American Agriculture

Louis A. Ferleger

Germany's Global Advantage

In this article, I explore how the transatlantic process transformed scientific activity and agriculture both within experiment stations and in the Office of Experiment Stations, an agency of the U.S. Department of Agriculture. German agricultural research significantly contributed to keeping American agricultural scientists informed about the latest scientific advances in their respective fields. Moreover, German exchanges involving experiment-station personnel, managers and scientists of the Office of Experiment Stations (OES), and the U.S. Department of Agriculture (USDA) influenced relationships between and among various groups who were vying for the resources that the American federal government had allocated to individual experiment stations. As American experiment stations expanded their work into new areas of investigation, partly as a result of the transatlantic process, they also developed new and different relationships with the business sector and agricultural organizations, as well as with the state.

In the nineteenth century and well into the twentieth century, various groups of American agricultural scientists from experiment stations and agricultural schools, as well as the OES and USDA personnel, traveled to Germany to observe and study firsthand the agricultural work at institutions of higher learning and experiment stations they had heard and read so much about. When the scientists returned to the United States, they told their colleagues and anyone who would listen about the important and innovative scientific work being carried out in German experiment stations. As a result of these exchanges, some directors of American experiment stations hired German scientists, while others sent their personnel to Germany to acquaint themselves with the latest advances and approaches to agricultural research. As more researchers returned from trips abroad, they waxed eloquent about the high-quality soil and field-crop projects they saw, as well as expressing their concerns about the extent to which American agricultural research lagged so far behind similar efforts in Germany. Unlike American experiment stations in the late nineteenth century, German experiment stations were internationally known for their high-quality investigations. The character and quality of German investigations were so frequently cited throughout America and parts of Europe that one could imagine some nations requesting a transplant or a clone from some German station to assist them in their efforts to improve agriculture. Germany's experiment stations were invoked as the most concrete example of what Alfred True, the head of OES from 1893–1915, believed was the central mission of experiment stations: to further the progress of agricultural science by engaging in original research.

Over the years, as these transatlantic exchanges continued, more and more managers and scientific personnel across the nation, whether they had visited German experiment stations or not, began to compare the character and quality of investigations carried out in German experiment stations with their own work. In addition to transatlantic exchanges, the American agricultural-science community was aided by the OES when they decided to include more information in their publications. In editorials and elsewhere, the OES encouraged scientists to pay closer attention to their German counterparts by increasing the number of English translations of German field, soil, and dairy investigations in the *Experiment Station Record*, a publication that listed and reported on agricultural-science activities across the nation and the world. While the OES published other documents, including experiment-station bulletins, farmers' bulletins, miscellaneous bulletins, monographs, and circulars, the *Record* was the one publication agricultural scientists relied on, more than any other, to inform them about diverse approaches and technologies to assist their efforts to uplift American agriculture.

One critical aspect of the work carried out in German experiment stations was the emphasis on scientific investigations that involved indoor laboratory experiments. These experiments involved the combining of the sciences of biology, chemistry, and, at times, physics. The emphasis on experiments of this nature meant that the majority of German stations were not locked into carrying out hundreds of similar field tests or frequent fertilizer investigations to determine which brand was supposedly the "best." For many years, fertilizer experiments dominated research activities at American experiment stations because of pressure from farmer groups and state officials.[1]

The success of German experiment stations can also be viewed as indirectly being an impediment to ongoing scientific work across the world. As Mark Finlay's pathbreaking work has shown, German experiment stations were not a model—but they did contribute to the slow development of similar scientific work elsewhere. It is, of course, the case that each nation had its own internal history that significantly determined the extent to which it promoted and funded original agricultural research, but the success of German experiment stations at a minimum may have hindered scientific work elsewhere, especially in Europe.

It is against this background that German experiment stations sustained their global competitive research advantage in agricultural science. In many European countries, there was little incentive to support the establishment of a network of experiment stations or agricultural-science efforts in general, including educational programs, as long as they could send their scientists to Germany for training, and borrow the best of agricultural science from the Germans. The problem with relying on Germany was that their agricultural-science innovations might or might not be useful to a specific country, depending on the extent to which the country's resource endowments (soil, climatic, and crop conditions) were similar to what German agriculturists faced.

The experiments carried out by German agricultural scientists were specifically oriented towards increasing the stock of useful agricultural *and* scientific knowledge. As a result, they involved unusual learning processes—what others have called "organizational learning."[2] The emphasis on indoor laboratory testing meant that the learning process was as important as the success rate. By emphasizing laboratory testing which involved organizational learning, scientists could work on long-term projects to increase the stock of useful knowledge for all scientists, irrespective of their relationship to the experiments.

The German experiment stations put in place an organizational structure to ensure that a core group of scientists within the station could carry out high-quality long-term experiments while simultaneously another small group could react, when necessary, to short-term and immediate problems. The emphasis on long-term research was on experimentation, not just results. Agricultural research projects were carried out that did not necessarily center on ongoing cultivation or processing difficulties, but that instead focused on some scientific problem related directly or indirectly to agriculture in general. The scientific orientation of these projects involved principles that were common to nineteenth-century German science; that is, that scientific research could ultimately contribute to scientific knowledge, as well as to specific problems confronting German agriculturists. The German investment in agricultural science and the emphasis on "the generation of innovation through organizational learning [is] inherently uncertain. The investment strategy resulting in a higher-quality, lower-cost product cannot be known in advance. Furthermore, what is learnt, as the innovation process evolves, changes the conception of the problems to be addressed, the possibilities for their solution, and therefore the appropriate strategy for continued learning."[3] In the German case, it is noteworthy that German experiment stations had sufficient financial backing not only from the business sector and/or agricultural organizations but also from the state to support and encourage investments in organizational learning.

Many German experiment stations, such as the ones in Prussia, Wurttemberg, and Bavaria, were organized to carry out high-quality experiments in the areas of animal metabolism, seed control, agricultural chemistry, plant physiology, soil tests, and crop-specific investigations. Autonomous and decentralized, each station had a detailed plan associated with its set of projects, explicit procedures for experimentation, appropriate and high-quality equipment, and instructions on how to write up the results of the experiments. There was no master plan, however, for how to build and sustain an experiment station. The size of the experiment station often differed by location, while the nature of the work carried out varied, depending on the circumstances of local and regional agricultural conditions and the extent to which a station received full financial backing from government sources and/or partial subsidies by business and agricultural organizations. Despite the diversity in experiment-station work, "throughout the 1860s, 1870s, and 1880s, Germans' reputation in the agricultural sciences was unsurpassed . . . by 1900, virtually every Western nation had employed German citizens to direct newly established institutions." [4]

In the late nineteenth century, if you were interested in the state of agricultural science in general, you consulted the Germans and sent your best people to their laboratories, experiment stations, or institutions of higher learning. Moreover, if you wanted to determine the state of the field in a specific area, you read what the German scientists had written and discovered about the topic. Finally, if you wanted to build an experiment station or expand existing facilities, you visited German stations and duplicated the aspects of their stations that suited your purposes.

What activities did German experiment stations engage in that attracted so many European and American scientists to their facilities? In 1889, for example, sixty-three German experiment stations employed 73 directors and 222 scientific specialists, plus hundreds of other workers, and engaged in the following kinds of activities:

> Twenty-nine stations exercise control of fertilizers, twenty-seven of feeding stuffs, and thirty-three of seeds, by analyzes and inspection of commercial wares. Four stations are charged with the inspection of foods and beverages. Eight stations are organized with especial reference to more purely scientific research. Fifteen are conducting investigations in vegetable physiology, nine in animal physiology and nutrition, two on soils, three in dairying, four in sugar-beet culture, two in fruit and vine culture, one in agricultural physics, eight in chemistry or chemical technology, four in agricultural technology, two upon commercial agricultural products (especially wine and tobacco), and three upon beer brewing. Nine of the stations have vegetation houses for experiment in vegetable physiology, nine have experimental fields, seven have feeding stalls for experimental purposes, four have experimental gardens, two are equipped with Pettenkofer's respiration apparatus, and one with a horse dynamometer.[5]

Prior to 1870, some argue that Germany was not the world's leader in agricultural science. In fact, "Belgium, the Netherlands, Britain, and Denmark, were on what may be called the 'efficiency' frontier in 1870. With their specific resource combinations, these countries had realized the highest levels of agricultural production per hectare and per head."[6] In these years, agricultural-science developments in chemistry in France and England were closely watched by German scientists who organized and carried out experiments based on this important work. By 1870, German scientific inroads in agricultural research were well established. While many factors contributed to the resurgence of German agriculture, "it was the Germans who set the example in the organization of a more or less nation-wide system of agricultural research and extension services, largely sponsored by the state. Between 1870 and 1914 a number of core countries adopted the German . . . [approach], as did the United States and Japan, but in the United Kingdom and France these institutions were only set up after the First World War."[7]

Germany's agricultural success and its emphasis on organizational learning relied on the "high degree of interdependence and mutual interaction between government policy formation in diverse areas, from the fiscal to the socio-political."[8] As a result, the agricultural sector significantly contributed to the nation's industrial development. It also enabled the nation to feed its rapidly growing population, expand food exports, reduce imports, and become relatively more self-sufficient in foodstuffs. Germany's agricultural productivity grew faster than any other European nation. Between 1850 and 1880, German annual average agricultural productivity grew 1.5 percent, with France and Belgium standing at 1.1 percent and the Netherlands, United Kingdom, and Europe recording productivity rates that were half or less than those of Germany.[9]

Over the 1880–1920 period, German agricultural productivity growth far outstripped all of Europe. Experiment stations played a prominent role in boosting Germany's agricultural productivity. The stations, usually located near or within institutions of higher learning, benefited by the large increase in students attending universities, many of whom decided to seek careers directly in agricultural science or a closely related field. From 1870 to 1900, the number of students doubled, and was more than two and half times larger in 1920 than 1900. While student growth rates increased in Belgium, the Netherlands, and France, no country except the United States added as many students as Germany (almost 100,000) between 1870 and 1920. [10]

Individuals and organizations in European nations, as well as in the United States, invoked Germany's agricultural dominance to promote various educational programs that they believed would support and expand agriculture and science in general. The German educational advantage was a cause of concern in England because of the nation's poorly funded and underdeveloped educational infrastructure. In 1870, English cabinet ministers argued for more funds to support the promotion of scientific education, and mentioned the problems England would face if it ignored the strides the Germans were making in technical and scientific areas. English agricultural organizations also built research laboratories that were similar to German facilities, specifically in chemical applications, plants, and soils. For example, in 1897, the Rothamsted Station received a donation to support research in plants and soils, and built a "Pot Culture Station" that closely resembled laboratories carrying out similar experiments in Germany.[11]

The Netherlands' efforts to support agricultural science were influenced by the success of German experiment stations. From 1880 to 1920, there were several attempts by the Netherlands (as well as by Belgium) to build, maintain, and promote agricultural science so that they could compete agriculturally with Germany. While the ability of any nation to sustain long-term agricultural-science-oriented activities in experiment stations depends on many factors, critical among them was continuous and committed funding, usually from government sources.[12] Sustained government support in agriculture in the Netherlands was "almost non-existent until the First World War."[13] In different ways, but with similar results, the lack of government support in France made it extremely difficult for the nation to establish a network of experiment stations similar to Germany. This may explain why French agriculture had "far too many marginal farms operating, and . . . most peasants have no easy access to capital for improvements. French agriculture increasingly became a museum with exhibits ranging from the medieval to the ultramodern."[14]

The expertise and success of German experiment stations made it unlikely that a nation could catch up quickly, or even approach the level of scientific knowledge accumulated within German experiment stations and agriculture in general prior to 1920. In order for non-German nations to compete with Germany's abundance of organizational capabilities, they would have had to support and sustain an accelerated effort involving a combination of business, government, and agricultural organizations who would have been willing and able to increase spending on research activities in agricultural science. The only country to approach and surpass Germany after 1920, the United States, had to transform its agricultural infrastructure under very different conditions because of mixed support from the business sector and statewide and national agricultural organizations. In the case of the United States, the state (i.e., the federal government) put in place a structure that was transformative because it encouraged and supported organizational learning to accelerate original research activities, both within the USDA as well as at individual experiment stations.[15]

Transatlantic Exchanges

Throughout the nineteenth century, American scientists who returned from trips to Germany mentioned the fascinating combination of institutional connections that were characteristic of German experiment stations. Some scientists believed that the important and innovative scientific work being carried out in German experiment stations would be difficult to achieve unless there was a dramatic change in how agricultural science was carried out in the United States. During the antebellum period, several prominent American agricultural scientists visited German stations and scientific institutions. Others sought advanced degrees from German institutions of higher learning that had programs in agricultural science, particularly chemistry. While many realized that it would be difficult to replicate the German approach in the United States, they did recognize that particular aspects of German agricultural experimentation and research were important.

In the 1850s, Samuel W. Johnson, an early leader in agricultural science in the United States and chemist at the Connecticut State Agricultural Society, went to Germany at about the time the German experiment-stations movement was sweeping the country. He studied there for a few years, and his experience in Germany reinforced his lifelong dedication and commitment to promote agricultural experimentation and research in the United States. Throughout his life, he encouraged others to visit Germany, and attempted to "institutionalize research in agriculture" in the United States based on what had been achieved in Germany. [16]

In the years before the Hatch Act, future directors of American experiment stations who had traveled to Germany used the transatlantic experience as a basis for their views on what an equivalent American system of experiment stations might accomplish. Germany had over seventy experiment stations by the mid-1870s, so that when Dr. George Cook, the first director of the New Jersey experiment station, visited experiment stations in Germany in 1870 and 1878, he remarked that it was "like being admitted to a new world." Cook recruited scientists who had been trained in Germany, including Dr. Arthur Neale, who was appointed the first chemist of the New Jersey experiment station, and who noted in his resumé that "He had studied at the University of Griefswald, in Germany, and worked in . . . Halle as assistant to Prof. Max Maerker." [17] J. H. V. Scovill, from Cornell University's College of Agriculture, who had visited German experiment stations, wanted the New York station to focus on what he had seen, that is, "farm systematization." By this, he meant the German emphasis on having "experimental stations, model experimental farms, or experimental farms." Professor George C. Caldwell, who taught agricultural chemistry at Cornell University, wanted the New York station to adopt the German emphasis on agricultural chemistry, noting that "'thirty or more' German experiment stations . . . employed 'an able chemist and one or more assistants' to solve agricultural problems." In the debate surrounding the Hatch Act, several prominent scientists cited the achievements of German experiment stations as exemplifying what the United States might expect from its investment in agricultural science.[18]

Other American agricultural educators and scientists who were active in the experiment station movement also sought out personnel whom they had met in Germany, or those who had been educated in German institutions of higher learning or had visited agricultural facilities there. For example, Evan Pugh and S. W. Johnson, both of whom played a critical role in the development of agricultural education and experiment stations in Pennsylvania, met in Leipzig, Germany. Johnson, in particular, had worked and been taught by Liebig, and had been trained at both the Leipzig and Munich universities.[19]

A large number of American agricultural scientists had German roots and had received advanced degrees at German universities. For example, Eugene W. Hilgard received a Ph.D. in chemistry from Heidelberg University in 1853. He played a prominent role in developing agricultural educational and scientific programs in Washington, Michigan, Mississippi, and especially in California. In the early 1870s he "proposed a vibrant collaboration between the state college and local agricultural societies centered on a series of experimental farms or stations. He recommended that this system, common in Germany, be brought to the United States." The agricultural scientist Wilbur O. Atwater based his proposals for a station in Connecticut on his experiences in Germany, where he had studied. Charles A. Goessmann, a professor of chemistry at the Massachusetts Agricultural College and director of the experiment station in 1882, had grown up in Naumberg, Germany, and received a Ph.D. from the University of Gottingen. Charles W. Silver, an agricultural chemist who had studied agricultural science at the University of Halle, promoted education and research at the Illinois Industrial University, a forerunner of the experiment station.

George Chapman Caldwell, a professor of agricultural chemistry and one of the leaders at the agricultural school at Cornell University, had studied in Europe, but in particular at the prominent German university in Heidelberg. Edwin W. Allen, who took over as director of the OES in 1915 when Alfred True moved to head the federal extension agency, had been trained as a chemist in Germany, which undoubtedly enhanced his stature at OES (where he had worked since 1890) and his chances of heading the OES.[20]

In one issue of the *Experiment Station Record*, the director of the Delaware College Experiment Station, A. T. Neale, recounted in exacting detail (five pages of text) his trips to many stations in Germany, especially to the beet-sugar district of the Province of Saxony, and in particular his time spent at the world-renowned Halle station with one of the giants of German agricultural science, Professor Max Maerker.[21] In a May 1891 *Record* editorial, the editor again noted the impressive achievements at the Halle station in Prussia, stating that it is "the largest station in Europe." The editorial notes how experiment stations in Germany moved from the countryside to the city so that they could be close to universities, to maintain close contact with the scientific community.[22]

The German experiment stations were unusual not only because of collaboration among agricultural associations, government, and business, but, as an 1890 *Record* editorial suggested, because of "the greater specialization of work and the relatively larger proportion of abstract research in the German stations. The individual stations confine themselves to fewer subjects of investigation and study them more deeply. Relatively more attention is given to work in the laboratory, the green house, and the stable, and less to that of the farm, garden and orchard."[23] Over his entire career at OES, Alfred True repeatedly mentioned the German emphasis on indoor laboratory experiments—what he called original research—as the major problem confronting American experiment stations. True believed that if you did not engage in and support original research projects, what we now call "organizational learning" could not have (or was unlikely to have) taken place. American experiment stations carried out far too many tests and studies that were responding to immediate concerns; solving these problems might alleviate short-run agricultural difficulties, but such an approach did not by itself generate long-term improvements in agricultural practices or productivity.

To encourage original research, as well as strengthen the organizational learning process at American experiment stations, many scientists—but especially Alfred True and Secretary of Agriculture James Wilson—wanted the federal government to provide specific funds for the direct funding of "original research" projects. They and others encouraged Congress to pass legislation to provide designated funds to support original research in agricultural science. Such legislation was put in place when Congress passed the Adams Act in 1906. As a result, American experiment stations received another infusion of funds, but this money had to be spent on science-based research. The act specified that each state would receive $5,000 per year of federal subsidies to aid agricultural-science investigations at state experiment stations. The USDA and the OES also continued to encourage state governments to appropriate more funds to supplement federal aid to agriculture for station activities. USDA and OES encouragement and support also led to state legislatures across the land appropriating more funds to experiment stations to support original research, as well as routine station activities. The Act not only allocated special funds for original research projects that were nontransferable, but also included specific monitoring mechanisms that the OES could use to assure the consistency, reliability, and originality of the experiments carried out.[24]

Transatlantic exchanges prior to 1906 probably contributed to the passage of the Adams Act. These exchanges between American and Germany involved both American scientists visiting German stations and German scientists visiting American facilities. One German commentator who had visited America in the late nineteenth century noted that "American agricultural science lagged behind Germany's in its sophistication."[25] This so-called "sophistication" is critical in the organizational learning process because the first stage of scientific learning usually takes place in the laboratory, and then over time is transformed, refined, or modified (during the post-basic-development research process) as more application-oriented (development) research is carried out. As a result, some original research projects eventually yield practical applications to improve cultivation practices and boost productivity. By focusing on experiments in laboratories, greenhouses, and stables, German experiment stations were seeking—and secured—more generalizable, as well as specific, applications that could be further developed and utilized in the fields, gardens, and orchards.

At the beginning of the twentieth century, when Germany was starting to fall behind American inroads in agricultural science, it still stood far above its European competitors. German experiment stations continued to carry out original agricultural research, just like the Americans, to boost productivity as well as expand efforts to be globally competitive. It was also the case that more transatlantic exchanges between the United States and Germany continued well into the twentieth century. As late as 1904, some American agricultural colleges were still organizing classes in German and urging administrators to support German modern-language classes, so that their agricultural students could learn German and read scientific results from original sources.[26]

American funding of agricultural science mirrored certain aspects of the German experience. The state, however, played a different role in the United States after the passage of the Hatch and Adams Acts. First, even though American agricultural science was achieving some startling results, most U.S. experiment stations did not emphasize indoor laboratory experiments to boost agricultural productivity until early in the twentieth century. Second, while increased funding was available, the battle over how the additional resources for experiment stations should be allocated did not cease, partly because American stations had to confront various agricultural groups or state legislators or state agencies that sought to redirect station activity away from scientific research to more immediate agricultural problems.

These individuals, groups, and agencies wanted agricultural scientists to focus their efforts on solving local or regional problems. Directors of state experiment stations increasingly found themselves being pushed and pulled in several directions. One group, elected and appointed state-government officials who funded part of station expenses, believed station work should be centered on an agenda of statewide crop-specific problems. This approach was opposed by officials from the OES, particularly Alfred True, who monitored station work and expenditures on behalf of the USDA. The OES wanted station work to center on analyzing feed stuffs, dairying, seed investigation and control, systematic variety tests, and long-term detailed field studies in a few lines of inquiry that may have been important either locally or regionally, but that emphasized cooperative work in the field and laboratory. And lastly, farmers and farmers' groups wanted experiment stations to focus their efforts on immediate or current agricultural difficulties plaguing specific farmers.

The previous examples have highlighted some of the transatlantic exchanges by American agricultural scientists, and how scientists viewed German agricultural research, training, and the organization of experimental work. Unfortunately, there is no data set available that recorded the number of visits American scientists made to Germany, or the number of times station or OES or USDA personnel cited or quoted German work. It is possible, however, to glean some other aspects of the transatlantic process of exchanges and interactions by examining accounts of the process that appeared as citations, articles, notes in the *Experiment Station Record,* as well as other sources. These sources are inherently limited, since we do not know what the editorial policy of the *Record* was, but it appears that even with several changes in the editorship of the *Record,* German scientists and Germany's progress in agricultural science appeared more frequently than the work of any other nation.

In the fourth issue of the 1890 *Record,* the editor describes the progress achieved by German stations since they established their first experiment station in 1851. The editorial notes include three pages of text and three pages of statistics that present a detailed portrait of German experiment stations. In the March 1891 *Record,* the editorial notes include a change of policy of what will be included in the publication, namely: "With the present number of the Record a beginning is made in giving brief accounts of European inquiry in lines in which our stations are working." The editor notes that work in Germany, France, and England at experiment stations, as well as laboratories and universities, will be reprinted in the *Record* because "the questions investigated there are the same as those on which our stations are working, or involve the abstract principles on whose solution the successful work of our station depends." The editorial concludes that the abstracts selected will be limited because of space, but will focus on accounts that "are most intimately connected with the work of our stations in certain lines."[27] These abstracts were probably more influential than many realized, since the American station agricultural-science community carried out many experiments that were reported in the *Record,* and noted that the experimenter was following or building on an experiment by a German scientist—such as the long report that appeared by H. W. Wiley on sugar beets in 1890. Over the next twenty years, the *Record* included hundreds of articles as long or longer on virtually every aspect of German agriculture science.[28]

In 1897, Dr. J. T. Anderson, first Assistant Chemist at the Alabama experiment station, replicated fertilizing experiments on cotton "according to the methods employed for other crops by Dr. Paul Wagner, the German investigator." A New Jersey experiment-station entomologist, Dr. John Smith, visited Europe twice, especially Germany, in 1900 and 1910, "studying their methods of insect control and of the teaching of entomology."[29]

Transatlantic exchanges promoted experiment-station agricultural research, despite various ongoing battles over the extent to which station work should center on local and regional problems. The president of the American Association of Agricultural Colleges and Experiment Stations and director of the Pennsylvania experiment station, Henry P. Armsby, noted in his presidential address in 1898–99 that "The German experience gave unmistakable proof that the Liebig-like investigators, though admittedly professional teachers, owed their discoveries, first, to their intensive scientific training and, second, to their remarkable freedom to use their time and their skills in research, not in undergraduate teaching duties. Furthermore the German experience showed conclusively that the most noted agricultural scientists, when permitted greatest freedom to do basic research, produced the discoveries having the most useful and practical application to farming . . . American college authorities need not fear that American researchers, if given similar latitude, would ignore the farmers' welfare. If American colleges did not adopt the German policy . . . they could not produce the type of meaningful research which alone could retain them, in future years, the popularity currently attained by station efforts."[30] In this speech and many more similar ones, station directors, scientists, and OES and USDA officials proclaimed that station research would help farmers, and urged college authorities, state legislators, farmers, and others to support station personnel engaging in original research.

Transformation of American Agriculture

Although transatlantic exchanges clearly opened up new avenues of research for American agricultural scientists, it is difficult to pinpoint the extent of the influence these exchanges had on agricultural productivity. Past studies have documented that agricultural research has yielded high returns on investments throughout the late nineteenth and twentieth centuries. Scholars have estimated an annual rate of return on American agricultural research expenditures of 65 percent from the end of the Civil War to the middle of the 1920s. For the reminder of the twentieth century, the rate of return estimates range from 33 percent to 65 percent higher than the earlier period. More impressively, several studies strongly suggest that federally sponsored research has significantly contributed to overall productivity growth rates.[31]

What impact did the transatlantic process have on the record of agricultural achievement illustrated by the previous statistics? It is possible that both the rate-of-return numbers and productivity growth rates would have been considerably lowered if these exchanges between American and German scientists had not occurred. The transatlantic process was knowledge enhancing, as well as a serious source of competitiveness for American agricultural scientists. It involved transformative experiences that accelerated ongoing debates on the nature and character of agricultural science and work carried out in experiment stations. The scientists who immersed themselves in the transatlantic process, either by visiting Germany or by closely following the results of German original research, had a difficult time gaining support for original research in the United States because they had to fend off various local, statewide, and national groups that wanted station work to address immediate, crop-specific problems.

The results of the research carried out by experiment-station personnel (as well as cooperative work with the USDA) changed the lives of American farmers. Better farm techniques, higher yields, improved pest control, to name a few advances, certainly benefited farmers and improved their economic lives. Farmers' concerns, however, were usually local and regional. Agricultural scientists' research concerns were abstract, global, and scientific. It is likely that supporting an approach to agricultural research that emphasized maintaining high-quality research activities in the name of science confused or angered farmers nationwide. It is hard to imagine that farmers who were confronting problems associated with railroads, banks, global markets, declining prices, overproduction, and reduced incomes cared much about the long-term benefits of agricultural science.

While further research is required, it appears that the transatlantic process in American agriculture, in particular the exchanges among German and American scientists between 1850 and 1920, was a critical link to the United States' success in expanding the experiment-station infrastructure and upgrading the quality of U.S. agricultural research nationwide. However, while American experiment-station scientists were in a race to catch up with the research achievements of the German agricultural-science community, they chose not to make the many serious immediate problems facing the ordinary American farmer their number-one priority. As a result, although the years between 1880 and 1920 were years of great change and achievement for American experiment-station personnel and agricultural-scientific advance, they were also years of great frustration for many American farmers. During this period, American farmers faced many serious problems, and their frustration with government organizations, including experiment stations, ultimately resulted in social upheaval and organized protest movements. It was not until the post-1920 period that

American farmers finally reaped some of the rewards of the long-term investment in original agricultural research, which ultimately changed the nature and character of farm life.

Notes

1. *Experiment Station Record* (1892–93): 625; idem (1894–95): 256; idem (1895–96): 633–34; idem (1898–99): 710; idem (1899–1900): 804.
2. Louis Ferleger, "Arming American Agriculture for the Twentieth Century: How the USDA's Top Managers Promoted Agricultural Development," *Agricultural History* 74 (2000): 211–26.
3. William Lazonick and Mary O'Sullivan, "Finance and Industrial Development. Part I: The United States and the United Kingdom," *Financial History Review* 4 (1997): 7–8.
4. Mark R. Finlay, "Science, Practice and Politics: German Agricultural Experiment Stations in the Nineteenth Century," (Ph.D. diss., Iowa State University, 1990), 301–4, 367. See also Daniel Rodgers, *Atlantic Crossings: Social Politics in a Progressive Age* (Cambridge, Mass.: The Belknap Press of Harvard University Press, 1998), 319, 321, 324–25, 327, 330–31.
5. *Experiment Station Record* (1890): 175–76.
6. J. L. Van Zanden, "The First Green Revolution: The Growth of Production and Productivity in European Agriculture, 1870–1914," *Economic History Review* 44 (1991): 219.
7. Ibid., 237; Finlay, "Science, Practice and Politics," 333–34; Colin Heywood, "Agriculture and Industrialization in France, 1870–1914," in *The Nature of Industrialization*, ed. P. Mathias and J. Davis (New York: Blackwell Publishers, 1996), 112.
8. John Perkins, "The Organisation of German Industry, 1850–1930: The Case of Beet-Sugar Production," *The Journal of European Economic History* 19 (1990): 550–51.
9. J. H. Clapham, *The Economic Development of France and Germany, 1815–1914* (London: Cambridge University Press, 1955), 209–10.
10. Heywood, "Agriculture and Industrialization in France," 47; Clapham, *The Economic Development of France and Germany*, 177–78, 203, 214; G. Wright, *France in Modern Times* (New York: W. W. Norton and Co., 1995), 261–62; H. V. Molle, "Het Belgisch landbouswbeleid in de wisselwerking tussen economisiche en sociale toestanden, politiek en administratie 1884–1984," *Agricontact, koerier van het Ministerie van Landbouw* 154 (1984): 1–141; R. Mitchell, *International Historical*

Statistics, Europe: 1750–1993, 4th ed. (New York: Greenwood Press, 1998), 894–98, table 12 on 751. On the United States, see Louis Ferleger and William Lazonick, "The Managerial Revolution and the Developmental State: The Case of U.S. Agriculture," *Business and Economic History* 22 (1993): 67–98.

11. Harry W. Paul, *The Sorcerer's Apprentice: The French Scientist's Image of German Science, 1840–1919* (Gainesville: University of Florida Press, 1972); J. J. Beer, *The Emergence of the German Dye Industry* (Urbana: University of Illinois Press, 1959), 15–16, 111; G. Haines IV, "German Influence Upon Scientific Instruction in England, 1867–1887," *Victorian Studies* 1 (1957–58): 218, 236; Finlay, "Science, Practice and Politics," 341–46; Sir E. John Russell, "Rothamsted and Its Experiment Station," *Agricultural History* 16 (1942): 161–83; Sir E. John Russell, *A History of Agricultural Science in Great Britain, 1620–1954* (London: George Allen and Unwin Ltd., 1966), 174, 195–96; Nicholas Goodard, *Harvests of Change: The Royal Agricultural Society of England, 1838–1988* (London: Quiller Press, 1988), 167.

12. Finlay, "Science, Practice and Politics," 327–31; Molle, "Het Belgisch landbouwsbeleid"; Ferleger and Lazonick, "The Managerial Revolution."

13. Michael Wintle, "Agrarian History in The Netherlands in the Modern Period: A Review and Bibliography," *Agricultural History Review* 39 (1991): 68.

14. Wright, *France in Modern Times,* 263; Heywood, "Agriculture and Industrialization in France," 109.

15. Ferleger, "Arming America Agriculture."

16. H. C. Knoblauch, *State Agricultural Experiment Stations: A History of Research Policy and Procedure* (Washington, D.C.: GPO, 1962), 14–17; Norwood Allen Kerr, *The Legacy: A Centennial History of the State Agricultural Experiment Stations, 1887–1987* (Columbia: Missouri Agricultural Experiment Station, 1987), 4–5, 11. In the 1880s, Johnson and Wilbur Atwater, a chemist who had spent two years carrying out research in German experiment stations, also sought to have American stations located next to institutions of higher learning that had agricultural schools, also a hallmark of German stations. See Kerr, 22–24.

17. Kerr, *The Legacy,* 3; Carl R. Woodward and Ingrid N. Waller, *New Jersey's Agricultural Experiment Station, 1880–1930* (New Brunswick: New Jersey Agricultural Experiment Station, 1932), 19, 128, 214. Cook also had influence on other experiment stations precisely because of his emphasis on German approaches to agricultural science. On his

contribution to the Arkansas agricultural experiment station, see Stephen F. Strausberg, *A Century of Research: Centennial History of the Arkansas Agricultural Experiment Station, 1888–1988* (Fayetteville: Arkansas Agricultural Experiment Station, 1989).

18. Alan I. Marcus, *Agricultural Science and the Quest for Legitimacy* (Ames: Iowa State University Press, 1985), 66–67, 154, 156. The editor of the local agricultural paper focusing on livestock disagreed with Caldwell and argued that German experiment stations spent too much time on chemical problems and not enough on other pressing issues. See also other comments either in support of or against the German approach (68, 70).

19. For a discussion of the ways agricultural education in Germany affected similar efforts and experiment station work, see Alfred Charles True, *A History of Agricultural Education in the United States, 1785–1925* (Washington, D.C.: GPO, 1929), 69, 127, 193, 258.

20. Steven Stoll, *The Fruits of Natural Advantage: Making the Industrial Countryside in California* (Berkeley: University of California Press, 1998), 49; Kerr, *The Legacy*, 58; True, *A History of Agricultural Education in the United States, 1785–1925*, 161–63, 178, 189; 259; Marcus, *Agricultural Science*, 72. See also similar attempts in Massachusetts and the invoking of the German approach (Marcus, 83). Finding trained specialists to handle the myriad problems confronting station scientists was a source of concern as well for the OES. In one *Record* editorial, the editor wrote about how the German Empire's approach to procuring qualified personnel worked, and how the experiment stations sought government support and involvement so that the chemists who were hired to examine food materials were as qualified as the scientists who carried out station work. See *Experiment Station Record* 2, no. 11 (1891): 626–27.

21. *Experiment Station Record* 2, no. 3 (1890): 93–97.

22. *Experiment Station Record* 2, no. 10 (1890): 542–46.

23. *Experiment Station Record* 1, no. 4 (1890): 177; George Grantham, "The Shifting Locus of Agricultural Innovation in Nineteenth-Century Europe: The Case of Agricultural Experiment Stations," in *Technique, Spirit, and Form in the Making of the Modern Economies: Essays in Honor of William N. Parker*, ed. Gary Saxonhouse and Gavin Wright (New York: JAI Press, 1984), 201.

24. Louis Ferleger, "Uplifting American Agriculture: Experiment Station Scientists and the OES in the Early Years after the Hatch Act," *Agricultural History* 64 (1990): 5–23.

25. Finlay, "Science, Practice and Politics," 375–79.
26. Julius Terrass Willard, *History of the Kansas State College of Agricultural and Applied Science* (Manhattan: Kansas State College Press, 1940), 462.
27. *Experiment Station Record* 2, no. 8 (1891): 389–90.
28. *Experiment Station Record* 1, no. 4 (1890): 175. For other citations of abstracts, see vol. 2, no. 3 (1890): 93–97; vol. 2, no. 4 (1890): 140; vol. 2, no. 8 (1891): 389–90, 459; vol. 2, no. 9 (1891): 522–35; vol. 2, no. 10 (1891): 542–43; vol. 2, no. 11 (1891): 627. Also, see *Experiment Station Record* 2, no. 11 (1891): 684–85; vol. 2, no. 12 (1891): 759–63; and other citations in various issues of the *Record*, 1890–1910. On the quoting of German work on sugar-beet research, see *Experiment Station Record* 2, no. 12 (1891); *Bulletin* 30: 748–49.
29. *Ninth Annual Report of the Agricultural Experiment Station of the A & M College, Auburn, Alabama* (Montgomery, Ala.: Brown Printing Co., 1897), 14.
30. Knoblauch, *State Agricultural Experiment Stations*, 76–77.
31. This paragraph is based on Ferleger and Lazonick, "The Managerial Revolution," 89. For other studies, see Robert Evenson et al., "Economic Benefits from Research: An Example from Agriculture," *Science* 205 (1979); Zvi Griliches, "Research Costs and Social Returns: Hybrid Corn and Related Innovations," *Journal of Political Economy* 66 (1958): 419–31; Vernon W. Ruttan, "Bureau Productivity: The Case of Agricultural Research," *Public Choice* 35 (1935); Ferleger, "Arming America Agriculture."

Drylands, Dust Bowl, and Agro-Technical Internationalism in Southern Africa

Sarah T. Phillips

In the late nineteenth century, Americans developed certain techniques for dry farming, or raising crops without irrigation, in areas of low or unpredictable rainfall. These methods for growing grain in arid regions drew international interest, and South Africans began applying them in the Orange Free State and in the Transvaal. Because there arose on the Great Plains of the United States a concerted dry-farming movement that attracted attention in South Africa, an analysis of agro-environmental adaptation in the semiarid regions of each nation extends beyond the purely comparative.[1] The use of dryland techniques enabled white settlers in North America and South Africa to farm areas previously thought to be of marginal use for raising large quantities of small grain. Because the U.S. land-grant colleges and the experiment stations of the U.S. Department of Agriculture played the primary role in the development of dry farming in North America and its promotion overseas, state intervention and state support sustained this process.

The cash-crop production of winter wheat under dryland conditions is the lens with which this paper examines the transmission of method and technology from the plains of one nation to the veld of another. Wheat, grouped with rye and oats as a winter cereal, is best suited to a cool, moist growing season. Wheat sown in the autumn, if capable of surviving the extremes of cold and possible drought, will yield grain in greater abundance than the same variety sown in the spring. Winter wheat is better able to overcome the effects of spring dryness due to its larger reserve of root growth, and the cold growing season and an early maturation date protects the crop from hot summer winds, insects, and disease. For these reasons, winter wheat tended to expand as far as the climate would permit. In the United States, farmers grew dryland winter wheat as far north as South Dakota and in some sheltered foothill regions of Montana. Farmers in South Africa grew only winter wheat, as the heavy summer rains and high temperatures of the summer rainfall area proved incompatible with successful wheat production.[2]

This transatlantic story does not conclude with the successful transmission of dryland methods, however, because the dry-farming movement also contributed to the American Dust Bowl of the 1930s, and the Dust Bowl received tremendous international attention. In fact, Dust Bowl narratives hastened the formation of concerted soil-conservation efforts by governments in both East and Southern Africa. The perceived threat of soil erosion on a grand scale, induced in large part by impressions of the denuded American plains, justified accelerated state interventions in African agriculture in the 1930s and 1940s. In turn, the compulsory terracing schemes and grazing limitations imposed on African populations led, in many instances, to peasant resistance and independence movements. In South Africa, white farmers greatly expanded dryland wheat production after World War II, aided immeasurably by mechanization and state support. Because American soil-conservation officials publicized their solutions to the problems of dryland agriculture in the 1930s and 1940s, the South African government was inspired to adopt certain conservation measures in a new extension program developed in the 1940s. Officials there believed that dry farming could be scientifically controlled, because the Americans had conquered the Dust Bowl.

During the course of the early twentieth century, there arose a nexus of methodological interchange between the agricultural frontiers of America and South Africa—first in the early years of the twentieth century with the dissemination of a system of dry farming, and then in the 1930s and 1940s with a set of prescriptions for managing its unstable aspects. The significance of this interchange is twofold. First, North America played a significant role in the extension of agricultural practice and policy before the

Dust Bowl, and before the political and economic hegemony of the United States after World War II. This was part of a process of "agro-technical internationalism." Information and technology flowed along new, global routes, rather than within the local systems of exchange that had previously characterized older forms of smallholder cultivation. Second, the international movement of dryland methods and Dust Bowl narratives strengthened the state in Southern and East Africa. In East Africa, it is clear that such intervention energized peasant resistance and independence movements. In South Africa, apartheid-era land policy purposely supported white farmers and marginalized the African population. The "transatlantic radicals" in this case consisted of new crops, new farming methods, and an emerging ideology of government-sponsored agricultural modernization that employed soil conservation and increased productivity as its justification.

The Development of Dryland Farming in the United States and South Africa

Around 1910, when white South Africans first began experimenting with dry-farming techniques, they acquired information from American publications and from American agricultural scientists. This pattern continued well into the twentieth century. This is not to suggest that indigenous, moisture-conserving methods of cultivation had not been developed in South Africa, or that Americans exercised the only influence on wheat (and maize) expansion in that country. The evidence, though, points to the overwhelming role of North America in the larger process of expanding the cultivation of dryland wheat, not only in South Africa, but in other subhumid and semiarid areas of the world as well.[3]

In fact, the United States had a head start in developing agricultural techniques for crop growing in arid lands. The American government played the most significant role in these developments. The U.S. Army assured settlers fresh supplies of land throughout the nineteenth century by confining the Native American population to reservations. The agricultural frontier, subsequently encouraged by such liberal land policies as the Homestead Act of 1862 and the Expanded Homestead Acts of 1908–1916, pushed westward onto the plains, despite their reputation as a Great American Desert. A daring subsidization of the railroads thrust the transportation facilities beyond the crop farmer, thus ensuring the railroads' interest in securing immigration and settlement of the prairies and plains.

The settlers came from a wide variety of countries and climates, bringing with them a diverse array of farming experiences from which to pick and choose. The Morrill Act of 1862 and the Hatch Act of 1887 provided a network of agricultural colleges, experiment stations, and extension scientists to improve and promote agricultural systems in every state and territory. Abundant land and manpower shortages stimulated the development of labor-saving machinery, which in turn engendered a favorable climate for larger, more extensive experimentation. American farmers also benefited from one of the largest internal markets in the world, as well as from a substantial foreign demand for their grain. A large, active Department of Agriculture (USDA) searched the world for new varieties of farm products and funded vast agricultural trials and experiments. After all, the varieties of wheat, sorghum, alfalfa, and livestock refined in the western regions of the United States originated in Europe, Asia, and Africa. Finally, the USDA generously exported its knowledge. In 1928, an agronomy professor in the Transvaal remarked that "the liberality of the Department of Agriculture in Washington in giving information and assistance to others is a byword among students of agriculture." Notably, the same professor maintained that "the South African need offer no apology for studying American progress with the expectation of acquiring valuable lessons. The general similarity of climate, an approximately contemporaneous development, the success which has attended the imitation of many American practices, and the enormous expenditure of money, time, and effort devoted to agriculture by the Americans, warrant his doing so."[4]

Farmers in Utah, California, and Washington probably devised methods of growing crops without irrigation independently of the major thrust of westward settlement. Still, the development of dry farming as a modern movement, sanctioned by conference networks and government investigations, was linked with the outpouring of migrants onto the Great Plains after the Civil War. Encouraged by unusually high levels of rainfall, and by the railroads that whisked their crops to market, the settlers brought corn and soft winter and spring wheat to Kansas and Nebraska, and spring wheat, oats, and barley to the Dakotas and beyond. Faced with drought in the late 1880s and 1890s, farmers diversified by turning to livestock and hardy forage crops—such as alfalfa and the sorghums. In Nebraska, Kansas, and Oklahoma, they also planted Turkey Red, a hard, drought-resistant variety of Russian winter wheat tested by the Kansas State Agricultural College.[5]

The settlers adapted to the environment by experimenting with a variety of wheat-cultivating methods. Kansas farmers, for example, developed the lister for corn, and later appropriated the implement for use in their wheat fields. The lister was essentially a double plow that cut the stubble and left the rough surface in alternating ridges and furrows. Listing saved time and effort, because a farmer could work his fields three times faster with the lister than with the old moldboard plow. The seed was drilled, not broadcast, in the protected furrows, and as the young plants grew, the surface was gradually worked down with a "ridge-busting" disc cultivator. Most importantly, the farmers had found that listing prevented soil blowing, and provided shelter and moisture for the fragile young crop.[6]

By the end of the nineteenth century, Kansas farmers combined listing with the techniques of Russian Mennonite immigrants—who, legend has it, planted the first crop of Turkey wheat in Kansas. The immigrants brought with them methods of cultivation honed in the Crimea, where the soil and climate resembled the dry prairie regions of the central United States. They plowed early, as soon as possible after a crop was harvested. They followed this initial plowing with repeated surface cultivation until the autumn seeding time, in order to check the growth of moisture-robbing weeds. Often, they allowed the field to lie in a cultivated fallow throughout the summer and following winter. This enabled the soil to soak up a season's moisture for the wheat crop of the following year. By the early twentieth century, farmers in Kansas practiced a routine rotation of winter wheat, a cultivated summer fallow, and a subsequent crop of winter wheat. Because 75 percent of the rains fell between the months of April and September, the cultivated summer fallow allowed for sensible, yet continuous wheat cropping.[7]

The ridge-and-furrow wheat cultivation in Kansas, however, came to be disputed by adherents of the smooth-surface methods advanced by Hardy Webster Campbell, a homesteader in South Dakota. In the 1890s, after he struggled with five years of drought, Campbell advertised and promoted his techniques. He emphasized that scant rainfall could be stored in the ground by increasing the retention capabilities of the soil: first, the ground must be thoroughly pulverized by discing, leaving the surface smooth. The subsoil should be packed, thereby strengthening the root bed and drawing ground water upward by capillary action. The soil would need protection from evaporation, requiring that the farmer cultivate with a disc harrow after each rain to build up a fine dust mulch. Most importantly, it was crucial not to let weeds grow during fallow periods, as they would plunder the precious moisture. Finally, less seed was needed in packed soil than in normal soils. "Percolation, evaporation, and capillary action," Campbell wrote, "will be found more interesting the more the reader understands them. . . . You will then comprehend why the plowing should be reasonably deep and the under portion made fine and firm, while the top should be fine, but loose and dry." Gradually, he emended his methods to advocate a mulch of soil lumps and clods, not one composed of a dust blanket.[8]

Hardy Campbell energetically publicized his system and helped to establish a dry-farming experiment station in Colorado in 1894. Thereafter, state associations, railroads, and business organizations adapted his techniques to promote the expansion of farming into previously marginal areas. Newly introduced drought-resistant plants, such as durum and Preston wheats and the sorghums, became the crops of choice. As historian Mary W. M. Hargreaves has shown, the "Campbell System" promised both to conquer the arid West and to eclipse farming practice in the East. The promotional propaganda of dry-farming advocates lured hundreds of thousands of settlers onto the Great Plains. Indeed, dry-farming operations in eastern Montana, the western Dakotas, and the central plains constituted the greatest addition to cultivated acreage in the United States after 1900.[9]

The Morrill and Hatch Acts paved the way for experimental dry farms in almost every western state. Railroad companies also operated model farms, hoping to entice settlers. The first Dry-Farming Congress was held in Denver, Colorado, in 1907, and subsequent Congresses gathered in Utah, Wyoming, Montana, and Washington. These conferences provided a forum for debate, and Campbell's influence waned. The USDA in particular took a cautious stance toward further development of the arid regions. In 1905, the USDA had established the Office of Dry Land Agriculture under the leadership of E. C. Chilcott, a former agronomist in South Dakota. Though Chilcott continued to advocate the use of soil-preserving tillage techniques, he warned that no set of scientific prescriptions could ever ensure success in the risky arid regions. Supporters of Campbell hardly welcomed these views. For example, John A. Widtsoe, an agronomist in Utah, continued to promote Campbell's techniques and theories (apart from the need to pack the subsurface of the soil). During this decade (1900–10) of experimentation and debate in the United States, a few South Africans began to adopt some of these methods of dryland agriculture.[10]

Winter wheat was not unknown in South Africa. Dutch farmers in the southwestern Cape Province, where rain fell during the winter months of June, July, and August, grew wheat almost from the moment they arrived in the seventeenth century. As early as the 1830s and 1840s, missionaries in Basutoland (in the summer rainfall area) recorded wheat cultivation during the dry season in *vleis,* or areas of year-round moisture, and the Sotho also planted more wheat in the late nineteenth century to feed growing grain markets in the emerging mining centers. In the early twentieth century, however, American advances in dryland wheat attracted considerable attention from the outside. Delegates from Canada, Australia, Brazil, Russia, and the Transvaal attended the Dry-Farming Congresses, and many of these conferees returned home and published news of American developments. Several works published by South Africans during this time provide evidence of early interest in American dryland techniques. William MacDonald, a visitor to the 1909 Dry-Farming Congress in Wyoming, wrote an article entitled "The Principles of Dry Farming" that appeared in the *Transvaal Agricultural Journal* in 1909. In 1911, the International Agricultural Institute in Rome published Macdonald's "Dry Farming in Transvaal." H. S. D. du Toit, an agronomist who studied in the United States in the early twentieth century, published *Drogeland Boerdery (Dryland Farming)* when he returned to South Africa in 1913.[11]

Convincing evidence for early dryland wheat farming in South Africa comes from Timothy Keegan's study of the southern highveld. The discovery of diamonds in 1867 at Kimberley, and of the Transvaal gold reefs in 1886 brought railroads, cash, and urban markets for agricultural products. Because agricultural commercialization and the "exploitation of the soil" advanced the furthest in the Orange Free State, the region provides a case study of the processes by which it became the granary of South Africa's industrial centers. Beginning early in the twentieth century, the state provided white farmers with access to loan capital. In 1907–08, the former Boer republics established land banks, supplanted in 1912 by the Union Land Bank. These land banks signaled the beginning of a continuous program of state-financed white farming.[12]

Guarantees of state support engendered three periods of financial boom and productive expansion: 1893–95, 1908–13, and the mid-1920s. Though maize grown in summer always remained the predominant crop in the Free State, wheat production flourished during the first boom years of the twentieth century. The total area of the Free State planted in wheat increased almost twofold from 1904 to 1911. This increase was especially marked in districts of the "Conquered Territory," stretching along the border of Basutoland (Lesotho). By 1918, however, census statistics reported that the area sown with wheat in the Free State had fallen. In 1919, a departmental committee sent to investigate the possibilities of wheat production found "that the shortage of seasonal labor and the uncertainties of dryland wheat cultivation were the major reasons for the decreases in acreages in the Orange Free State."[13]

Except for a small region of year-round rain on the south coast, rain in South Africa falls either in the winter rainfall area of the southwest, or in the summer rainfall area of the rest of the country. Between 65 and 90 percent of the total rainfall comes during the summer months in most areas of the Union. As in the United States, moisture generally decreases from east to west. The rate of evaporation is more crucial to agricultural success, though, than the amount of precipitation. Because regional rates of evaporation in South Africa are considerably higher than evaporation rates in the United States, the rainfall in South Africa is less effective than that occurring within similar isohyets in America. Only in southwestern Texas, for example, does the evaporation rate approach that of South Africa. For this reason, the areas in South Africa that receive between 20 and 30 inches (500 to 760 mm) of rainfall, such as districts in the eastern Orange Free State, more closely parallel U.S. land west of the 20-inch (500 mm) isohyet than a comparison of annual rainfall might initially suggest.[14]

By 1908, economic conditions in the Orange Free State favored the importation of dry-farming methods, and an official report used the phrase "dryland wheat cultivation." Without a South African description of this practice, however, it would be difficult to conclude that farmers in the Free State or the Transvaal had adopted American practices. Fortunately, though, several publications from the 1920s offer concrete evidence that South Africans had indeed borrowed American moisture-conserving techniques for growing winter wheat in both the Free State and the Transvaal. Farmers in these regions cultivated a summer fallow during the rainy season to accumulate moisture for the winter crop.[15]

The 1929 South African *Agricultural Handbook* includes a sample farm inventory that mentions the requisite implements for dryland farming—four plows, a disc plow, six drag-harrows, three cultivators, and a drilling machine. Notably, the inventory cites no tractor or combine harvester, the stock-in-trade of American wheat farmers by the late 1920s. Pictures of wheat harvesting show a self-binding reaper pulled by four horses. Herein lies the significance of the dryland wheat revolution that occurred in South Africa after World War II. Only after extensive mechanization could wheat farming proceed on the scale it had assumed before the war in the United States.[16]

The mechanization of agriculture in South Africa and the renewed interest in dryland techniques after World War II stemmed in large part from government support. After Union in 1910, the state drew upon the expanding mining sector to finance agricultural development in the form of land banks, agricultural cooperatives, and education. Tariff protection became the norm as a result of the 1924 Pact Government, an administration that was receptive to policies of state intervention. In 1926, sugar was the first commodity to benefit from an increased import duty. The Great Depression of 1929–32 further depressed agricultural prices, accelerating the drift toward comprehensive protections. Beginning in 1934, producer-dominated marketing boards enforced high tariffs and high internal prices for wheat, wine, maize, and tobacco. The Marketing Act of 1937 codified the existing arrangements by authorizing Commodity Control Boards to fix prices and monopolize marketing arrangements. Legislation in 1939 also increased support for agricultural cooperatives, which were enabled to carry out the handling and marketing of specified commodities. A hefty majority of farmers belonged to cooperatives by 1960, many participating in two or three.[17]

Influenced by massive state support, land under cultivation increased rapidly, reaching a peak of 97.9 million hectares in 1959. Economic historians have argued that South African farming underwent a revolution during the 1950s and 1960s, and that the agricultural landscape was completely transformed by 1970. This subsidization was an expensive undertaking. Between 1948 and 1966, the Department of Agricultural Economics and Marketing invested an annual average of 31 million rand. Of this figure, wheat received the most support—an average of 13.2 million rand a year. Furthermore, this support of wheat growing coincided with a change in consumer tastes. Specifically, urbanizing blacks began to favor bread over maize porridge, heightening the internal demand for wheat.[18]

With a shift in technology, a high protective tariff, and a growing internal market, the stage was set in South Africa for the postwar expansion of dryland wheat farming. The transfer of dryland techniques and the expansion of wheat acreage, however, was connected with the later export of Dust Bowl narratives. The story of prewar wheat farming in the United States will illuminate some of the causes and international consequences of the Dust Bowl.

The United States Dust Bowl

Due to the work of such scholars as Mary W. M. Hargreaves, R. Douglas Hurt, Harry McDean, and Donald Worster, the history of the northern and southern plains in the Dust Bowl era is well known (and quite contested). Yet part of the story—and the historiographical debate that accompanies it—bears repeating. The intention here is not to introduce new data or an original analysis of the Dust Bowl, but to develop a few themes as background information to the primary focus: the transfer of American attitudes about soil erosion and soil conservation to Southern and Eastern Africa. Foremost among these themes is the development of a set of beliefs about what caused the Dust Bowl, and what fixed it. These attitudes became embodied in the person of Hugh Hammond Bennett, head of the U. S. Soil Conservation Service and chief American propagandist in South Africa. A related theme is the role of governments in global information exchange and environmental intervention.[19]

Social and ecological conditions converged in the southern plains to create the disaster of the 1930s. While much of the country experienced unusually dry weather during the 1930s, the central plains states bore the brunt of repeated droughts. Though plains farmers everywhere faced withered crops and starving livestock, the residents of the southern plains suffered from dust storms and severe wind erosion. For the most part, they had arrived in the years following World War I, hoping to cultivate large sections of wheat with the aid of gasoline tractors and combine harvesters. As wheat prices dropped in the 1920s, the settlers borrowed money for more machinery and broke sod for more wheat. They used a new form of agricultural technology—the one-way disc plow—because it worked faster to break the sod and destroy weeds. It also laid bare large stretches of erodible soils that were particularly vulnerable to overcropping. Drought, which prevented the wheat from growing and holding the soil intact, first appeared in the summer of 1931, when one-third of the panhandle area of Oklahoma, Texas, western Kansas, southeastern Colorado, and northeastern New Mexico was plowed under, and the soil exposed. Strong winds whipped the dirt into dust clouds that wreaked havoc for the next several years. Federal officials estimated that a single dust storm in May 1934 carried away 300 million tons of fertile topsoil, some of it as far as the Atlantic Ocean. A 1936 survey of fourteen Dust Bowl counties disclosed that 54 percent of the land planted to grain had been blown out. That same year, nearly 20 percent of the cropland in forty-five counties lay idle, and one out of every four farm homes had been abandoned.[20]

Between 1925 and 1931, wheat acreages in the southern plains had expanded by 200 percent; in some counties, this figure increased to 400 or even 1,000 percent. The labor requirements of wheat farming had also nurtured a speculative cadre of "suitcase farmers," who appeared in the fields only during the minimum six weeks it took to plant and harvest the wheat. Furthermore, changes in nearby industrial employment sent settlers with no farming experience to the region. Labor cutbacks in the Texas, Kansas, and Oklahoma oil fields, for example, had forced workers to look for jobs elsewhere. Many of these middle-aged men migrated with their families to the southern plains, where they could rent, sharecrop, or purchase a small farm. A culture of transience and impermanence permeated the region. Consequently, listing, crop rotation, extended fallowing, and strip cropping were rare, and the advent of depression-era incomes ensured that such conservation measures were entirely absent when the dust began to blow.[21]

The drought and the Dust Bowl highlighted the problem of soil erosion, and drew the nation's attention to the plight of those caught in its vise. While many Dust Bowl residents, weighted with poverty and desperation, left their homes, most farmers remained in the area and profited from government relief and reconstruction programs. The Dust Bowl area, in fact, received more federal funds per capita than any other agricultural region. And in the plains states as a whole, drought-stricken farmers benefited immediately from federal crop payments, emergency cattle purchases, emergency listing funds, soil-conservation programs, relief grants, crop and seed loans, and relief jobs.[22]

While the federal government purchased some submarginal land in the Dust Bowl region and sponsored several resettlement communities, most Dust Bowl communities welcomed a different set of possible conservation remedies: technical measures to control soil erosion. This approach became embodied in the person of Hugh H. Bennett, chief of the Soil Erosion Service. During the 1920s, Bennett had drawn the nation's attention to the "national menace" of soil erosion, arguing that sheet and gully erosion explained lost fertility and decreased farm income. In 1929 Congress passed legislation authorizing several erosion experiment stations, and in 1933 Bennett received $10 million for additional conservation work. The new Soil Erosion Service (SES) established demonstration projects and worked with cooperating farmers to promote conservation measures such as contour plowing, terracing, strip cropping, pasture building, and stock-watering ponds. The SES supplied technical direction as well as the machinery, seed, shrubs, and trees. It also worked with the Civilian Conservation Corps to supplement labor furnished by farm owners. By the fall of 1934, the SES operated thirty-one demonstration projects in twenty-eight states.

In Jewell County, Kansas, for example, the SES showed residents how to increase grain yields and prevent gullies by terracing their land and plowing on the contour.[23]

Along with the CCC, the SES—renamed the Soil Conservation Service (SCS) under the Department of Agriculture in 1935—established several wind-erosion demonstration projects in the Dust Bowl area. Farmers signed on to the program, agreeing to cooperate with the SCS for five years. The benefits of the most basic soil-preserving measure, contour plowing, were appreciated by 1936, when a group of Texas farmers who had not prepared their fields watched one of their neighbors grow 160 acres of feed on his contoured land. The SCS also emphasized the utility of terracing, citing a study that concluded a two-inch rain could be converted into a seven-inch rain with the aid of terracing and contouring. In addition, conservation officials worked to implement the strip cropping of drought-resistant, soil-holding feed crops. Superior wheat and sorghum yields on the demonstration farms, along with a reduction in soil blowing, illustrated the benefits of such methods throughout the 1930s. By the end of the decade, 80 percent of farmers under SCS contracts attributed increased net farm incomes to the conservation program, 89 percent attributed increased land values to the program, and a full 95 percent aimed to continue the conservation methods after their contracts ended.[24]

In 1934, the year the Soil Erosion Service became the Soil Conservation Service, Congress passed the Soil Erosion Act. This legislation charged the government with the task of supporting a large conservation program. Because the SCS believed the federal government had no constitutional right to enforce land-use regulations, it wanted to encourage the states to impose such requirements on landowners. Accordingly, the SCS designed a model state law in 1936 and called it *A Standard Soil Conservation District Law.* By 1937, four Dust Bowl States—Kansas, Colorado, New Mexico, and Oklahoma—passed similar legislation (Texas had passed a law in 1935 authorizing wind-erosion conservation districts). Local initiative would establish the districts, and the farmers within each would unite in the fight against erosion. Thirty-seven of these districts existed in the Dust Bowl states by the summer of 1939. Though the legacy of the Soil Erosion Act and the conservation districts remains uncertain, most believed it was the proper step to take at the time.[25]

Donald Worster, the most influential Dust Bowl historian, argues that these arid regions, characterized by patterns of cyclical drought, inherently could not withstand the destructive capacity of the new technology.

Farmers and the capitalist system that supported their endeavors refused to recognize these limits, and the disaster came about because "the expansionary energy of the United States had finally encountered a volatile, marginal land, destroying the delicate ecological balance that had evolved there."[26] Yet some have maintained that Worster's explanation does not by itself clarify why the Dust Bowl occurred precisely where it did, or why it failed to appear in other mechanized, semiarid regions of the wheat belt. Other work suggests that the Dust Bowl was the product of a specific time and a specific place, not the result of dryland farming in general. Whatever the Dust Bowl's cause, government conservation assistance clearly enabled many residents to remain wheat farmers. And Hugh Bennett's prescriptions— contour plowing, strip cropping, crop rotations, shelterbelts, and grazing management—also constituted the greater part of his message to South Africans.

Soil Erosion and the American Experience in South Africa

Shifts in technology, high protective tariffs, and a growing internal market provided the background for a postwar expansion of dryland wheat farming in South Africa. What is remarkable about the reintroduction of dry-farming techniques after the war, however, is that the "wheat bonanza" happened at all. The American Dust Bowl publicized the dangers of farming in marginal lands, and officials in South Africa imbibed the reactionary literature that followed. Even the South African farmers and specialists involved confessed that that "the United States dustbowl was still very fresh in memory and monoculture was a long dirty word . . . Nevertheless when one of the professors asked what crop rotation plans [we] had in mind, [we] laughed and said, 'Wheat for the next 99 years.'"[27]

Serious consideration of soil erosion in South Africa had historically emerged from worries about settler agriculture. Though hints of a "veld degradation orthodoxy" appeared in the eighteenth and nineteenth centuries, the belief that South African pastures had deteriorated gained more widespread acceptance in the twentieth century. F. E. Kanthack, a Cape official, publicized the connection between soil erosion and bare, deforested, or overgrazed land in 1908 and 1909. Another article that appeared in the *Rhodesian Journal of Agriculture* in 1913 also lamented overstocking and the nighttime *kraaling* (central penning) of livestock, a practice that wore tracks and *dongas* (gullies) into the ground. The author denounced crop farmers for up-and-down plowing of slopes and clean cultivation, which left the soil vulnerable to rain and wind erosion. He recommended alternating stock paddocks, contour plowing (plowing either perpendicular to the prevailing winds or the prevailing watershed), and strip cropping. Such prescriptions foreshadowed the basis for state intervention to halt soil erosion, which was established by the drought of 1919–20.[28]

Horrific levels of stock losses accompanied the drought. It decimated the supply of wool, the nation's primary agricultural export. The government instructed the South African Drought Investigation Commission to look into the disaster. After more than one hundred public meetings in the semiarid region of the mid-Cape, the committee blamed the losses of 1919 on faulty veld and stock management. Overgrazing, overstocking, herding, the scarcity of drinking places, and the *kraaling* of animals at night had deteriorated the vegetal covering, reducing the ground's capacity to hold water. Rain rushed over the bare earth, carving *dongas* and sweeping away the plant-holding capacity of the ground. The report characterized this soil erosion as that "insidious evil creeping in unseen like a thief in the night and robbing us of our national wealth." Significantly, the committee held the small stock farmer responsible for the damage.[29]

The report specified three categories of soil erosion: surface erosion by wind, surface erosion by water, and erosion by *donga* or *sloot* formation. Erosion of all three kinds was proceeding at an alarming pace, thus provoking the committee to recommend *"immediate and prompt action if retrogression is to be arrested."* The report also placed all forms of erosion in two other divisions: the erosion on cultivated lands, and veld erosion. Though erosion on cultivated lands was "a matter of extreme importance, the area thus far covered by your Commission in its investigation has not included any portions in which erosion of cultivated lands is very serious, and . . . your Commission has decided not to deal with it here."[30] More research is needed to determine whether cultivated lands had escaped serious erosion, or if the committee simply failed to visit regions marked by it.[31] In any case, this report, a landmark recognition of soil erosion, blamed the stockholder of the mid-Cape, not the wheat or maize farmer of the ex-republics. Many publications, including Leppan's *Agricultural Development* (1928) and the *Handbook for Farmers in South Africa* (1929), reiterated the Drought Commission's conclusions. Jacks and Whyte's *Rape of the Earth* (1939), a "world survey of soil erosion" that greatly influenced South African officials, also summarized its findings. One could reasonably maintain that South Africans continued to associate truly debilitating erosion with range mismanagement, not with cultivation. This probably contributed to an ideological climate favorable to dryland wheat expansion after World War II.[32]

A more persuasive explanation for confidence in wheat monocropping probably lies in an examination of state aid to farmers facing erosion difficulties. In general, conservation efforts on behalf of white farmers constituted an important part of the general expansion of government agricultural involvement. The National Soil Erosion Council was established in 1929 to direct conservation activities, and the 1929 *Handbook for Farmers in South Africa* included a substantial section on soil erosion. The author calculated that "nine of our principal rivers carry away more than 187,000,000 tons of soil every year, or enough to cover a depth of one foot an area comprising 91 square miles." Though recognizing the dangers of wind and sheet erosion, the *Handbook* concentrated on the most visible form, the *donga*. "The best remedy for soil erosion is to take care that no dongas are born on our farms. . . . But unfortunately there are already so many thousands of them that we will have to use all our energy to stop or retard this evil."[33]

The *Handbook* implored farmers to plant vegetation in and along gullies. In drier areas, "the Union Forest Department also supplies exotic trees and plants able to withstand drought and cold, some of which could undoubtedly be planted successfully for the purpose of closing up dongas." The *Handbook* further instructed the farmer in the methods of installing wire netting and dams in order to direct silting, and it included three photographs and two diagrams of the recommended process. "When once a start is made, the benefits will be apparent. . . . Sometimes these dongas run through several farms, and it is only by the closest cooperation of the neighboring farmers that a success can be made in checking soil erosion." In 1934, the Agriculture Department set up pasture research stations to investigate erosion, and offered some conservation extension services to white landowners throughout the 1930s. Much of the impetus for this increased propaganda came from the American Dust Bowl, and the onset of World War II apparently led many officials and conservationists to regard themselves as waging another war against a fierce new enemy—soil erosion. Under the Soil and Veld Conservation Act of 1941, the state could designate severely eroded regions as "Conservation Areas" and order that conservation measures be installed. But the state rarely used this power, viewing such actions as extreme. All in all, the available conservation funds could only entice farmers to change their methods until 1946, when the Soil Conservation Act empowered the Department of Agriculture and local committees to intervene (to a certain extent) in white farming practices.[34]

The few years prior to the passage of the 1946 legislation witnessed events that illuminate the subsequent expansion of dry farming in the Free State. Historians Peter Delius and Stefan Schirmer claim that many South African officials in the early 1940s "saw a state-run soil conservation programme as the best way to transform agriculture into a sector that would be able to contribute comprehensively into a dynamic and efficient postwar economy." In 1943, a government report on the "Reconstruction of Agriculture" concluded that the state could aid cash-strapped white farmers by continuing the marketing system and expanding the conservation program.[35] In 1944, a visit from Hugh Bennett, the director of the United States SCS, helped to publicize the U.S. soil-conservation experience. On his two-month tour through South Africa, Bennett insisted he rarely saw "so much as a single field in which any kind of soil protection or soil-building rotation was being practiced." He outlined his impressions of South African farming in a pamphlet of twenty-eight pages, published by the South African Department of Agriculture and Forestry. He declared:

> Many farmers do little or nothing to check wastage and impoverishment of their lands by erosion and over-cropping. They run goats, sheep, cattle, donkeys, and horses through their fields to take off the last vestige of vegetative residue needed to replenish the prevailing deficiency of organic matter in the soil; they plow up and down slopes to hasten run-off and erosion; and they go on cultivating fields year after year to soil-depleting crops, without rotation to soil-building crops, such as grass and legumes. Accordingly, the State must help—supply the necessary technical knowledge to get the job done, and perhaps certain machinery, seed, and planting material the farmer may need but cannot get.[36]

To combat such problems, Bennett recommended the same remedies enacted within the United States and for the American Dust Bowl of the 1930s. South Africa, Bennett argued, needed to establish soil-conservation districts, on the American model, directed mostly by local farmers. In addition, he urged the immediate implementation of contour plowing (he included several photographs of wheat farms in the winter rainfall area eroded due to up-and-down plowing); strip cropping; crop rotation; windbreaks of grasses, shrubs, and trees; *donga* control; and veld management. Moreover, Bennett called for a huge investment in technical personnel— "the conservation organization of the Department of Agriculture probably needs in the neighborhood of a *thousand men* as quickly as it can get them and train them . . . Conservation work is way out behind in South Africa; it needs to be caught up with and the start should be now." Most importantly, he stressed that due to his techniques, the United States was prospering. "We have had just as bad erosion as anything I have seen in South Africa; we have had prodigious dust storms and donga erosion, and vast areas affected by sheet erosion. We have stopped the dust storms . . . we know how to handle the donga and the sheet erosion. . . . As the results are increasing yields and farm income, the farmers like it . . . I hope some such plan as I have discussed will be adopted and pushed. It will cost a great deal, but everybody will like it and it will pay magnificent dividends to the Nation."[37]

According to Wellington Brink, Bennett's adoring biographer, "the Chief—they called him that over there—was top-notch copy. Newsmen made a big fuss over him. They dogged his heels, followed him through the fields. The war on erosion vied for the front pages with the war being waged on the Axis. . . . Soon the headlines were screaming 'Wealth of Nation Washing Away—Wheat Belt Must Be Tackled Now.'"[38] One South African cartoon portrayed Bennett as a medical specialist leaning over the sickbed of "South African Erosion."[39] Encouraged by Bennett's tour, the Department of Agriculture issued two reports in 1944 and 1945 stressing the need for conservation farming. These papers listed several policies needed to improve agricultural methods. Notably, many of these recommendations mirrored Hugh Bennett's suggestions—contour plowing, strip cropping, shelterbelts, crop rotation, and grazing management. The Soil Conservation Act of 1946 included provisions for the implementation of these practices, thereby sanctioning government intervention in the use of private property. The legislation provided for a National Soil Conservation Board, and for the establishment of local soil conservation committees to monitor conditions and to persuade farmers to alter risky practices. At the same time, the government greatly increased its agricultural extension work.[40]

Government conservation assistance, that is, accompanied the postwar expansion of dryland wheat, as the very soil-conservation agents Bennett had recommended (and the 1946 legislation had funded) took charge of the process. They aided in the expansion of mechanized wheat farming, but other responsibilities included providing "a free service to farmers by way of surveying contour-banks and dams and drawing up farm plans."[41] Thus, farmers in the Free State engaged in industrial-scale dry farming in the late 1940s because conservation agents were confident that they could control the process. After all, Hugh Bennett certainly believed his techniques had controlled the dust storms in the United States (though factors other than state intervention probably averted later Dust Bowl appearances in both the United States and South Africa).[42]

Rural Change and Racial Consequences

A question not yet addressed is how these developments affected Africans. It is possible to suggest that agro-technical internationalism radically changed rural relations and rural welfare in two related ways. First, the importation of dryland techniques represented part of the general process of agricultural modernization and commercialization. With the penetration of capitalist agriculture in the Orange Free State and the Transvaal, white settlers grew militant in demanding a plentiful and evenly dispersed rural labor force. As more and more white farmers bought land and sought labor, they worked to curtail the independence of African peasant producers, and required labor from blacks in return for grazing and cultivating rights. Eventually, whites paid wages and restricted land rights entirely. Whether the advance of white agriculture depended on the repression of blacks, or whether state support launched and maintained the white capitalized farm economy; whether Boer nationalism was the guiding force, or whether the British were also co-conspirators—the result was the same: Africans experienced steadily diminishing access to land, to subsistence and market production. By mid-century, 87 percent of the land was reserved for whites and 13 percent for blacks (who by the year 2000 accounted for more than three-quarters of the population).[43]

Second, the international movement of Dust Bowl narratives, agricultural specialists, and conservationist ideas accelerated the demise of African farming in the "white" areas and supported stepped-up intervention in the "African" areas. While the problems of settler agriculture had initially prompted interest in conservation, this concern was transferred to the peasant producer. The notion that Africans were simply poorer farmers with little concern for conservation practice justified the move to a wage-labor system under which whites exerted full managerial control of their farms. Furthermore, South Africa and the colonial states in East Africa—emboldened in part by the American experience—embarked upon similar schemes for "bettering" and "developing" African agriculture.

Though the timing and exact nature of the transition from squatting to labor tenancy, and from labor tenancy to wage labor in South Africa varied by region, state power underpinned each transition. The Natives' Land Act of 1913 set the direction of twentieth-century land policy. Essentially, it declared that the different African reserve systems in each province would be the only areas where Africans could legally acquire land. Sharecropping and renting would also be phased out over time, and only labor tenants or wageworkers would be allowed to live on white-owned land. Most historians agree that the motivation for the legislation stemmed from white farmers anxious to secure labor, and certain that "kaffir farming" robbed them of that entitlement. "A native will rather pay rent and squat, and do as he likes, than live rent free and work," wrote a correspondent to the *Farmers' Weekly*; " . . . this is the root of our difficulty."[44]

In the Free State, where, as Timothy Keegan demonstrates, "conflict over access to rural resources and control over productive enterprise crystallized earliest," only sustained landlord action and collusion enforced the legislation. Though one would be mistaken to pinpoint 1913 as the decisive turning point due to the fact that enforcement varied by region and that squatting and sharecropping continued, it is clear that the 1913 Land Act profoundly altered rural relations and outlooks. "The sharecroppers," Keegan writes, "quickly lost their social optimism and their faith in self-improvement . . . [they] no longer had the self-confidence to build schools, carve desks, and hire teachers . . . those who sought to elevate themselves or their children found that rural production provided them less and less with a viable base." In fact, the 1913 legislation became a major concern for African politicians. Solomon Plaatje, a leading member of the ANC, documented the effects of the law in the Free State, and published an influential book in 1916 entitled *Native Life in South Africa*. He recorded the plight of the sharecroppers: their homes confiscated, their cattle dying. Having no choice but to become labor tenants or to trek, many crowded the roads. "The South African native," Plaatje wrote, "found himself not actually a slave but a pariah in the land of his birth."[45]

While it seems Plaatje may have exaggerated the immediate effects of the Act, the law did present capitalizing farmers with a potent legal weapon in clearing land of squatters and controlling all production on their land. During this time, farmers increasingly desired to manage all of their holdings, as they experimented with the new scientific ideas disseminated through the Agriculture Department's publications and applied technical concepts to enhance yields. Resistance, of course, was widespread. "In the main," Martin Murray writes, "rural Africans only reluctantly submitted to capitalist discipline at the point of production and . . . waged a heroic yet eventually losing rearguard battle to preserve their access to the land." In the Middelburg district of the Free State, farmers throughout the 1920s struggled to impose labor service agreements on those Africans wishing to remain on the land, and to evict those who would not submit to the new terms. Resistance took the forms of theft and destruction of farm property. On one night in early November 1924, "unknown arsonists" even set fire to several stacks of freshly harvested winter wheat scattered across several farms, prompting widespread fears of a "native uprising."[46]

A series of crucial structural changes also took place during the 1920s and 1930s. From 1918 to 1939, the number of farms increased by 41 percent, and during roughly the same period the number of owner-occupied farms increased by 57 percent. Crop production increased as land formerly held out of cultivation (for speculative purposes, or for rent income from squatters) became occupied by commercial farmers. Land values rose along with land occupation, and thus farmers put the land to more intensive use. As a result, the land farmers made available to labor tenants for grazing and cultivation dwindled. Labor tenants struggled to maintain their access to land by threatening to leave entirely (and thus renegotiating the terms somewhat), or by moving on, generally west or south into more arid regions, where access to land might be secured on more favorable terms.[47]

The depression of the 1930s, while hitting rural economies hard, also brought about major state aid. White farmers received considerable sums of money from the land banks, they drew funds from the government for soil-conservation works, and by the late 1930s almost every commodity was protected by a complex system of price supports and marketing cooperatives. A major problem, though, threatened to rip the rural seams asunder—labor migration. In search of higher wages and better working conditions, many Africans left. This prompted efforts to beef up the machinery and implementation of "influx control," the notorious "pass laws" that restricted labor mobility.[48]

The 1940s saw continued labor shortages in the countryside. The war effort created higher wages in the towns, and the 1948 report of the Fagan Commission remarked that many males were going to the towns and leaving their families on the farms. The Tomlinson Commission later confirmed this observation when its report showed that 40 percent of the increase from 1936 to 1951 in "the number of Bantu urban residents" could be traced to departures from the farms. White farmers denounced the labor-tenant system and the loss of manpower. Calls emanated from every rural corner—district congresses, farm journals, newspapers, agricultural unions—for "only one solution: the farm labourer must be a farm labourer and that only."[49]

This labor shortage intensified just as commercial grain farming expanded after World War II. In the short run, mechanization only increased the need for labor, especially during the harvest season, as at first machines tended to replace animals—tractors instead of oxen and horses, for example.[50] The South African Agricultural Union proposed that "the Native community be encouraged to advance in two main groups, agricultural and industrial," and the Transvaal Agricultural Union proclaimed that "the ruling practice of allowing Native labourers to leave their masters for a portion of any year and to be employed in towns is one of the principal causes of labour wastage . . . the Native must be given a choice of becoming either an industrial worker or permanent farm labourer."[51]

With the 1948 victory of the Nationalist Party, these recommendations came to fruition. The Natives' Land Act (1913), Native Service Contract Act (1932), Native Trust and Land Act (1936), and Native Laws Amendment Act (1952) served as the legal basis. Labor Tenant Control Boards, which could emend or end labor contracts, extended their operations and geographical reach. A prison labor system supplied farmers with convict workers. Labor bureaus, first instituted in 1951, controlled "the numbers of people allowed to enter the urban areas and [directed] labor to those areas most in need of it . . . once a rural person got a 'farmworker only' stamp in his pass, it was virtually impossible for him ever to break from that category legally." And after 1952, as a result of the Group Areas Act, no African person was allowed to remain in a town for longer than 72 hours without special permission. Thus, the postwar Free State "wheat bonanza" must be viewed in the political context of the postwar Afrikaner state: increased state capacity and agricultural expansion went hand in hand with racial dominance in the countryside.[52]

This dominance took increasingly virulent forms as the century proceeded. The labor shortages of the postwar era became labor surpluses by the early 1960s; farmers now wanted smaller and more skilled work forces to manage a still-increasing amount of machinery, especially combine harvesters. This problem merged with another—the "blackening" of the countryside. As the most capitalized white farmers succeeded, those not able to keep up with their neighbors sold out and moved to the towns. At the same time, the rural black population continued to increase. "Now that farm labour was no longer in short supply," wrote members of the Surplus People Project, "it was a development that the government could no longer

tolerate." Legislation in the 1960s abolished labor tenancy across entire regions. The state directed settlement to designated townships and to the reserves (*bantustans*), where population increased dramatically and where
few acquired access to land. A concerted campaign to clear the "black
spots," or places where Africans had held title to the land before 1913, also
commenced. Millions of people "found themselves in barely planned rural
slums which were urban with respect to their population density and lack
of agricultural opportunity, but rural in relation to facilities, services, and
employment."[53]

Significantly, proponents of the removals often employed an environmental argument—that white operational control would not only boost
production, but would also promote better conservation practice.[54] Here is
evidence of the second (but intimately related) influence of agro-technical
internationalism: the impact of the American conservation experience on
postwar rural policy in Southern and East Africa. A historiographical trend
exploring this theme began in the mid-1980s, when two influential articles
on state-sponsored agricultural development appeared. Both William
Beinart and David Anderson noticed a connection between agricultural intervention (inspired in part by the U.S. experience) and post–World War II
resistance to colonial/state authority. In the colonial states of East Africa
and in the settler states of South Africa, Beinart maintained, "the most
acute phase of rural anti-colonial struggle in the 1940s and 1950s coincided with heightened government commitments to 'development.'" David
Anderson opened his article with a similar idea—that "the 'second colonial
occupation,' with its 'do good' justification for meddling in African agriculture, heightened political consciousness by giving African farmers something to complain about."[55]

While it is clear that conservationist concerns arose from many different
quarters, both Beinart and Anderson assign a large role to the Dust Bowl
and to American personnel such as Hugh Bennett. Due to relations of "kinship and comraderie," the colonial states of East Africa looked to South
Africa for guidance, and both sent representatives to the United States to
view the measures of the U.S. Soil Conservation Service. "Even when the
Colonial Office tried to draw upon more appropriate examples from
Africa," Anderson remarks, "they discovered that all roads led back to
Hugh Bennett and the American SCS."[56]

The literature on the postwar rural-development schemes is quite large,
so only a few examples will be touched upon here. In East Africa, soil conservation had materialized as a vital concern by the late 1930s. State

intervention took different forms in Kenya, Uganda, and Tanganyika, but for the most part officials were united in support for conservation measures such as stock culling, terracing, and water-retention structures, with increased cash-crop production a corollary, or, in some cases, the primary goal. These development schemes have been studied so extensively because many seem to hold the keys to understanding the sustained resistance of the decolonization era. David Throup, for example, locates the birthplace of Mau Mau in Kenya within the second colonial occupation of the 1940s, when Britain abandoned the policies of indirect rule in favor of a new developmental strategy that required an interventionist administration. In the 1930s, the Kenyan government became concerned with the issue of farm degradation and soil exhaustion in the native areas. Land alienation, population growth, and the demarcation of reserves contributed to shorter fallow periods and the cultivation of crops on steep hillsides. In the 1940s, field administrators blamed small traders and commercial cultivators for "mining the land," and they decided to revive traditional land authorities in order to implement an extensive terracing campaign. Here, Throup places the Murang'a peasant revolt at the roots of Mau Mau, for he argues that there existed a close correlation between the areas in which the chiefs pushed terracing in the late 1940s and the centers of Mau Mau support in the early 1950s. The terracing campaign, along with a host of new agricultural regulations, created wide resentment against the chiefs, and allowed rural radicals and urban militants to organize a protracted challenge in 1947 and 1948. The militants later resurfaced as Mau Mau leaders in the early 1950s. [57]

Tanzania witnessed similar scenes. There, officials initiated five development projects in the late 1940s—in Mbulu, Usukuma, Kondoa, Usambara, and Uluguru. In his study of Usambara, Steven Feierman puts these schemes to combat soil erosion squarely in an analysis of the development of organized resistance (TANU). There, the government saw declining yields as a problem of soil erosion, rather than a problem of scarce land. Officials assumed that the land would not be able to support future populations, and in 1950 they implemented plans for labor-intensive conservation measures, for removing land from cultivation, and for removing people from the mountains. Specific techniques most prominently included the building of terrace-like *matuta* (ridged, raised squares). The very process of building these ridges felt foreign, and the core of resistance stemmed from women who were forced to build the ridges, thereby converting land that was reserved for the poor into land for cash-cropping men. The resistance was emboldened by Julius Nyerere's 1956 arrival in Shambaai, and 1957 saw the defeat of the Usambara Scheme.[58]

In South Africa, where conservationist anxieties originally stemmed from settler agriculture, attention turned to African producers. To be sure, blacks had long been criticized as poor stewards of the land, but events of the 1930s—falling yields, droughts, population pressure, a soaring migrant-labor level—infused this view with a new urgency. The 1932 Native Economic Commission, charged with analyzing conditions in the reserves, described a "race against time" to avert "the destruction of large grazing areas, the erosion and denudation of the soils, and the drying up of springs." Images of the Dust Bowl further informed the South African analysis of the native areas. "Africans," Beinart writes, "were constructed as unscientific overexploiters of grazing, of trees, and of land, who displayed an irresponsible attitude to future needs, either because their agrarian systems were inadequate in themselves or because old systems were inappropriate under new conditions." In this belief, South Africans found support from none other than Hugh Bennett. "Over there," Bennett remarked to an American audience, "they call the blacks 'natives' . . . and those natives haven't made any advancement in five thousand years." In a different piece, Bennett remarked that a farm in Natal had lost all its topsoil and most of its subsoil due to the "overpopulation, overstocking, and the improvident farming methods" of the native labor tenants.[59]

The solution (known as "betterment") was first introduced in the 1930s and 1940s, but was strengthened after 1949 and became inextricably connected with the Nationalist policies that matured into the Bantusan plans. The first betterment proclamation (1939) included villagization, stock reduction, the division of land into arable and grazing categories, and fencing. Efforts resumed after World War II, and the various schemes triggered ripples of resistance that delayed implementation. The betterment discourse and rhetoric merged with the population removals discussed above. While first designed to combat soil erosion, betterment projects evolved into a justification for removals and a place to deposit blacks from other areas.[60]

Not stated directly, but implicit in the previous discussion are the following themes: first, that despite actual signs of soil erosion, such intervention was coercive in nature; second, that officials habitually overlooked local methods of environmental control; and third, that by confusing land scarcity with land degradation, the state obfuscated the actual needs involved in agricultural development and soil conservation. In fact, the "land question" was probably the most significant factor in hampering the work of black conservation organizations, such as the African National Soil Conservation Association.[61] It should be noted, however, that the present South African government is examining plans for compensation and land restitution.[62]

Conclusion

Wheat farmers in the summer and winter rainfall areas of South Africa adopted American dryland farming techniques in the first decade of the twentieth century. Though it had decreased in importance by 1919, sources from the late 1920s indicate that dryland farming of winter wheat persisted, especially in the Orange Free State along the Basutoland border, and in parts of the Transvaal. After World War II, the general mechanization of agriculture, a sheltered domestic market, and heightened internal demand encouraged an increase in the scale of dryland wheat cultivation in South Africa. Officials there were confident they could learn from the Americans' experience with soil erosion, and that the Free State could avoid extensive wind damage.[63] The American experience also bolstered state-sponsored schemes to modernize African agriculture. Officials combined technical concepts derived in part from Dust Bowl narratives with an ideology of racial dominance to enact coercive policies of agricultural modernization. In some instances, such projects provoked fierce resistance, often leading to independence movements.

On the view that an "agrarian radical" may consist of any agent that upends rural life so as to forever alter modes of living and working, this paper emphasizes the transformative nature of agro-technical internationalism. Because the American state played the primary role in the early development of the country's agricultural areas, the United States was positioned by the beginning of the twentieth century to serve as the principal exporter of technical and empirical concepts. Global routes for the transfer of agricultural information had been forged at the beginning of the century, and the existence of these established paths made possible the dissemination of dry-farming practices, the circulation of Dust Bowl narratives, and the movement of a specific set of beliefs about environmental management.

This chronology of dissemination demonstrates that North America played a significant role in agricultural extension before the Dust Bowl, and before the political and economic hegemony of the United States after World War II. Indeed, the international routes of information exchange maintained by the Dry-Farming Congresses, academic researchers, and the USDA eventually made possible the rapid circulation of Dust Bowl accounts and the stories of environmental degradation (and regeneration) that so influenced policy in Southern and East Africa.

Notes

This is a revised version of "Lessons From the Dust Bowl: Dryland Agriculture and Soil Erosion in the United States and South Africa, 1900–1950," *Environmental History* 4 (April 1999) © Forest History Society. I would like to thank James McCann, Louis Ferleger, and Deborah Fitzgerald for their help with the revision.

1. E. B. Dickinson, "Wheat Development in the Orange Free State: Some Recollections," *Fertilizer Society of South Africa Journal* 2 (1978); William Beinart and Peter Coates, *Environment and History: The Taming of Nature in the USA and South Africa* (London: Routledge, 1995). Though "dryland farming" or "dryland agriculture" now refers to all rain-fed agricultural systems, I will use the terms interchangeably with "dry farming" to designate a specific set of agricultural techniques developed in North America and imitated in other arid regions.

2. Mark A. Carleton, "Successful Wheat Growing in Semiarid Districts," in *Yearbook of Agriculture, 1900* (Washington, D.C.: GPO, 1900), 534; J. H. Arnold and R. R. Spafford, "Farm Practices in Growing Wheat," in *Yearbook of Agriculture, 1919* (Washington, D.C.: GPO, 1919), 124; James C. Malin, *Winter Wheat in the Golden Belt of Kansas: A Study in Adaption to Subhumid Geographical Environment* (Lawrence: University of Kansas Press, 1944), 22.

3. Works on dry farming by Australians and South Africans are discussed in G. Plehn (a German diplomat stationed in Denver, Colorado), *Das Trockenfarmen im Westen der Vereinigten Staaten von Nordamerika* (Hamburg: L. Friederichsen and Co., 1913).

4. Hubert D. Leppan, *The Agricultural Development of Arid and Semi-Arid Regions with Special Reference to South Africa* (South Africa: Central News Agency, Ltd., 1928), 215, 197–98.

5. John A. Widtsoe, *Dry-Farming: A System of Agriculture for Countries Under a Low Rainfall* (New York: Macmillan, 1911), 354–61; Mary W. M. Hargreaves, "The Dry-Farming Movement in Retrospect," *Agricultural History* 51 (January 1977): 149–65; Malin, *Winter Wheat*, 186–87; Mark A. Carleton, "Hard Wheats Winning Their Way," in *Yearbook of Agriculture, 1914* (Washington, D.C.: GPO, 1914), 398.

6. Malin, *Winter Wheat,* 210–45.

7. Carleton, "Successful Wheat Growing," 538–40; Elwood Mead, "The Relation of Irrigation to Dry Farming," in *Yearbook of Agriculture, 1905* (Washington, D.C.: GPO, 1905), 426–27; Malin, *Winter Wheat,* 245; R. Douglas Hurt, *The Dust Bowl: An Agricultural and Social History* (Chicago: Nelson-Hall, 1981), 72. Hargreaves points out that by the 1860s, farmers east of the plains in the Red River district had also experimented with summer fallow in cultivating wheat; see "Dry-Farming," 150.

8. Hargreaves, "Dry-Farming," 152; Hardy W. Campbell, *Campbell's 1902 Soil Culture Manual,* reprinted in *Readings in the History of American Agriculture,* ed. Wayne D. Rasmussen (Urbana: University of Illinois Press, 1970), 172; Hargreaves, *Dry Farming in the Northern Great Plains, 1900–1925* (Cambridge, Mass.: Harvard University Press, 1957), 87–88.

9. Hargreaves, "Dry-Farming," 154; Hargreaves, *Dry Farming,* 19.

10. Widtsoe, *Dry-Farming,* 372–78; Hargreaves, "Dry-Farming," 155.

11. James McCann, *Green Land, Brown Land, Black Land: An Environmental History of Africa* (Portsmouth and London: Heinemann, 1999). See papers by Australians and South Africans mentioned by Plehn in *Das Trockenfarmen.* William Beinart cites the works of Macdonald in "Soil Erosion, Conservation, and Ideas about Development: A Southern African Exploration, 1900–1960," *Journal of Southern African Studies* 11 (October 1984): 57.

12. Timothy Keegan, *Rural Transformations in Industrializing South Africa* (London: Macmillan, 1987), 206, xii. Keegan focuses on the nature of capital accumulation in the Free State to emend the radical thesis that the repression of a servile black tenantry was essential to the rise of commercial agriculture. He concludes that a new industrial imperialism fostered rural white populism and state aid for white farmers, factors more decisive than the need for cheap labor in industrializing the agriculture of the highveld.

13. Keegan, *Rural Transformations,* 203, 211, 107–8. Land area in South Africa was measured in "morgen" before the widespread use of metric units; one morgen equals 2.1 acres.

14. Union of South Africa, Department of Agriculture, *Handbook for Farmers in South Africa* (Pretoria, 1929), 336; Leppan, *Agricultural Development,* 200–201.

15. H. D. Leppan and G. J. Bosman, *Field Crops in South Africa* (South Africa: Central News Agency, Ltd., 1923); Leppan, *Agricultural Development;* Union of South Africa, *Handbook of Agriculture.*

16. Union of South Africa, *Handbook,* 608, 363.

17. Stuart Jones and André Müller, *The South African Economy, 1910–1990* (London: Macmillan, 1992); Francis Wilson, "Farming, 1866–1966," in *Oxford History of South Africa,* vol. 2, eds. Monica Wilson and Leonard Thompson (Oxford: Clarendon Press, 1971), 104–71.

18. Jones and Müller, *South African Economy,* 141; Wilson, "Farming," 165; Beinart and Coates, *Environment and History,* 67.

19. In addition to works by Mary Hargreaves, R. Douglas Hurt, Harry McDean, and Donald Worster, the reader is referred to *Great Plains Quarterly* 8 (spring 1986), an entire issue devoted to Dust Bowl scholarship. For a fascinating inspection of plains historiography as postmodern puzzle, see William Cronon, "A Place for Stories: Nature, History, and Narrative," *Journal of American History* 78 (March 1992): 1347–76.

20. Works Progress Administration, "Areas of Intense Drought Distress, 1930–1936" (Washington, D.C.: GPO, 1937); Hurt, *Dust Bowl;* Carl C. Taylor, Helen W. Wheeler, and E. L. Kirkpatrick, *Disadvantaged Classes in American Agriculture* (Washington, D.C.: GPO, 1938). Also see Donald Worster, *Dust Bowl: The Southern Plains in the 1930s* (New York: Oxford University Press, 1979).

21. Hargreaves, "Dry-Farming," 161; Hurt, *Dust Bowl,* 17–31; Harry McDean, "Federal Farm Policy and the Dust Bowl: The Half-Right Solution," *North Dakota History: Journal of the Northern Plains* 47 (summer 1980), 28–30.

22. Hurt, *Dust Bowl;* David B. Danbom, *Born in the Country: A History of Rural America* (Baltimore: Johns Hopkins University Press, 1995), 225; Richard Lowitt, *The New Deal and the West* (Bloomington: Indiana University Press, 1984), 39; Henry A. Wallace, "Report of the Secretary of Agriculture to the President of the United States," 10 December 1935, in *Yearbook of Agriculture, 1935* (Washington, D.C.: GPO, 1936), 60.

23. Douglas Helms, ed., *Readings in the History of the Soil Conservation Service* (SCS Economics and Social Sciences Division, Historical Notes No. 1); Hugh H. Bennett, "Huge Waste by Soil Erosion: The Nation Begins a Survey," *New York Times,* 14 May 1933; Soil Erosion Service, Memorandum for the Press, 5 October 1934, Misc. Papers of Hugh H. Bennett, 1926–1934, National Archives RG 114, entry 21, box 8; Neil Maher, "'Crazy Quilt Farming on Round Land': The Great Depression,

the Soil Conservation Service, and the Politics of Landscape Change on the Great Plains During the New Deal," *Western Historical Quarterly* 31 (autumn 2000): 319–39.

24. Hurt, *Dust Bowl.*

25. On the origins of the model state law, see Douglas Helms, "The Preparation of the Standard State Soil Conservation Districts Law: An Interview with Philip M. Glick," U.S. Department of Agriculture, Soil Conservation Service, 1990.

26. Worster, *Dust Bowl,* 5. For a critique of Worster, see Harry C. McDean, "Dust Bowl Historiography," *Great Plains Quarterly* 8 (spring 1986).

27. Dickinson, "Wheat Development," 73–74. "Wheat bonanza" comes from Beinart and Coates, *Environment and History,* 68.

28. The term "veld degradation orthodoxy" comes from Beinart, "Soil Erosion, Animals, and Pasture over the Longer Term," in *The Lie of the Land: Challenging Received Wisdom on the African Environment,* ed. Melissa Leach and Robin Mearns (London: International African Institute with James Currey and Heinemann, 1996); Beinart, "Soil Erosion," 55–56, 61. For eighteenth- and nineteenth-century conservation efforts, see three articles by Richard Grove: "Early Themes in African Conservation: The Cape in the Nineteenth Century," in *Conservation in Africa: People, Politics, and Practice,* ed. David Anderson and Richard Grove (Cambridge: Cambridge University Press, 1987), 21–39, "Scotland in South Africa: John Croumbie Brown and the Roots of Settler Environmentalism," in *Ecology and Empire: Environmental History of Settler Societies,* ed. Tom Griffiths and Libby Robin (Edinburgh: Keele University Press, 1997), and "Scottish Missionaries, Evangelical Discourses and the Origins of Conservation Thinking in Southern Africa, 1820–1900," *Journal of Southern African Studies* 15 (January 1989): 163–87.

29. Union of South Africa, *Final Report of the Drought Investigation Commission* (Pretoria, U. G. 49, 1923); *Drought Investigation Commission Interim Report, April 1922,* reprinted in *Desertification: Environmental Degradation in and around Arid Lands,* ed. Michael H. Glantz (Boulder, Colo.: Westview Press, 1977), 252.

30. *Interim Report,* 252, 254 (italics in original).

31. I suspect the latter, as Leppan in 1928 recommended that dryland farmers in the northwestern Free State and the southwestern Transvaal adopt the inexpensive American practice of listing to prevent the soil from blowing (204).

32. G. V. Jacks and R. O. Whyte, *The Rape of the Earth: A World Survey of Soil Erosion* (London: Faber and Faber Ltd., 1939).

33. Union of South Africa, *Handbook*, 343, 346.

34. Ibid., 347–50; Peter Delius and Stefan Schirmer, "Soil Conservation in a Racially Ordered Society: South Africa, 1930–1970," *Journal of Southern African Studies* 26 (December 2000): 731; Beinart, "Soil Erosion," 60–61; "Introduction: The Politics of Colonial Conservation," *Journal of Southern African Studies* 15 (January 1989): 152; Farieda Khan, "Soil Wars: The Role of the African National Soil Conservation Association in South Africa, 1953–1959," *Environmental History* 2 (October 1997): 441.

35. Delius and Schirmer, "Soil Conservation," 732–35.

36. D. Hobart Houghton, *The South African Economy* (Cape Town: Oxford University Press, 1964), 59–60; Hugh H. Bennett, "Land—and the Union of South Africa," *Survey Graphic: The British and Ourselves* (May 1945), 233; Bennett, *Soil Erosion and Land Use in the Union of South Africa* (Pretoria: Department of Agriculture and Forestry, 1945), 9–11.

37. Bennett, *Soil Erosion*, 26–28.

38. Wellington Brink, *Big Hugh: The Father of Soil Conservation* (New York: Macmillan, 1951), 137–40.

39. "Die Spesialiteit: Daar's hoop as elkeen sy plig doen" (The Specialist: There is hope if everyone does his duty), reprinted in *The Land* 4 (spring 1945), 131.

40. Houghton, *South African Economy*, 60–61; Beinart and Murray, "-Agrarian Change, Population Movements, and Land Reform in the Free State" (Working Paper No. 51, Land and Agriculture Policy Centre, Johannesburg, 1996), 77–79. For a critical assessment of the Soil Conservation Act of 1946, see Delius and Schirmer, "Soil Conservation."

41. Dickinson, "Wheat Development," 73.

42. After WWII, many wheat farmers in both regions invested in groundwater irrigation systems. In South Africa, farmers responded to new pests and weeds by rotating their fields more frequently and diminishing the amount of time the soil lay bare. See Beinart and Murray, "Agrarian Change," 79.

43. William Beinart, *Twentieth-Century South Africa* (Oxford: Oxford University Press, 1994), 10, 261; Charles Van Onselen, *The Seed is Mine: The Life of Kas Maine, a South African Sharecropper* (New York: Hill and Wang, 1996), 8.

44. Quoted in Francis Wilson, "Farming," 129.

45. Keegan, *Rural Transformations*, xii, 195; Beinart, *Twentieth-Century South Africa*, 54; Laurine Platzky and Cherryl Walker, *The Surplus People: Forced Removals in South Africa* (Johannesburg: Ravan Press, 1985), 85.

46. Martin J. Murray, "'Burning the Wheat Stacks': Land Clearances and Agrarian Unrest along the Northern Middelburg Frontier, 1918–1926," *Journal of Southern African Studies* 15 (October 1988), 74–75, 80; Beinart, *Twentieth-Century South Africa*, 50. Also see William Beinart and Colin Bundy, *Hidden Struggles in Rural South Africa: Politics and Popular Movements in the Transkei and Eastern Cape, 1890–1930* (London: James Currey, 1987); and Ted Matsetela, "The Life Story of Nkgono Mma-Pooe: Aspects of Sharecropping and Proletarianism in the Northern OFS, 1890–1930," in *Industrialization and Social Change in South Africa*, ed. Marks and Rathbone.

47. M. L. Morris, "The Development of Capitalism in South African Agriculture: Class Struggle in the Countryside," *Economy and Society* 5 (August 1976): 292–343; Van Onselen, *The Seed is Mine*, 7. As sharecroppers like Kas Maine ventured into drier regions to secure more independence, they found that interactions between blacks and whites—especially between black tenants and white tenants or "poor whites"—were more common and amicable than in the wetter, more capitalized farming regions. See Charles Van Onselen, "Race and Class in the South African Countryside: Cultural Osmosis and Social Relations in the Sharecropping Economy of the South Western Transvaal, 1900–1950," *American Historical Review* 95 (February 1990): 99–123.

48. Beinart, *Twentieth-Century South Africa*, 113; Colin Bundy, *The Rise and Fall of the South African Peasantry* (Berkeley: University of California Press, 1979), 234. Also see "South Africa: The Development of Labor-Repressive Agriculture," in Stanley B. Greenberg, *Race and State in Capitalist Development* (New Haven: Yale University Press, 1980).

49. Morris, "The Development of Capitalism," 334–35.

50. Though many, like Kas Maine, ceded their relative independence when tractors obviated the need for sharecroppers' oxen (Van Onselen, "Race and Class" and *The Seed Is Mine*).

51. Quoted in Morris, "The Development of Capitalism," 335–36.

52. Wilson, "Farming," 146–49; Platzky and Walker, *Surplus People*, 104, 108; Stanley B. Greenberg, "The South African Agricultural Union: Managing the Transition to Capitalist Agriculture," in *Race and State in Capitalist Development* (New Haven: Yale University Press, 1980), 87.

53. Platzky and Walker, *Surplus People*, 121–22; Beinart, *Twentieth-Century South Africa*, 198; Beinart and Murray, "Agrarian Change." Also see Cosmos Desmond, *The Discarded People* (London: Penguin Books, 1971); Michael Morris, "State Intervention and the Agricultural Labour Supply Post-1948," in *Farm Labour in South Africa*, ed. F. Wilson, A. Kooy, and D. Hendrie (Cape Town: David Philip, 1977); Ellen Kuzwayo, *Call Me Woman* (London: The Women's Press, 1985); William Beinart, "Agrarian Historiography and Agrarian Reconstruction," in *South Africa in Question*, ed. John Lonsdale (London: James Currey, 1988); and Colin Murray, *Black Mountain: Land Class and Power in the Eastern Orange Free State, 1880s to 1980s* (Edinburgh: Edinburgh University Press, 1992).

54. Beinart, *Twentieth-Century South Africa*, 196.

55. William Beinart, "Soil Erosion, Conservationism and Ideas about Development: A Southern African Exploration, 1900–1960," *Journal of Southern African Studies* 11 (October 1984): 52; David Anderson, "Depression, Dust Bowl, Demography, and Drought: The Colonial State and Soil Conservation in East Africa During the 1930s," *African Affairs* 83 (1984): 321.

56. Anderson, "Depression, Dust Bowl," 327, 340; C. Maher, *A Visit to the United States to Study Soil Conservation* (Nairobi: Department of Agriculture, 1940).

57. David Throup, *Economic and Social Origins of Mau Mau* (London: James Currey, 1987).

58. Steven Feierman, *Peasant Intellectuals: Anthropology and History in Tanzania* (Madison: University of Wisconsin Press, 1990). Also see Pamela A. Maack, "We Don't Want Terraces! Protest and Identity Under the Uluguru Land Usage Scheme," in *Custodians of the Land: Ecology and Culture in the History of Tanzania*, ed. Gregory Maddox, James Giblin, and Isaria M. Kimambo (London: James Currey, 1987); and Kate B. Showers, "Soil Erosion in the Kingdom of Lesotho: Origins and Colonial Response, 1830s–1950s," *Journal of Southern African Studies* 15 (January 1989): 263–86.

59. Delius and Schirmer, "Soil Conservation," 720–31; *Report of the Native Economic Commission*, quoted in Platzky and Walker, *Surplus People*, 93; William Beinart, "Introduction: The Politics of Colonial Conservation," *Journal of Southern African Studies* 15 (January 1989): 159; Hugh Bennett, "Africa: Another Continent to Mend," *The Land* 4 (spring 1945): 132; Bennett, "Land and the Union of South Africa," 10.

60. Delius and Schirmer, "Soil Conservation," 723–31; Bundy, *Rise and Fall*, 226; Beinart, *Twentieth-Century South Africa*, 129–30, 205. For case studies of betterment projects, see two articles in a special conservation issue of the *Journal of Southern African Studies* 15 (January 1989); Fred Hendricks, "Loose Planning and Rapid Resettlement: The Politics of Conservation and Control in Transkei, South Africa, 1950–1970," and Chris de Wet, "Betterment Planning in a Rural Village in Keiskammahoek, Ciskei."
61. Farieda Khan, "Soil Wars," 446.
62. Beinart and Murray, "Agrarian Change."
63. Of course, most farmers in the United States and South Africa today rely on pumped groundwater or water harnessed by dams and ditches, not on dry-farming methods per se. Such "technological fixes" as contour plowing, stubble mulching, and strip cropping are not everywhere employed, and wind erosion continues at alarming rates. And, like other highly-capitalized monocultures, wheat growing depends on large quantities of harmful chemical inputs— fertilizers, herbicides, and pesticides.

Contributors

Rusty Bittermann is Chair of the History Department at St. Thomas University, where he is working with his colleagues to develop an innovative World History curriculum. His research focuses primarily on the rural history of Atlantic Canada and the British Isles and has been published in the *Canadian Historical Review, Labour/LeTravail,* and *Acadiensis* as well as various edited collections. His most recent work on Prince Edward Island land issues appears in John McLaren, Andrew Buck, and Nancy Wright, eds., *Despotic Dominion: Property Rights in British Settler Societies.*

David A. Y. O. Chang is Assistant Professor of History at the University of Minnesota. He is completing a book on race, nationalism, and the politics of land tenure in eastern Oklahoma. His publications include a forthcoming article on Native American and African American nationalist and emigration movements, to appear *in Crossing Waters, Crossing Paths: Black and Indian Journeys in the Americas,* edited by Tiya Miles and Sharon P. Holland.

Gregory S. Crider is Chair and Associate Professor of History at Wingate University. His research in Mexico and Central America has focused on labor, culture, politics, and social relations. Current writing projects include *Workers with Guns: Making Sense of the Mexican Revolution in Atlixco, 1900-1950* as well as a cultural biography of Mexican labor boss Luis Napoleón Morones.

Louis A. Ferleger is Professor of History at Boston University. He is co-editor *of Slavery, Secession, and Southern History.* He is completing a book on southern farmers after the Civil War.

Reeve Huston is Associate Professor of History at Duke University. He is author of *Land and Freedom: Rural Society, Popular Protest, and Party Politics in Antebellum New York,* and currently researching a book on conflicts over the meaning and practice of democracy in the United States between 1815 and 1840.

Marixa Lasso is Assistant Professor of History at California State University-Los Angeles. Her dissertation was entitled "Race and Republicanism in the Age of Revolution: Cartagena, 1795–1831."

James C. McCann is Professor of History and Director of the African Studies Center at Boston University. He is author of *Maize and Grace: African History, Corn, and Africa's New Ecology, 1500–2000* (forthcoming), *Green Land, Brown Land Black Land* (1999), *People of the Plow: An Agricultural History of Ethiopia* (1995), *and From Poverty to Famine in Northeast Ethiopia* (1987).

Sarah T. Phillips is Assistant Professor of History at Columbia University. She specializes in twentieth-century U.S. history, with an emphasis on politics, the state, and the environment. Her articles have appeared in *Environmental History* and *Agricultural History*.

James C. Scott is Professor of Political Science and Anthropology at Yale and Director of the Program in Agrarian Studies. He has run a money-losing small farm (sheep, bees, eggs) for 25 years now. His most recent book is *Seeing Like a State: How Certain Schemes to Improve the Human Condition Have Failed* (1999). On explicitly agrarian themes he has published *Weapons of the Weak: Everyday Forms of Peasant Resistance* (1985) and *The Moral Economy of the Peasant: Subsistence and Rebellion in Southeast Asia* (1976).

Daniel Samson is Assistant Professor of History at Brock University in Canada. He has published in *Acadiensis* and *Left History* in addition to editing *Contested Countryside: Rural Workers and Modern Society in Atlantic Canada, 1800–1950* (1994). He is currently working on revising his dissertation, "Industry and Improvement: State and Class Formations in Nova Scotia's Coal-Mining Countryside, 1790–1865" for publication

Susan Sleeper-Smith is Associate Professor of History at Michigan State University. Her recent monograph, *Indian Women and French Men: Rethinking Cultural Encounter in the Western Great Lakes*, was published in 2002. She co-authored *New Faces of the Fur Trade* and has published in *Ethnohistory, Journal of American History, Journal of the Early Republic,* and *Journal of Indian Culture and Research*.

Thomas Summerhill is Assistant Professor of History at Michigan State University. He specializes in nineteenth-century U.S. social and political history, with special emphasis on agrarian insurgencies. In addition to several articles, his book, *Harvest of Dissent: Agrarianism in 19th Century New York*, is forthcoming in 2005. He has held fellowships at the Yale Program in Agrarian Studies and the Smithsonian Institution.

Michigan State University Press is committed to preserving ancient forests and natural resources. We have elected to print this title on Nature's Natural, which is 90% recycled (50% post-consumer waste) and processed chlorine free. As a result of our paper choice, Michigan State University Press has saved the following natural resources*:

9	Trees (40 feet in height)
3,917	Gallons of Water
1,575	Kilowatt-hours of Electricity
432	Pounds of Solid Waste
848	Pounds of Greenhouse Gases

Both Michigan State University Press and our printer, Thompson-Shore, Inc., are members of the Green Press Initiative—a nonprofit program dedicated to supporting book publishers, authors, and suppliers in maximizing their use of fiber that is not sourced from ancient or endangered forests. For more information about the Green Press Initiative and the use of recycled paper in book publishing, please visit *www.greenpressinitiative.org.*

*Environmental benefits were calculated based on research provided by Conservatree and Californians Against Waste.